The Advent

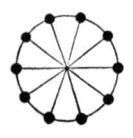

Whatsoever is contained in this book, O Devi, comes From You.
What is there to dedicate to You?

THE ADVENT

G DE KALBERMATTEN

This 2002 edition privately printed in the USA

Copyright © HH Mataji Nirmala Devi Shrivastava, 1979

Introduction

It really came as a great surprise to find myself writing this book. Like everybody else, in my adolescence, I had played with the idea of writing something one day: a novel, some poems... but not the Advent! I should confess that I felt and still feel awkward to write about the coming and message of HH Mataji Nirmala Devi. The reasons for this are few. My poor command over English language and style, the vastness of the subject, its complexity, but clearly, the greatest drawback is my own inadequacy to be a worthy messenger for such a news.

Without any false humility, I have to plainly state that there are many people who have progressed much further than myself into the new state of consciousness that this book is meant to introduce. They are more evolved, mature, and are far better models of what this book is all about; they are my teachers in many different ways. I would like to express here both my thankfulness for their guidance and deep reverence for what they stand for. Each of them are living flames that truly enlighten. Words and thoughts arranged in chapters cannot have this pretention.

Yet, despite my shortcomings in the spiritual life, I feel I should introduce HH Mataji's revolutionary yoga to a larger public. My chief concern in this attempt is to pass on invaluable informations to all those, in the West, East, North and South who are seeking the meaning of their life. All those who cannot any more be tamed by artificiality and organized lies, all those who cannot be lured by phony satisfactions, all those who, in a word, seek the Truth are brothers and sisters in a great quest which began thousands of years ago. They are those who deserve to know what is now really going on: the triggering of the culminating step in the human evolution.

I have exposed this tremendous development to the minds of Western intellectuals. Yet I believe that Easterners can find the reading profitable. Indeed developing countries are, to a large extent, following the pattern of the "advanced" Western industrial countries without always realising the seriousness of the present crisis in the overdeveloped Western culture.

G DE KALBERMATTEN

Contents

Introduction	v
PART ONE—DAYS GONE BY	1
PART TWO—THE UNIQUE DISCOVERY OF SAHAJA YOGA	17
1. Between you and me	19
2. Encounter with Sahaja Yoga	27
PART THREE—REVELATION	49
3. The revelation of the cosmic within the human microcosm	54
4. The instrument of awareness	64
PART FOUR—ELUCIDATIONS	97
5. The virtue of dharma	99
6. Religion and Religions	132
7. Evolution in consciousness	152
8. After self-realization	176
9. Tantrism as an expression of evil	197
10. Collective salvation before the coming of the Rider	232
PART FIVE—THE DIVINE MOTHER	247
PART SIX—THE OLDEST QUEST	301
11. The philosophical roots of the ideology of development	304
12. The great dilemma	333
PART SEVEN—ASSUMPTIONS TO CHALLENGE	351
13. Assumption number one: Past Religions and Mythologies are nothing but superstitions	353
14. Assumption number two: The Devil does not exist	366
15. Assumption number three: We have made the world a better place to live in	386
APPENDIX	413
GLOSSARY	416
ABBREVIATIONS	420

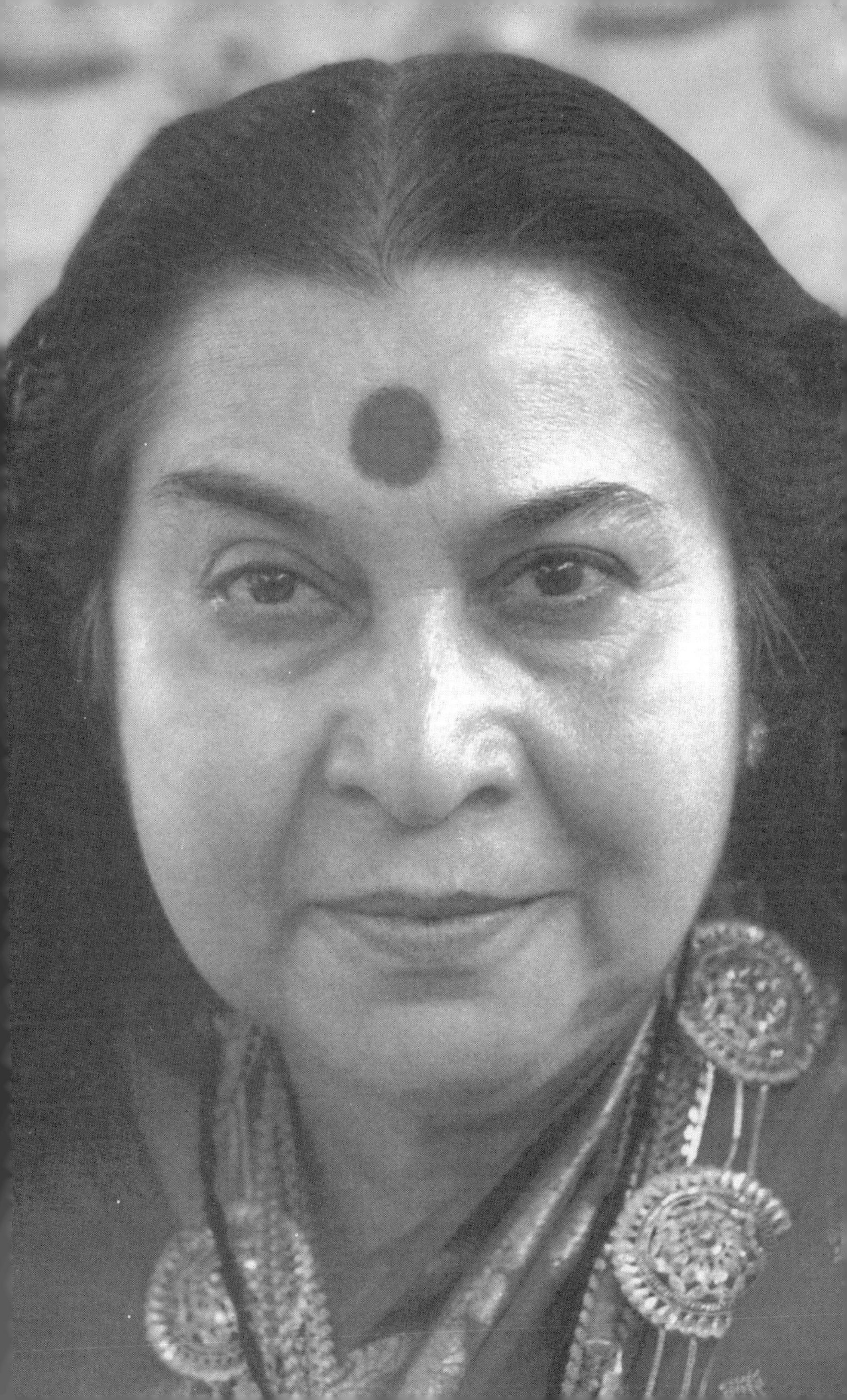

Part One

DAYS GONE BY

When I enter into the oldest image of my memory I see a little boy in a red overcoat sitting in the snow. Everything is white around me. Thick snow flakes fall gently in the silence. Actually I do not pay too much attention to them because I am very busy eating snow. I have woollen gloves. I find the taste of snow through the taste of the wool extremely interesting and I am at royal peace with the whole world.

A couple of days later, something shocking happens. It is the second image. There is snow in the second image also, but the snow is heaped into hard icy balls and these balls are thrown at me. Can you believe it? I find the experience most distressful. I must tell you the story. It was a sunny and merry carnival day. My elder sister had a little fox mask and I had a huge, superb elephant mask. We wanted to join the children of the village to play with them. But when we arrived on the village's central place they begin bombarding us with these stupid snow balls. We run away, somewhere, to hide and cry. My elephant mask was torn apart. I do not understand anything about this world but I do not like it. Thank God I have a sweet and lovely Mummy. I can go back to our chalet where she is waiting for me (that is what I assume anyway) and I shall have kisses and dry clothes and hot chocolate.

So, in life there were icy snowballs and hot chocolates. I tried to avoid the first and seek the latter but with the passing of years, this delicate maneuvre became increasingly difficult.

While growing up, I found out that the adults expected me to become reasonable. Now, I don't know whether you know, but 'adult' and 'reasonable' are two strange notions.

Adults and those beings that you always see from below. They have long legs and talk loud all the time. 'Reasonable' means that you have to become as incomprehensible as they are. To be sure adults are helpful: they open the door, they push the lift button, they keep big dogs away. They also have lovely cars. But they do not make any sense at all. If you are wise you can get a relief from adults. Christmas day, for instance, you can take all the presents they give you under the living room sofa where they cannot see you and there you can quietly open the packages. But these situations are rare. Ultimately, you can only deal with adults by letting them believe that you have become reasonable. To this effect don't look like you're having too much fun: adults have no fun. They are serious. They are important. You will further learn about important things in school. School is important.

In school you discover other children. Some of them are pretty nice, some of them are already adults, and some of them throw stones instead of snowballs.

It does not matter that much, because I can come back home for lunch. Also I am quite lucky because I have two adorable grandmothers. My grand maman de Sion (this is my home town in Switzerland) lives in a high ceilinged wooden room. There I climb into her bed and we talk for a long time together. She is not like the other adults, she understands: at Easter time she comes with us into the garden and looks for the eggs in the nests. She is so sweet and so mild, she prays to the Virgin Mary every day and I can always see love in her eyes. My grand maman de Seeburg (this is where my mummy comes from) has a beautiful mansion near the lake. From the balcony I look at the swans and the sunset. We are the best of friends. The poor thing is so scared because she listens to the catastrophes on the radio's daily news but then I cuddle her and she is all right. In the garage, there is a big American car that no one uses: maybe she will give it to me. The garden is full of the mysterious smells of the lake and it is so quiet also.

When I am eleven, my father puts me in the boarding school of a college run by the priests of a venerable medieval abbey. Sigh! At seventeen I managed, at last, to be thrown out of it. Quite a few things happened in between.

In this all-boys school, the obsessive concern was 'girls'. Conversations around the topic, aimed preferably at thick laughs. Some priests with a weird imagination are on the watch for the boys' guilty friendships. I was at first disgusted by this atmosphere. Then only shocked. Then I got used to it. It belongs, I guessed, to the process of becoming an adult. Let me do my homework: many forbidden books are available through classroom friends. Well...I educated myself all right, but in the process I unknowingly began to spoil my attention.

Religion belonged to the daily discipline and was stamped by the same official seal: boring, coercive, artificial. I strongly reacted against both of them and started reading novels during the daily morning mass. I gradually came to enjoy my status as the acknowledged leader of the rebellious elements. With a small party of companions we delighted in all kinds of naughty practical jokes. Among ourselves we would pledge our commitment to the lost spirit of gone by chivalry, chosen poets and nocturnal expeditions to the cellar of the Abbey to steal the canons' distinguished wines. It is quite thrilling to discover friendship by a midnight candle while tasting the vintages of a sleeping monastery.

We also found out that our favourite authors, artists and musicians had all been deeply annoyed with the prevailing stupidity of their society and that we could not have agreed more with their reactions. So we grew into intellectualism, dandyism and adolescent rebellion, proudly deciding that the greatest crusades are the hopeless ones. Sometimes, however, listening to the basilica's vaults echoing Gregorian chants, I would find myself wondering: "Maybe these hymns, once upon a time, were sung by priests who were full of joy." At fourteen I wrote in a sort of diary: "How can they make God so lifeless? How dare they? He is so great, God's greatness is what I can dimly catch a glimpse of."

Contemporary intellectuals were more busy defining the truth than finding it. I took to liking authors such as Socrates, Seneca, Villon, Pascal or Montaigne. They are not very trendy but, I thought, they are honest.

They are not like my professor of religion or my professor of philosophy (I was lucky with the professor of literature) talking about things they had half digested with half a brain. The second half marvelling at the smartness of the first one. In fact I am not quite fair to my professor of religion: he had found the truth. It did not cost him much more than the price of a pocket Bible. But I thought it was not expensive enough and I did not buy it.

I am sixteen, I am in Feiburg am Breisgau, Germany, for summer holidays. And I am madly in love. She is a German girl which is quite good for my German but that's not the point. I love her. Well, that's what I thought. In the summer school during class hours, we send each other little paper balls of feverish notes while the teacher is writing on the blackboard. She is complimenting me for how good I am in history and I just love compliments, especially from her. She wants to invite me to a party; I have never gone to a party!... but I will manage it. Now, the nasty parents come in the picture and I cannot see her. Therefore I cannot eat, I cannot sleep. We arrange, through her girl friend, secret meetings on the bank of a small lake in the Black Forest. How terribly romantic! One day, half closed eyes, she told me "give me a kiss". I was terribly impressed. I did not know what to do. At last I took my rain coat, put it on her head and kissed her through the rain coat. She was a bit surprised. But—I already had quite a talent at rationalizing things—I explained to her that it was a French trick. I think it worked. She was impressed and pleased to have such a knowledgeable French boyfriend.

End of summer. Back to college, rain and tears. I'm fed up with college anyway. Dialogues with my teachers become increasingly impatient.

—"Sir why is there Evil in the world?
—Because we have sinned.
—Then why did we sin?
—Because our nature has been corrupted by the original sin of our first parents.
—But sir, why should I be corrupted by a sin I have not committed?
—Human nature was corrupted so that it could be redeemed.
—Sir I am afraid I look as little redeemed as you do.
—Get out!"

My friends have been thrown out. Only tasteless people could possibly prosper in this college. Thus the rector, a considerate man in his own way, expelled me from the school, charge: "bad influence on his comrades." Three more years of college in my home town. Exams passed, 1968: University, Freedom, life begins.

I had firmly decided to enjoy it!

I had great holidays! Summer in Salzburg (Austria); so many friends from various countries. Listening to Mozart's concerts and taking baths in baroque fountains. I am in love with, well, a couple of girls. Summer in Florence (Italy): I am the guest and become the friend of an old lonely marquess who loves animals and Francisco d'Assisi. Being pennyless, he is selling paintings and furniture to feed the extravagant birds which are kept in the aviary of the park. But he had to feed them by himself and a couple of years later he died of exhaustion. I began to learn that life in a money oriented society is rather ugly when you don't have any. In the so called rich countries, not everybody is rich and few of the rich are happy. Later on while studying marxism in Bologna I would be quite satisfied to understand more scientifically how developed society became such a heartless mess.

But I was lucky indeed, my family was not poor. In Geneva I had my flat, my car, no real money problems and the possibility to do a lot of what I pleased at that very age when one develops a strong wish to have fun. In my summer holidays, I was trying to blend love, romanticism and some kind of historic landscape. I was a staunch believer in the possibility of engineering poetic happenings. So I was in love (that by the way, had become an adult word) on the French cote d'Azur, in the islands of the Aegean sea, etc... Of course the year is not made of summers only but in Swiss winters you can do a lot of skiing: sparkling, white snow, blue violet sky and speed. During this University time I also somewhat managed to get a degree in law but that was beside the point. The point is that I was seeking to taste an intensity of pleasure and joy through the various opportunities which were proposed to me. I can recall those days: going to Paris, Brussels or London to meet friends, having balls and parties in mansions and castles...And yet in this whirl-pool, I did not lose the preception of a deeply rooted drive to find an answer to a few basic questions. "What is this game about? How can I make people happy? How can I be happy (well, I look happy. But deep inside I am not). What is happiness, what is love, what is truth?" This was Pontius Pilatus' question but I did not intend to wash my hands.

Sometimes I would also feel something supremely adorable, existing far beyond us, totally elusive and yet as badly needed as oxygen. "Oh God wherever you are, don't you see that this world is going nuts? I am going nuts also. Please aren't you going to do something about it?" It was not unusual that this dialogue with the walls of my room would begin—and end up—in tears.

I was trying to make a poem or a romance out of my life but I was using the wrong material; aesthetics, the world of forms was a world of limitations. In beauty—be it of a statue, an idea, or a woman—I would see the draft of a model which was beyond my reach. I lost myself in drafts looking for the model. That exercise became increasingly frustrating.

In a similar way I could see that the minds of the great thinkers, poets, etc., had been enlightened by sparks of truth, sparks of one and the same fire shivering in the creations of arts and literature, in science, philosophy. But truth, itself, was completely beyond my grasp. I was honest enough to recognize it and proved to be also rather ironic towards people who did not have this honesty. I could see them only too well taking refuge in religions, creeds, ideologies, destroying the old golden calf to build new ones! God, the Nation, Progress, the Working Class, Youth. "Why are you worshipping youth", I thought disdainfully. "Youth is a blessing that does not know itself, an unfulfilled promise.." but I thought also "Youth is as old as hunger." I became sick and tired of this upper-class, unconcerned way of life I had shared in many European countries and agreed with Nietzche's "What makes Man vulgar is to think he lives for nothing." And what is this thing that makes life worth living? I did not really find anything worthwhile but the quest for what could be worthwhile. Sometimes I became extreme in my argumentation: "Either God exists, or He doesn't; if He doesn't let us blow the house up. But if He does, He certainly is worth looking for a bit further." Most of the time though I would not use the word "God" I would just wonder "What is going on?..." So, as many others I went further. I was not specially attracted by drugs to begin with, but at that time in Geneva, I had a Dutch friend fond of tulips and hashish, especially hashish. She kindly introduced me to her way of life. I found this kind of smoke interesting but in the last analysis, not helpful. All the while I was discovering with so many boys and girls of my generation that to love and to be loved helps to exist..but discovered also that love without the right balance does not give peace or fulfillment.

Lucidity is a mixed blessing; it all depends what it is that the light shows. I thought I was more lucid than many people around. Maybe I was right but, anyway, that was no fun. I could feel the pressure of society: inhumane, boring, cruel and stupid. I could see people trying to swim in the pea soup: running after entertainments or political creeds, seeking love or success with little understanding of the mechanisms that made them run. Still, I was running all right myself, thus growing increasingly annoyed with my own stupidity. I could chart my own story fairly easily:

I was born in 1949 in a well-off aristocratic family in Lausanne, Switzerland. This implied two things: I belonged to the postwar generation and to the privileged social stratum of a privileged country. These coordinates provided the framework of the story. I had known enough of material security and social status to realise that, although these privileged surroundings greatly helped to live in the world of man, they did not altogether provide me with what I was looking for. On the other hand I had gone through almost all the possible experiments the post-war generation went through: it did not give me what I was looking for either. Oh well! Let's go to sleep. I will wake up tomorrow. Existence sticks to the skin in its own ways. Somehow I will make it. Basically I was trying to remember the adolescent who wrote once: "May nothing ever appease my hunger; let it not diminish; may my thirst never be quenched; let it increase. For it is in being hungry and thirsty that I do not betray myself".[1] Meanwhile, I thought it would be idiotic to reject the world since one is merged in it. So, I accepted it, trying to smile about things or, better learning to laugh, first, about myself, in order to earn the agreeable right to laugh at others. I agreed with Chamfort's "The most lost of all your days is the one when you did not laugh,"[2] but I was not as cynical as he was. So, I had fun, listening to music, seeing friends, travelling, reading. One day follows another, the sun rises and sets, one day it rains and the next day it's sunny. I shave in the morning; I sing, I weep, I go to school, to the office, to the barracks, I come home, I go to sleep, I wake up—you see what I mean.

I went through the social rituals one must perform in order to reassure the members of the tribe. I did those things that esta-

---

[1] "Que jamais rien ne vienne combler ma faim. Qu'elle ne diminue point, que rien ne désaltère ma soif; qu'elle augmente. Car c'est en ayant faim et soif que je ne me trahis pas."

[2] Chamfort. Maximes: "La plus perdue des journees est celle ou l'on n'a pas ri".

blished people consider very respectable; I socialised in upper class circles, I received an Academic education in Europe and the USA, I became an artillery lieutenant, went into banking and international administration. I also did those things that Western anti-establishment people consider very respectable. I studied marxism with great care, I went into drug experiments, I visited various new religious movements, lived freely and in hippie communes, etc... As a whole, all these experiences proved to be fruitful and interesting... in pointing out what is to be avoided and what to be sought. I tried to seize all the fruits of all the trees, I tried to bite the fruit which would never leave my mouth. Of course I failed. I did not think the Devil could overpower me because I felt I was as innocent as he was shrewd. I made my little gamble with the Devil like dear doctor Faust and Mephistopheles.[3] I guess what kept me moving was my curiosity. I was of the opinion that an open minded boy could not ignore the findings of Eastern spirituality. So I read about it, and I also visited some masters imported from India. To my mind the teachings of Indian philosophy answer many outstanding questions pertaining to the genesis of the Universe, the relation between spirit and matter, the existential status of man, the path of liberation, etc...

On the other hand, after having visited some "masters" for a while I begin seeing the tricks that they play upon their followers. It was distressing to find out that most are fakes, many are corrupt and that they were using the energy of the people who blindly surrendered to them not to mention taking away their material possessions. I felt sorry for many of these disciples, but felt that some others deserved their lot. They seemed to assume they would obtain the Kingdom of Heaven at a discount price in the guru shopping centre, and were rather arrogant about it. "When I try to get anywhere near God I had better keep humble", I thought, "It is safer".

Bologna, Italy; old stones gazing at us. I love medieval streets, arcades, piazzas. A country full of beauty and sophisticated intellects where I am learning that aesthetics and intellect alone do not lead anywhere. The taste of a civilisation's decay can be savoury, poor Europe, but where is life going to spring up next?

---

[3]"When, to the moment, I will say, linger you now, you are so fair! My soul will belong to you". (my translation)

Through my studies I set out to chart the findings of the seekers of the past: Arjuna, Akhenaton, Kant, Karl Marx... Machiavelli is fed up with Augustine. He says "Let's forget morality because we cannot know anything about it". Well, he is looking at the pope; I understand the statement! But what then will guide human action? What integrates individuals in the community? Hobbes runs away from Cromwell's armies and writes "Self-preservation"... fair enough; it sounds logical but not inspiring. In the nouveau riche England Locke says "private property"... it sounds inspiring but only for the few who can accumulate it. Rousseau is not happy. Lenin and Mao Tse Tung see the contradictions, Yes. Lao-Tzu and Hegel talk about the synthesis... you mean in actual history? Marcuse says the synthesis cannot be. But he did not know about Patanjali and Zen Buddhism. My little brain is getting feverish: I guess the outline.

In 1974, when I was studying at the Johns Hopkins University in Baltimore (Maryland) I became convinced that only a radical historical happening could break the vicious circle of individual and collective disequilibria. I somehow reached the conclusion that the break-through would be an epistemological one—that is: it would occur in the field of the human awareness—and that the signs of the time pointed this event to be imminent. But I did not know where, when and how it would happen... maybe it was already happening.

"The" question could have been phrased in those terms: How to evolve a new faculty of perception (beyond the intellect) which represents an evolution in the phenomenology of awareness and not a regression? To go back to instinct is not going to solve the problems of civilisation because instinct and civilisation are nothing but a significant expression of the great human contradiction which cannot be solved by merely going back and forth between the poles of the contradiction. Furthermore, the standard psychic state of a Western man represents a fairly evolved level of rationalisation; that is an asset not to be neglected. One can consider as a regression the attempt to go beyond the mind's cognitive capacities through "instinctual" media such as drugs, sex considered as a "Weltanschauung", indulgence in pseudo-mystical and pseudo-animist types of parapsychological enquiries. The present day type of Californian circus, fake gurus, false prophets, Science-fiction and so-called "new churches" were only showing that the necessity of an epistemological breakthrough was in the air. Playing with hegelian concepts, I would say that the present moment of world history is to actualise a potential which is reaching maturity in this second half of the Twentieth Century in the same way, say, that the Nineteenth Century brought forth the material breakthrough. Evidence of such potential could be found in a careful analysis of religious, artistic and literary manifestations as well as in definite patterns of behaviour in the most advanced societies.

Actually the theoretical hypothesis was nicely framed. But it was an empty frame. Unless I came upon the actual happening of the cognitive breakthrough, all these considerations were leading me nowhere. Of this I was painfully aware.

There are days when I do not sound too good myself. Days such as this one:

"I don't get out of bed before three O'clock p.m. because I don't know what to do outside of it—

I don't know how to exist.

I don't know what to do.

I don't know how to feel.

I don't know whether I should think or not.

I just don't know.

I'm feeling sad. I'm feeling lost."

I'm fed up with friends whose parking meter is blocked on "sex". I begin wondering at my own behaviour. A few years ago I used to think, like most of us that sex love should provide the optimal chance for happiness and fulfillment. We all had accepted "free love" as a matter of course; it was the dogma of our way of life. But how many of us are truly enjoying ourselves? No so many indeed! There is so much insecurity. People are afraid of loving someone because they are afraid of suffering: the elected partner might leave them tomorrow for someone nicer! What is the right relationship? I would not like my own little sister to go with a man who should leave her after some time. Then, why do we behave like butterflies? Even when I am with a girl-friend my attention restlessly wanders around. This restlessness does not give any joy! Thus I decided to settle down, trying to enjoy friendship and love without sex.

I'm fed up with University professors who do not know what matters and what does not. A new type of paralysing sophistry has developed in Academia, under the respectable label of analytical thought. Analytical thought helps to think clearly, and to be sure this is a respectable function. But this contribution is merely methodological or instrumental. To think clearly or not about something is one thing. The thing you are thinking about is another one. This is simple objectivity. You may think clearly about peanuts and think in a confused way about the Universe. To deduce that peanuts is the substratum of the Universe is a pretty foolish step to take but it is one commonly taken in contemporary Academia.

There is nothing Universal about the University's knowledge. It is an orderly chaos of particulars..everyone cultivating one's private little province without any relation to the whole. Lucky me, I'm getting my M.A. degree! At once I jump in a 1954 Packard via New Orleans, Los Angeles. I like travelling; life is fun again; I'm going to see the Grand Canyon and swim in the Pacific Sea.

I completed my cycle of "American" experiences, in going as deep into the Californian counter-culture as I could without hurting myself too much. Maybe they had the answer I was looking for! An answer, I knew, existed: I could feel it in the beauty of the world, in the writing of the sages, in loving or being loved, and yet I could feel it and know at the same time that something prevented me from being one with it. I could sometimes reach "that stage" through very short instants of blissful intensity. Again and again, I had been trying to break the invisible wall between me and Reality, me and myself, me and the unity of love. Were we not, all of us, looking towards the same goal? All, brothers and sisters, trying to pierce through selfishness and confusion, to break through dreams and illusion, to wake up, to be free, to reach the point where we could look around and say: "Yes this I was, am and will always be. The world is shivering with my joy. I am, you are and we are one".

In California, I reached the end of the road.

I had tried my best, I was honest, I was analysing myself rather lucidly in psycho-analytical and socio-economic terms, etc... I was confronting situations, others, myself with as much openness and love as possible. I could, at last, see the solution, but could not catch up with it. The kingdom I was looking for was so near me—only a nerve's thickness away maybe—but it was desperately out of reach. The proximity of the unattainable was agonizing. I knew the answer was within me; I would hurl myself at the door but could not open it. It was exhausting.

I remember one evening near Pacific Palisades (Los Angeles), left stranded on the beach, kneeling toward the ocean and the coming night, muttering my little "prayer on the Pacific": "My Lord, my love, it is You I seek, it is You I want, It is You I seek, it is You I want. Help me to rejoin You. All of You who have the power to help me, help me to rejoin Him."[4]

Well, I had done what I could, but I knew I could not do any more. From Virginia's "blue ridges" to the wooded hills of Boulder Creek (California) I had shared the anguishes and hopes of a generation of seekers, beautiful people, lost people, a lot of them heading towards a dead end. All avenues seemed to have been explored. Going everywhere and nowhere. Who could say: "You are wrong", "You are right"? No one knew. I did not know what to do anymore; I was writing in Berkeley:

Neither here
Nor there
But sleeping within
Is the thing I'm looking for, And yet, to wake up,
Should I stay here, should I go there?
Oh Beloved, free me from my blindness.

In Berkeley I got from an Indian friend of mine, a very bright and sweet boy, the address of a person living near London. He told me, "She is truly a Mother and She is Divine. She took birth in the past as Seeta, Radha, the Holy Virgin Mary; She is the promised Avatara of the Shakti and She has come again for the sake of Her children. Oh, you cannot know...you should go and see Her."

"But Rajesh; how can you say things like that?

—You can feel, Grégoire, you can actually feel it.

You can feel tremendous energy coming out of Her, like vibrations, and it changes your state of consciousness!"

By that time I knew how to refrain emotional and mental reactions to such an apparently crazy statement; experience only can be trusted: "So, I thought, maybe, maybe not. Let's see". My feelings and thoughts were not exactly serene though. On one hand, the enormity of my friend's statement made it very difficult for me to consider that he could possibley be right. We had been

---

[4]"Mon Seigneur, mon amour, c'est Vous que je cherche, c'est Vous que je veux, c'est Toi que je cherche c'est Toi que je veux. Aide-moi a te rejoindre. Vous tous qui avez le pouvoir de m'aider, aidez moi a Le rejoindre".

waiting for so long!...It is almost inconceivable to believe that, at last, a true divine Incarnation was actually living in this world, eating, sleeping, unknown to the world and yet preparing its redemption. On the other hand the signs of the time were pointing towards something at the same time incredible and imminent. We were among the false prophets of the last days announced by Jesus, in a growing conjuncture of spiritism, drugs, sexual aberrations pointing toward social dissolution. In the developed countries, technology was out of control. In the developing countries sheer misery was out of control; the physical survival of mankind looked like an awesome challenge. If ever the world stage was to be set up for the coming of the Ultimate Redeemer, it had to be now.

As the existing mess was man and especially male-made I found it rather satisfying that the Incarnation might be of the feminine gender (the Hindu "Divine Mother" "Mataji"). It cast an exciting light on christian dogmas also. So I began to be attracted to the idea of meeting my friend's teacher. "If this is so, what am I doing here?" I packed up, got a ride to Chicago. Flew to the East Coast, and from there, to London where Mataji was staying. The last lines written in the USA betray joyous expectations.

Bring forth that for which I'm striving
Help me
To let you
Take me
In your hand.

✦ ✦ ✦

The power which controls powers is love.

✦ ✦ ✦

The great adventure, the fantastic ride, the unknown way.

✦ ✦ ✦

When I look back at these twenty-five years I must say that I have been extremely lucky. I had not been eaten by lions, neither stabbed or stoned. I did not have to drink an unhealthy potion like Socrates nor did I blow half my brain cells like an acid freak. I did not even take a train to Siberia. I had been above all comforted by the thought that my quest was not particularly original. Looking for the answer to the same questions which had been debated by so many monks, kings, poets, philosophers, madmen and saints. Debates which echoed in the chamber of Pharaoh, the courtyards of Akbar's Fathepur Sikri, the cells of buddhist and cistercian cloisters. Very old questions indeed...Today, as yesterday, they are at the core of the evolution of thought and society.

Is there any answer? Can "THE ANSWER" be found? I had been hopeful, desperate, cynical...Until the day I met a most adorable, impressive and mysterious super human being: Her Holiness Mataji Nirmala Devi.

Part Two

THE UNIQUE DISCOVERY OF SAHAJA YOGA

"The new revolution in your awareness has to take place otherwise all human achievements have no meaning. It would be like arranging all the electrical decorations for the marriage without the electrical current. But when the light will be ON, you will see the Bridegroom and the Bride."

H.H. Mataji Nirmala Devi.

1

Between you and me

The average intellectual person has a marked taste for understatements and he should be quite uncomfortable to be confronted with big words such as Universal evolution, Cosmos, Man, Destiny, Self-realisation, God and Devil; How awkward! He should also wonder about the author's strange audacity to use them. Moreover what is going to be divulged about the advent of HH Mataji, Sahaja Yoga and collective consciousness can appear so incredibly beautiful that the best intentioned reader might consider the author of this book as merely a particularly impertinent specimen of a rightly disliked category of writers: people writing about things they do not know. And if we assume that, for the sake of impartiality the reader is prepared to consider the academic hypothesis that the author could know what he is saying, then the puzzling question arises: what sort of people can possibly talk about the Kingdom of God and know what they are talking about?

I will not avoid words such as Destiny and God because these powerful verbal symbols precisely cover the matter of this book. As for the extent of my knowledge, let me quote, for the time being, the *Kena Upanishad*:

> "I cannot say that I know Brahman fully, Nor can I say that I know him not. He among us knows him best who understands the spirit of the words: Nor do I know that I know him not".

If you view yourself as a seeker, you should also be prepared to investigate the concrete possibility of experiencing the fulfilment of the Quest in case this possibility materialises. How can I share my own experience with you? A book is a particularly trivial tool to this end, yet, I do not have any other way to reach you. Why do I want to reach you? I guess joy is perfect when it is shared. All my Sahaja Yogi brothers and sisters want you to enter into the city of the joy of God. I am writing on their behalf. Also I was never terribly attracted by the "individual enlightenment model" if darkness was to hang around my precious undisturbed Self, keeping other people in sorrow. So, this is an attempt at communication. I know I am not qualified to write about HH Mataji and Sahaja Yoga, yet, if you receive something of the message, my presumptuousness in doing so might be forgiven.

I am fully aware of the basic futility of bringing into some sort of conceptual framework a reality which completely transcends our own conceptual abilities because, anyway, it is the source of everything that exists, inclusive of our mental powers. The ocean can comprehend the drop of water and not vice-versa. And when this Ocean is the Ocean of the Divine Love words are left on the shores! Now I know why all the great saints said the joy of Self-realization cannot be described. Before I was like a drop away from the Ocean but now I know how it feels to be dissolved in the Ocean. Discursive intelligence and analytical minds cannot imprison in their constructs that sacred love which sustains the organic diversity of the all pervading Oneness. None of the things which are written in this part of the book are of a nature to be laid down in words, none of them can be contained in letters, sounds, ideas. I assure you, I very much hesitated to take up this pen. It has been written down though for a precise reason; not in order that it may be believed, but so that experience itself may be understood; This work is a very humble invitation to experience. Despite tremendous seeking and a maddening urge to know myself the deep concern I always felt was not for my personal evolution but for the emancipation of all the ardent and true seekers. And the age which is dawning is one of the collective understanding of the meaning of existence; this writing is nothing but a first, modest homage to that great understanding. Now the process of understanding is not at all mechanical and blind belief is actually a hindrance to its achievement. After self knowledge one realizes that belief and disbelief are like the twistings of the individual ego attempting to evade truth.

First of all, whatever truth is, it "is" by its very nature, independently of my being able to grasp it or not. Truth is truth, "in se et per se", perfectly self-sustained and complete: if there is somewhere in the country a piece of landscape with say, a river and a tree, it exists whether I see it or not. Actually, truth is what-is-which-is-existing, it is the radiance of existence. But now, what has been often argued is the following point: if there is somewhere a river and a tree but I do not see it, then I do not know it: it might well exist "in itself", it does not exist "for myself" and since it does not exist for myself, as far as I am concerned, it does not exist. The statement "there is a river and tree" is true in itself but it is not true for me and if it is not true for me, how can I accept that it is true in itself ? *The next step not to be taken is to assert that since it is not true for me it is not true at all.* This grave mistake has been made quite a lot in these positivist days. This mistake, be it said in passing, is the expression of a rather classic error of logic, the sophism of generalisation: "What I perceive is. Hence I perceive what is. Hence what is not perceived by me is not". This is the typical illusion of intellectual optics believed by contemporary thought. Fairness would require to add, at the end of the last proposition: "for me". I know reasonable and honest thinkers are aware of this.

The "for me" changes the whole setting and allows the discriminating intelligence to go further in assessing its own cognitive coordinates.

The discriminating intelligence says: "O.K., I do not see the river and the tree but it does not mean that they do not exist, it just means I do not know whether they exist or not". This was the stage reached by Emmanuel Kant in *the Critique of Pure Reason* and the stance advocated by Socrates, Buddha and Lao-Tsu: "know what you know and know what you do not know and know that you know what you know and that you do not know what you do not know". This has always sounded good to me and I suppose the reader can go along these lines and agree with me. After all, this is conventional wisdom. The logic and immediate implications of this position appear in the following statement: Truly I am to tell you about the river of the water of life and about the tree of life which is the path of the sacred Kundalini[1]. But, most probably, you never walked into the inner landscape where they are to be found and thus you cannot believe me; nor should you! However you should not reject my saying either; how could you? You have not gone into this secret place, you have not looked for yourself, have you? And even if you have, can you say that you reached your destination? Can you confidently say that you have found it and that it is same as what has been described in the Scriptures?

Therefore, the way this book can be of some help to you is the following: it can suggest to you that the matter is worth your attention; you can decide to walk towards this country so that you can see by yourself the river and the tree and then, you will be in a position to believe your experience. This is what this attempt is all about; to announce it, to invite all of you to awake, arise, and begin to walk on the path of revelation, while telling you also something about the proper direction. If you can harken to that much for yourself, I promise God will also do something for you as he has done for such an unworthy soul. But help yourself first so heaven will help next. Please believe me, only the dawning of realization, your rebirth, your true Baptism will bring true knowledge to the seeker. When something is laid down in propositions, it obviously becomes subject to objections and controversy; this is the rule of the verbal world. But let the reader acknowledge the true extent to which he can evaluate something which is neither a piece of philosophy or a religious mainifesto but merely a sign post on the road of truth. It is the signal on the road of your own seeking. All great saints describe that in most human beings there is a well hidden magic garden where the flowers of God's love are blossoming. There everything is beauty, freshness, joy, innocence and love. There is the river and the tree. I must announce very humbly that I have really been led to that place. This paradise that we often believe to be so very far is, in fact, quite near. It cannot be lost as long as we have the longing to find it. Seeking is the point. This book is dedicated to all the seekers of truth. May all of us be blessed by the truthfulness of our Quest and Divine Love be our guide! Forget weariness and the past toils of the journey! A day of mighty hope, a day of perfect joy is now dawning upon this world.

---

[1]The residual divine energy within man which rests in a potential state until the moment of self-realization.

If you are not concerned I should quote HH Mataji Nirmala Devi:

"How can I make you hungry. I have cooked for you a very nice meal but if you are not hungry you will not eat it and fuss about it. Those who are hungry will demand it".

Please, do not pretend you are not concerned.

"Hypocritical reader, my fellow-man, my brother" are the words which open Baudelaire's main collection of poems, reminding the reader not to pretend to be detached from existential issues which vitally concern him. I do believe that the true path of liberation should concern any human being. Verily the water and the tree of life I am to talk about concern each of you for the tree has its very roots in everybody's being, it is the core of the spiritual and psycho-somatic process in each and every human body. I am writing this fantastic statement not as a result of years of long compilations of esoteric writings but as the result of a practical immediate, and inwardly felt experience, that I could simply call: the experience of the present.

Let us try to visualise a horizontal line between the *past* (which is stored within the super-ego side of the mind) and the *future* (which is worried about by the ego side of the mind). Somewhere, on this line, there is an ungraspable spot, a geometrical point called *now* which actually breaks the line into its past and future segments. The present is an invisible point on the line because it cannot be quantified in time units like the past (i.e. 1789 AD, 1800 BC) or the future (i.e. 1985, 2000) and yet the irritating paradox is that, from the human standpoint, only the present is; the past is no more and the future not yet.

If our meditation can enter within this invisible point (by thoughtless meditation) it swells it like air in a balloon so as to have past and future absorbed in it: (*see* Fig. 1); the intensity of the all pervading Present is enjoyed because super-ego (past) and ego (future) have been renounced. To enter the invisible point of the horizontal line is like breaking through geometry into a dimension which opens beyond multi-dimensionality itself: there is the Kingdom of God, the magic garden. So very near and yet so far. How to enter it?

The so-called mystic writers say that the Kingdom is within

you, the gate is within you, the key is within you, the path is within you... but it has to be cleared first.

Fig I:

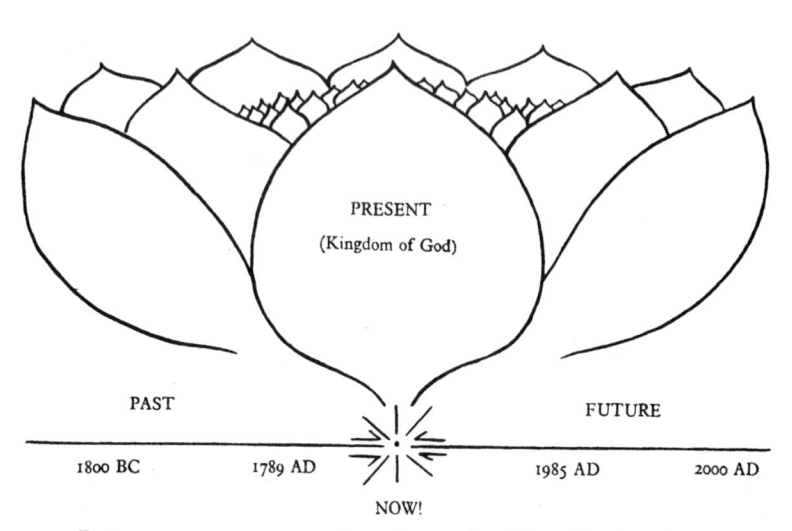

PRESENT
(Kingdom of God)

PAST — 1800 BC — 1789 AD — NOW! — 1985 AD — 2000 AD — FUTURE

Let me try to express in a figure (*see* **Fig. II**) the landscape of our realization:

Fig II:

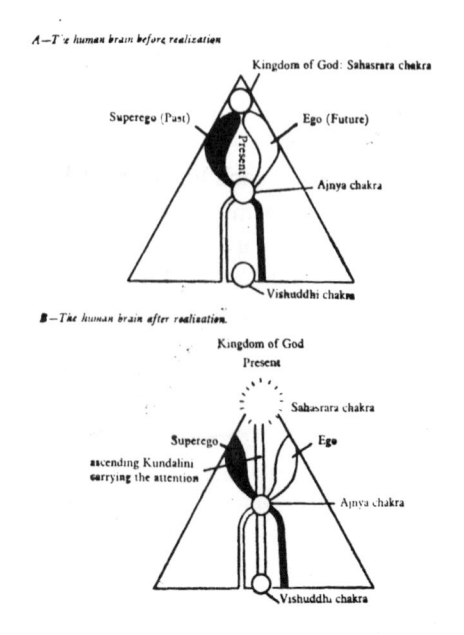

A — The human brain before realization
- Kingdom of God: Sahasrara chakra
- Superego (Past)
- Ego (Future)
- Present
- Ajnya chakra
- Vishuddhi chakra

B — The human brain after realization
- Kingdom of God
- Present
- Sahasrara chakra
- Superego
- Ego
- ascending Kundalini carrying the attention
- Ajnya chakra
- Vishuddhi chakra

THE UNIQUE DISCOVERY OF SAHAJA YOGA

The kingdom is the merging of the Kundalini in the seventh chakra (subtle psycho-somatic center) at the top of the brain (Sahasrara) the abode of the awakened Shakti (divine energy). This chakra has been described in the great mandala of the Shri-Chakra in Shri Shankaracharya's work the *Saundarya-Lahari*: The Flood of Beauty. It has been referred to as Buddha's thousand petalled lotus.

The gate is the sixth chakra on the path of Kundalini between and above the eyebrows (ajnya), referred to as the "third eye", it is the abode of Lord Jesus Christ, the one who has mastered the Buddhi (intellect) and is the Bouddha. (*see* Figure III, p. 39).

The key to that gate is the child-like surrender coming from the heart chakra (anahata) abode of Lord Shiva, which has been referred to by Lord Jesus: "Truly, I say to you, whoever does not receive the Kingdom of God like a child shall not enter it." Luke 18.17.

The path is the inner channel within the spine (Sushumna nadi) referred to as the Tree of Life. It is the path of Kundalini, the residual divine Energy within Man. However there is a gap in this subtle channel. (The gross manifestation of this gap outside of the spinal chord is expressed as the gap between the solar plexus and the vagus nerve of the parasympathetic nervous system). Also the path as well as the chakras (psycho-spiritual centres of energy on the Sushumna nadi) might be constricted or closed because of the loads resulting from previous karma, spirit possessions, nervous troubles, etc. Hence the path has to be cleared first. But, as we will explain later, this cannot be done by the seeker himself because his attention cannot reach his own Sushumna. We understand now the role of the true Master (guru): he is the one to water the seed of life with the vibrations of divine energy that flow like rays, from his being. When the holy vibrations enter into the being of the seeker they fill the gap within the Sushumna and thus form a bridge on the path of Kundalini's ascent. This seed of life will manifest into the Tree of life; when Kundalini is spontaneously awakened by the vibrations of the guru, She realises that She is being invited by the Divine authority of a highly evolved realised soul. She thus rises, piercing six chakras (chakra bhedah) in the central channel (Sushumna).

The water of life is firstly the river of cool vibrations emitted from the Primordial Divine Energy (Adi Shakti). It has been identified in the scriptures as the wind of the Holy Ghost[2] (the breath of the pneuma of the Greek fathers) or the Holy river Ganga falling down from Lord Shiva's head. They are also the Chaitanya of Shri Shankaracharya. At the moment of self-realization, the subject can indeed feel these vibrations as a cool wind, or, depending upon the force, as a cool river flowing into the finger tips and later his hands and his whole being. At the stage of God realization the water of life, referred to as "amrit" or nectar, is felt as a shower of indescribable bliss pouring down from the Sahasrara, into the central and autonomous nervous system.

---

[2]"When the day of Pentacost had come, they were all together in one place. And suddenly a sound came from heaven like the rush of a mighty wind and it filled all the house where they were sitting... and they were all filled with the Holy Spirit". *Acts of Apostle 2*. After that, the tongues of fire (Kundalini) appeared on each of them.

2

Encounter with Sahaja Yoga

> "You will know the truth and
> the truth will make you free".
> John 8.32

> "When the masks are removed there is Self-knowledge which is the knowledge of God.
> To know the Self is to be the Self because there are no two Selves. Hence knowing is being. Consciousness is existence". —Shri Ramana Maharshi

When Newton, Rutherford or Einstein discovered those laws which brought well known revolutions to scientific thinking, they were merely unveiling some of the innumerable aspects of the phenomenology of Energy which were hitherto unknown. Moreover thanks to Einstein, Heisenberg and Niels Bohr, contemporary scientists are aware that the observer is interacting with the object of the observation by his very act of observing: being within time and space, the observer is himself a part of, or masked by, this space-time physical cosmos he is observing. Depending on the observer's standpoint, the same phenomena can be identified by two different, contradictory and yet valid experiments, generating different series of interactions. This is because physical experimentation unveils only specific aspects of phenomena, not the totality of the real, and the selection of these aspects depends upon the specific background of the scientist. For instance, the same phenomena of the physical world have been validly—and differently— explained by Newtonian physics or Einstein's theory of relativity. If this is so, scientific knowledge cannot give the last word on the nature of the Universe. It also exposes the way in which Man corresponds with the global cosmic ecology he belongs to: knowledge, discoveries and the resulting interactions constantly modify the relation between Man and the cosmos.

Unknown laws of reality express phenomena which are existing but which have not yet entered Man's consciousness; as such, they are potential knowledge. The evolution of human consciousness is to actualise this potential knowledge by apprehending these laws; the findings evolve a new relation between Man, himself and the world; to know means to transform. Man is in a perpetual state of becoming because he constantly strives for knowledge and discovery: When the newly discovered laws belong to the material realm man can eventually transform the latter by harnessing them to his profit, by applied knowledge i.e. gravity, electricity, atomic energy, etc. When the laws belong to the psycho-spiritual realm, knowledge itself, causes an inner transformation. The quality of our perception is important because it actualises a corresponding quality of reality; this is magic, transformation, creation!

The power of God's Love is so tremendous that we can purify our attention merely by turning it towards the Divine Love. Indeed there is this innermost knowledge of which Shri Krishna said:

"By the single sun
This whole world is illumined:
By its own knower
The Field is illumined".
—*Bhagavad Gita XIII*

Absolute knowledge is the entry into living truth. Into that truth which is living light and living joy. This is where our Lord Jesus Christ, is waiting for us.

Absolute knowledge is absolute transformation: this very creative dimension of epistemology is today finding its most powerful expression in my teacher Mataji's discovery of Sahaja Yoga.

"Know Infinity and you become infinite". Many of us know this basic message of the ancient wisdom and accept it. But how can I have that experience? Does it take one second or a hundred lives? What happens? What about my next door neighbour? These questions can only be answered by concrete experience and not verbal juggling. All the possible speculations about the inward alchemy of consciousness have already been proposed by the seekers of the past. If there is any truth in these, let the truth manifest itself. If the mutation is feasible, let it happen.

Early in August 1975. The plane has taken off from Philadelphia International Airport. In a couple of hours I will land at Heathrow. I am reading Tolkien's *The Two Towers* as I am too excited to sleep. Sad to leave friends behind but my attention is already on my meeting with HH Mataji.

I shall remember for a long time my first trip from Victoria Station to Oxted (Surrey), where HH Mataji is living. I am sitting in a second class coach of one of those cute little British trains, considering half afraid and half amused: "Hey Greg you might be on your way to find the grail in your cute little blue and yellow train or you might put yourself in a mess once again. Well, she sounded quite nice on the phone". The train reaches Oxted. I register a couple of fast heart beats but I am more excited than anxious. Somebody is waiting for me at the station: he looks pretty normal. Through a lovely and quiet countryside, I walk to HH Mataji's home. I ring the bell: the door opens. HH Mataji comes into the hall. "Mes hommages Madame"...I offer my homage. I had bought flowers at Victoria Station.

What happens when I meet HH Mataji is rather stupefying. In a few minutes I feel I am known by somebody who makes me feel like "back home" or "the return of the prodigal child". I am welcomed by somebody endowed with essential goodness, simplicity and love. It is difficult to express these feelings. I do not know HH Mataji and yet I know her. For the first time, since a long, long time I feel completely relaxed and begin to speak to her with absolute confidence and simplicity.

She is asking me questions about my family, my health and why I have only a little shirt because I am going to catch a cold. I answer. I tell also that I have been looking for something, it is truth I guess, but I have not found it and I am tired. She smiles. She says smilingly, "I will have to test you." I burst out laughing, "Oh you can test"—How was the travel?—the travel was all right. We take a cup of tea. Her voice is so sweet, so tender. I can feel she is absolutely honest. I am wrapped in a deep, soothing motherly love. And I become very fond of her. Everything is so simple. Everything will be all right. The house is silent. Sunshine enters through the window. She says she knows me. I know she does. She does: it is strange and beautiful. Within myself, something resurrects, something I had almost forgotten: my own goodness, my own dignity. I am so very happy. Peace has come in me. Mataji, who are you? She wears a white saree.

We did not spend hours talking. After some time I entered a new state of consciousness in the only way that my intelligence could accept: I knew that this little mind of mine could not comprehend Reality but that Reality should comprehend it. It roughly happened in this way.

HH Mataji asks me to sit in front of her and to stretch my hands towards her. It seems to me that she goes into a deep concentration and makes quite a few movements with her hands and arms. These movements indicate that HH Mataji is trying to raise something from my navel to the top of my head but with my eyes I cannot see anything: Some of the gestures also suggest that she has some kind of invisible weapons in her hands. Some others remind me of the ritual postures of very old statues. All the time I am staring at her. She is so utterly beautiful, full of humility and humanity with an indescribable glow of inward majesty. During the process a little later I begin to feel a sort of cool breeze flowing into my hands, like a river of vibrations. This breeze forces its way into my open palms, despite my incredulity. I certainly did not remember then, that one word the Greek fathers used to designate the Holy Spirit was "pneuma" meaning "breath". Nor do I think about "Chaitanya Lahari" the Water of Life or the river Ganga. I just do not understand at all what is going on but I know something is happening...that I do not understand; this by itself, is quite interesting, the more so that I am now feeling localised sensations within my body, along the spine, as if some parts of my body unknown to me are coming into existence. The more puzzling fact is that HH Mataji seems to know exactly what is going on: "it is in the heart chakra". Yes, indeed, I am feeling something in my chest. HH Mataji directs her hand towards my back near the heart area and after some time the slight pain vanishes...and reappears at the base of the throat: "it is in the Vishuddhi chakra," says she smilingly: again, she puts a specific finger on the backbone at my throat. My eyes begin to cry and I feel a burning in my forehead. There, she applies "tika" or the red powder with which Indian women adorn their forehead at the spot supposed to be the seat of the "third eye". She explains, "This tika is vibrated and will help dispel the negative vibrations which, at the moment, are jammed in your Ajnya". She says at this chakra: "Think of Jesus Christ and that he gave his blood for the human emancipation". Slowly the tension in my forehead dissolves and my whole head is filled with a sensation of lightness or acute lucidity. It is also a very soft and pleasant feeling. As the tension in my head melts away, a space is created, so to speak, which gives me complete relaxation and I feel I am completely silent but fully aware. My eyes become a bit heavy and I close them. But soon the strain leaves my eyes and I feel I am acquiring a new quality of vision. Again I open my eyes and I am looking at HH Mataji and grow evermore fascinated, maybe a bit like a child entering a fairyland. Sometimes I am catching a glimpse of very swift lightning, of a golden dust whirling around her shape. I can also distinctly see— I do not know how to say it—various personalities who appear through her expressions while she is talking to me. There is a lady, a Madonna overflowing with compassion and love. Her eyes express such a depth of knowledge, such tremendous love that I am bewildered, really trying to drink this in, to fill myself with it. I see also a young woman, exquisitely lovely, adorable as cannot be named, who laughs like a little girl (she laughs with her eyes also). But her laugh resounds like the trembling of Power itself. Now, another young woman with an expression of disgust on her face, as the incarnation of the integral purity would have to look at something filthy. HH Mataji is talking; with a gentle and loving voice she explains: "Your Kundalini is your own mother. She has been with you in your past births. Even when Kundalini is not active it is aware of your past deeds, she is the witness of your good and bad deeds". I get a fright. She goes on pensively, "You have made mistakes, the chakras are damaged, it will take time to heal them". She then notices that I am growing increasingly anxious and says at once: "Don't you worry. Everything will be all right". This statement carries such a powerful expression of motherly love that my fears vanish. The room is merged in a golden, moving light or so it seems to my dilated pupils; I feel enveloped in a bath of soothing energy of Joy. HH Mataji is saying: "Kundalini has risen. The parasympathetic nervous system is being activated. You do not need to do anything. The process of your second birth is sahaj, spontaneous." I am delighted that I am not supposed to mentally strive for something because if my mind is simply to relax and be watchful I am avoiding the danger of suggestion or autosuggestion. On the other hand I am embarrassed to witness something happening to me, which is at the same time obvious and obviously out of my control. I am not in a state of hypnosis though because my intellect can and does argue: "Is it that? Is it really that?" Who is this person, in front of me, who is working as a catalyst of energies unknown to me, energies that I feel coming in my body in waves of vibrations? What about my karmas. Has she dissolved them? Will this bliss last? Suddenly I come to realise that these vibrations have an impact on my awareness also; I am softly entering a dimension where everything in the room has begun to change and yet remain the same; a majestic silence is growing within me. The noises of the mind disappear: it is as if something more real, more intense, reveals itself in the already manifested reality of myself, the air, the yellow curtains and the table: something simple and essential, this very thing I have been hunting for so long. Simple. Direct. Immediate. Obvious. Blissful. Something called Reality. This Reality that I had, in vain, tried to encompass is slowly, gently encompassing me. This is a bit too much! I cannot really face the possibility that I have reached the end of such an intensive and continuous quest. I feel sleepy...and, with HH Mataji's blessing go to sleep.

When I wake up a delicious Indian dinner is ready and I must say, I don't bother about anything but enjoying it. HH Mataji is looking at me and I can perceive pity and compassion. She looks distressed by my condition. I am like a little baby whose great bliss is to enjoy his mother's exclusive attention. "My time is free for a couple of days", she proposed, "why don't you stay here a little longer; in your case it will take some time to stabilize; as it is you are not well". Of course I knew I was ill and had gone headlong into the wrong paths of a misled search.

The following days I found out indeed that my state is not too bright. Sometimes I feel the vibrations, sometimes I don't; there is pain in various parts of my body; my mind gets restless again. HH Mataji grants me many sessions of vibrations therapy. I go into states of bliss and then slip back again into confusion. One time, fed up with myself, I tell HH Mataji that I'm afraid I'm completely useless and beyond repair. HH Mataji asks me "how do you feel now?" At that very instant I feel like I am dissolving in an indescribable sensation of bliss creeping in my whole body, I close my eyes. A little later HH Mataji softly says, "I think you should not get upset". Lo! bliss has gone! I am stupefied at this experience. It clearly proved that Mataji has an absolute mastery over the phenomena of energy-awareness. She can lift me to the seventh heaven in the twinkling of an eye if she so desires; it is perfectly amazing! "Then the struggle is here for me to clean my mechanism myself"; I accept the idea. It is fair. It conforms with my idea of human freedom that, in some way, I participate in the process.

As it is, my Kundalini does climb, and I get surprising vibratory information; the cool waves coming up in my hands, while I am opening them towards HH Mataji, generate different sensations in the different fingers and parts of the hand. The sensations in the fingers often happen to be connected with a sensation within the body and I come to discover that each finger and part of the hand is connected with a specific psycho-somatic centre (chakra) in the body. The various sensations, little feelings of burning and pain, seem to indicate where are the psychic or physical problems; the full dimension of this experience is better expressed when I add that I am also receiving this sensory information from other people.

Indeed, the following days, resting in Hyde Park or Holland Park, shopping in London, taking the train at Victoria Station to meet HH Mataji, I realise that the localised sensations, either in my fingers or in the parts of my body where the chakras are located, correspond sometimes with a thought, sometimes with the proximity of other people, sometimes I feel it without knowing why. I find out that I feel in my body the chakras of other people when putting my attention on them. Inversely HH Mataji's servant who is a realized soul, while stretching his hands towards me knows exactly which of my chakras is under stress; I am, at first, a bit embarrassed! HH Mataji says: "This is collective consciousness. You are aware of your centres as well as of those of others".

I can recall countless instances of such cases. For instance in a session with Sahaja yogis in London, we are trying to raise the Kundalini of an Indian doctor. I feel pain in the right finger corresponding to the ajnya chakra; the man is puzzled and confirms that his right eye is very weak. Another day, I phone a friend of mine who has heart trouble and I immediately feel the pain on the left side of my heart chakra. These are very simple examples but, of course, the information provided by the vibrations does not refer only to physical troubles. I get related by vibrations to my own psycho-somatic instrument of awareness and to those of the people who surround me. When I confront "negative" vibrations (expressed by burnings or pains) my own vibrations spontaneously react against them. Now that I am tuned with this vibratory state of original Energy, my own body acts as a catalyst for this energy.

I am annoyed because, obviously my condition is not very good. My system has been damaged by my past mistakes. Yet I feel, somehow, that I understand why I committed them. I feel I behaved like a naughty little boy who crept out of the house to play in the mud in order to attract his mother's attention. Now this longed for attention is on me and I enjoy it thoroughly.

During this stay in her house I was at the same time puzzled and elated! I was realising I had finally reached what I was looking for: a cognitive instrument which did not rely on drugs or anything counterfeit or artificial, an inward tool of awareness which did not exclude any part of myself but integrated them in this higher synthesis the philosophers of yore had been looking for. This was the epistemological breakthrough, the revelation of the secret, the Mutation.

Then, a bitter paradox manifested itself in this mind which had been left free to witness and evaluate the whole process: having searched for so long, I could not believe I had actually reached the goal: "It is too beautiful to be true! Why should it happen to poor me?"

I was amazed to confront a specific difficulty, which, I believe, is going to confront a few intellectuals of this generation: we have formed the habit of searching, wondering, wandering, above all analysing to such an extent that it has become a pattern of life. In a state of constant mobility, our mind is investigating this, investigating that; we cannot give up "the Quest" and the magnetic attraction of its mythical status. In a way, we can say that, having rejected so many things as not true "not this, not that"—we could be likely to disregard truth also because we do not know how to tell the difference. Also an intellectual's ego is always trying to supress the spiritual sensitivity: it hangs like a curtain between me and my Self; it wants to spread an asphyxiating cloud of murmurs, doubts, questions, crooked thought processes, biases and nonsense. I am getting really fed up with the pettiness and the stupidity of my ego! Though I know it is the truth I am facing, I cannot identify with it: I am in a way denying it! Because of this negativity of my ego I am one of the slowest to settle down into my self-realization.

The first days of my encounter with Sahaja Yoga, in HH Mataji's home or walking in the Surrey countryside, my mind is still very agitated: I do not know how to accept, how to let something happen to me, how to be relaxed; I want to understand and control everything that is happening to me while being unable to do it. Waves of questions arise, one after another: "If this is so, it is the opening of the Golden Age! How are we going to reach all the seekers? They must know it. How will they accept it? Can they renounce harmful life styles? Shall I stand on my feet? Can we make it?" My sympathetic nervous system at times, goes wild. There is a struggle in my head, as my heavily conditioned mind cannot relate to what happened to it; I do not know how to ride the horse of the mind (ego and super-ego). But, eventually I again come to experience this state of thoughtless awareness, firstly only for a few seconds, and then after a few days, more often, and for longer periods. In this state, I merge into a silent intensity that I can only describe by the word 'bliss'. All the noises, fears and anguishes of the mind are swallowed up by the inward intensity of being. I am there, without present or past, without attractions or repulsions. I feel much closer to my real identity; a very old world wakes up in me. My relation to the outer-world becomes the one of a witness, just seeing things as they are. Then again, the clouds hide the azure. All the while, with an amazing patience, HH Mataji explains to me the working of the Divine Energy, the genesis of the cosmos, the history of the divine incarnations. With a crystalline acuity she describes the moment of evolution we are going through and what the alternatives are. I am suspended by her words. They form a sparkling torrent of wisdom, intelligence, knowledge. HH Mataji also gradually answers all my personal questions, telling what my problems are and why things are happening this way. She knows all about the conditionings of our minds, the modern times and its problems. It is a feast of the mind! My intellect is surprised at her knowledge.

I am considering HH Mataji with an awe growing out of tremendous respect. I have again seen some of her aspects. One evening HH Mataji is sitting on a chair, in the dining room, wearing a white saree with red garments. The black, blue and brilliant night of her hair fall on the shoulders. Her eyes are closed. I am sitting at her feet. The face I am contemplating is neither of a man or of a woman, ageless, resting in its own divinity, a cosmic, almighty figure. I wonder where HH Mataji has gone and my head is filled with an awareness of the galactic spaces' silent infinity.

The other instance, which occurred the day before I was to leave Great Britain, was rather dramatic. I was depressed to be leaving HH Mataji and my mind was very disturbed as the dislodged shadows were fighting within my head to maintain their grip.

HH Mataji is fed up with them and I behold a frightful, terrible and yet perfectly beautiful and divine vision. She is seated. Wreaths of golden white clouds spring from her form. The air in the room is palpitating with energy. The face is animated by a glowing inward radiance. It has become as white as snow in the sunshine. Sharp eyes are piercing me. The expression I behold in awe is like that of a royal eagle. I am afraid, I look at the carpet. Disturbances have left my mind. Peace is settling within me. The next day, when I leave her home my mind is resting in a peaceful state of thoughtless awarness.

I recall this blessed week as the most astonishing time in my life, a time vibrating with unexpected climaxes of revelation and discoveries, bathing in an all encompassing atmosphere of motherly tenderness and love. I am enriched with the memories of a very blissful time. At times, peace was overwhelming. For instance, she would ask me to look at a painting without thinking. I could do it and the joy that was in the heart of that paintings' creator would pour into me like a cool river of breeze. I was thrilled. The quality of silence felt in such occasions can be illustrated by the following comment of HH Mataji: "When the waters of the lake of the mind are still, it reflects the beauty of its surroundings and the undisturbed joy of the Creator". Yet, in many instances, I was fed up with myself, depressed by the weakness of my restless mind and by its incapacity to identify once and for all with the truth it could witness.

I am today in a better position to explain what happened during my first encounter with Her Holiness Mataji Nirmala Devi.

In Sahaja Yoga the moment of self-realization means instant bliss for the great saint who has prepared himself for it for thousands of years of successive rebirths. But somebody who jumps into it from a less advanced state will, logically enough, have a different perception of the experience. He will need much more time to realize the greatness of the jump and to clean himself from the accumulated conditionings. Other people who damage their instrument by inbalanced lives, by drug taking, over-involvement into sex, etc., may encounter certain problems and their growth into the new awareness can be slower. This has largely been my case... ! For two years I could not remain in thoughtless awareness for longer than a short period of time. Sometimes people just touch Realization and they have to work on themselves with determination in order to consolidate their position. Sahaja yoga teaches us how to do it. The seekers who have damaged their chakras should be patient with themselves. HH Mataji says "your Kundalini is patiently waiting for the time of her manifestation. As your own mother she will never hurt you. With loving care she will first gently cure your physical body and repair the chakras". Kundalini is not rushing her way through damaged chakras. We should understand the delicacy and the rhythm of the evolution which is gradually transforming our awareness. As the process is spontaneous and natural, it manifests according to the subject's condition. An aspect of Sahaja Yoga which commands my immediate respect is that this yoga leaves you free: it does not propel you into a state of perception which is over-powering.

HH Mataji's granting of a new awareness is spontaneous and effortless. Effortless in the sense that the mind of the sadhaka has just to relax during the process, avoiding efforts, auto-suggestions and wishful thinking, remaining open and ready to witness the truth of the experience. The experience itself cannot be mistaken for any counterfeit suggestion or spirit's possession, precisely because you can lucidly watch it with your mind, while its reality is attested to by the body's sensations. HH Mataji brings into a beautiful perspective the effortlessness of Sahaja Yoga. She says: "Everything that is very important is effortless; for example breathing, has to be very simple and effortless. That is why your self-realization takes place effortlessly." Indeed, it is so simple! The Kundalini spontaneously rises in the physical presence of HH Mataji or when she is awakened by Her vibrations.

At any time, a Sahaja yogi acts as a free agent with the great advantage however, that his increased power of discrimination and vibratory awareness immensely helps him to correctly evaluate the terms of the alternatives and to make the right ethical choices. This freedom explains some of the difficulties that may confront some of us after realization but it also leaves us with the challenging capacity of being an actor in the drama of our own ascent. With Her unique sense of humour, HH Mataji says: "Sahaja Yoga can start your motor car; if it needs repair, Sahaja is also a repair shop...But without starting the car, how will you move? The starting is effortless".

In order to enable you to better understand this happening I wish now to present in the *Figure III* the Tree of Life which is formed by the chakras and the three channels of energy with which they are connected.

—The Kundalini is sleeping in the triangular bone above the pelvic plexus, waiting for the time of Her manifestation.

—The chakras are the subtle centres in the spinal chord and the brain. They manifest outside the spinal chord as plexuses and they control the organs of the physical body as well as the neuro-endocrinal system of the corresponding region of the human body.

—The three energy channels (nadis), together with the seven chakras, manifest the autonomic and the central nervous system as well as the specific functions of the two hemispheres of the brain: the ego dominated part of the brain (left hemisphere) is connected with the right side sympathetic nervous system (pingala nadi) while the super-ego dominated part of the brain (right hemisphere) is linked with the left side sympathetic nervous system (ida nadi).

—The Void shown in the diagram is not the blessed emptiness of the Zen buddhists. It corresponds to the state of awareness (Bhavasagara, Ocean of illusion) in which we are lost in igronance and confusion. To overcome this, the Kundalini has to raise through this part of the body.

In other words the physical health of the subject as well as his psyche's character depend upon the type of inter-actions within the subtler energetic structure of the nadis and the chakras.

The imminence of a revolution in medical and psycho sciences is better shown by stating that a Sahaja Yogi has the power to monitor this energy. He can, for instance, use his hand as a multi-purpose transmitter of the energy. This is one of the greatest aspects of Sahaja Yoga! You actually get the power to cure people with your bare hand as the dynamic force of Divine Love (Chaitanya) is emitted through your hand and your Being. *Figure IV* (*see* page 40) shows how the hand is linked with the central psycho-somatic system.

THE UNIQUE DISCOVERY OF SAHAJA YOGA 39

Figure III: *The human microcosm*

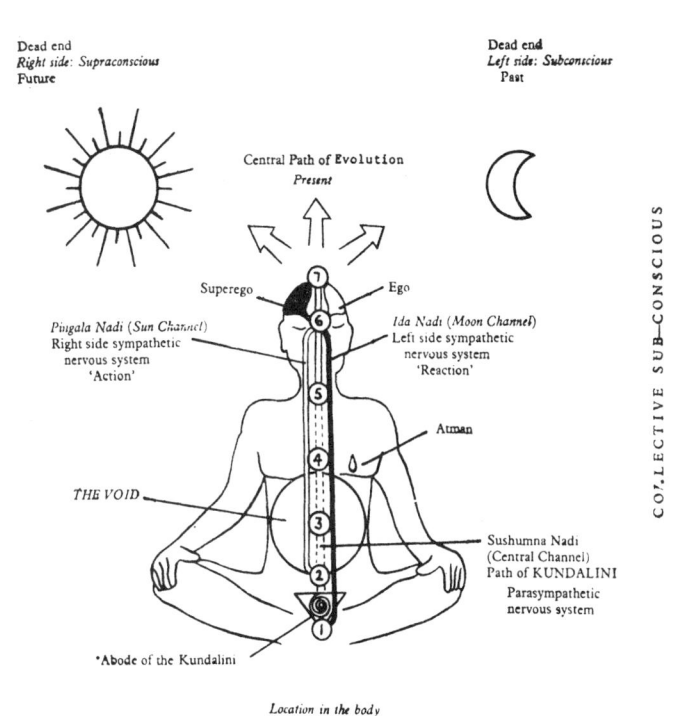

Dead end
Right side: *Supraconscious*
Future

Dead end
Left side: *Subconscious*
Past

Central Path of Evolution
Present

Superego

Ego

Pingala Nadi (*Sun Channel*)
Right side sympathetic
nervous system
'Action'

Ida Nadi (*Moon Channel*)
Left side sympathetic
nervous system
'Reaction'

Atman

THE VOID

Sushumna Nadi
(Central Channel)
Path of KUNDALINI
Parasympathetic
nervous system

*Abode of the Kundalini

COLLECTIVE SUPRA-CONSCIOUS

COLLECTIVE SUB-CONSCIOUS

Chakra	Location in the body / Gross Expression	Manifest on the Physical Level (General description)
7. Sahasrara (1,000 petals)	Limbic area	Vibrations
6. Ajnya chakra (2 petals)	Crossing of optic thalamus	Pineal and Pituitary bodies
5. Vishuddhi chakra (16 petals)	Cervical plexus	Arms, Neck, Mouth, Nose, Eyes, Ears, Lower Brain.
4. Anahath or Riddhaya chakra (12 petals)	Cardiac plexus	Heart, Lungs
3. Nabhi or Manipur chakra (10 petals)	Solar plexus	Liver (part) Stomach
2. Swadhistan chakra (6 petals)	Aortic plexus	Partly sex and elimination, Liver (part), Spleen, Pancreas, kidney, lower part of abdomen.
1. Mooladhara chakra (4 petals)	Pelvic plexus	Sex, elimination
*Mooladhara	Coccyx	Parasympathetic Nervous System (dormant)

Figure IV:

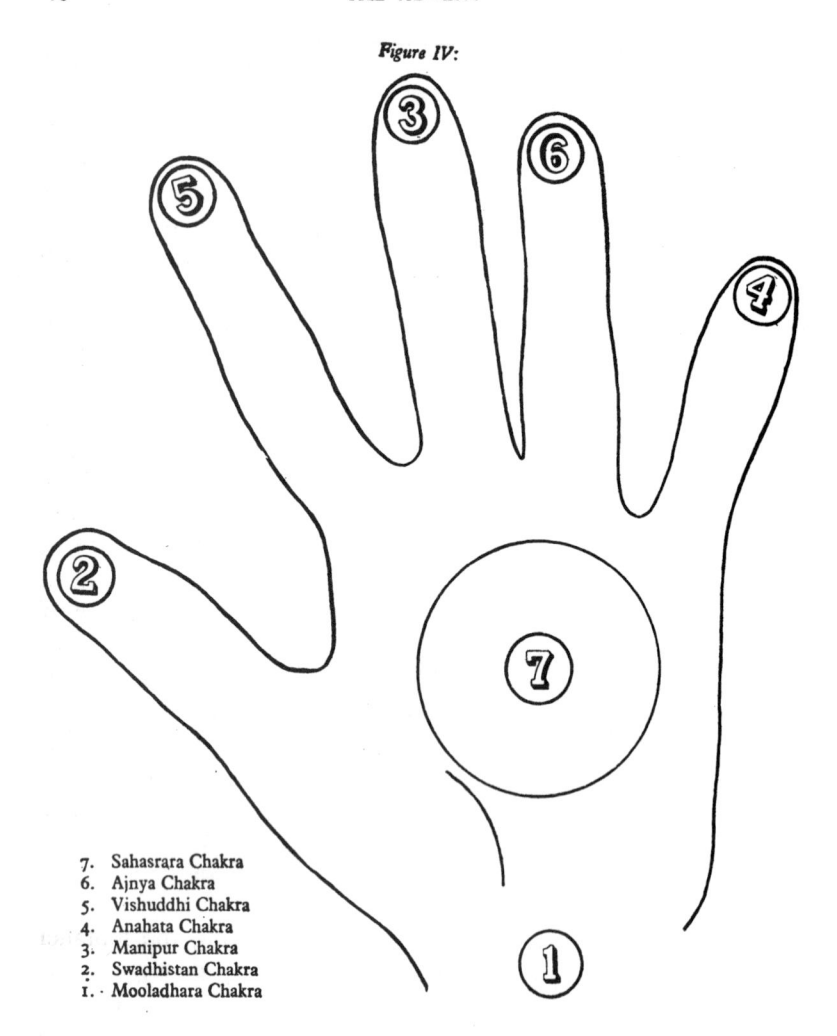

7. Sahasrara Chakra
6. Ajnya Chakra
5. Vishuddhi Chakra
4. Anahata Chakra
3. Manipur Chakra
2. Swadhistan Chakra
1. Mooladhara Chakra

—This graph shows how each of the fingers of the hand sends forth and receives the differentiated vibrations of the corresponding chakras. This process starts after realisation and is felt by the Sahaja Yogi through the medium of physical sensations. (central nervous system).

It is one thing to read about the chakras in the Ancient Tibetan or Hindu scriptures and it is quite another one to actually feel them in the body. The newly discovered vibratory awareness casts a new light on the perennial human problem of discriminating between right and wrong because the integrated awareness of dharma manifests of the physical level itself. In other words, if there is something "wrong" you become spontaneously aware of it. One day, a person looked at me on the underground escalator, and, intercepting this glance, I felt pain in my eyes! Another time, I was thinking of a very sweet nephew of mine and ..my head became light and filled with a sensation of well-being, etc., etc.

HH Mataji always gives a full explanation of these happenings. When a man puts his finger in a fire he withdraws it quickly because his central nervous system informs him that it burns. A Sahaja yogi develops this kind of spontaneous reflex action towards any kind of surroundings (emotional, mental, spiritual) because the central nervous system and the autonomous nervous system (sympathetic and parasympathetic) are integrated by the raising of the Kundalini with the spiritual awareness of Dharma which is one of the aspects of the cosmic consciousness.

The moment of self-realization corresponds to the rising of Kundalini, within the spinal chord, (Sushumna nadi—the Tree of Life), making its way through the void and breaking through the apex of the brain (*Brahma Randhra*): the connection with the all pervading Primordial Energy is thus established. Then this energy can be felt by the newly integrated nervous system as vibrations. In my own early experiences I felt the awakening of my Kundalini a couple of times as a pleasant feeling of coolness from the bottom of my spine. Other Sajaha Yogis had other experiences. A friend of mine in India told me that he actually heard the sound made by the Kundalini piercing the fontanel membrane. Another one recalls, after the same experience, a sensation of bliss melting down from the top of his head. Another one, having closed his eyes, saw elliptic movement of light spreading from the Ajnya chakra and lightening his head.

Let us quote only a few among so many realized Sahaja Yogis. Rajbai J. Modi writes in *The Divine Mother*:[1]

"My personal experience of awakening of Kundalini took place in the first week of January 1972. Rev. Mataji touched the six plexuses for a few seconds and powerful force started

---

[1] *The Divine Mother*, Z. S. Moray edit. (Bombay) p. 9.

rising from plexus to plexus and ultimately to the brain. While this was going on, I was very deep in meditation. Mataji finished her job in seconds and I was going very deep into Dhyana with immense joy and pleasing sensations all over my body. My eyes could not be opened and meditation continued. My body was warmer, I was with myself as if fully drunk, but completely conscious. Later on Dhyana was even more interesting and deep. On the 27th January 1972, when I was at Bordi, late in the night after the programme some of us were staying along with Mataji. Mataji told me to close my eyes and touched my Sahasrar. Within seconds she said, "Realised!" She asked me to think, but I could not keep the link even for a few seconds. Afterwards I went to sleep. Next morning, one elderly person had a slight pain in the heart and I tried giving vibrations. To my surprise he said, "I am feeling better". This is how it started and has continued ever since.

Just after the realisation a sensation of the flow of energy was felt by me. Mataji asked me to give vibrations to a person who was to be realised. To my amazement I found that the flow was hot in nature. Mataji told us there is a little resistance as he was getting awakening of the Kundalini, and then the flow become cold. Mataji told us that now the power was flowing down the sympathetic system (Ha and Tha i.e. Surya and Chandra nadi) thus cooling it. Suddenly I felt that the vibrations were coming back to me on one hand. So Mataji closed her eyes and with her powers (Sankalpa) she brought the vibrations in both the hands. She opened her eyes and asked me if it was coming in both the hands. When I said yes, She asked me to ask the person whether he was thoughtless. He nodded his head, said his eyes cannot be opened. Mataji asked him to wait. After two minutes, he opened his eyes and found his eyes were glowing. He told me he got perfume of very strong fragrance of roses. He also saw very strong light. When I asked him to feel the vibrations from his fingers, he said he can feel the flow. There are numerous instances of such realization and countless numbers of jagruti (awakening)..."

David, a Sahaja Yogi from London says about his encounter

with HH Mataji : "I felt incredibly kind of happy. I felt very high, the pressure in the head melted away; every time she looks at me coolness surrounds me." Miriam declares that: "As soon as she put her attention on me I felt the vibrations." For Lindsay it was "like flying with the Tao. Wow! It was so beautiful. I was just silent. I felt so much love. It is my heart which decided." Christine: "A couple of weeks before meeting HH Mataji I started to feel full of joy and... I don't know how to say it... incredibly happy just to exist. I saw Her for the first time in a friend's flat. When She entered into the room the palms of my hands started tingling and then there was a cool breeze. I felt completely at peace. Completely there. It was a second birth. Everything was new." Tony, one of my friends, was meditating in a room with the picture of HH Mataji. Young children of visiting friends came into the room and asked what he was doing. He answered smilingly: "I am taking power from this Holy Lady. Do you want to try?" So, the little band sat down. They all stretched their hands towards the picture. After some time a girl remarked: "Hey there is a lot of wind." She paused for a while and then asked thoughtfully, "How do you switch off?" The common thread running through all the various experiences of realization is that the phenomenon has been triggered by the proximity and/or meeting with HH Mataji. After months of critical observations I have reached the indisputable conclusion that She is the absolute master of Kundalini. Just by Her glance or even through the help of Her photograph one can achieve awakening and also self-realization. Moreover, no one so far has been able to render such a comprehensive, integrated and detailed knowledge of Kundalini.

"Sahaja Yoga" means spontaneous union. It expresses the fact that what is potential, in-born within us should manifest itself naturally and spontaneously, "like a seed grows into a tree."[2] However a tree does not grow in the midst of a waterless desert and the process of self-actualisation is initiated and stimulated by the "Water of Life", the vibrations of Divine Love that HH Mataji is pouring. Incredibly enough, after a while, the Sahaja

---

[2] For instance the sensations of exquisite fragrance are perceived when the roots of the tree (the Mooladhara chakra) are very strong. It is reported that the cell of Saint Catherine of Siena was perfumed with such fragrances.

Yogis have themselves the power to radiate these vibrations!! As stated above there are many cases of realization given by HH Mataji's disciples, through these vibrations, or more correctly, there are countless cases of realization given by these vibrations through HH Mataji's disciples even in big cities like Delhi, Bombay, London or Los Angeles. Which masters can bestow such tremendous powers on their disciples? There is indeed something very special about the advent of HH Mataji!

Two years later in Kathmandu, I am working with an international development Agency. I can describe my position as follows: My mind has greatly improved in its capacity for discrimination and its ability to focus the power of attention: I can watch, almost like projected on a cinema screen, the pictures and images of conditionings and interferences and thus, I do not identify with them any more or generate for myself the consequent negative karma. Sometimes I can see to which aspect of my past they relate. I have an increased power to stop the thought-waves I dislike. Without any difficulty I have totally changed my life style and I feel physically much more healthy and inwardly much cleaner. Exactness of perception evolves proportionally to this inside cleanliness. When I face difficulties I can "see" them and it is an enormous advantage. I am dealing much better with every aspect of daily life.

Actually I do not yet live in thoughtless awareness but I can reenter it whenever I want. Slowly but surely this is changing my cognitive relationship with myself and with the world. Perhaps I can express it thus: I am opening myself to a world just more real than the material one, although it encompasses this latter and so to say, magnifies it. It is truly a world more real than the one most people consider to be the real one: it asserts itself with direct obviousness and naked simplicity; it is known by the integrated perceptive faculties of my being and not merely by the body, or the thoughts, or the emotions alone. It is neither a thought, or a feeling, or a sensation but, somehow, all these together in a joyous silence and still something else. This new world—which I suspect to be the most ancient one expresses a quality of transparency and freshness, simplicity and joy, innocence and spontaneity, purity and holiness; it manifests a dimension of the sacred and the beautiful, an affirmation of truth and excellence. I know I had lost it and I am now recovering it. In the depth of my most ancient memory dawns that which was, is and will be.

May be I should also add that, since my realization, I have had experiences of various orders. For instance I had some "parapsychological" experiences and extra sensory perceptions such as: conscious action in the sleeping state (outside of my physical body) seeing and talking to spirits sometimes fighting with them, hearing a majestic chorus of angels and divine music in my head, etc. But I do not focus my attention on these matters. The main thing is to put one's attention on the inner consciousness of the Self. I felt my own Kundalini two times as an incredibly fantastic blissful feeling, like a shower of grace and divinity pouring softly from the Sahasrara down the whole body. The second of these experiences was connected with a vision of HH Mataji as a majestic crowned queen, clad in a royal purple garment, seated on a golden throne and holding various weapons in her many hands.

More recently in Bombay I had the privilege of being in a car with HH Mataji. We were five Sahaja Yogis on our way to the seaside to look at a possible site for an ashram. I was not well and had a bad cold; HH Mataji put her hand on my neck. I swooned. I was about to lose consciousness. I felt a tremendous shivering rushing from the bottom of my spine to the top of my head. Half fainting, I laughed. In my mind and in my heart only one thought, "Deliverance. She is the Deliverer." Since that blessed minute my capacity of staying in thoughtless awareness improved.

You know, it is not easy to describe life after the second birth because it is so very simple. This life which had been disturbed by moods of boredom, frustration or despair and by all kinds of tensions, this same life turns into joy. It all happens inside. It is there and nothing can take it away from you. Hence the Sahaja yogis feel so strong now; we know it is the strength of love which enables us to help others and ourselves. This knowledge itself resides in our heart as an ocean that is deep and endless and yet silent.

We feel very confident on the basis of these new experiences. It is a fact that we are now in a position to know Reality in the environment and ourselves. We perceive exactly what things really are through vibratory information! When social masks and facades are thus pierced by a direct, spontaneous and immediate sensation one no longer shows off or is abused. Furthermore, the new perception reveals a nexus of vibratoy interactions which define the fields of the cosmic ecology. Not only people, but places and objects, living beings, organic and inanimate matter, the complete substratum of reality can reveal a certain degree of goodness or dharmic quality. It is indeed on the basis of these findings that we are beginning to understand the true nature of the cosmic battlefield, the Units of Psychic Interferences and the way to trace one's path as a detached and playful witness of the great show! Understood also is the fact that there is an instrument of knowledge through which Man could spontaneously avoid the wrong course of action and remain undisturbed by negative influences. We can see that, at last, it has become possible for Man to achieve the knowledge of Reality. This is the stage of history in which Mankind will understand his true place in the cosmic ecology. And, above all, life becomes a long delight; this is, after all, what matters—isn't it?

I have begun to grasp the true significance of some old scriptures. For instance the perception of the wind of the vibrations from the Holy Spirit has been hinted at by Lord Jesus in a statement I never could understand before:

"That which is born of the flesh is flesh, and that which is born out of the spirit is spirit. Do not marvel that I said to you 'you must be born anew.' The wind blows where it wills, and you hear the sound of it, but you do not know whence it comes and whither it goes; so it is with everyone who is born of the spirit." Nicodemus said to him "How can this be?".—John 3.6.

How can this be? I could not know before I could feel the vibrations. And how could I explain it to this American "Jesus freak" I met who was explaining what it means to be second born by referring to the Bible.[3] The poor thing! He is not going to know what he is talking about unless and until he feels the breath of the vibrations.

---

[3]What Sri Shankaracharya wrote for the orthodox Hindus is valid here : "The study of the scriptures is useless so long as the highest truth is unkown, and it is equally useless when the highest truth has already been known" in *Vivekachudamani* (Calcutta 1926. 9th edit. July 1974) p. 21.

In thoughtless awareness we get in touch with our own Self (Atman). This is why the growth in this awareness is so essential.

As the Self is not limited by our physical, emotional and mental bodies, knowledge of the Self implies knowledge of the cosmos. The latter knowledge also expresses the field of the Self's manifestation through a vibratory transformation of the Divine Energy.

"He who knows, meditates upon, and realizes this truth of the Self, find that everything—primal energy, ether, fire, water, and all other elements—mind, will, speech, sacred hymns and scriptures—indeed the whole universe—issues forth from it."—*Chandogya Upanished.*

The spontaneous yoga opens a new dimension to human consciousness: the Kingdom of God. The revelation of Sahaja consciousness is God's greatest gift to Mankind.

It really becomes possible to relate to the sayings of the past Avatars (Divine Incarnations) and masters not merely through a longing of the soul for a glimpse of understanding but thanks to the naked reality of experience:

"Being asked by the Pharisees when the Kingdom of God was coming, he answered them; "the Kingdom of God is not coming with signs to be observed; nor will they say, 'Lo, here it is' or 'There'. For behold the Kingdom of God is in the midst of you."—Luke 17-20

Oh! wake up! Don't you know that it is what you have been looking for?

HH Mataji's discovery of Sahaja Yoga is historical in the double sense that it comes at a specific, preordained point in history and that it is going to shape the course of future history. She is completing the grand task of all the great Incarnations of the past. It is not a hazard that the Sanskrit expression for the Golden Age is Satya Yuga: the Age of Revelation. Maybe we should have taken more seriously Joachim of Fiore (1145-1202), a Cistercian Monk who lived in Southern Italy. He predicted that after the age of the Father (that we know to be Krishna—Jahwe) and the age of the Son (Jesus—Mahavishnu) the third age to come would be the Age of the Holy spirit (the Primordial Energy, Adi Shakti), to bring about knowledge and integration. The year 1260 would inaugurate the third Age and the coming of the Kingdom of Heaven on earth. Well, the timing might not have been accurately predicted but the scheme is worth a few thought.

The Fifth of May 1970, in India, the One who incarnated in the person of HH Mataji Nirmala Devi discovered, from the human standpoint and for the benefit of the human race, how to complete the full mastery over Kundalini rising and how to make, out of it, a collective phenomenon. Thus She made a historical possibility out of the necessity to evolve, at mass level, the new category of perception necessary to break through the contemporary chaos of society. Thereby the gap between the Finite and the Infinite is to be in fact closed. The Golden Age opens before Mankind by the grace of this absolutely unique personality.

Before my visit to HH Mataji I was full of expectations. I had my own ideas of how a Divine personality should look and behave. However, all this mental build up dissolved before Her exquisitely simple and innocent nature. I came to forget that She is regarded in India as an Incarnation of the Adi Shakti and that I should relate to Her from that point of view. But the very nature of my experience gradually helped me to remember it. Along with thousands of others, I got the proof of Her absolute genuineness and amazing spiritual stature. And we got not only all the knowledge pertaining to the new consciousness but also the actual techniques and powers to spread it around us ! We are thus absolutely convinced that HH Mataji Nirmala Devi is "The" Divine Incarnation of the present time. These words are true. They are the Truth. Part Five of this book is more specifically dedicated to the great news of Her Advent. You will be inclined to wonder about Her true nature when I will divulge the Great knowledge of Sahaja yoga that was granted to so many Sahaja yogis by Her Grace. You will certainly be amazed at the originality and completeness of this knowledge. So, with humility, I place before you these precious pearls of revelation.

Part Three

REVELATION

"Then He looked in my eyes and said: "My blessing shall be upon you."
When He said that I felt as it were a gust of wind rushing through my body. And I was no longer shy."

Jesus, the Son of Man
Kahlil Gibran

"Saha" means with; "Ja" means born; "yoga" means union. Sahaja Yoga implies that every human being is born with the potential to be united with the Divine (the Infinite, the Reality) and that this potential is actualised by Sahaja Yoga, a technique of spontaneous, effortless salvation. ("Yoga" also means technique or ability).

In one of Her favourite images HH Mataji says that "the Kundalini, the residual divine power, resides in the triangular bone at the base of the spine. It is the germinating power of the seed of your being. This seed sprouts through Sahaja Yoga. I am like the gardener who pours some water on the seeds which he has planted in his garden. At first, only a few flowers come up, but at the time of the blossoming the phenomenon of en masse self-realization is manifested. This Divine love that I pour is your own right for this is the culminating point of the human evolution which has been promised by the Scriptures."

As previously said, if the seeker is in the required condition, his Kundalini rises in the presence of HH Mataji; for Kundalini knows who HH Mataji really is. Kundalini reaches the third eye (Ajnya chakra) without causing the slightest pain; one feels completely calm and thoughtless but one is absolutely aware. She (Kundalini) penetrates the last centre, the Sahasrara and there pierces through the fontanel membrane. The seeker begins feeling the cool breeze of the vibrations (Chaitanya Lahiri).

It is so simple that it is unbelievable! So that with a touch of humour, HH Mataji remarks: "Everything that is important has to be very simple. Suppose you had to make an effort or read books in order to learn the technique of breathing...you could not have existed."

The preceding stages of the human evolution followed one another without the awareness of Man but now, HH Mataji says "the evolution from the human stage onward will take place in a human style, that is with awareness. You will be conscious of the happening and manifestation of the evolutionary process. An egg does not know how it becomes a bird but human beings have to know and feel their evolution as Sahaja Yogis".

What does HH Mataji mean by a "human style"?

In the field of scientific investigation, any great discovery appears to be a revelation from the Universal Unconscious to a specific researcher. The discovery is then broadcast for the benefit of the entire human community. Then comes the elaboration and culmination of the process. Take, for instance, electricity: the laws, properties and applications of electrical energy manifested as soon as the human beings started using the discovery. Sahaja Yoga proceeds along the same lines.

One should remember that any discovery is prepared by a succession of stages, an ascent in knowledge. Similarly, in Sahaja Yoga we relate this culminating step of our spiritual ascent to all the previous ones, to all the discoverers who brought forth this last jump into collective consciousness. When we enter into this new consciousness we start using the new techniques, properties and applications of the discovered energy. We can thus directly relate to the previous discoverers which are the focal centres of a human personality and exist as deities in the various centres of the spinal chord. These deities are the organizers who orchestrate the patterns of living matter, bodily processes and psychic happenings that make up a functional human being.

After mastering Sahaja Yoga one develops techniques to handle the new vibratory awareness.

The deities on the central evolutionary path (sushumna) can really be contacted by chanting their names. When we take the name of a specific deity (mantra) we feel the vibrations indicating a reaction at the corresponding place in the body. When a chakra is constricted, the Kundalini is checked in Her ascent and one can sometimes see Her with the naked eye, pulsating in the centre concerned. By taking the name of the deity which controls that particular chakra the obstacle can be removed. We become conscious participants in God's cosmic plan.

All that is taking place now has been prophesied by the Scriptures of different civilisations. Sahaja Yoga manifests the breakthrough onto the new evolutionary plane for which the human race has been waiting. This knowledge has come to us through the Universal Unconscious. Now it is time to broadcast it. The beauty of Sahaja Yoga blossoms in en masse realisation. The individual yogi (microcosm) spreads to the society (macrocosm) the knowledge of the great primordial cosmic being: THE VIRATA. That is the culminating revelation that explains, integrates and fulfils all the previous revelations. It is the fulfilment of the social contract between God and His creation, Man.

Twenty years ago a scholar was writing about Sahaja:

"It is in identity of enjoyment, in the inexpressible experience of unity that one reaches the state of SAHAJA, of non conditioned existence, of pure spontaneity. All these terms are, of course, difficult to translate. Each of them attempts to express the paradoxical state of absolute non duality (advaya) that issues in mahasukha, the "Great Bliss"."[1]

Today, by the Grace of HH Mataji, this state is open to the human race.

---

[1] Mircea Eliade, *Yoga Immortality and Freedom*. Bollingen series. (Princetown 1969) page 268.

3

The revelation of the cosmic within the human microcosm

"This body is a palace and it is the house of God. Within it God kept the infinite flame."

—Satguru Baba Nanak

Like any other scientific discovery, Sahaja Yoga is merely actualising a knowledge which was hitherto potential. However, because of the radical nature of this discovery, the subsequent transformation undergone by the knower is actually a mutation. Indeed, it is said in the *Mandukya Upanishad*: "Whosoever knows AUM, the Self, becomes the Self." The object of Sahaja is not merely the knower himself as in any psychological theory: it is the knower's Self, the Atman. The knower the object of knowledge and the act of knowing are spontaneously synthesized by a cognitive happening into one awareness. This is the meeting point of truth, consciousness and joy.

During the past millenia the mechanism which makes this sacred alchemy possible has been protected with utmost secrecy by the very few initiated. The time has come however when old mysteries should be exposed to Man's consciousness and intelligence because this time is the time of the Holy Spirit, as it has been announced by Lord Jesus. True, the early Christians expected its immediate manifestation but this is because they had forgotten the words of Peter:

"But do not ignore this one fact beloved, that
with the Lord one day is as a thousand years,
and a thousand years as one day."
—*The Second letter of Peter 3.9*

The evening of the second day draws nearer and the time is coming. All those who were waiting for its in their previous lives should now listen. Sahaja Yoga is revealing to them the long sought for knowledge of the super human realm.

We know that self-realization, the second birth, marks the entry to the Kingdom of God which still has many provinces that we may not know. Therefore, we are merely inviting you to enter it and to explore it for yourself. To this effect let us unveil the meaning of the instrument (yantra) in-built in each and every individual, the Kundalini that brings about our rebirth. It is the psychosomatic instrument by which the advent of the Kingdom of Heaven can be actualised on earth. However, this account will not be complete. Let us hope that HH Mataji Herself will, one day, grant us a book fully displaying the process of Man's second birth and spiritual ascent. She indeed promises, "I will tell you all the secrets."

The structure of our evolution is much subtler than mere matter and cannot be found under the scalpel of the surgeon although it is located at specific places within the human body. But people with greater perceptive powers have been able to see it in meditation. Today some of these saints have shown that they know all about it and about the fantastic coming of HH Mataji.

The human psycho-somatic spiritual instrument that the Sahaja Yogi experimentally discovers within himself through vibratory awareness is not a random structure. In this respect, we have been able to check the discovery of HH Mataji by the experience of vibrations and experienced the truth of what is now being brought to the public's knowledge. We are thus fully convinced that Her Knowledge is genuine, primordial knowledge.

"God is one" say the great religions and Sahaja Yoga alike. But this should not mean that He is like a lump of sugar or the Rock of Gibraltar. Even a lump of sugar contains thousands of crystals. And when we say "God is energy" we ought to remember that energy is convertible and can be put to many uses. Oneness does not exclude plurality. The body of a human being is made up of about sixty million, million cells. It contains many organs such as heart, brain, liver, etc., which go on performing perfectly many various functions. One single human being performs so many more functions, has many aspects and establishes many different types of relationships. He can be a brother, a father and a son all at the same time. The idea that God is one should not imply that He has only one attribute, or aspect, only one function: "The One who is all pervading, all doing, almighty, and who is far more minute and vaster than Man has to be much more complex in Its manifestation and yet perfectly integrated." HH Mataji goes on: "When the One starts manifesting its many aspects, the creation takes place".

HH Mataji tells us that, before the creation of this material world we know around us, various aspects of the One God expressed His various aspects in various divine forms. The oldest religious traditions of this planet, e.g. the Aryan Vedas, have been informed of the existence of these divine forms or deities who exist in other strata of existence.[1] The relationship between these deities represents the pattern through which the Original Divine Energy is generating the whole cosmos. This implies that the working of universal evolution depends upon the interactions of these various forms of Divine Energy. When we consider all of them together through the perception of their essential unity we see them as the components of the Great Primordial Being. This being has been revealed by Shri Krishna, in a mighty vision granted to Arjuna. (See the *Bhagavad Gita*). It is named the VIRATA. In Her own book to come, HH Mataji will tell us about the genesis of the Virata and of the whole cosmos.

In the same way that the air is blown through the holes of the flute in order to become music, in the same way the Holy Spirit (Adi Shakti) manifests God Almighty through seven of His main aspects which correspond to the expressions of God, (devatas, deities) respectively worshipped by the different world religions. There are seven holes but the air is one. In the same way there are seven main aspects of the Virata. These seven aspects correspond to the seven Adi Chakras (original centres) in the cosmic body of the Virata. But the Virata is one, expressing also the unity between the Primordial Witness and the Primordial Actor. In other words the Virata represents the full expression of God brought forward by the Holy Spirit. But the integrated manifestation of the Virata to the human beings did not take place in the past history of the human race.

The Virata encompasses everything that exists. For instance

---

[1] The existence of super-human beings is recorded, as explained later (Chap. XIII) in all the mythologies.

the devas and other higher beings are occupying one of the strata of existence which are contained in the ego (the collective supraconscious) of the Virata. Inversely, hell represents one stratum in the super-ego (the collective subconscious) of the Virata. Seraphs, cherubs, angels do exist. Some of them perform important functions. The Archangel Gabriel (Hanumana) and the Archangel Michael (Bhairava) manage respectively the collective supraconscious and the collective subconscious. As the cosmic body which reveals the Holy Spirit (or Divine Energy) the Virata can be compared to a prism refracting the light into the colours of a rainbow. Or, to use another image, we can say that the Virata is like an "Energy manifesting Cosmic machine". As such, the machine consumes and digests Energy and the wastes of this Energy, the excretions of the Virata, are the demons.

It should be easier for an ant to understand human civilisation than for us to understand the mind of the Virata. Maybe we could try to call it the all-pervading consciousness and attention, the omniscient knower and creator of truth. The Ancients perceived it as the all powerful Destiny. From the point of view of modern psychologists, it appears, maybe, as the Universal Unconscious.

The link between the Virata and historical evolution develops chiefly in two ways. Firstly some of the deities can take a human birth (Divine Incarnation or Avatar) and actively lead Mankind. Secondly the original cosmic structure of the Virata is integrally represented at the micro-cosmic level in each and every human being as the spiritual instrument of our perfectibility. Hence self-realization implies the awakening of the Virata within us. In the body of a realized person the chakras (the psycho-somatic centres) are reflections of the corresponding original or Adi Chakras of the Virata. On these Adi Chakras, the deities preside, and radiate the Energy. HH Mataji says that, through self-realization, the human microcosmic computer is connected with the cosmic programme. The information starts flowing through the nervous system in the form of vibrations. Actually the temperament, personality structure and destiny of every human being depends upon the relationship between this inner instrument and the cosmic Archetype but before realization we are not aware of it. We just undergo various moods and nervous conditions without knowing much of what is happening and why. It is because this cosmic structure can exert such a powerful impact on our daily life that it is important now to present it.

The Virata is represented here in the *Figure V* as an anthropomorphic, graphic image. It should be obvious however that the

Figure V: The Cosmic Structure of the Virata

The mind of the Virata is the Universal Unconscious

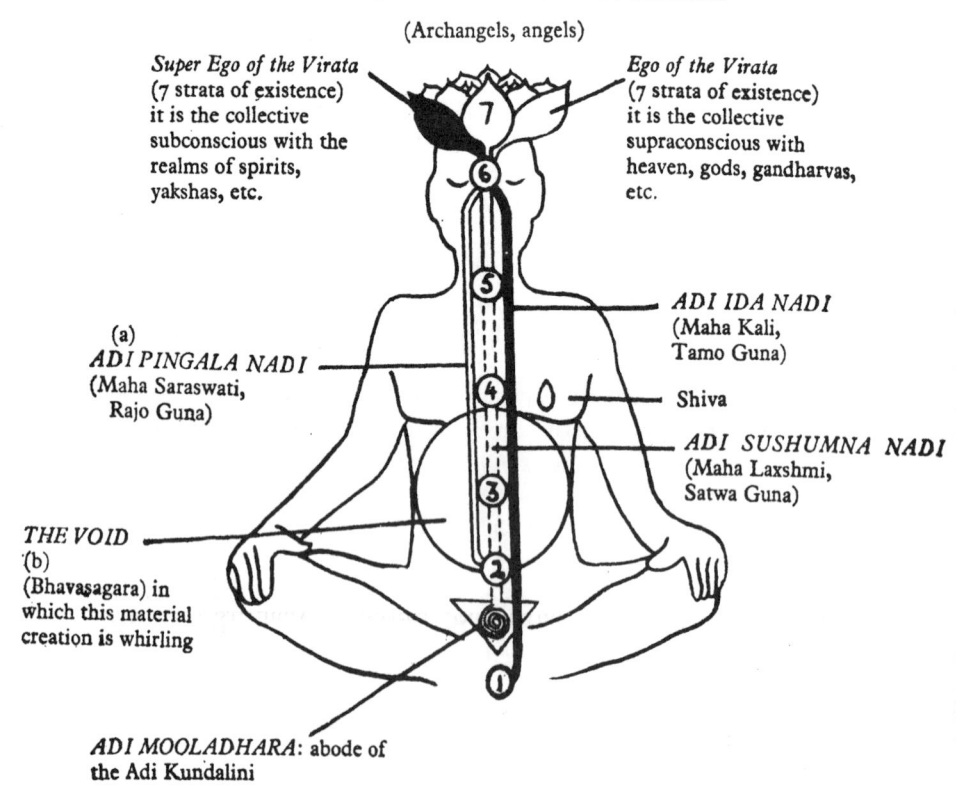

(Archangels, angels)

Super Ego of the Virata
(7 strata of existence)
it is the collective
subconscious with the
realms of spirits,
yakshas, etc.

Ego of the Virata
(7 strata of existence)
it is the collective
supraconscious with
heaven, gods, gandharvas,
etc.

ADI IDA NADI
(Maha Kali,
Tamo Guna)

(a)
ADI PINGALA NADI
(Maha Saraswati,
Rajo Guna)

Shiva

ADI SUSHUMNA NADI
(Maha Laxshmi,
Satwa Guna)

THE VOID
(b)
(Bhavasagara) in
which this material
creation is whirling

ADI MOOLADHARA: abode of
the Adi Kundalini

(a) Adi means primordial.
(b) Bhavasagara means the Ocean of illusion. It is the state of consciousness of the human race. We are located within the stomach of the Virata, in that organ which discriminates what is to be kept (for the sustenance of the cosmic organism) and what to be rejected. The deity controlling this space is Dattatrya, the Primordial Master (Adi Guru).

Virata is totally beyond physical dimension, existing in a stage of Awareness-Energy that we cannot conceive. However Awareness can be experienced and it is the purpose of the Virata to lead Mankind on this Path of Awareness. Although the full Virata was shown to Arjuna by Shri Krishna, the Incarnations of the sixth and seventh chakras, Lord Jesus Christ and Kalki were not yet, at that time, manifested by a personified expression. At the time of this writing, Kalki is not yet manifested.

I should like to repeat that, while any specific aspect or centre of the Virata may have been, in the past, worshipped by the various religions, the understanding of the complete morphology of the Primordial Divine Being, the Supreme Lord of Revelation, has never been possible before the coming of Her Holiness Mataji Nirmala Devi.

From the point of view of the human microcosm:

—Each chakra corresponds to :
—a specific aspect of the divine,
—a specific physical-psycho-energetic role in the evolution of the human individual,
—a specific level of implementation of the universal evolution of the Virata.

—The basic structure of each human being follows the pattern of the structure in the Virata. It is the instrument (yantra) of the cosmic and microcosmic (individual) evolution. But it is fully manifested only in the Virata.

CHAKRAS OF THE VIRATA		PRESIDING DEITY	ASPECTS OF GOD
7. Sahasrara Chakra		Mataji Nirmala Devi + Shri Kalki	—Realisation, Integration, Collective Consciousness.
6. Ajnya Chakra	left	Shri Mahavira	—Non Violence to Self
	centre	Lord Jesus Christ + Virgin Mary	—Resurrection, Forgiveness Mastery over the cosmic forces, Light of Truth.
	right	Shri Gautama Buddha	—Non violence in others.

5.	Vishuddhi chakra		Shri Radha +Shri Krishna	—Greatness of God, Playful Witness, Conscience, Divine Diplomacy.
4.	Anahata Chakra	left	Shri Shiva + Shri Parvati	—Existence, Bliss in Self.
		centre	Shri Durga	—Motherly protection Security and Confidence
		right	Shri Sita + Shri Rama	—Ideal human behaviour Fatherly protection.
3.	Manipur or Nabhi chakra		Shri Vishnu + Shri Laxshmi	—Evolution, Dharma, Well Being.
2.	Swadhistan chakra		Shri Brahma + Shri Saraswati	—Creativity, Aesthetics.
1.	Mooladhara		Shri Gauri	—KUNDALINI, Virgin purity
	Mooladhara chakra		Shri Ganesh	—Innocence, childhood, Wisdom, Anger with sinners.

The Deities controlling these chakras are the "chief organizers" of the Divine Energy.

CHANNELS

The channels of Energy identified as PINGALA, IDA and SUSHUMNA nadis represent, in the body of the Virata, the triple mode of operation of the Holy Spirit's energy; they correspond to the "moods" of the Virata (the Indian cosmology speaks of the three gunas).[2]

1—The Ida Nadi of the Virata (Tamo Guna, passive mood) is controlled by this aspect of the Holy Spirit which is Mahakali (the existence power).

2—The Pingala Nadi of the Virata (Rajo Guna, active mood) is controlled by this aspect of the Holy Spirit which is Mahasaraswati (creative power).

3—The Sushumna Nadi of the Virata (Satwa Guna, revelation through evolution) is controlled by this aspect of the Holy Spirit which is Mahalaxshmi (evolutionary power).

From the point of view of the human understanding we can

---

[2] See in the *Bhagavad Gita* the chapters XIII, XIV, XVII, XVIII, as well as various Upanishads.

very superficially identify the three gunas as follows:[3]

Mahakali's field, tamo guna, represents the all pervading desire of existence in the nucleus of every atom, electromagnetic vibrations in matter, life force in plant and animals, pulsation of life in higher animals and in the human beings where it exists as desire and controls the emotional body. It has been variously conceived for instance as the Taoist Yin, the thesis of the Hegelian dialectics, the notion of "nature" when opposed to "culture"; it is the female, negative, passive, etc.; it has been, for instance, magnified by Man in baroque architecture, romantic literature, poetry and music. The temperaments who try to reach God by the sublimation of this field are known to follow Bhakti Yoga, the yoga of devotion.

Mahasaraswati's field, rajo guna, represents the mood of the Virata which creates the causal essences, elements, masses of matter, constellations, and finally solar systems and our earth. It controls the mental body of the human being. This field has been conceived for instance as the Taoist Yang, as the antithesis of Hegelian dialectics, the notion of "culture and civilisation" as opposed to "nature". It is the male, positive, active, etc.; It has been magnified by man in classical music and architecture, in rationality, law, social organisation, philosophy, in science and technology. The temperaments who try to reach God by sublimation of this field are known to follow Karma Yoga, the yoga of action.

Mahalaxshmi's field, satwa guna is the dimension in which the Virata itself is the goal, leading the way of Universal Evolution in sending forth various incarnations (Avatars) to guide it. The actual deities are "seated" on the chakras of the Virata, in His Sushumna (Central channel). This mood can be said to be the one that brings forth the Divine Revelation, synthesis and integration. It has been perceived by man as a system for equilibrium, synthesis and harmony, conceived as the synthesis of the Hegelian dialectic; it has been magnified by those feats of human genius expressing the perfection of rhythm such as the pyramid of Cheops, Shah-Jehan's Taj Mahal or the Athenian Parthenon on the acropolis. Every manifestation of perfection in the arts, philosophy,

---

[3] The Indian cosmology tells that Mahakali is the Shakti of Ishwara, Mahasaraswati the Shakti of Hiranya Gharba, Mahalaxshmi the Shakti of Virata. These are the three personified aspects of the Virata's nadis. All these Sanskrit names were found by very ancient Sages.

etc., relates to this field. Jnana Yoga (yoga of awareness) is meant to bring the practitioners onto the Sushumna channel.

The supreme yoga of integration which encompasses them all in awakening the residual divine Energy within man (Kundalini) is Sahaja Yoga.

This triple distinction of the Original Energy does not represent only the three modes of operation of the Virata. It controls on the gross side the triple aspect of our autonomous nervous system: the right side sympathetic nervous system by the activity of a creator (by rajo guna); the left side sympathetic nervous system by the existence power (by tamo guna); and the para-sympathetic nervous system by the evolutionary power (by satwa guna).

Furthermore the whole of the cosmic pattern is at work in the human body. The chakras in the human body reflect the various levels of energy emitted by the cosmic organizers, that is, the deities on the primordial chakras. Before realization we can say that the deities on the human chakras are sleeping, and thus the full integration of the personality does not take place. Yet the chakras perform vital functions. They carry the code of the organism's potential for evolution and spread the instructions through the nervous system.[4] When excessive stress breaks the connection of the sympathetic nervous system with the chakras these instructions can no longer keep the organic cohesion of the system. Cancer settles in. After realization, the deities on the chakras are awakened and the whole of the human awareness system (biological, endocrinal, spiritual) is integrated. The connection between the cosmic structure of the Virata and the human nervous system should be accepted as a hypothetical proposition until it can be experimentally verified during and after realization. Then, proof can be given that various chakras react to the mantras or invocation of specific deities. For instance the subject can feel that an invocation to Shri Vishnu or Shri Laxshmi can release the pressure he was feeling on the navel, (Manipura or Nabhi chakra). It has been demonstrated quite a few times that the Kundalini may not cross

---

[4]cf "Cells from the orbital area of a frog embryo can be removed and placed somewhere in its stomach region, but there they produce new gut lining and not internal eyes. There is a co-ordinating system which ensures that cells in a particular area, although each is potentially capable of doing anything, do what is required of them there." Lyall Watson, *The Romeo Error* p. 34.

the space between the vagus nerve of the parasympathetic system and the solar plexus if the Primordial Guru is opposed in one of his past incarnations e.g. Muhammad, Zoroaster, Nanaka, etc. Once the vibrations or Chaitanya connect our awareness with the cosmic programme, we gradually come to experience the living communion between ourselves and the Virata.

The deities on the Adi Chakras of the Virata express various aspects of the Divine. For instance Lord Ganesha is the transcendent purity of divine childhood. Lord Shiva is the Self, the bliss of absolute existence. Lord Jesus Christ is the truth of the light of God. With the gradual opening of the corresponding chakras in our body we develop these respective qualities within us. It is the wish of the Divine Love that the children participate in the perfection of God. After realization, the divine qualities blossom within us and we enjoy our own virtues. A realized poet joyfully wrote to HH Mataji: "Now the sandal wood has started enjoying its own fragrance."

When Socrates was reminded of the advice carved in the temple of Apollo in Delphi: "KNOW THYSELF", he knew that to know oneself actually gives the key to the knowledge of the whole universe. It is a puzzling experience to realize that the scheme which guided the genesis and evolution of the Universe is integrally represented within man.

4

The Instrument of Awareness

"Oh Friend! this body is His lyre"—Kabir

"Play your stringless lute"—A Zen Koan

Let us turn our attention towards the human microcosm. First of all we should acknowledge that the sages of the past knew more about it than the modern man. For instance in the *Rig Vediya Purush Sookta* we can read:

> "This body is a city which cannot be conquered (Ayodhya). There are nine doors with nadis everywhere and the prana works through them...by these we act and know. But the most important among them is sushumna which goes through the spinal chord to the brain. In this nervous system there are plexuses which control various parts of the body; they are called chakras...You have to remember that these chakras are really in the spine and in the upper part of the brain."[5]

Similarly Guru Vashista is reported to have told Shri Rama:

> "There are two very subtle nadis called ida and pingala. In this house of flesh they are placed left and right and nobody knows about them. And in this mechanism of the body there are three pairs of lotus which are superimposed on a thread.

---

[5]*Rig Vediya Purush Sookta*—Commentary on the first mantra of Purush Sookta by Sampurnanand, Sharda Prakashan Pub. (Benaras 1947) p. 19-20. (free translation).

The vital energy (prana) works through them."[6]

These and many other comments are fully substantiated by Sahaja Yoga.

In the human body, there are three main channels (nadis) through which the energy circulates. They control complex interconnected sets of smaller channels within the whole body. The gross expression of these channels corresponds to the physiology of the nervous system. The central system can be described as follows: Within the spinal column, we have the central channel known as SUSHUMNA; the gross manifestation of this channel is termed the parasympathetic nervous system. At the right side (in your own body) of Sushumna we have the channel known as PINGALA NADI which corresponds to the right side sympathetic nervous system. At the left side of Sushumna we have IDA NADI which corresponds to the left side sympathetic nervous system. Placed on the central channel we find the seven centres (chakras) which control our physical, emotional, mental and spiritual bodies. The chakras are expressed as plexuses outside the spinal chord. We have the same number of plexuses and subplexuses outside as the number of chakras and their petals inside the spinal chord. Very little is known about this system to medical science which terms it the autonomic nervous system: the system which works on its own. The autonomic nervous system is described in clinical anatomy as the part of the nervous system concerned with the innervation of involuntary structures such as the heart, smooth muscles, and glands throughout the body. It is distributed throughout the central and peripheral nervous system. It can be divided in two parts: the sympathetic (left and right) and the parasympathetic. The activities of the sympathetic prepare the body for an emergency. The activities of the parasympathetic aim at conserving, restoring and balancing the energy. The sympathetic portion of the autonomic nervous system is localized in the thoracolumbar region while the parasympathetic portion is found in the cephalic and sacral regions. The connection between this system and the activity of the psyche is now being explored through the neuro-endocrinology of the brain. The connection of this system with the spiritual evolution of the subject is totally unknown

---

[6] *Yog Vashista*, Kalyan edit. January 1961 p. 319 (free translation).

to present day scientists. Actually, this knowledge was the privilege of a few initiated Buddhist and Hindu masters. It is difficult to know how much or how little of it was revealed to the various mystic seers of the Middle-East but today, we can confidently expect that a new science of man will soon unveil the complex totality of these energetic phenomena.

Now, let us quote again Her Holiness Mataji Nirmala Devi:

"When the human foetus is about two to three months old in the mother's womb the column or rays of consciousness (emitted through the all pervading original Energy), passes through the brain; it gets refracted into channels corresponding with four aspects of the nervous system which are:

—Parasympathetic nervous system: Sushumna nadi: the Central Path
—Sympathetic nervous system (right): Pingala nadi: the Sun Channel
—Sympathetic nervous system (left) : Ida nadi: the Moon Channel
—Central nervous system : it is our physiological link with the material world.

The set of rays that fall on the Fontanel bone (apex of the head known as Taloo) pierces it in the centre and passes straight into the medulla oblongata through Sushumna" (In his comments of the stanzas 11 and 12 of the *Aitareya Upanishad* Shri Shankaracharya observes that the Lord Consciousness enters the body at that spot, "the crown of the head," "where the parting of the hair occurs"). "The energy, after manifesting the parasympathetic nervous system settles down in three and a half coils in the triangular bone placed at the end of the spinal chord (Mooladhara). This residual primordial Energy is traditionally known as KUNDALINI. On its way downward Kundalini bestows the respective Deities on the chakras. The parasympathetic nervous system is the medium through which we receive the divine Energy. But as soon as a human child is born and the umbilical chord is broken, a gap is created in the Sushumna, manifested outside, as we already mentioned, by the gap between the solar plexus and the vagus nerve of the parasympathetic nervous system."

As soon as the child is removed from his mother's breast he undergoes an experience of separation, deprivation, which is retained in his subconscious. The scream of the protesting infant asserts his separate identity. It proclaims the establishment of his individual ego. Reactions to the new, changing environment develop the super-ego. Later, when activity builds up on the two sympathetic nervous systems, ego and super-ego swell up like balloons and cover the two hemispheres of the brain. There is no outlet at the top of the brain to release the waste of the psychic energy; it accumulates there.[7] The fontanel bone calcifies and the subtle Energy gets cut off completely. A new microcosm is born. Then, the human being identifies himself as a separate identity and his mind becomes the field of tension between ego and super-ego.

With the growth of the individual, the development of the creative and mental faculties inflates the ego (termination of the Pingala channel) while the super-ego (termination of the Ida channel) is everyday storing further conditioning. Psychic energy goes back and forth between these two poles, sometimes managing to settle on the equilibrium point (the Ajnya chakra on the Sushumna channel). But the contradictions which define the set up of the human psyche exert a constant influence on the subject's behaviour and also determine to a large extent his inward evolution. For various reasons the dialectical movement of the psyche may lose its equilibrium. The symptoms are the following: quick irritation or exasperation; Irrational moods of fear or of feeling depressed. When the psychic energy as attention (chitta) swings from the extreme of the ego to the extreme of the super-ego the subject finds it difficult to cope with the resulting tensions. If these tensions have reached the breaking point, nervous breakdowns, neuroses, psychoses, etc., manifest the advanced stage of the process. In a system thus shattered, the Units of Psychic Interference easily enter through the Nabhi or Ajnya chakra. For the sake of convenience I am coining "UPI" for Unit of Psychic Interference, as a broad generic symbol for entities such as "spirits", "ghosts", "djins" which can and do intrude our awareness system. Their existence will be discussed later on.

The environment plays a very crucial role in maintaining the balance of the psyche. If the child is brought up in a happy, well disciplined, united family he develops a dharmic personality. The

---

[7]In a factory, a lot of waste goes up in smoke. If there is no chimney this smoke would be trapped in the building.

moral character of his parents and their absolute fidelity to each other gives him the right model of emotional maturity. This child feels secure and is fit to fulfil his role in the evolutionary process. Thus it is said that the greatest reward for the good deeds of the past life is to be born in a dharmic family. Of course, the innate balance is also the result of the previous lives' experiences.

When the energy does not move far away from the equilibrium point, the chakras on the Sushumna channel are not distorted and the subject's life manifests this element of harmony and balance. In this condition, simple people live in contentment. Philosophers and scientists are more likely to receive from the Universal Unconscious the hints which will provoke creative development in their respective fields of thought. Artists express in their works the aesthetics of truth. The vibrations of these people are cool and they can get their realisation very quickly because the Sushumna channel is ready for the ascent of Kundalini. Innocent children and youngsters who are enjoying a harmonious familial enviromnent often belong to this category, their parasympathetic system keeps the balance between Ida and Pingala. Those who keep themselves on the Sushumna enjoy a mature psychic life, free from the mental discussions and melodramatic infatuations that seem to be the rule of today. They do not play mental and emotional games which are marginal expressions of Reality.

In relation to our presentation of the Virata's cosmic programme, let us mention again the threefold psychosomatic structure channelling His triple energies.

—IDA NADI corresponds to tamo guna ("passivity")
—PINGALA NADI corresponds to rajo guna ("activity")
—SUSHUMNA NADI corresponds to sattwa guna ("balance")

As we said, Sahaja Yoga takes the aspirant beyond these three gunas and their corresponding yogas (bhakti yoga=yoga of devotion, karma yoga=yoga of action, jnana yoga=yoga of knowledge), because in its essence, Sahaja Yoga is the Kundalini Yoga, the yoga of the Divine Energy within Man. It raises a new flow of integrated Energy inside the Sushumna.. The Kundalini and the one that She has enlightened are not subjected to the influence of any of the gunas, (not even to the influence of Satwa guna which implies the quest for equilibrium, happiness and wisdom) for the Kundalini integrates and transcends the gunas, when She moves from Her sleeping condition to Her awakened state. HH Mataji used to smilingly ask : "Can you conceive of an Energy which thinks, organises, feels and loves?" , Shri Krishna is reported to have said "how hard it is to break through my maya (illusion) made of the three gunas" yes it certainly is... until Adi Shakti decides to intervene.

The parasympathetic nervous system (PNS)

"There is a strange tree, which stands without roots and bears fruits without blossoming; It has no branches and no leaves, it is lotus all over"—Kabir

The Sushumna and the chakras, this traditional theme of the Eastern mystical poetry, are the subtle focus of energy which controls the working of the parasympathetic system. We can say of this system that it is our communication channel with the Infinite. Provided that the Sushumna can be opened again for the ascent of Kundalini it pumps the all pervading original Energy and powers it into our chakras. The parasympathetic fills in the vitality that the sympathehic is meant to use. The first dilates the chakras; the second constricts them. The path of the Kundalini energy is the Sushumna within the spine. On the cosmic level Sushumna is nothing but the right way of evolutionary ascent (dharma) which is also in-built at the microcosmic level of the individual. It is the central path mentioned by Gautama Buddha, which goes through the "narrow gate" of the Ajnya Chakra, referred to by Lord Jesus Christ, before reaching the divine Kingdom of the Sahasrara chakra at the top of the brain. As before said the chakras are seated on this central path which represents, at the microcosmic human level, the way of dharma (virtue) and sattwa (righteousness). The channel corresponds to the cosmic path carrying different centres adorned by the incarnations sent forth by the Holy Spirit at different periods of our evolution. This path is the one to be followed for our spiritual ascent. It is the Tree of Life whose fruits can be tasted only by the authorised person, that is, a subject whose Kundalini has risen with due "protocol". Indeed, the mishandling of the Kundalini and the chakras because of the ignorance or perversion of the teacher can be extremely dangerous for the practitioner, on the physical as well as the spiritual plane: plexuses might be completely blocked and the path broken down, thus seriously threatening the aspirant's chances of realization. This is because the interference of a non self realized or unauthorised guru amounts to an insult to the dignity of the Kundalini. It goes against the protocol of Divinity and the deities of the different chakras might recede. If this is the case, it is very easy for a "guru" versed in the art of black magic to introduce a UPI into the chakra. The chakras which happen to be most exposed to intrusions are the nabhi and the ajnya chakras.

When properly invited by vibrations, the Kundalini leaves Her abode in the triangular pelvic bone and, following the Sushumna path, She makes Her way through the six chakras awakening the deities until She reaches the seventh one. Depending upon the condition of his chakras, the subject can feel the movement of the Kundalini's ascent, a fact which has been experienced by thousands of Sahaja Yogis throughout the five continents. Actually, in many instances, if the lower chakras are blocked the ascent of the Kundalini can be seen with the naked eye when the aspirant prostrates himself before HH Mataji because the Kundalini pulsates at that place. I heard it through a stethoscope as a throbbing (like the heart throbbing). Sometimes, blessed with a mystic vision one can witness the whole process of Kundalini's ascent.

On the way to the Sahasrara, Kundalini has to cross the Ajnya chakra: this is no mean achievement! You cannot "open the third eye" without the rising of the Kundalini.

> "Strive to enter by the narrow door, for many, I tell you, will seek to enter and will not be able."—Luke 13.24

> "Enter by the narrow gate: for the gate is wide and the way is easy, that leads to destruction and those who enter by it are many. For the gate is narrow and the way is hard, that leads to life, and those who find it are few".—Matthew 7.13

Here, Christ warns us against the entry of the attention into the Ida and Pingala channels and refers to the way of the Sushumna.

The mind cannot know lasting peace and thoughtless awareness cannot settle unless and until the Ajnya chakra is fully opened, a process corresponding to the cleansing of the chitta (thinking or attention principle). In some cases this might take time. Indeed this chakra, controlled by Lord Jesus, proves to be extremely sensitive: it will not let any disturbance reach the Holy City of the Sahasrara which is the Kingdom of God within human beings.

The moment of Self-realization corresponds to the breaking through the fontanel bone (Brahmarandra) at the top of the brain, by the ascending Kundalini. HH Mataji calls it "Baptism done by God's authority". This opening has actually been felt by some Sahaja Yogis. Others felt the energy coming down from the Sahasrara into Ida and Pingala. In most of the cases thoughtlessness is felt and the physical perception of the vibrations indicates the integration of the central nervous system with the spiritual awareness. Thus the individual soul (Atma) can be connected with the Cosmic consciousness termed also as the Universal Unconscious (Paramatma). The Universal Unconscious is the mind of this Virata who told Arjuna: "this entire creation is pervaded by my invisible form. I contain all creatures, none contain me" (*Bhagavad Gita* 9).

Thoughtlessness, Emptiness, the Zen "Void" brings us to the Universal Unconscious. Bodhidharma, the father of Chinese Zen who writes on "Wu-hsin" ("no-mind") says of the Unconscious:

"It is like the celestial drum, which, while lying still, spontaneously and without conscious effort, produces varieties of exquisite sound in order to teach and discipline all beings. It is again like a wish-fulfilling gem which, without conscious effort on its own part, creates spontaneously varieties of form. In like manner, the Unconscious works through my conscious mind, making it understand the true nature of Reality; it is wisdom, it is the master of the triple body, it functions with utmost freedom...The Unconscious is the true Mind, the true Mind is the Unconscious...

Only let us be awakened to the Unconscious in all things in all our doings—this is the way of discipline, there is no other way. Thus we know that when the Unconscious is realized all things cease to trouble us."[8]

---

[8]Quoted in D. T. Suzuki *Essays In Zen Buddhism. Third series.* Rider and Co. (London, 1970) p. 23.

Thoughtless awareness is the first step towards merging with the Universal Unconscious. From thoughtless awareness the Sadhaka goes into the deeper stage of doubtless awareness and further into higher levels of Awareness Energy of which I am not able to speak.[9] Can we now see the cognitive implications of Kundalini's awakening of the Parasympathetic system?

Man elaborated concepts of God and himself through whatever he could perceive of the Unconscious. It is from this Unconscious, C.G. Jung contends, that mankind has always drawn its gods and demons, all the primordial images which form the basis of the great systems of thought, "all these thoughts that are superiorly powerful and without which man ceases to be a man". It is from that Unconscious that we receive creative inspiration, conscience, intuition of truth, etc. Messages often reveal themselves in dreams. Human beings can follow a hidden guidance through these intuitions and hunches. But, as Erich Fromm sees it, the modern man is increasingly repressing his inner voice and thus also losing the sense of discrimination between good and bad, truth and falsehood.

So we have to become conscious of the Universal Unconscious within us. The individual unconscious, represented by the sleeping Kundalini in the Mooladhara, is nothing but a part of the Universal Unconscious. Kundalini's awakening of the parasympathetic and the consequent link between the individual consciousness and the Universal unconscious, breaks through the cognitive barrier which used to mark the absolute limit of the rational man's field of knowledge: direct perception replaces intellectual opinions. In the words of HH Mataji:

> "The breakthrough into the Unconscious breaks the barrier between the limited human awareness and reality."

Actually, after self-realization, the central nervous system becomes aware of the autonomous system. "Auto", in the sense

---

[9] At the moment of realization : thoughtless awareness-collective consciousness
—Next stage of awareness : doubtless awareness-communion in collective consciousness
—Further stage : complete self-realisation-mastery over the elements
—Yet a further stage : God Realization.

given here by HH Mataji, means the Self. That very Self (Atma) which is one with the Universal Unconscious (Paramatma).

Hence at the first jumping into the Unconscious the inward, spiritual sensitivity expresses itself in physical sensations. The wind of the Holy Spirit carries the messages of the Unconscious. Feelings of tingling, light burning, numbing of the finger tips manifest. But what do these sensations mean? "Someone who knows has to decode it" says HH Mataji. Maybe the instructions from the Divine to mankind could be interpreted only through the Divine incarnating among human beings to give them the key of the code?[10]

Last but not least, it is not possible for man to use this energetic phenomenon for evil purposes. Indeed, self-realization happens spontaneously because, from our point of view, it corresponds to the mobilisation of the parasympathetic energy. This mobilisation is possible mainly when the required amount of "goodness", or dharmic balance is keeping the subject on the central track of Sushumna. A wicked man is "technically" unable to get realization. Furthermore, when we strive for it, try to do it, make efforts to get it, we are working with the sympathetic nervous system and we cannot but miss the point. One will better understand now why the traditional notion of God's grace emphasizes aspects such as surrender, availability, letting something happen. Our Divine Mother wrote: "What an achievement it is when we realise that human minds cannot be taken to reality but that reality has to engulf the human mind in its loving ocean". Of this, the mystics, saints, sages and seers of all ages, Kabir, Saint John of the Cross, Gazzali, Ramakrishna, Meister Eckhardt, etc., etc., were well aware. As Kierkegaard keenly put it:

"Who should the striving person want to be like except God; but if he, himself, is something or wants to be something, then this is enough to prevent the likeness".

"When the sea puts all its efforts and assembles all its strength precisely then, it cannot reflect the picture of the sky... but when the sea is quiet and deep, then sinks the picture of the sky in its nothingness".

---

[10] For instance the founder of a spiritual movement in Japan got his enlightenment the very year HH Mataji visited this country. However they did not meet.

When the sea is quiet and deep one is bathing in the void of thoughtlessness which is the Self's perception of itself. But the blissful condition demands that the attention-energy rests on the Sushumna without undergoing lateral movements. To maintain oneself there is a rather difficult feat as the great Zen Master Rinzai Gigen (died 867) reminds us in his *Rinzi Roku* (*the sayings of Rinzen*):

> "O Venerable sirs, here lies indeed the point where learners have to apply themselves wholeheartedly, for there is no room here even for a breath of air to pass through. It is like a flash of lightning or like a spark of flint-stone striking the steel. One winks and the whole thing passes away. If learner's eyes are vacantly fixed, all is lost. As soon as the mind is applied to it, it slips away from you; as soon as a thought is stirred it turns its back on you."[11]

Indeed without the Divine Mother's very special grace which is materialised in Sahaja Yoga only a few individuals in any one century would attain self-realization. These were extremely highly placed human beings who had to struggle hard, back and forth on ida and pingala nadis. But how could the mass of the people follow them? Yet are the masses indifferent to the truth? Are they not seeking true happiness and peace?

Sorry, one cannot successfully strive to be peaceful...and yet peace is what we seek. Nor is the finite human being in a position to join Infinity and yet he longs for it. Today, we are in a position to say that this contradiction can be overcome at the level of the human psycho-somatic structure because the divine love is rescuing Mankind from the existential dilemma. We ground this claim on the basis of experience, observations and findings we have made on countless occasions. Our experience demonstrates two major facts:

> —The parasympathetic system has the potential to be the agent of the transformation of awareness,
> —This potential can be actualised by bombarding the subject with the vibrations of Chaitanya.

---

[11]quoted in *Zen Buddhism and Psychoanalysis* Erich Fromm, D. T. Suzuki, R. De Martino; Harper Colophon books (New York 1960) p. 40.

At the time of writing these lines I know alraedy that many readers will be in a position to verify these propositions by themselves. The understanding of this experience however will be facilitated by an adequate perception of the working of the sympathetic nervous system.

The sympathetic nervous system (SNS)

"The psyche is an autonomic regulation system. There cannot be equilibrium, or autoregulating system without opposite forces capable of counterbalancing each other."[12]
—C.G. Jung

The sympathetic is the medium through which we programme ourselves—and are programmed—in the course of our daily life as well as in the transmigratory course of successive births and deaths. It is largely according to the condition of our sympathetic nervous system that our destiny takes its shape. When we gain some control over our SNS we also acquire a corresponding degree of control over the subsequent course of our life or lives. However the SNS cannot but evolve into three dimensions: time, space, causality: it cannot reach the divine; enlightenment is beyond its reach as it evolves through action (Pingla) and reaction (Ida). These two movements create the psychic waste, smoke or fumes which fill the balloons of the ego and super-ego, at the end of the pingala and ida channels. These balloons inflate, meet at the top of the brain and trap us into our finite limited "I"-ness.(See Fig. II)

A. The right side sympathetic nervous system uses the energy of Pingala Nadi, the Sun channel, at the right side of Sushumna. It caters to the emergencies of the active consciousness and culminates in the ego on the left hemisphere of the brain. When our attention passes on the right side we are involved in thought, planning, organisation, the future, etc. When this channel is overstressed there is overload on the mental body and this explains many of the symptoms of mental restlessness or exhaustion affecting intellectuals, bureaucrats, technocrats, etc. Also the ego is inflated. In the best cases, after death, temperaments extremely involved in pingala

---

[12]C. G. Jung *Psychologie de L'Insconscient.* George et Cie (Geneva 1973) p. 116 (my translation)

nadi can reach the seven strata of heaven which are in the collective superaconscious (the ego of the Virata). There the invisible masters are dwelling but these strata are an evolutionary dead-end, in the sense that the complete union with the Supreme cannot be achieved along these lines. In the worst cases, rajasic temperaments become egotistical monsters, real devils, who seek to dominate or subdue their fellow human beings through the medium of powers they have eventually acquired; many so-called Hatha Yogis, seeking the mastery of the body and Rajah Yogis seeking the mastery over the mind, are overcome by rajo guna. Of course we do not need to be such a pseudo yogi in order to have a "big ego". The ego belongs to every man's psyche and the problems it generates belong to every human being even if they are not yet aware of it. It is not easy to control the ego because it can hide itself very well. The psyche influenced by the ego exhibits a strong tendency to build up expectations, to pass (limited) judgements. This is indeed a trait common to many of us. More specifically in the psychoanalytical disciplines, this field is the part of the psyche's life on which Adler focused his researches, and the result of his findings is the famous Will-to-Power theory.

B. The left side sympathetic nervous system uses the energy of Ida Nadi, the Moon channel, at the left side of Sushumna. This channel's network corresponds to the subconscious life of the psyche (the libido) and it culminates in the super-ego, on the right side of the brain where all past experiences are stored. When our attention passes on the left side we are involved in feelings, the past, recollection, affective moods. When this channel is overstressed there is overload on the emotional body and then, through the medium of the super-ego, the mind appears open to all sorts of conditioning, from benign psychological cases to instances of possession. Inflated super-ego results in an extremely conditioned psyche, affective disturbances, emotional stresses, etc. Temperaments exceedingly involved in tamo guna, in the worst of the cases see-saw after death into the seven strata of hell, in the collective subconscious, (super-ego of the Virata). There the demons and depraved spirits (the buddhist word is "preta") are dwelling.[13]

Today, the implicit confusion between sex and self-reali-

---

[13]As a spirit will always try to avoid dwelling in the nether regions he becomes an UPI whenever the opportunity arises.

zation is disturbing more than a few westerners. This part of the psychic life has been the object of Freud's attention and one can find much about it in the theories of Libido, Eros and Thanatos, pointing towards the notion of conditioning. The average psyche exhibits the super-ego's influence through the tendency of habit formation.

As long as the Sushumna channel is closed, the energy of the sympathetic system cannot be connected with the parasympathetic and our attention which is engrossed in this energy also cannot penetrate into Sushumna. Hence it goes from left to right, right to left, in an endless elliptic movement.

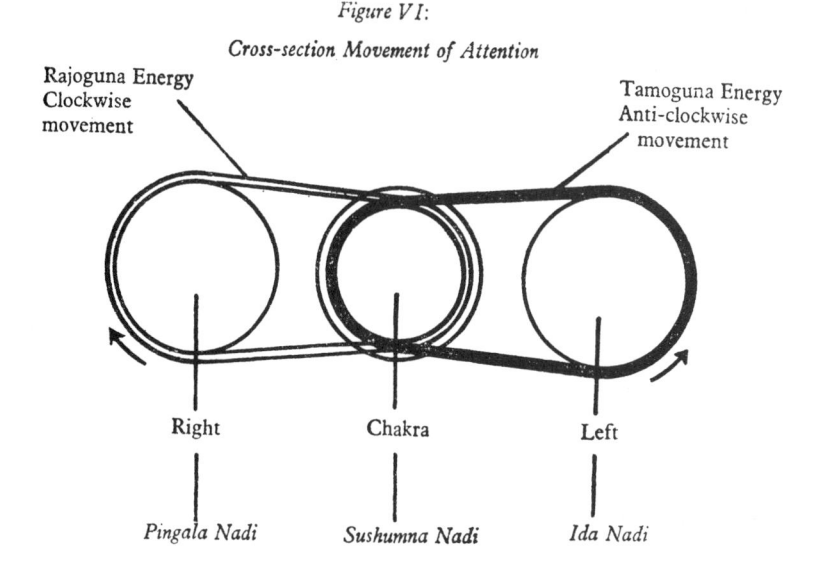

Figure VI:

Cross-section Movement of Attention

Rajoguna Energy Clockwise movement

Tamoguna Energy Anti-clockwise movement

Right — Chakra — Left

Pingala Nadi — *Sushumna Nadi* — *Ida Nadi*

The cosmic bipolarity perceived by many a system of thought expresses the perception of the two alternative ellipses[14].

The art of Sattva (equilibrium through Righteousness) that is mastered through a dharmic (virtuous) life appears to keep this movement in some sort of balance. Thus the attention is gathered

---

[14] Actually the western cosmology perceived the world as duality and eventually, as a trilogy whenever the perception of the sattvic synthesis asserted itself. But the cosmic oneness beyond the three gunas and the three aspects of the autonomic nervous system remained ever elusive.

together on the point where the ellipses are meeting.[15] It is at this junction point that, as an alternative to left and right movements, Sushumna exists in the vertical dimension whereby the attention can ascend. This mastery that was sought by the sages of yore is extremely difficult to gain but offers of course, the optimal conditions of success for the raising of the Kundalini.

As a matter of fact, what usually happens in a common man like you and me is that, when one side of the SNS (sympathetic nervous system) is drained by over-involvement, as a reaction, the opposite side will be affected next.[16] Man becomes a prey of the gunas, of the perpetual back and forth movement of the psychic energy. That is what the harp player told Siddhartha Gautama: one cannot play the right music when the strings of one's instrument are too tight or too loose...a statement which led to Buddha's enlightenment. When my strings are too loose (through overactivity of the left SNS) I am going to make them too tight (overactivity of the right side) and vice versa. The process can be stretched over several rebirths but one can observe it within a single life also C. G. Jung concluded rightly that psychic life seems to be ruled by the regulative function of opposites or contradictions that Heraclitus called "enantiodromyon": everything ends up in its contrary. The same phenomenon, perceived at the cosmic and historic level, is expressed through the Toist Ying-Yang Cosmology and the Hegelian and Marxist dialectic. Jung thought he found the answer and a way to solve the contradiction between Freud and Adler which deeply disturbed him as he perceived that both were correct although expressing contradictory theories.

Contradictions indeed exist, at the cosmic level of the Virata between its tamoguna and rajoguna (a contradiction subsequently perceived by man in matter) and at the human microcosmic level, between the right and left SNS. Our economic theories evolved from our perception of the law of contradiction in the

---

[15] See the Tibetan symbol of the vajra.
[16] When the movements of the energy are too heavily attracted by the opposite poles, the temperaments of the people take to extreme, unbalanced and sometimes pathological behaviours (e. g. Sadism-Masochism).

cosmos.[17] Our psychological theories evolve from our perception of the law of contradiction in the microcosm.

Contradictions are "natural", we all agree, but whatever is natural needs not be good for the evolution of man.

It is fair enough to become aware of contradictions but it is even better to overcome them. Are your strings too tight? Don't make them too loose. But how to get the right tuning? In Sahaja terms the question gets translated: how to overcome the perpetual back and forth movement between the left and right side SNS? and this means in turn: how to overcome the Action-Reaction process between the ego and the super-ego so that the awareness can be turned on the Self? The answer to this question cannot be a theoretical or an intellectual one as it implies the awakening of the energy of the parasympathetic nervous system (Kundalini). We are not going to awaken it by reading or thinking about it. This was the oldest riddle, the ancient dilemma. It generated the difficulties of the human quest for reality. Without finding the rythme of spontaneous righteousness within ourselves, we will not be able to implement it in society.

The standard psychic state (SPS) is the state of the normal human being (homo sapiens) whose awareness is clouded by the ego and the super-ego. It depends mostly upon the sympathetic nervous system and thus man acts and reacts partially according to the effects of external conditionings.

Between the insignificant case and the acute one we find the UPIs and cross the border of psychic pathology. In an evolutionary perspective the SPS of the homo sapiens is only one stratum of consciousness open to man. Although it is in this stratum that the conscious perception of the majority of the people is evolving it

---

[17]"Dialectics is the teaching which shows how opposites can be and how they happen to be (how they become) identical—under what conditions they are identical, transforming themselves into one another—why the human mind should take these opposites not as dead rigid, but as living, conditional, mobile, transforming themselves into one another"

Lenin *Conspectus of Hegel's "The Science of Logic"* collected works (Moscow 1958) vol. 38 p. 97.

See also Mao Tse Tung's brilliant essay *on Contradictions* : "The fact is that the unity or identity of opposites in objective things is not dead or rigid but is living, conditional, mobile, temporary and relative: in given conditions, every contradictory aspect transforms itself into its opposite" Mao Tse Tung *on Contradictions* selected works (Peking 1965) p. 340.

would be a mistake to define it as the only existing one because the only one perceived. We cannot apply the logical principle of non contradiction to the field of psychology: Man is (in a state) A and therefore he is not (in a state) B; because the human psyche moves in the multidimensional geometry of those depths where man can, at the same time, be and not be. Ultimately, in thoughtless awareness, geometry itself is abolished. Indeed psychic geometry, the domain of emotional and mental forms, is the field of the SPS, that is, the field defined by the activity of the SNS. To go beyond this stratum of consciousness means to go beyond forms and logic.

In the super-ego aspect of the standard psychic state I am affected by energetic phenomena which are not mine, I can be and not be at the same time, that is, I am alienated from, my Self, my real identity, from my Joy, Truth and Consciousness. That is why the SPS is a state of alienation and existentialist philosophy defines the human condition in terms of this alienation. Of course alienation is significantly worsened by the intrusion of UPI's. The homo sapiens cannot avoid operating principally through the SNS, through this very system which cannot by itself get immune to the UPIs. He is in a state of alienation which does not recognize itself as he is not aware of the conditioning. He has not, usually, developed the sattvic discriminating power which would help to break the identification with the alienating, intruding factor. If one considers abnormal the fact that the human psyche is affected by forces in a way which is beyond its very understanding one could say that the SPS, the state accepted as normal, is in fact abnormal. In this way we can find the roots of all the human suffering. Today, abnormality has gone so far that the gutters of hell pour into our cities: depravity, violence, etc.

Modern psychoanalysis is quite aware of the problems of the modern man's psyche which is affected by all kinds of disturbances. It has demonstrated that some threatening psychic contents can intrude from what they call the collective unconscious into the individual unconscious. From there these contents guide, condition disturb the mind; they impact on the subject's psychic health and can start anguish, fears, conflicts, neuroses, abnormal interpersonal tensions, depression, etc., etc.

Alas psychoanalysis cannot go much further than identifying symptoms and bringing only a partial relief. It is not equipped to really identify the UPI as the ultimate pathogenic factor. Classical psychotherapy usually proposes the mobilisation of the conscious psyche of the subject which is to identify—and thus exorcise the agonizing shade dwelling in the subconscious. Techniques to this effect are the "Diagnostiche Assoziationsstudien" the diagnostic study of mental associations, the analysis of dreams which give to the victim of the UPI the possibility to verbalise the perturbed condition (speech analysis). This possibility allows the subject to withdraw from his previous identification with the UPI. This act of discrimination of the conscious side of the psyche is the psychic liberating act, whereby in some instances the UPI is expelled from the subject.

This established process is basically correct but its shortcomings are many.

—Once the subject's attention is withdrawn from a misidentification what happens to it? What prevents it from falling under another misidentification?

—The agonizing and mysterious sensation cannot be properly reduced to the UPI which causes it. The UPI is not recognized as such, that is as *not* belonging to the subject's mind, a vulgar parasite not to be feared but to be thrown out.

—Without vibratory awareness the UPI cannot be dealt with at the very moment of its intrusion. Medical sciences intervene too late, when it is firmly rooted in the psyche causing all sorts of disturbances. Psychiatry is alerted by these symptoms. But what is needed to prevent sufferings is preventive action.

—Without the opening of the chakras on the central path of Sushumna and of the psychic space of thoughtless awareness we miss the firm ground from where we can project the power of discrimination. When a UPI dwells in the system, the subject often seeks and feels an intensity of physical and psychic sensation through the UPI's sensations; the confusion between the victim and its parasite is extremely difficult to dispel as the subject is carried further away from Sushumna.

—Last but not the least modern science completely ignores the nature of the strata of existence. It throws all the unknown in the "unconscious" basket. It is a total confusion! With Sahaja awareness we can recognize

    i the Universal Unconscious (paramatma) the pure mind of God, approached in the holiness of thoughtless awareness,

ii   the collective subconscious impacting the human super-ego,

iii   the collective supraconscious impacting the human ego.

Once you know this scene you also know who are the actors, what is the game and what is your role in it. It is great fun to play it!

Our psychiatrists have chiefly investigated the super-ego aspect of the standard psychic state. It is high time to turn our attention towards its ego aspect, the more so that, in the West, it thoroughly conditions our behavioural pattern.

Ego exists as a by-product of pingala nadi's activity. When this activity succeeds the ego inflates. In short the ego gets possessed by itself. At this stage the mind is not threatened by psychic intrusions but by self deception: ego's job is to keep you out of reality. It has a ptolemaic conception of the psychic galaxy, seeing itself as the centre of the universe. Even the existence of God and His power is challenged.

An egoist cannot see things in a right perspective for his intelligence is devoid of wisdom. He coins new words, elaborates new theories to justify his ends. This introduces us to the genesis of racism, fanaticism, orthodoxy, etc. The egoist furthermore picks up all kinds of vices, becomes adulterous and cruel, insults the chastity of women and takes great pride in doing so: "What's wrong? I like it!" He talks of liberty, freedom, achievements but is the slave of his lust and greed. He is "competitive". As he uses his mental side he usually proves to be very clever, tactful and cautious, keeping the social image up while deceiving, betraying, oppressing others.

If the ego eventually becomes very effective and successful, it starts emitting overpowering fields of microwaves which capture the attention of people who are stuck with the opposite psychic pole: the extreme of the super-ego. A club is thus formed. It can begin in drinking parties and end up into nazism or terrorism. The combination of extreme ego and super-ego then becomes a collective monster. But you need not go that far to endanger human collectivity. The egoist boastfully breaks the laws which maintain the integrity of the family and the cohesion of society. He plans and preaches, writes books and last but by no means least, makes movies; the super-ego crowd follows; the attention of the masses is drawn away from the central path of evolution.

People whose attention crosses into the area further to the right of the pingala channel enter into the collective supraconscious where they are possessed by the dead spirits (UPIs) of egoists. Thus supported they become more subtle and efficient.

It is easy to cure a person suffering from disturbance of the left SNS because they are unhealthy, disturbed, paranoid and are anxious to get rid of their ailments. But egoists are incorrigible: "Nothing wrong with me"; they make others paranoid, sick and unhappy. But they are fine.

I should not end up this digression on the PNS, the SNS and therapy without mentioning a few more points.

— Acupuncture has identified the network of nadis that channel the energy of the SNS and operates on this limited basis. Unlike Sahaja Yogis, the acupuncturists, cannot reach the PNS core of the life force system.

— Sahaja Yoga does cure cancer. Overactivity of the SNS causes a chakra to be disconnected from the PNS. As we said, the cells of the body can no longer decode the instructions for life sent forth by the organizing deities. The chakra continues emitting energy, but, without being regulated by the PNS function this energy becomes destructive and starts the mutation and proliferation of the cancerous cells. The chakra science can eradicate the very first cause of the disease in resetting the distorted chakra in its original abode on the Sushumna.

— The positions of the chakras in the subtle body correspond with the location in the physical body of important hormone producers (pineal and pituitary bodies, thyroid, thymus, adrenals, ovary and testes...) Western medicine dismisses the possibility of the chakras having a biological meaning because it could not locate a circulatory system, nerve or lymph vessel network that connected these points together. But in Sahaja Yoga we find out that ida, pingala and Sushumna nadis connect all these centres and they consist of as many concentric channels as there are chakras. To each chakra corresponds a specific channel. Sahaja curative techniques operate through this subtle integrated network. It has a regulating effect on these glands and the bodily processes they control.

The above points should be understood with the following remark in mind. You cannot realise the Divine in laboratory tests. It does not flow into the test tube. Sahaja science cannot be established or refuted by traditional science for this latter could not control the conditions of a "scientific" chakra experiment. Indeed one has to respect the divine protocol of the deities of the chakras and of the Kundalini. In order to find out about Sahaja Yoga the seeker should first get his Self realisation. He then gradually discovers that, with realisation, he gets good physical and psychic health and much more than this. The gunas, gradually, cease to delude and confuse: the left SNS no longer represents a potentially dangerous channel between the collective subconscious and the individual libido. It carries the blessings of Mahakali (the Deity controlling Ida Nadi): the sadhaka enters into the living tissue of the divine cosmic interdependency. The right hand SNS no longer tends to inflate the ego but carries Mahasaraswati's blessings: the sadhaka creatively develops the assertion of his Divine identity.

The Kundalini

What makes all the difference between Sahaja Yoga and any other type of yoga is that Sahaja Yoga is the culmination of all the yogas as it is the yoga of the actual awakening of Kundalini. The serious seeker should go and ask any serious master of Eastern mysticism:[18] he would tell you that the supreme yoga is the Kundalini Yoga, not because it excludes any other form of yoga but because it integrates them and transcends them. Guru Vashista asserts that: "Kundalini is the seat of absolute knowledge."[19] Kundalini is inborn in us and manifests Herself spontaneously when Her time has come.

The awareness of the presence of the Divine Energy within the human body was considered by the sages and rishis of yore to be the highest knowledge; it was revered with a sacred respect and hidden from the multitude by a strict esotericism. The Kundalini, its path and the chakras have been glorified in Eastern mysticism by many initiatic writings, and by countless monuments of art

---

[18] But he should avoid this parasitic legion of doomed fools, self-appointed Messiahs, false prophets, etc., who are crawling around us.
[19] Yog Vashista (op. cit.) p. 144.

and architecture.[20] It has been the highest knowledge granted to man, the holiest goal of the ancient paths of Initiation, often symbolised by the sacred fire or the sacred serpent for the Kundalini and the tree or the ladder for its path. Moses saw it in the burning bush and the Christians calling it the Holy Spirit, worship its manifestation as tongues of fire over the heads of the apostles during the Pentecost reunion. It is most probable that some priests of Ancient Egypt and South America could have had access to specific aspects of the Kundalini's tantra (instrument) thus obtaining various siddhis (magic powers); but it is unlikely that they had access to Kundalini Herself. The great Buddhist masters of the Mahayana or Vajra variant considered that the existence of the path of liberation within man himself was the deepest secret they had to keep intact and transmit to a few deserving disciples. The degenerated understanding of certain lamaic or tantric sects cannot affect the original purity of this tradition. One finds symbols of Kundalini in many different cultural legacies such as Mercury's serpent which is an alchemical symbol for the process of psychic metamorphosis. The gnostics understood the serpent to represent the spinal chord and the rachidian bulb. We can try to understand Kundalini as follows.

In the first divine strata of existence part of the Primordial Divine Energy (Adi Shakti, Holy Spirit) does not manifest itself

---

[20] In *The Foundations of Tibetan Mysticism*, Lama Anagarika Govinda exposes the relationship between the mantra "OM MANI PADME HUM" and Kundalini yoga. The form of the Buddhist "stupa" is interestingly described as representing the superimposition of the chakras.

The onion shaped bulb of the Islamic mosque represents the Sahasrara, etc. The famous Tree of Jesse window of Chartres Cathedral is also a picture of the Sushumna.

Dr. Pramila Sharma of Delhi who has studied the links between the ancestral teachings and Sahaja Yoga points out that Kundalini Yoga is described in vedic and tantric texts. We can name the Arunopanishad of Krishnyajurveda, the Bhavarichopanishad of Rigveda, the Upanishads of Atharveda, Yogopanishad, Yogashikhopanishad, Kathopanishad, Yogkundaliniupanishad, etc. In the *Puranas* we have the Devi Bhagavatpuran, Markendayapuran, Shri Bhagavatpuran, etc. In the *Sanhitas* : Hathyoga Sanhita, Layayoga Sanhita, Rajyog Sanhita, Rik Sanhita, Shiv Sanhita, etc. In the *Yoga Texts*: Hathyoga Pradrepika, Goraksh Padhti, Tantrasar, Yogakarnika, Yogavashistha Shatchakra Nirupan, Sidh Sidhant Sangrah, Kularanava Tantra, Saundarya Lahari, Subhgodayam, Lalita Sahasrarnam, etc. Kundalini has been chanted by saints such as Shri Kabir, Nanak, Dadu, Buleeshah, Gyaneshwar, etc.

but remains stored in the Virata until the time of its cosmic manifestation has come. This "sleeping" Divine Energy is Adi Kundalini, the Primordial Kundalini of the Virata. The Adi Kundalini is personified in Shri Gauri, the Mother of Lord Ganesha. She represents the shining innocence of the Divine Holy Virgin.[21] At different periods of the cosmic evolution HH Mataji says, She progresses from chakra to chakra. When she appears in a specific chakra the corresponding Deity is fully awakened and a major step of evolution set into motion. In the stratum of existence of this material world, the existence of the Divine Energy of Kundalini is similarly hidden within the human microcosm, in each and every one of us. HH Mataji says: "the Kundalini Power is the embodiment of the "will power" of Bhagawati—the Divine Mother—She is awakened by Bhagawati's will power or volition".

Let us now relate Kundalini to the evolution of the present day human beings with respect to their level of cognitive faculties.

An animal is spontaneous but it is not aware of that force which gives him instinct. A man however is no longer spontaneous because he programmes himself by reason, through the activity of rajo guna, while the animals are confined to tamo guna. The present human state is a state of the mind's development which was meant to prepare man's cognitive instrument for awareness. The state of the human being is the state of the separated identity, the egg state: man considers himself to be an autonomous, autarchic being. This step in the phenomenology of consciousness was necessary to enable man to perceive his own ego. The perception of the ego is indeed necessary to oppose the conditioning of the super-ego. The ego-man, the egg-man is a myth but it is a necessary one because, through this myth, the instrument for perception of the "I-ness", the Self, is completed. Meanwhile, on the historical stage, man believing that he is King of himself asserts his monarchy over the material world. He rises in dignity and power, he intervenes in evolution like a master, handles creation and destruction and becomes the steward of the world.

The egg state corresponds to the state where the energy of the Kundalini is enclosed within the triangular bone of the pelvic plexus

---

[21]She also is most powerful. The pattern of womanhood has been evolved according to the Archetype of Shri Gauri. Therefore the greatest power of a woman is her chastity.

at the bottom of the spine. Man's psychic life and cognitive faculties depend upon the right and left side sympathetic nervous system (rajo guna and tamo guna) and upon the possibility of reaching an equilibrium between them (Satwa guna).

Now the state of the separated identity is also the state of the split consciousness, the unhappy consciousness (Unglückliche Bewusstsein) of Hegel's Phenomenology of Spirit. When encompassed in its ego-shell man enjoys the freedom of the individual egg. But not too surprisingly, the state of isolated egg implies limits. Man's growing awareness resents them. While being aware of being a finite being, man is also aware of an Infinite dimension within and outside of himself, aware that he is more than a separated shell. However he does not know how to reconcile the Finite and the Infinite. This is the core of the great metaphysical debate over the essence of human nature and the purpose of human destiny. Moreover the freedom of the ego-man is a freedom of choice between this and that which appears also as the freedom between good and evil. When this freedom is coupled with ignorance, then, mistakes, sins and sufferings are brought to the world. This is the core of the perennial ethical debate over the essence of human nature, the problem of the existence of Evil in the world.

At last, this growing awareness longs for a spontaneous harmony beyond the movements of the gunas, beyond metaphysical contradictions and ethical mistakes. In the "egg-man" state, man is not spontaneous nor is he integrated within or outside of himself and his action brings social injustice. Hence the evolved human being seeks to be free from the myth of the ego, from separateness, contradictions and ignorance. This evolution of awareness took millenia but it has been completed within this Kali yuga (from Shri Krishna's death to the present day) and this completion has called for the Incarnation of the Great One who grants us the promised knowledge by which we can be convinced. HH Mataji Nirmala Devi has come to experimentally reveal the knowledge of Kundalini. Opening for us the dimension of the spontaneous synthesis between the Finite and the Infinite, thus completing the grand task of the previous incarnations. Indeed *The opening of the fontanel bone (brahmarandra at the top of the brain) by the rising Kundalini is the opening of the egg's shell*: the new man, the new Adam is born. The immediate and experimental knowledge of Kundalini which is the message of Sahaja Yoga might well be said to open a new cycle of universal history. It should be emphasized, once again, that this puzzling statement is substantiated by the experiences of countless people.

The process of the Kundalini's ascent can be described as follows. The Kundalini can be compared to a rope made out of many threads. She rises by unfolding her coils piercing every chakra. The width of the Kundalini, that is, the number of the threads, starts diminishing as She ascends if the higher chakras are not open or if the spot to pierce in the chakra is constricted. Of course, if the lower chakras are open, the Kundalini rises as a whole but then, if the higher chakras are not open, only a few threads pierce through chakras and reach the Sahasrara. The Kundalini does not force Her way upwards; She caters to the needs of the chakras, cures the disease caused by the constriction of the chakras and subsequent recession of the deities; She awakens them. The awakened deities clear the path for Her ascent. Now if the lower chakras are not cleared we obviously run into difficulties. For instance, the drama of the western seekers is that they totally ignored the psychosomatic imperative at the roots of sexual morality: "respect your own chastity!" The deity of the lowest chakra, the Mooladhara chakra, is Shri Ganesh who is the personification of the divine child's innocence (He later incarnated as Lord Jesus Christ). When we indulge in unbalanced sexual behaviours, when our attention gets obsessed with sex,[22] we are damaging the foundation path of the Kundalini. It has been found with many young westerners that, as their Mooladhara chakra is in jeopardy, the force of the Kundalini's ascent is very weak and the sensitivity to vibratory awareness quite poor. It has also been found that these difficulties can be overcome. However, if such is our condition, we need twice as much perseverance and faith as a simple and innocent man because, as stated already, our progress might be slow, and we will be challenged by all sorts of doubts. During this transition we are to check the agitation of our intellect which will have been shattered by too much previous adharmic behaviour. Difficult as it may seem, this self-control is possible because the Kundalini is already helping us.

Let us describe a slow motion ascent of Kundalini. (In a few

---

[22] For instance looking at depraved movies, reading "erotic" books, imagining immoral sex activities etc., etc.

very evolved beings self-realisation takes place in the split of a second and is established for ever). When the Kundalini rises without confronting major problems on the lower chakras it reaches the Ajnya chakra and spreads on to the lower brain plate, like a cloud which brings a sort of sweet heaviness or a sleepy feeling. We can say that, first, the Mother puts us to sleep. The second feeling is when the vital force of Kundalini melts down on the Ida and Pingala, as if the clouds of vital force start pouring bliss. These two channels carry it down to the Manipura chakra and a new impulse of Kundalini's force joins it. (All the while the head feels gradually lighter as if its load is being taken away). Then, the triple force (Mahalakshmi, Mahasaraswati, Mahakali) rises in the Sushumna and opens the Ajnya. The Ajnya crossing creates the thoughtless awareness. The pupils start dilating, the head becomes clearer. Advanced disciples, at this point, have seen Christ's light within themselves. One feels the silence of the Sahasrara. At Sahasrara Kundalini's force accumulates. A release of pressure starts as the Brahmarandra opens. At this great moment the subject feels the cool breeze of the vibrations: this is "realization". There are many people who have become "awakened" (Jagruti) and also have some curing power but they cannot remain in thoughtless awareness; they touch it for a minute or so. However the process of the Kundalini oozing out works out with time and ultimately the subject reaches a stage of deeper awareness that we can call "doubtless awareness". With many people the experience has been one of a quick and permanent ascent; some felt as if two balls of ice fell in their hands, and started melting. The cooling crept into their being. However the subject's perception of his own realization is not always that clear. If the Vishudddhi chakra is stretched or constricted, then, one does not feel the vibrations despite realization, that is, the piercing of the Brahmarandara.

It may be worthwhile to summarize this chapter on the instrument of awareness by graphic representations.

After realization the new world opens. To quote HH Mataji Nirmala Devi, as soon as our attention moves to our inner consciousness we can move on everybody's Kundalini. As the thread (sootra) of a necklace is passing through every bead of the necklace, the inner consciousness (Kundalini) is also passing through every human being; thus collective consciousness is achieved. I have discovered this to be true especially in Bombay and Delhi with

90 THE ADVENT

A.—Before realization

Figure VII

UNIVERSAL UNCONSCIOUS
Continuous Present
Archangels   Cherubs   Seraphs

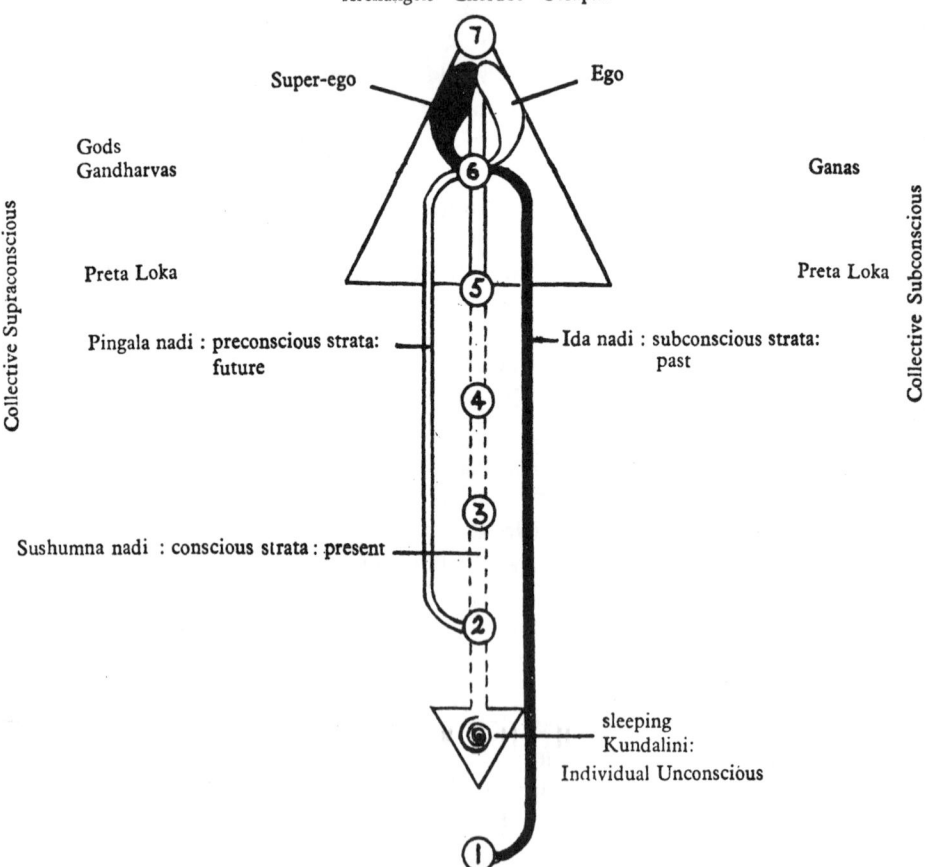

Super-ego — ⑦ — Ego

Gods
Gandharvas   Ganas

⑥

Collective Supraconscious   Collective Subconscious

Preta Loka   ⑤   Preta Loka

Pingala nadi : preconscious strata: ——   ←— Ida nadi : subconscious strata:
future   past

④

③

Sushumna nadi : conscious strata : present ——

②

sleeping
⓪   Kundalini:
Individual Unconscious

①

i. Before realisation, the conscious strata (the enjoyer of the present) is a very narrow thread of consciousness represented in the above graph by the Sushumna channel. The attention of the subject is permeated by the thoughts from the preconscious strata generating the ego and the moods from the subconscious strata generating the super-ego.
ii. There is no direct link of awarenes with the Universal Unconscious. The Kundalini is sleeping.
iii. The deities on the chakras are not fully operative. There is no link of awareness between the chakras: the personality cannot be integrated.
iv. The consciousness is trapped in the egg of the brain (ego and super-ego).

B.—After Realization

Figure VIII
UNIVERSAL UNCONSCIOUS
Continuous Present

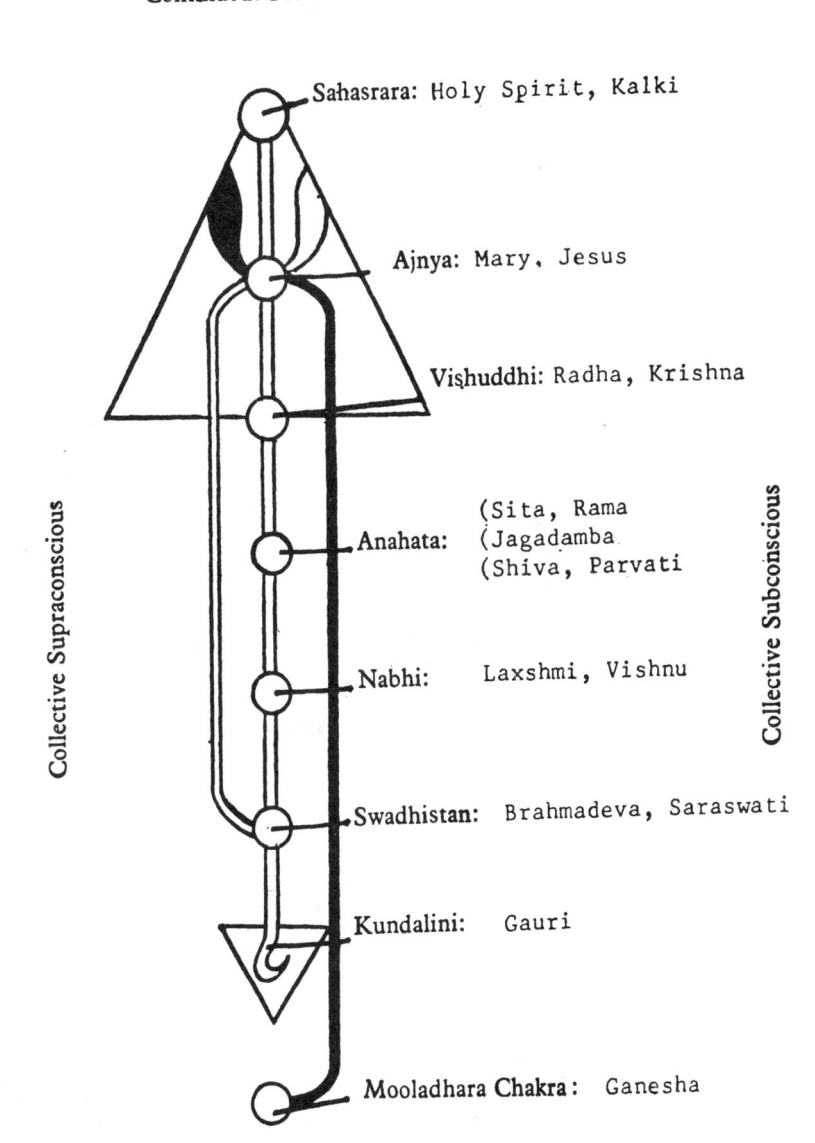

Sahasrara: Holy Spirit, Kalki

Ajnya: Mary, Jesus

Vishuddhi: Radha, Krishna

Anahata: (Sita, Rama
(Jagadamba
(Shiva, Parvati

Nabhi: Laxshmi, Vishnu

Swadhistan: Brahmadeva, Saraswati

Kundalini: Gauri

Mooladhara Chakra: Ganesha

Collective Supraconscious

Collective Subconscious

After Realisation

i. The awareness space of the conscious mind has increased. Ego and Super-ego gradually drop down and are sucked back into Pingala and Ida.
ii. The ascended Kundalini establishes a direct link with the Unconscious. It manifests as the flow of vibrations.
iii. The Deities on the chakras are awakened. They are the reflectors of the original deities on the Adi Chakras of the Virata and they "organize" our awareness accordingly. As they are linked together by the ascended Kundalini the personality becomes integrated. They decode and respond to the messages from the Holy Spirit. They read other human beings as awareness systems. They direct our spiritual growth.
iv. Collective Consciousness is achieved. The attention is drawn inside because of the inward happening of Kundalini's rise.
v. In a fully mature realized being, the Deities ascend from their place of work in the chakra, to their own seats within the Sahasrara. This is the stage of complete Divine integration.

other Sahaja Yogis. When we are together the intensity of our awareness deepens and I do not know exactly how it comes on but I know that we radiate a considerable flow of energy when we are collectively meditating. Within the vibratory field of awareness we generate, we propel each other further into the depth of our awakened consciousness: Old and young, high court judges and children, housewives and students: everybody is sharing this fantastic feeling. We are enjoying ourselves, enjoying each other, sharing the Joy of God. We are bathing in that communion of love that we frantically sought for so long. It is overwhelming! No more talks of universal brotherly love! It has become a truth, a part and parcel of our consciousness.

There are only a few thousand Sahaja Yogis at the moment because HH Mataji Nirmala Devi started the whole process of collective emancipation only a few years ago. Moreover a living process takes time to manifest. But because of the properties of collective consciousness and the liberation of energy it involves, a snowball effect of spreading the new consciousness can be expected, despite the fact that the atmosphere is saturated with all kinds of not-so-good vibrations.

Furthermore the greatest proof of the genuineness of Sahaja Yoga is that in given conditions, every Sahaja Yogi has himself the power to grant realization by raising the Kundalini! Thus the power of the seeker's own Self starts manifesting.

However we have to be aware that this dazzling realm of godliness cannot be reached by the mere striving of the intellect's curiosity, or indeed, by any of our human efforts, and this is the result of the nature of the Kundalini: we cannot "tame" our Kundalini but we can surrender ourselves to Her. Like Lord Ganesha is surrendered to His Immaculate Mother. I am repeating, that the Kundalini is beyond the gunas and hence beyond our control. Therefore, Sahaja Yoga transcends the other forms of yoga which merely aim at controlling the ego-identified mind by destroying the ego. The Kundalini does not destroy but overcomes, transcends...Here we should clearly understand the following:

Mukti (Liberation) is the breaking point of the ego's shell by the Kundalini and yet it is not enough to break the ego because, once the ego is broken, gone also is the protection that it gave to the individual psyche. One might then fall under the domination of the invisible masters of the supraconscious or the dead spirits and other forces of the subconscious who act through the superego. (At this point, conditioning reveals some frightening aspects). The true liberation can only be the liberation from the ego (rajoguna, right side SNS) and the super-ego (tamoguna, left side SNS). This can be achieved only by the Kundalini's clearing of the central path (satwa guna, parasympathetic nervous system). Any other so called "liberation" leads to a further enslavement process: nothing is basically changed in the mechanism of misidentification but its object. The pseudogurus who advocate new kinds of meditations or transcendental experiences capitalize on the disciple's ignorance of the role of the super-ego. When these fake teachers are at the same time wicked and powerful they can enter through the super-ego into the subject's psyche; to this effect they exhort the disciple to overcome the ego because, obviously, a strong ego would oppose their ways.[23]

The true identification with the Self is only possible when the Kundalini is settled in the seventh chakra. The explanation goes as follows:

HH Mataji tells us that the three aspects of the Primordial Witness (God Almighty, Sadashiva), the Primordial Energy (Adi Shakti, Holy Ghost) and God the Son (the Christ, the Buddha) are all expressed within the human microcosm:

—The Adi Shakti, the Energy, the Holy Spirit is manifested

---

[23]The ego itself can be intruded by supraconscious U.P.I.'s which give additional creativity.

within man when Kundalini awakens from Her potential state at the bottom of the spine and actualises Herself in the Sahasrara: *this is the state called self-realisation*, the manifestation of the Kundalini aspect of the Holy Spirit in the Sahasrara. Lord Jesus said: "What is the Kingdom of God like and to what shall I compare it? It is like a grain of mustard seed which a man took and sowed in his garden and it grew and became a tree, and the birds of the air made nests in its branches." Luke 13.18. The psychosomatic and spiritual instrument is manifested by the rising of the Kundalini. And again, "To what shall I compare the Kingdom of God? It is like leaven which a woman took and hid in three measures of flour till it was all leavened". Luke 13.20. The alternative phases of potentiality and actuality of the Shakti-Kundalini are the substance of this statement.

—The Child God, the AUM, the bread of life is also expressed within man. He resides in the Mooladhara chakra as Shri Ganesha where He looks after the protocol of Mother Kundalini. His evolved form resides as Lord Jesus Christ in the Ajnya chakra where He keeps the Gate of the City of the Holy Spirit, the Sahasrara. He is manifested within man when He opens the Ajnya on the path of the ascending Kundalini, thus totally purifying and enlightening the mind (buddhi).

—God Almighty, the Witness is manifested through the Self within man when He is united with the Shakti who has settled in the Sahasrara.[24] The Self is the Soul, the Atman, personified by Lord Shiva who resides within the human heart, at the left side of the heart chakra. The limbic area in the brain is the Kingdom of God. We can say, in a way, that it is the heavenly space where

---

[24] "Thou are diverting Thyself in secrecy with the Lord, in the thousand petalled lotus, having pierced through the Earth situated in the Muladhara, the Water in the Manipura, the Fire abiding in the Swadhistana, the Air in the Heart (Anahata), the Ether above (Vishuddhi) and Manas between the eyebrow (Ajnya) and thus broken through the entire Kula path." Shri Sankaracharya *Saundarya Lahari* stanza 9. The Katha Upanishad is more technical : "Radiating from the lotus of the heart there are a hundred and one nerves. One of these ascends towards the thousand petalled lotus in the brain. If, when a man comes to die, his vital force passes upward and out through this nerve, he attains immortality". HH Mataji compares the Self with the flame and Kundalini with gas energy. When they touch ignition takes place.

one rests before entering into the sacred presence of God the Almighty (Sadashiva). He resides beyond the Sahasrara and can be approached through the hole in the fontanel membrane (baptism). When the human attention appears in the presence of God Almighty, the Self, which is His reflection in the heart, gets enlightened and starts emmitting cool vibrations (the breeze or the wind).

Then the Witness and the Energy complete in the Sahasrara of the enlightened one the cosmic play intiated at the dawn of time. It is the play of God's Self-recognition within the creation. We are all invited to join it.

PART FOUR

ELUCIDATIONS

5

The Virtue of Dharma

The Sushumna and the chakras are the royal drive to be adorned and garlanded for the rising of Kundalini. Therefore all the scriptures and saints suggested that the best way to prepare this path is to lead a dharmic, virtuous life. All the Sahaja Yogis of the five continents now bow to the dictates of all the real Gurus, prophets and masters.

When Kundalini transfigures our awareness in Her ascent, our cognitive faculties merge in a new dimension: the physical, emotional, mental, spiritual beings in us are synthesised by the spontaneous force of the primordial energy. In other words we are perceiving through one unique, fully integrated instrument: as previously said, the vibrations are felt in the fingers or even in the toes!...as well as in any single part of the body depending upon the case. The whole of the human body is a temple of the transformation.

The Sushumna is the channel of the Mahalaxshmi energy. It represents the evolutionary line of Lord Vishnu the protector aspect of God Almighty who is the embodiment of dharma. The opening of the Sushumna therefore implies spontaneous dharma-consciousness and because of the above mentioned integration Dharma is felt at the physical level through the awakened central nervous system. Hence as soon as the new born Yogi confronts negative vibrations he becomes aware of them by physical sensations.

A senior civil servant went to HH Mataji asking for realisation. We all tried our best to help him but his Kundalini would not cross the level of the nabhi chakra (the abode of Lord Vishnu). Meanwhile the Sahaja Yogis present in the room had pain in their stomachs. A couple of hours later we learnt from locals that this man had made a corrupted use of the public money entrusted to him; the nabhi is Shri Laxshmi's chakra as bringer of wealth and comfort to dharmic people and vice versa; the chakra had recorded his misdoings. On another occasion we could not explain why a beautiful work of art emitted very bad vibrations; it turned out that the artist had killed his father. A man who was secretly deceiving his wife was badly caught on the nabhi chakra (dharma) and on the right heart chakra (seat of Lord Rama, the ideal husband and father), etc., etc.

The experiences gained in raising people's Kundalini as well as those gained through the awareness of our own chakras indicate that the different chakras are more particularly affected by specific sins. For example:

—*The Mooladhara chakra.* Without a proper understanding of sex this chakra is upset and the general condition of awareness-energy will be correspondingly weak. In this respect, the reeducation of the attention is a lengthy process but a rewarding one. The right side is affected when there is constipation or repressed sexuality such as puritanism.

—*The Swadhistan chakra.* It is often strained when our activities are too much dominated by the ego. Pain is felt in the loins. This chakra is also completely broken down in some instances of sexual misbehaviour. The right side will be affected by too much planning, overactivity. Artists are generally weak on this chakra because they strain their creative energy to its limit. Diabetes is caused by an imbalance due to excessive mental activity. Lethargic temperaments are weak on this chakra.

—*Manipur (Nabhi) chakra.* This chakra gets heavy and disturbed by the ingestion of fermented drinks, certain meats and drugs. It is also affected by any misdoing related to money, material accumulation or something basically wrong in our lifestyle. Liver troubles are the result of too much stress on the right nabhi and swadhistan. Liver patients are disturbed in their attention and awareness.

—*Anahata chakra.* Tensions load this chakra especially when the familial relation to the father (right side of the chakra) or the mother (left side) involve emotional or other problems. When this chakra is caught the subject is in a state of insecurity. The left side is affected by threat to the physical existence and overactivity (athletism). The right side is affected when ideal patterns of human behaviour are not respected.(e.g. husband-wife, father-son, dutiful citizen relationships). Excessive disturbances lead to breast cancer, heart attacks, etc.

—*Vishuddhi chakra.* This chakra is affected by any form of lack of self-respect in thought words, or deeds; by self-denial; by bowing to a wrong person; by dominating or being dominated; It is also disturbed by smoking. Pain can be felt in the throat, ears, etc.

—*Ajnya chakra.* This most sensitive centre does not let any impurity ascend to the Sahasrara and will be specially affected by erratic thought waves and a wrong use of our eyes, by playing mental and emotional games. It is affected by too much reading, too much television; by the inability to forgive or to ask for forgiveness; by the touch of demonic "gurus". Because the Ajnya chakra controls the optical nerves as well as the pineal and pituitary bodies, the control of one's eyes is a sine qua non condition to the control of the attention. For instance, when we walk in a street, we should not glance endlessly at every passer-by. The sadhaka has to apply steadfast attention to clear the Ajnya, a process which lasts several years. The reactions of the Ajnya cause burning on the forehead and in the back of the head as well as headaches. It affects our sight; if there is a UPI one may become suddenly blind.[1]

—*Sahasrara chakra.* The complex thousand petalled lotus contains in a subtle form all the others. It is jammed and painful especially when the subject does not surrender to the manifestation of the truth that he has witnessed. Dogmatic people are caught on the Sahasrara. So are also those clinging to their mental set-up, concepts and opinions about spirituality.

There are many permutations and combinations of chakras but in this book they cannot be described in detail.

[1] "I was looking at my Ajnya chakra from within my head. It looked like a kind of elongated ball shining like the sun. I saw also black dots turning around it " Bohdan Shehovych, a Russian doctor who is also a Sahaja Yogi could see UPIs attacking his Ajnya.

Through various vibratory information man is becoming instinctively or better, spontaneously aware of the right and wrong: the time has come for him to be authorised to taste the fruits of the Tree of knowledge of good and evil. Our experiments have taught us a few very simple guidelines for behavioural soundness. Among those:

—A person who works too hard or is very lethargic must bring himself towards the centre and avoid extreme behaviour.
—A person who worries too much about money, possessions, their upkeep or one who is vain about them can never rest in contentment.
—A person who pays too much attention to success, fame, outward appearance develops artificiality and lacks wisdom and profoundness.
—A person who thinks and plans too much ultimately becomes frantic and can never tune in with the Divine.
—A person who leads a licentious life loses the awareness of the divine qualities. Women in this world, when regarded as mothers or sisters (except for one's own wife), can be enjoyed in all innocence and spontaneity.
—A person who is religiously narrow minded has to open his Sahasrara by believing in all the great religions and all the great incarnations.

Self realisation implies the stage of awareness in which dharma is self-conscious. However, before this stage is reached, it is very important to be conceptually aware of dharma and to conform one's behaviour to its requirements (the so called useless "moral conduct") so as to maintain our parasympathetic instrument fit for the raising of Kundalini.

Before the opening of Sushumna it seems to be of great importance to lead a dharmic, moral and balanced life, so that our attention does not involve itself too far either on pingala or on ida nadi (right and left sympathetic nervous system). The danger of doing so results from the fact that, unlike Sushumna, these two channels are not expressing the evolutionary line of man's perfectibility. Sushumna, Pingala and Ida, the three main channels of energy built into the microcosmic human psycho-somatic instrument, are connected with different strata of existence at the cosmic level. So, if we are overly involved in pingala nadi we will, after our death, be attracted by the collective supra-conscious. In the case of ida nadi we will join the collective sub-conscious. For man these realms are evolutionary dead-ends, leading to potentially unhappy reincarnation on earth. On the other hand, the one who gets stuck in the lower strata of these realms might be kept in hell or come back on earth as a spirit, our famous UPI. Only the Sushumna leads to the Kingdom of God. As we said, at the very extreme of ida nadi we find totally conditioned, possessed personalities. At the extreme of pingala nadi the oppressive, egoistical monster manifests itself.

That is why—HH Mataji tells us along with the earlier teachers—the extremes are to be avoided. Moderation keeps one nearer the central channel. The innocence and spontaneity are retained by a person who does not take his attention away from this channel. And Shri Ganesha, the God of innocence is at the same time the god of wisdom: "In ruling men and in serving Heaven, the Sages use only moderation. By moderation alone he is able to have conformed early (to Tao)" Lao Tzu goes on to state very clearly that Tao implying here Dharma, is this disposition which makes men "UPI-proofed".

"Let Tao reign over the world, and no spirits will show their ghostly powers.
Not that the spirits have no more powers,
But their powers will not harm men".[2]

If we take our attention away from the central path to the left or right sides and seek "liberation" from dharma, maybe because of the influence of the environment, the movement of the energy constricts the chakras on the central channel. When the attention goes too much in one direction, ultimately the course of life might lead towards physical and psychic disintegration. If the extreme movements from one side to another precipitate themselves, the delicate flower of human awareness becomes crumpled, the mechanism is confused. People suffer all kinds of diseases. For many people the psychic energy constantly oscillates between

---

[2]Tao Te Ching in the translation of Chiu Tao-Kao. Unwin publisher (London 1972) p. 74 and 75.

right and left, left and right sides of the sympathetic nervous system. This tendency leads to alternative conditioning of the super-ego (ida nadi) and assertion of the ego (pingla nadi). When the pendulum's swing is too violent people merely exhaust their life's energy in contradictory and uncontrolled psychic process (e.g. alternatives of self-justification and guilt, pride and despair, etc., etc.). The broken down chakras are then opened to the UPI's, cancer may set in.

The ancient ideal of Greek esthetics and ethics which sought to avoid every kind of excess and laid paramount emphasis on the notion of harmony expressed a noble cultural understanding of these secret energetic laws. Dharmic people are indeed much less likely to be the prey of Maya (delusion) Moira, Anangke (destiny), Hubris (Pride) or Fortuna.

> "and blessed are those
> Whose blood and judgement are so well co-melted
> That they are not a pipe for Fortune's finger
> To sound what stop she please." (Hamlet III.2.62)

Those (Shakespeare might not have known it) are blessed by Dharma which gives balance and firmness on the Sushumna anchorage.

Sahaja Yoga reveals that a dharmic life keeps the energy's movements in an equilibrium which offers the optimal chances of success for the rising of Kundalini: when the chakras are not laterally strained or squeezed they can be pierced in their centres by the ascending power and thus, pave the way for the breakthrough of awareness. Then, in the words of my friend Gavin Brown: "If you are identified with Dharma you are on the thread of all existences; what you do is what is necessary: Fulfil life and love, satisfy yourself and God, complete the circle."

Maybe we could better understand now the rationale behind the old rules of moral behaviour. To act against Dharma, or, in old-fashioned terms to commit a sin amounts to act against one's self-awareness. Sin is a deviation from the path of the evolution of the consciousness.

In this respect HH Mataji explains the following:

"The sensitivity of the chakras becomes dull after the first few shocks to them. Then, a human being starts living with all the shocking habits very easily. He exists but in a very superficial way as he does not want to go down into his depths, because in this movement, he has to first face the shocks that are stored within. He tries to forget them as that helps him to exist. But mere existence is not enough. It is insulting, frustrating, debasing and degenerating. Many courageous people really want to face themselves. Sahaja Yoga will help those."

The process will require our patience and collaboration. The greatest asset of a seeker throughout difficulties and mistakes, is the ability to search in all earnestness and honesty[3]. Indeed we can get realisation even with a damaged instrument but, as mentioned before, it will take time for the Kundalini to consolidate the new stage of awareness.

When the chakras and nadis are damaged by Adharma we are a bit like a cracked cup which does not retain water; we can perhaps better understand the relationship between dharma, our psycho-somatic instrument and self-realization by listening to HH Mataji's description of Lord Buddha's samadhi:

"Buddha had dharma. His body was clean. His mind, his attention did not find any joy in worldly greed or desires. His cup was ready and it emptied when he became tired of his searching efforts and surrendered. That was the moment in which the Divine vibrations poured like torrential rain; the Shakti filled his cup and made him the "Shakta", the Enlightened one. So when you are taught to keep to virtue you are warned to keep the cup intact and clean."

By the grace of God the water of His love has the property of slowly repairing the cracked cup in which it is flowing. However, if the cup is totally broken, logically enough very little hope is left; it would be better for us to avoid exploring the breaking point between the crack and the fracture.

---

[3] The earnest longing for the Truth is the vital aspect of this Bodhicitta (desire for Supreme enlightenment) which is described in the Mahayana Buddhist texts as the key to bodhisattvahood. See Maitreya's instructions to the young Buddhist pilgrim Sudhana in the *Gandavyuha sutras*.

Those who are not aware that I am talking about rather serious matters probably fail to consider that the consequences of our actions (karma) follow us in the after death and largely condition our further destiny. Let us swiftly elaborate on that:

When the heart ceases to beat we know that the soul (atman) has left the aggregates it had assembled for a short while in order to enjoy the human experience of existence. The individual's consciousness withdraws from the bodily organs which supported it. The Atman and the Kundalini depart. The content of the consciousness gathers together in the Kundalini which start reducing in size up to one or two centimetres; then Kundalini leaves the body carrying the chakras which are loaded with the content of consciousness that is the karma of this past as well as previous lives (total memory). Firstly the deceased in the Kundalini form attends the corpse for about thirteen days (c.f. the traditional importance of funeral rites to appease the spirit of the dead). Then, depending upon the content of the chakras and the condition of the Kundalini, he becomes attracted by the field of energy corresponding to it and proceeds towards the related stratum of existence. In the Virata, the preta loka (realm of spirits) has many layers. The interaction between this abode and the individual consciousness determine the next human birth. At the time of the child's conception both Atman and Kundalini incarnate again.

With the naked eye a Sahaja Yogi may see a UPI hanging around: These entities show up as small round dark spots sometimes alone or sometimes with their Kundalini. The Kundalini is bruised, chakras are darkened or even stretched outside, etc. The malformations thus physically observed in a centimetre wide shape are an expression of the stigmas of sin on the UPI's consciousness. They strongly suggest it is better to try avoiding sin while being in a human shape. Some desperate people choose death as the solution. But it is not. For no one dies. Only a tiny part (the physical components evolved from the earth and water elements) drops out at the time of "death". All the rest remains. Dissatisfied and tortured souls linger on near the conscious areas of the Virata (ghosts, djins, etc.) ready to manifest as UPIs. It is much worse to suffer in the spirit stage than in the human one. With a physical body one can help oneself but without it the state of suffering is hell. Also, in this state one cannot improve the chances of evolution while being exposed to further sin (becoming a UPI).

It is not in my power to quote the innumerable scriptures which warn us to avoid sin but I would merely refer the perturbations of our psychic life to two basic sins we are committing: the sin against the Father and the sin against the Mother.

—Every man is potentially the one who can represent for his child, the expression of absolute security in the face of life and destiny. Thus he somewhat incarnates the tutelary aspect of God, the Almighty. Lord Jesus said: "Your Father knows what you need before you ask Him". The sin against the Father is a sin of mistrust against the divine Providence. The psyche wants to comprehend everything, to control everything, intending to be the tutor of Destiny as well as the accountant of the little artificial security that it manages to insure. The pathology generated by this hopeless fight expresses itself in the mental and emotional bodies as a worried spirit constantly hunting an elusive security; one builds up a sand castle of "security" and identifications. Fame, power, material accumulation are some of the names of this game of dupes which usually takes the form of useless aggression. We should make a clear distinction between poverty and material deprivation. The first implies the impossibility to guarantee survival. The second is a matter of attitude; it is a relative, artificial, socially conditioned concept. Even a rich man can feel deprived. I remember a rather amusing sight in the harbour of St. Tropez (France): near each big private yacht there would be a bigger one. Owners would look at each other's boats with envy and jealously.

But a realized soul, his attention withdrawn inside, enjoys his own virtues. He is materially satisfied and does not waste his attention in superfluous accumulation of possessions. Whenever the need arose, I saw so many of them happily sharing their extra money. Spontaneously, generously without showing off. HH Mataji remarks: "A realized soul is a Badshah (Emperor). Like Shri Sainath of Shirdhi, he can sleep on a stone and enjoys the comfort of a mother's lap."

—Every woman is potentially the one who can be for her child, the expression of the supreme recourse to love, thus incarnating an aspect of the Divine. Furthermore the expression of holy innocence, purity, sublimity is represented by her chastity which also manifests a fundamental aspect of the Divine Energy. The sin against the mother is attacking this status when the sexualised psyche sees women as objects of carnal consumption[4]. Through this degradation, it is an entire conception of the universe which is debased and tends towards the cloaca. The vitiated spirit projects its vision on the world and turns it into a vast sewer. The pathology generated by this perversion expresses itself as an extremely conditioned psyche.

Of course the reader is already aware of the parallel between these two sins and our psycho-somatic structure. The sin against the Father is done through pingala nadi and the ego. The sin against the Mother through ida nadi and the super-ego. Interestingly enough, if somebody is excessively developed on one of the sides he will be inclined to commit the sin corresponding to the other side, thus expressing the perpetual movement of action and reaction between the two nadis. This statement is true not only for individuals but also on a collective level. For instance the Western, industrial countries have evolved themselves chiefly on the sun line (pingala nadi) as they are ego-oriented. In those countries the sin against the Mother is now very commonly committed; there is little true respect for womanhood and motherhood left any more.

We might fear that social disintegration is in store for a society which feels no shame in degrading its women. In the Eastern world which has evolved chiefly on the moon line we find that it is above all the sin against the Father which is now committed. In most of those so called poverty ridden societies the drive for economic survival is presently turning people into robbers and cheats, who will try to make money at any cost. Work ethic often seems to be an alien, irrelevant concept.

In terms of our discourse it is clear that both of these sins are against Dharma, but with respect to self-realization we can almost say that the worst of the two is the sin against the Mother. The psycho-somatic explanation goes as follows: It is extremely important to realise that, while the sin against the Father endan-

---

[4]Lord Jesus warned us not to have adulterous eyes. Having sex with the eyes instead of enjoying a sane sexual relationship with one's wife does not give any fulfilment and just wastes the energy. It insults the motherhood of women. It goes against the Ajnya Chakra. But people in the so called Christian countries do not mind in the least ignoring Christ's warnings.

gers various chakras (nabhi, vishuddhi, ajnya) the sin against the Mother directly attacks the mooladhara chakra which is the foundation at the basis of the whole edifice.

The believers in sex liberation do not know how badly they damage themselves! We have given realisation to many of them in England and India. What usually happens however is this: the Kundalini rises at once, more easily than for, say, an average Indian man. This suggests that the subject had a great background in spirituality, having possibly been a saintly seeker in previous lives. But to our great amazement after a few minutes and sometimes a few seconds, the Kundalini falls down to Her abode. This indicates that the broken down Mooladhara chakra cannot support the ascended Kundalini; on the contrary it sucks Her down. We then have to delicately explain to our liberated friend that free sex is not conducive to the growth of awareness. If we have the courage to do so, the subject feeling insulted by our backwardness, might well decide at once that Sahaja Yoga is not the true way of spirituality. My Indian friends were often puzzled at what they rightly considered to be surprising reactions. But Western Sahaja Yogis, rather aware of the situation of sex relations in developed societies have expressed more fatalism than astonishment. How many people in the West are really interested in the truth? How many are prepared to give up their misidentifications for the sake of truth? Do they think that they are going to pick up God en passant, by the way of their fancies? These questions bother us.

The shakti of Shri Ganesha is wisdom. It is wisdom which makes you accept and recognize dharma; it is wisdom which gives you balance between heart and mind. Shri Ganesha knows what is right and wrong and He will not compromise. To call His blessings we should respect the holiness of women and consider them as reflections of the virgin Adi Shakti Gauri: but for one's wife, all women in the world are mothers or sisters. Alas, in the modern times our perception of women is conditioned by a decadent culture; unnatural and degrading relationships are socially fashionable. People have made such a silly fuss over sexual liberation that I wish to elaborate a bit on the matter.

Sex, HH Mataji states is quite good and natural; sexual harmony is a very beautiful and sacred link between husband and wife. She actually encourages Sahaja Yogis to get married[5] for a successful marriage gives balance and maturity. The Divine wants us to enjoy life, to enjoy ourselves, to enjoy each other. Delights of softness, tenderness and pleasure are best relished in the precious love of the husband and wife's physical intimacy.

During the two years I spent in Nepal and during my visits to India I have been quite impressed to see how people in a rural environment often are spontaneous, open and happy despite extremely difficult material conditions. When comparing these features with corresponding behaviours in the West, one can put forward a couple of sociological observations relating to sex, sexual conduct and family structure.

Thank God I did not visit India as a tourist! I avoided big cities where Indians are sometimes more westernised than westerners, and carefully avoided hotels, clubs and other tourist traps. It is rather unfortunate that most of the foreigners miss the general social pattern of India as we mostly meet Indians who are foreigners in their own country and know nothing of their own culture.

We can say that, as a rule, the behaviour of a family member is automatically kept in check by the awareness that the greatest responsibility is towards the children; they also know that whatever the parents do or think becomes for the children a pattern to follow. Henceforth, selfish and arbitrary behaviour by a member of the family is not tolerated. If, say, a married man runs after another woman he will be cut off from the family and rejected by society. The public reprobation will stick to him whatever he tries to do. This is because, in the Indian subcontinent, the family is still the fundamental unit of society and the child is the centre of the family.

From his early childhood, the child is provided with a set of inter-personal relationships through which he can spontaneously evolve psychic balance and emotional maturity. Such relationships are with the mother, father, older sister, younger sister, older

---

[5]Repressed sexuality and artificial asceticism as encouraged in some traditions of priesthood are not, repeat not, a condition for spiritual ascent! The great rishis of the Vedic ages were married. Actually, repressed sex negatively affects the mooladhara chakra and the general balance of the psyche. Moreover, in the cycle of rebirths repressed people can see-saw into their opposite and become most licencious and depraved.

brother, younger brother, aunts, uncles and grand parents on the father's side, relatives on the mother's side, etc. Each of these relationships has its own emotional coefficient, emits its own fragrance and the child is thus enveloped in a delicate variety of expressions of love. He gives and receives love through the subtle prism of this familial structure. The nuances in the expressions of love, in the ideal family, fully meet the emotional needs of the child. He is the little king in the sweet kingdom of familial love: lovingly teased by brothers and sisters, directed by the parents, adored by the grand parents, protected by his uncles and spoiled by his aunts, etc. This love-web is enjoyed not only during childhood; it remains very much actual through the various phases of life. A man will not look at a woman as a potential wife but as a sister or mother (depending upon the age of the woman) because such are the models of emotional relationships he has evolved through his childhood and adolescence. When the time of marriage comes, the bride of the groom is selected through a collective decision in the family after consulting their horoscopes. This collectiveness dignifies the social dimension of marriage and integrates it in the familial puzzle. Then, and only then, the partners in the new couple discover a new type of relationship; the love between man and woman as husband and wife. One specific expression of this relation appears in physical love. In many cases marriages are emotionally and physically successful. Physical love is enjoyed through the freshness of a new discovery, in the tender intimacy of exclusiveness. Exclusiveness makes it precious and sacred; it provides the right framework to enjoy it fully. It makes sex all the more enjoyable because it insures the optimal tuning of the partners' neuro-psychic instrument[6]. The fullness of physical love is a function of respecting the psychological specificity of sex: this latter is only one aspect of the husband-wife relationship which, itself, is only one among many types of inter-personal relationships and behavioural rules. We will elaborate on this later on. In any case one does not enjoy sex by reading books or seeing movies about it; this kills the joy. HH Mataji says: "can we enjoy the fragrance of flowers by reading or learning?"

---

[6] "Erotic life blossoms only when the spirit and instinct meet in a happy concordance" C. G. Jung *Psychology of the Unconscious* (Geneva 1973) (my translation). page 61.

The institution of marriage within the larger context of the family is meant to provide the protective framework in which physical love can happily blossom.

Alas, things are somewhat different in the West. Because of historical reasons (two World Wars, capitalist mode of production, loss of religious perceptivity, etc.) the familial cell has been tremendously weakened. The rudest attacks on the family are now being conducted by various types of liberation movements; women's liberation, sex liberation, homosexual liberation, etc. In a Western family, the child, very often is not protected. Parents and grand parents are barely to be seen, parents are busy with their own business and only devote marginal time to the education of the children which is left to the school. (Moreover some parents are busy organising their love affairs all their lives. They never grow out of the love story syndrome and you find a lot of old people indulging in it.) The nursery or the school become the child's educational training ground. In this soil, the seeds of love do not sprout too well and the children reach the time of puberty having been completely frustrated emotionally, and without even knowing that they have been deprived. They have little experience of the delicate variety of feelings through which love can be channelled: furthermore, deprived of the loving familial environment which was meant to bring about the child's psychic balance, children develop a subconscious craving for emotional intensity. Then at the time of adolescence they are confronted with the ready made answer to their quest for love: school mates, environment pressures and official education policy only to often focus the adolescent's attention on the paradise of sexual promiscuity.

Actually it is very difficult for such a child to resist the tremendous cultural conditioning of the Western society which presents sex as the only medium to feel any intensity of feeling apart from violence and pain. Indeed, this leit-motiv pervades the media such as films, books, magazines, etc. Visual arts, mass media, songs, etc., are marketing women as objects of pleasure. The message is widely broadcast and broadly accepted, because, in the alienating urban life of an advanced industrial society, physical intercourse seems to offer the only escape from the pressures of the environment (which itself is the result of too much activity on pingala nadi, hence, to balance it the movement towards ida nadi is inevitable). Such a society itself sponsors sex as an outlet for frustrated energies because such an outlet helps the people tolerate the absurdities of the system. Amazingly enough our "developed" countries which exhibit familial irresponsibility to a frightening degree feel in a position to propose models for world development: "what about the population problem in the developing countries?" Yes sir; and what about our own problems? Your daughter is fourteen, she is a drug addict and does not remember how many boys she had. What about minding our own business? Are we the only capable people, are we in charge of world affairs?

In the USA and Europe, only too often, children are left without any criteria, models or guidance. They are lost without even being aware of it. Thus young boys and girls enter the cycle of sexual experiences. The story is usually told in the sweet terms of a juvenile romance but reality is quite different. The real story, is often saddening. Countless western youngsters, boys and girls, have told the same story. When they meet they want to enjoy themselves, enjoy togetherness and friendship in all simplicity but this is not possible for the following reason. As soon as a boy, say meets a girl, the natural spontaneity of the relationship is destroyed because, automatically, in the boy's brain, the attention goes into expectations of sexual activities with this girl.

The same process eventually happens in the girls' mind. If they resist the suggestion they get uneasy and embarrassed: the innocence of the relationship is lost and so is the joy: as the confusion express itself through the eyes they perceive it in each other and can feel uncomfortable without knowing why. If on the contrary they are overpowered by the suggestion they will identify themselves with it and try to have a "love affair" together. But in this instance physical love is not fully enjoyed because the two partners relate to each other through a disturbed neuro-psychic condition. Because of quickly vanishing emotional and physical satisfaction the relationship will break and the quest for a new partner begins. They think they are enjoying themselves but HH Mataji very much questions this: "If there is satisfaction, why should the mind shift from one person to another?" They believe in 'fun'. They might call themselves 'gay'...but the truth of the matter is that sex without privacy and sanctity loses all its joy-giving quality; when it is made public, vulgar or cheap it becomes repulsive to the finer and subtler dimensions of the human awareness. (This is not a matter of opinion but an absolute fact; it can be verified by vibrations).

In the process, psychic balance is completely lost; everything might be 'sexualised' by the subject's sickened mind: nature, situations, travelling encounters, holidays are perceived as the framework of sexual expectations and this obsession kills the spontaneity of sex and the joy of life.

In terms of Sahaja Yoga we would say that such involvements ruin the Mooladhara chakra at the bottom of the spine and the swadhistan chakra which is above it. Thus the very foundations of the Kundalini path are seriously damaged. The immediate consequences of this damage appears to be the loss of psychic balance whose expression was spontaneity and innocence. With the loss of this balance, dharma (or virtue) cannot be intuitively perceived any more; it means that the Manipura chakra is affected also. The attention is no longer controlled because the deities in the first three chakras recede into sleep. Then sex becomes the main feeler. The right and left side sympathetic systems (pingala and ida nadi) are activated and drained to the detriment of innocence and Dharma (sustenance). In the process the fourth centre, Anahata chakra, is disturbed: affective frustration and a sense of insecurity results. The Vishuddhi chakra is then drained off by which self respect and dignity are weakened. The Ajnya chakra being the counterpart of the Mooladhara chakra is spoilt simultaneously and thus the "sex focused awareness" settles in the psyche (mainly in the super-ego) from there it controls the eyes, and invades the field of thought. That is, the sexualisation of the consciousness progresses from the subconscious to the conscious in which the subject with a poor capacity for discrimination begins to misidentify himself with this nonsense. The attention is wasted as the eyes, so to speak, flirt on their own. The big problem when one's awareness is thus weakened is that one does not notice it... precisely because it is weakened and numbed. Logically enough when the awareness itself is affected there is no awareness of the damage. Hence some people just go on and identify themselves with all kinds of silly business. They think everything is perfectly all right...!

People who are not yet identified with this perversion of the psyche know that something is wrong with them but they do not know how to regain innocence, spontaneity and joy: they suffer quite a bit. Human relationships can become a kind of hell: where joy is absent, physical pleasure cannot stay very long. The impact of unbalanced sexual behaviour is felt at the physical level also: doctors are very worried by the increase in the troubles of male potency: cerebral sex is the passport for impotency; eroticism, in all its forms, destroys potency because it disconnects the physical sexual arousal from its natural emotional environment (i.e. being in privacy with your wife). After a few years of artificial excitement, sexual activity no longer responds to natural stimuli. Doctors worry about all this but they do not perceive the causes. They are also concerned by the increase of cancer in the sex organs which seems to depend somehow on the frequency of the sex act and on the age of the first indulgence. The great majority of "liberated" women cannot experience any orgasm and the sinister joke of sex therapy completely misses the point. Further steps to complete destruction which many have crossed include: sexual perversions, violence, etc., all topics largely propagated by books, movies, and sometimes television programmes.

The subtle damage to society is much worse. A proper marriage represents the collective acceptance of the union by the collective social being and by the Great Being of the Universal Unconscious. If there is the proper love, attention and reverence within the marriage the Unconscious blesses the union with great joy and showers its blessings. Due attention given to the auspiciousness of every act maintains the link with the Unconscious: it keeps the deities awakened to bless the family. Blessings bring material prosperity (the blessings of Shri Laxshmi as a housewife or Griha Laxshmi) healthy food (the goddess Anapurna), etc. The family is tuned to the cosmic ecology. In this beautiful dialogue with the Unconscious the small things of life are garlands offered to the Gods and they fill you with peace and contentment. Days, events, relationships spontaneously drop like notes of a divine melody. Needless to say, this realm of subtle joys is totally destroyed by modern permissiveness and liberations: when you destroy the rules of the game there isn't any game any more.[7]

That is why you don't meet many spontaneous, relaxed, joyful people these days. Everybody seems tense, frantic and so

---

[7]Lord Rama truly blessed India by incarnating there. He taught the Hindu civilization the sense of the social boundaries ('mariada') of human behaviour. These mariadas are the rules of the game in which human beings can enjoy each other.

materialistic that, when income tax is raised by one penny there is a row in the country and a debate in parliament.

Back to sex behaviour in the West I must confess that I am rather frightened by the magnitude of these phenomena which are spreading under the seal of social legitimacy. How can one revert these "Upish" trends? Most people are not even aware of them and democracies are not equipped to impose a (very necessary) ruthless censorship on the prostituted media. What is going to happen to all those who are overpowered by this ugly case of collective possession? People behave in a pathological way and think it to be "natural"! Alas, animals are luckier than us because they have no consciousness that they can pollute. All this is sheer nonsense of course but alas, today many people agree with Diderot: "Better to be mad with the madmen than to be wise alone." Youngsters adopt irresponsible modes of behaviour because it is a fashion to do so. The old have no wisdom as they have grown old without it. Because of the collapse of the family there is no institution which can check the pathology of sexual behaviour in the West. Elders follow the trend.

Should one laugh or cry? The old want to show they are young because they have no faith in their dignity, wisdom and maturity. You can see so many romantic sugar dadies of 60 years having moving love affairs with 16 year old school girls. While in "developing" countries elders are wise, respectable and enjoy social recognition.

Indians do not know how blessed they are in a way, to have grown up in a protected society; they should reject the influence of the permissiveness that materialist societies have generated. In those societies, people have unknowingly crossed the subtle border line between freedom and licence; still running after freedom they have fallen into enslavement and are not even able to see it. Let developing countries' new generations learn something from these stupid mistakes instead of following us and moving towards their doom with double the speed.

Of course even with this sort of conditioning, a subject can get realisation. But he has to recognise that a mistake is a mistake; he should ask for forgiveness. If he goes on identifying with his past behaviour, how can the grace of the Shakti be operative? Such a subject should not only recognise his past mistakes but he should be very patient with the process of his spiritual ascent because the Kundalini will take her time to repair the chakras and clear the nadis. I know some will say that I am exaggerating. Well, I intend to focus on the darker sides of the picture because nobody in the West seems to be aware of them. And I am afraid that I do not exaggerate at all as I have seen this happening to hundreds of Sahaja Yogis in the West.

Others will wonder what need there is to impose one's ideas. My answer is quite simple: I intend very humbly to make people aware of their priorities, because I want to relate my own experience to theirs: If you are interested in sex, in money, in power... well go ahead...you might get them. But if you are interested in your own joy, in blissful awareness, in self-realisation, in God, know that it should not be confused with sex, money or power.

You who are reading these lines my fellow man, my brother, my sister..Perhaps I will sound quite rough to your ego but I intend to carry on my point. The time for niceties is over and I trust you are strong enough not to just space out..You who are reading these lines my fellow man, my brother, my sister, before deciding I am rude or overpowering please look into yourself. You also are an open structure, without any beginning or end that you can recall, beyond any possibilities that you could define. If you say: "I know who I am," please do not lie to yourself. Can you feel your chakras? Can you experience the manifestation of your Self as a collective being? You cannot... Deep down in your heart you know that your quest has been misled and its findings futile. But you do not want to admit it. Is it because you are afraid to look into nothingness that you do not dare confront your own divinity? Or is it that you are not that interested to know what your story is all about? How many lives are you still to spend to exhaust your dreams?... but you believe yourself to be awake, don't you? I hope you are, for now the time is short, and this generation will know it before the last sorting out by the Divine: please correct yourself.

At the eve of the year One Thousand, all the bells of Medieval Europe were ringing and people were mourning waiting for the imminent coming of the last days... which never came. So people quietly forgot about the coming of the Son of Man and the prophecy of redemption and destruction. But this moment of history ahead of us that the projections of the computers and the forecasts of informed scientists and thinkers announce as the potential apotheosis of man's self-made doom, this very time is the one of which it has been said:

"And will not God vindicate his elect, who cry to him day and night? Will he delay long over them? I tell you, he will vindicate them speedily. Nevertheless, when the Son of Man comes, will he find faith on earth?"—Luke 18.7

Are we fools that we believe Lord Jesus has spoken in vain?:

"As it was in the days of Noah, so will it be in the days of the Son of Man. They ate, they drank, they married, they were given in marriage, until the day when Noah entered the ark, and the flood came and destroyed them all. Likewise as it was in the days of Lot—they ate, they drank, they bought, they sold, they planted, they built, but on the day when Lot went out from Sodom, fire and sulphur rained from heaven and destroyed them all—so will it be on the day when the Son of Man is revealed."—Luke 17.23

The holy Koran warns:

"When that which is coming comes and no soul shall then deny its coming some shall be abased and others exalted." —Koran 56.1

True! It is almost impossible not to be sinful in a sinful society. But after all, we might have been our forefathers and ourselves brought this society to the wretched stage where it is now. And again we might also have been those who have been waiting for the fulfilment of the promise, who have endlessly sought this very thing which is now revealed to us by HH Mataji's Sahaja Yoga. So, let us repent, let us arise. Tomorrow belongs to us. We will conquer it by entering the Present. For the Present belongs to God and to those who belong to Him. That is where the tale of the great joy begins.

You, who are seekers, please awake, arise. The holiest of the holy, is here to save us. Our Divine Mother is all powerful: no one can challenge Her! But let us be humble in our hearts and minds, and consider our behaviour: Are we blameless? Could we stand in front of the Rider of the Apocalypse? Let us repent for our mistakes and sins, let us rejoin the child within us and ask for forgiveness. In the Ramayana Shri Rama told Vibheeshana: "When one comes to me for refuge, I cannot reject him," Shri Krishna said to Arjuna in the Gita: "Have no fear, cast off all doubt. I shall destroy all your sins." It is the heart of the Vaishnava faith that there is hope for the worst man if only he surrenders himself to the Lord. The very word "Islam" means surrender. And as the Father spoke, so did the Son Jesus also: "Just so, I tell you, there will be more joy in heaven over one sinner who repents than over ninety-nine righteous people who need no repentance." Allah, the Mighty, the Wise One is also the Compassionate, the Merciful. So let us not be confused or afraid. After all, what sins can overcome the Divine Love? HH Mataji says: "What foolish human ideas of destruction can bring forth the destruction of the Creation or its Creator who resides within us?" But we should look with lucidity and courage at what we have done and are daily doing. For instance how many of us, led astray by the arrogant complacency of our modern "permissive" society, how many could cope with the following statement:

> "You have heard that it was said, you shall not commit adultery. But I say to you that everyone who looks at a woman lustfully has already committed adultery with her in his heart."
> —Matthew 5.27

In this specific instance referred to by Lord Jesus, UPI vibrations and deprived spirits can go from one person to the other through the medium of glances. Are we above Shri Krishna's warnings?

> "Lust hides the Atman in its hungry flames, the wise man's faithful foe. Intellect, senses and mind, are fuel to its fire. Thus it deludes the Dweller in the body, bewildering his judgement."—*Bhagavad Gita III*

Surely, there are a few aspects of our behaviour that could be improved... It is high time that we assess our control over ourselves; let us strengthen our commitment to dharma, so that, when the day comes, we will not be scattered away. At this turning point of history which marks the end of the Kali Yuga the alternative is between integration or disintegration and the field of the alternative is our very being. Dharma is this power of inward sustenance and cohesion that gives the right balance. It is, in HH Mataji's terms, "the point where the gravity of sin does not act". We have only reasons for hope and rejoicing because the Sacred Mother has come for our emancipation. But She asks us all to co-operate.

Firstly let us not fall into the trap of psychological theories which encourage us to put the blame of our sins on someone, or something, else: the parents, the childhood, the society... The arrogance of the ego happily sticks to these theories and we go on, hurting, oppressing others and cheating ourselves. As HH Mataji says, "ego's job is to keep you out of Reality". Egoists live in a fool's paradise. Only after realisation can the identification of the mind with the ego be broken: I felt at first aghast to discover my own harshness, selfishness and incredibly clever way in which Mr. EGO was distorting my perceptions and thinking process!

But now to feel sorry, ashamed or guilty is a switch to the extreme of the super-ego and it again takes you away from the central path of Sushumna. Some people spend their days secretly enjoying how bad they feel, how terrible life is; it is all very romantic.

The drama of sadism and masochism is over once you jump into collective consciousness.

The happening is effortless but you might nonetheless wonder "what should we do to prepare ourselves for self-realisation?"— There is a modest, but indispensable beginning on the way to assert ourselves over the slips of our physical, mental and emotional bodies.

If a man loves a woman, let him marry her first. If a woman loves a man, let her marry him. And if two people do not love each other, what is the point of being together? HH Mataji exclaimed once:

> "If love cannot blossom in the optimum conditions of marriage how can it blossom out of it? How can the whole world know love?"

Let us rediscover the joy of sex in the sanctity of marriage. Let us forget drugs and other intoxicants such as drinking and smoking.

Let us turn our backs on greed, violence, debauchery and all the subtle forms these vices are taking today, under the seal of the new social legitimacy. This advice is nothing but the first measures to follow in order to bring some respite to our shattered psychosomatic spiritual instrument. I know that for many people this will already be too hard to follow, while it is quite easy indeed to dismiss me and my sayings. But don't you see, I am not even speaking about Sahaja Yoga? Don't we realise that these simple recommendations have been made countless times by the prominent teachers and seers of all the great religions? Have we forgotten the causes of the fall of many empires on this earth? Do we believe that all the saints of the past are a bunch of outdated fools and that we are the enlightened ones of the great "liberation"? Believe what we may, the judgement will be grounded on the truth of right and wrong and not on our beliefs. This is what Sahaja Yoga has already discovered through vibratory awareness.

In Kathmandu, to look after my pretty garden full of roses, cacti and pine trees I have a young Nepali gardener. He knows very little English, he did not go to school and is not aware that people construct theories about morality. But he is realised. He knows the dharma of people, places, objects, situations, "Yes this is good. Vibrations are good. I feel good in the head" or "it is bad. There is pain in my left hand. My feet are hot. I have headache." The apostles of liberation from dharma would find it hard to convert this boy because they would give him a burning sensation in his chakras even before opening their mouths.

We ought now to dwell a little bit longer on the virtues of the family, for this sacred institution is universally threatened by modern "enlightenment".

We know that cells in an organism are spontaneously (sahaj) organized by very specific living patterns and that the breakdown of those patterns means the death of the cell or its mutation into a cancerous threat to the surrounding tissue. The same holds true for the human individual.

Each individual is part and parcel of a subtle network of psychic life forces which maintains the balance of his personality: this precious network, or pattern, is known as "the family". If this network is disturbed the harmony of the personality is seriously threatened.

We find daily application of these subtle laws in our Sahaja Yoga practice:the left side of a young woman was burning all over; we told her, "something is very wrong on your emotional side";

She broke down crying and said that she had just gone through a divorce. The worst part was that her parents thought that it would bring her a great fortune. If there are troubles in your family, the disrupted family is fighting within you: you feel agitated, tired, insecure... Disorders are recorded in the chakras: the right side heart chakra (place of the father and of the husband), the centre and left side heart chakra (place of the mother), the left side nabhi chakra (place of the wife) are constricted. We were amazed to see that most of the seekers are so badly hurt by their family problems!

The personality structure can be completely bowled over when the family setting is too badly upset. If, say, the father is a drunkard, the mother a cheap woman, if the husband is a "play boy", dependents will be shattered. Their models of human behaviour are gone, their values finished! In a spirit of revenge they might themselves adopt harmful modes of behaviour.[8] What happens when one member of the family becomes arbitrary? He loses contact with the great Collective Being and malignancy starts which spreads to his family and then to whole society. The social cell has become cancerous.

With vibratory awareness we find out that someone who has given up family values starts emitting anti-family (antidharma) microwaves. The attention of another weak individual is attracted and "inoculated" with the vibratory injection. His behaviour will follow his attention. He changes his values. Cancerous mutation within society thus takes place unnoticed and undisturbed. The degenerating human cells of the social organism mutate one after the other.

HH Mataji intends to grant to the society an awareness by which it can defend itself. She thus demonstrates with absolute clarity the importance of the family. She said once:

"The goddess Laxshmi who is the power of our protector father Shri Vishnu is the one who manifests the beauty of the housewife in this Universe (Griha Laxshmi). The family, the vital unit of every society, is looked after by the mother. She is the mother-goddess of the family. The daughters are the beautiful goddesses and the granddaughters the angel goddesses." She says

---

[8]Sociological studies on the motivations of "professional" prostitutes show that, in many cases, their fathers had been very tyrannical or adulterous husbands and that they sought to avenge their mothers and punish the male by debasing other men.

of husband and wife that "they are not similar but both are equal, no doubt! One is the right and the other the left wheel of the chariot. If one wheel is bigger than the other the chariot cannot move properly. Both must be respected. The husband-wife relationship has to be absolutely informal; all artificiality must be dropped. They must love and also sometimes quarrel to show their concern. This is the sign of a healthy relationship. But a woman has to behave like a woman and man has to be like a man. Spontaneous fidelity, love and mutual sharing are the only way one can give and receive the joy of married life. The slightest deviation from conjugal fidelity must be absolutely avoided, and if committed, openly confessed. A person who does not believe in a one woman-one man relationship should not marry at all; why make another person unhappy? The effects of secret infidelity are of the worst kind and can ruin the whole society."

HH Mataji remarks that things went wrong for the couple with the monetisation of the economy. In the agrarian societies of the older days man and woman were performing equally valued social functions; the man chopped the wood, hunted, etc., and the woman cooked, looked after the household and so on. The ego of both partners was satisfied. But as soon as man brought money to the household he seemed to become more important. His ego inflated and he started depreciating his wife's position. You see, in a money-orientated society, money becomes the criterion! So, because the housewife does not earn money her activity does not receive an effective social recognition anymore. On top of this the moneyed male became only too often an erratic don Juan. Men flirt with their secretaries or sales girls and ill-treat their own wives. In a house where the mother is not respected the daughters may lose their sense of chastity; the arbitrary behaviour of men pollutes the atmosphere, throwing family and society off balance.

As men do not pay proper attention and respect to the married woman her ego is hurt. She may then give up her role as the left side operator catering to the needs of loving care, emotional balance and existence and she becomes ego-orientated. She takes up arms against men.

This movement can follow many patterns: a woman becomes careerist, activist, feminist, etc., or she starts enticing one man after another and thus satisfies her ego as men do.

When a woman gives up her chastity she can conquer (in

direct and indirect ways) that which made the social supremacy of the male: money... and accumulate much more power and wealth than men can. In the process she might well win the war of the sexes but she destroys everybody and easily mutates into a monster of domination. Emotional confusion overpowers society; homosexuality develops. "Man and woman are the counterpart of each other and can make their lives so very beautiful and joy giving". HH Mataji sighs, "when will man learn to enjoy his own things and his own wife instead of coveting those who belong to others?" The marriage between sex and money breaks the marriage between man and woman. The high priests of that gateway to psychic hell proudly challenge us for we are "inhibited" and "repressed". They say: "Why have virtues? Why have chastity?", and one might add, "Why true love and why evolution?"

In India, during the wedding ceremony, the bride is presented with nine symbols which represent the power of Shri Laxshmi. This symbolically indicates that, within the institution of marriage, the powers of the woman sustain the optimal path of evolution for herself and all those who surround her. If a married woman is seen in the morning people consider it very auspicious. Countless rituals are performed worshipping the married woman. If five of them are invited to dinner it is said the gathering brings very great blessings. Women have their own festivals, etc.

Let us all use our wisdom to recognise that dharma has to be respected and established in our full freedom. Freedom is essential first to establish morality as our own. If it is established by fear and coercion, HH Mataji notices, it does not last: "it falls off like plumes of a peacock attached to a crow." But there is no freedom in giving up wisdom, breaking the family and allowing the six enemies[9] of our being to overpower it. All customs and lifestyles that encourage permissiveness and "openness" to sin, "tolerance" towards evil, must be banned. A benevolent sponsorship is absolutely essential if, in the words of HH Mataji, "Democracy is not to become a demonocracy."

Do not consider me to be a righteous preacher who reprimands the wretched sinner. In the first part of my life, until the age of twenty-five, I have been at pains to commit most of the mistakes that this generation is committing.

---

[9]Lust, cruelty, vanity, jealousy, materialism, human attachments.

If today I can see what is a mistake and what is the right course of action it is not because I have acquired a superior knowledge through private insights. I know the truth because I met the One who could lead me to it; HH Mataji Nirmala Devi; it is a very simple story. Actually, I really think I am very human: this means "Human, all too human" as Nietzche's Zarathustra put it, with the well known train of weaknesses, confusion and ignorance. But let us also remember that human beings have been referred to as the salt of the earth, the light of the world and nothing less than God's own children! So, within the human possibility there is a wide scope for changes and mutation.

When I was an adolescent I found out that the guardians of the rules of morality, parents, educators, teachers did not know what the rules were all about. "You tell me that I should not do this because it is wrong. O.K. but why is it that it is wrong?" The answer used to be anything but convincing and so I usually decided to find out for myself, that is, to do the forbidden thing: to steal, to lie, to indulge in my sensual good-pleasure. The trouble when you are not realised is that your central nervous system is not aware of dharma. That is, you put your finger in the fire of sin but there is no nerve to report the damage to the brain so as to launch the corrective reflex action: i.e. withdraw the finger from the fire. So I went on, building up misidentifications and damaging my chakras. I met quite a few girls...I wasted a lot of time, attention and energy in this kind of situation. I happened to be sometimes happy but increasingly I seemed unable to taste whatever happiness is. I was exhausting a subtle potential of freshness and innocence; my sensations became imperceptibly more dull. My experiences have been in common with those of many young people I have met. A further mistake I wish I could have avoided was taking drugs.

When you "take speed" (amphetamines, etc.) you overactivate your pingala energy; through your ego you can enter into the collective supraconscious, that is, into the rajo guna of the Virata. Most drugs however act on ida nadi and propel the user into the collective subconscious, the tamo guna of the Virata. In that case the protective role of the ego is abolished and the subject can feel other identities than his own, go into the past, communicate with spirits. I was never that interested in drugs as such but I was curious. I discovered that drug-taking unveils strata of existence about which modern science simply has no idea. This finding was correct.[10] But the great priests of drug-taking completely overlooked the obvious price one has to pay for the trip into these provinces. Apart from the money, the fees are collected in kind:brain cells, nervous systems, bits of chakras... The stress on the sympathetic nervous system in the long run, causes cancer... Needless to say, drugs invite UPI's; the victims shake in front of HH Mataji, their hands shake violently, etc. (The interest of hallucinogenic drugs is that the seeker sees auras and lights surrounding HH Mataji. Some of them saw Her as a column of multicoloured glowing flames.)

One evening, in New York, while sniffing cocaine with friends, I was looking at a black girl. My attention shifted from the ego to the super-ego like a pendulum. At one point, as my attention came into the present, the vision I had of this girl imperceptibly changed. For a moment she looked absolutely beautiful and real, almost divine; the energy at that short time happened to be crossing on the Sushumna channel and her reality manifested. We shared a blissful moment of collective consciousness because I happened to be on my Sushumna as well. Perhaps a sort of love and beauty was felt. But we could not maintain ourselves in that state and we tipped into the subconscious. I saw in that area who was playing the game. On her face I saw the features of the spirit who had entered her—or was already stored there, I don't know—it was a XIXth Century white woman: absolutely sex-starved. I began feeling uncomfortable because this UPI was staring at me. Then my poor friend fell into the lower strata of the subconscious and I saw with my naked eye an ugly, demonic entity appear on her face. Of course now I have found out that among drug-users, there is a close interaction of any such phenomena. Because of the psychic promiscuity that cocaine generated I spent that evening struggling with awful UPIs within my own mind...Within a fraction of a second from bliss into hell. This is bound to happen sooner or later in this kind of psychic exploration because drugs, depending on their types, open wide the gates of the subconscious or of the supraconscious.

I could also recall the experience of a trip into the supracons-

---

[10]In this respect HH Mataji remarks: "Whatever is written is not scripture and whatever is unknown is not Divine."

cious. Once in the Californian hills, at a remote wooden house with good people around, I swallowed a drop of LSD. After some time I began feeling the throbbing of nature's energy, in the earth, the wheat, the trees and myself. I felt that I was at the same time very old and very new. Meanwhile my friend seemed to be merged in an ecstatic vision; I don't know what she saw but I think she entered into the supraconscious; she looked completely dazzled and subjugated by a vision of godliness. Days later she could not bear being separated from this artificial godliness she had been propelled into for a short LSD while. She created the myth that she had become divine and accepted it. One month later, she left her husband, and I think her child, to begin some kind of impossible celestial quest with other friends.

These two happenings pretty well summarise the drug story. If you expose yourself to evil spirits, in the subconscious, they will jump on you at the first occasion and enter your chakras as parasites of your energy. If you see godly beings in the supraconscious you can only see them, that is, you cannot become them and as they are saintly personalities they will never enter your psyche; if a UPI enters into you from the supraconscious it will be one of those oppressive "masters", a variety of egoistic spirits who want to use you for their own purposes. The victim is not aware of anything as he cannot use the discriminating tool of vibratory awareness to check the condition of his ego and super-ego, or, if aware of something being wrong, does not know how to put it right again and may get frantic.

Drug experiences can put you on to something unknown for some time; that is why they can be so attractive. You may even cross over Sushumna for a very short time, but you can never remain in the centre because lateral movements soon take over. Moreover it makes it more difficult to rest near the Sushumna in your actual, daily life because the autonomic nervous system is upset. We have found out that drug addicts take a lot of time to get their Self-realisation. If they do not give up drugs after realisation they cannot remain in the realised state—Drugs go against the human awareness; do not surrender your attention to them! Discard them completely! In the subconscious and supraconscious realms the human awareness becomes sub, or inhuman.

In my years of searching I have entered many different and sometimes strange provinces: this is the common story of Western seekers. We have gone into all possible trips: pop music, travelling, motor bikes, sex, surf, communes, gurushopping, etc., etc. "Tripping" means totally committing one's attention and the attention is the element which conditions our destiny's trajectory: Andre Gide says like the Buddha: "where my desire goes, there I shall go." We follow our attention and it is through our attention that we can free ourselves from the karma wheel or... get further enslaved. So, what one is tripping about is a relevant question and, as a rule it is better not to trip too much. That's exactly where Socrates was helpful to me ("know what you know"): I was never really tripped out, or became overly involved in anything; or even fully committed myself to anything because I never knew whether it was worth it and I knew I did not know it. I believed I was innocent, yet I harmed myself quite a lot. After discovering how I had hurt myself I started feeling bad, useless, guilty, I started repenting. This was a typical movement into the left side. The Ocean of HH Mataji's compassion saved me from these swings. Today, I thank Socrates for not allowing me to completely destroy myself. Whereas lots of fellow kids, lacking the Socratic carefulness, fully committed themselves into many different (and often damaging) trips: they did not know whether it was worth it or not, and they did not know that they did not know. They just assumed it was the right thing because it fitted the needs of the moment and/or because they liked it. The price to pay for such a mistake is just tremendous; it is heartbreaking to think about: how many friends do we have who are lost? Many, many, too many.

When I remember the year 1972 in Geneva, and the sight of adolescents fully committing themselves with heart and soul to a "satguru" who is known in India to be a despicable crook, I can only take their confusion as one index of the darkness of the time!

The Socratic device has been helpful to me especially when I went to different "gurus". They pretended to be this, to be that, to give this and to give that; my reaction was: "Maybe. Let's see. As long as I don't see, don't ask me anything, least of all surrender." The game is, of course, not an easy one because you are always tempted to believe that you are nearer to what you are looking for; and because the setting around these people is usually heavily suggestion-oriented, inducing individual or mass autosuggestion. And last but not least, these "gurus" know their job pretty well, whereas you are a naive seeker like a new born babe in the show, the little rabbit walking proudly into the wolf's lair.

Anyway, thanks to sound carefulness, I had a safety buffer. No doubt, I have been badly damaged but I have avoided the supreme danger: identification with wrongness, which, in too many cases, appears to be the point of no return, that is, no return towards the central Path of Evolution, towards Sushumna, the Path of Dharma within ourselves.

My body had more dharma than myself: it would protest against what I was using it for. I did not feel well in my skin and also got health problems. Mental activity would go on and on without me being able to stop it. Night sleep became thinner and thinner. But I would not understand the signals, My doctor in Switzerland kindly informed me: "you suffer from troubles of the neuro-vegetative system." I asked: "what is this?" he said "it is the system which depends upon the autonomic nervous system"; especially the parasympathetic system. I asked "what is this parasympathetic thing?", he answered, "...to be honest medical science does not really know anything about it". "...This was quite an expensive doctor and I did not find the answer helpful. I knew something was very wrong with me; I was nervously shaky and rather sick; no doctors could help me. In my relationships I had become increasingly paranoid.

The first day I was with HH Mataji Nirmala Devi in Hurst Gree, she had to excuse Herself a couple of times and go to the "bathroom". There, I could hear she was vomiting. She was taking my vibrations upon Her chakras to ease mine and the bathroom was the direct result. I did not feel too proud about it... I was very fortunate though because HH Mataji, at that time of the year, had some time to give me. For ten days she worked with amazing patience and love, healing the wounds of my adharmic life with the purity of Her vibratory powers. I could at the same time discover the damaging extent of my past mistakes and watch the progress of my recovery, at the physical as well as the psychic level.

It is when you withdraw from your weaknesses as misidentifications that you can see it; that is, you can see at the same time that it is not you, that it is noxious and that you had involved yourself in it. It is a painful process to clearly see one's own weaknesses but it is a salutary one; better go through it now than at "the last judgement"... It is because I have clearly seen my own weaknesses that I am urging you to take better care of your self. HH Mataji puts it in the following way:

> "You can cleanse your clothes if you can separate your clothes from you. You clean them without feeling guilty about it because you know you are not your clothes."

Sahaja Yoga is unveiling the innermost secrets that the guardians of our moral rules could not explain. There is no longer any need for us to weaken our evolutionary chances by damaging experiences. The deep meaning of religious teachings and moral rules express various aspects of the one and only truth.

As I said, it can be proved at the time of Kundalini awakening. The power of God that loves, thinks and organises, when perceived as vibrations, starts giving direct information. The human awareness can thus have a dialogue with the Universal Unconscious which is the power of the Holy Spirit.

Every time an opportunity arises, I have seen HH Mataji, assisting human beings in their ascent with an attention and dedication so total that I really marvel at it. But the boundlessness of HH Mataji's compassion is not at stake here. It is not feasible that HH Mataji could devote Her time to each of the innumerable individuals who desire to achieve human evolution. Mankind at large should strive to make Her work easier. It is now the responsibility of everybody to seriously consider what line of behaviour optimizes the potential of the individuals' evolution.

If somebody leads an adharmic life the chakras and the nadis will be affected. But the inverse proposition is not true; the psychosomatic structure can be affected without major moral mistakes of the subject; the physical health or just the vibrations of the environment play an important part. We have seen that even born realized souls slip down in their awareness and compromise with the falsehood of the world. Many very good and sincere people turned up with damaged chakras simply because they lived in a negative environment. That is why this society is to be changed. Radically.

I might as well give you a last warning. In Nepal they have a saying which goes "Avoid the tiger, the fire and the guru". Better indeed to have no guru at all than to have a fake one! The false prophets of the last days of this Kali Yuga are let loose. They are the foes of Shri Krishna and Christ, the masters of Adharma. They are committing the worst sin against the Father because they are talking in his name to attract and doom the lost seekers. Some of them are guilty of the most abominable sin against the Mother as they are fornicating with their disciples, pretending to lead them to God. And they are committing the sin against the Spirit because they are committing these crimes with a full knowledge of their doings. The Koran echoes: "who is more wicked than the man who invents a falsehood about Allah and denies the truth when it is declared to him?" (39;32). Do not become their loot. For them, the Bible and the Koran said, there will be no pardon. HH Mataji makes no mystery of the fact that He has doomed them: "the people who try to befool the innocent seekers and exploit them by dirty habits are permanently doomed to hell".

There is indeed one ultimate mistake in which some of our contemporaries seem to delight, a mistake which is as old as the North Indian tantrikas or the sects of the "Brethren of the Free Spirits" who flourished in Europe from the Twelfth to the Sixteenth Century. Their favourite quotation was Paul's "to the pure all things are pure" (Titus 1.15). The idea being "I am so perfect, united with God, etc., that whatever I do I cannot sin"; on this stimulating assumption whoredom has now become the ladder to Heaven...The clearest comment I can propose to you on the confusion between sex and spirituality is made in the *Vivekachudamani* of Shri Shankaracharya:

> "Whoever seeks to realise the Self by devoting himself to the nourishment of the body, proceeds to cross a river by catching hold of a crocodile, mistaking it for a log."[11]

And I will end up this chapter in the words of the *Apology of Socrates*:

> "This, O Athenian citizens, is the truth; and I tell it without concealing or suppressing anything, whether great or small, and yet I am well-nigh sure that it is this very frankness which makes me so hated."

---

[11] Shri Shankaracharya *Vivekachudamani* or the "Crest-jewel of Discrimination". Translation S. Madhavananda. (Calcutta 1926. Ninth Edition 1974) p. 31.

6

Religion and Religions

> "And he to whom worshipping is a window,
> to open but also to shut, has not yet
> visited the house of his soul whose
> windows are from dawn to dawn"
>
> —Khalil Gibran *The Prophet*

With the intellectual modesty so typical of their time, the 19th Century philosophers declared with Feuerbach that God was dead. They did so with a marked elation because they thought that the death of God meant the birth of man. Actually they were only half wrong. A principle which used to rule mind and societies had effectually been killed by 19th Century thought but it was not God. It was the concept of God. Such a development proved to be a mixed blessing. In losing the awareness of "God", people freed themselves from the transcendental criteria which provided some sort of moral frame and they sank remorselessly into the crass materialism which is the bane of today's societies. But, on the other hand, by liberating our minds from the religious dogma, in getting rid of human concepts, ideas and images about God we have opened for ourselves the possibility to rediscover, through the immediacy of a living experience, what the truth is behind and beyond those dogmas. We have spent the three-quarters of this century in exploring the first consequence: unbridled materialism, in its Capitalist or Marxist form. It is now time for us to explore the bearings of the second consequence of the death of the concept of God: the possibility of the direct experience of God, which leads to a new experience of human evolution. In the age to come all theories and concepts of religion will be checked against the direct experience of the subject's consciousness. We can do it through Sahaja Yoga. Actually, we are doing it daily.

Yes, Socrates! Yes, Buddha! Yes Lao Tzu! There is this level of knowledge where we know what we know and what we do not know. Before this level is reached, man erects in structures, in dogmas, in systems whatever he can grasp from the truth. In this specific sense all religions, cosmologies, ideologies are partial, and incomplete interpretations of the truth. The common people then get caught in the trap of the "Superior truth" that others are in charge of interpreting for them according to criteria which often have nothing to do with truth. On the contrary, Sahaja Yoga is offering us self-sufficiency in knowledge. To understand this proposition let us expose now what is a concept.

In order to see myself I need to look in a mirror: I am not able to see my face directly. In the same way, to look at reality outside of myself (the object, the world, the show) reality inside of myself (The Self, the subject, the witness) uses the mind as a mirror. The human mind is the medium through which we try to perceive reality or truth. We want this mind to reflect the full truth of what we are and of what things are. This is where the problem of knowledge begins. What we perceive through the mind is not reality itself but a representation or a reflection of reality. The mirror is not the thing. Another word for "representation" could be: "the concept". Now, one of the uncongenial features of this mirror appears to be that it is not very clean. The mind undergoes all sorts of variations (actions of the ego, reactions of the super-ego) which affect the directness and objectivity of its perceptive capacity. We are looking at reality through a tinted mirror, with changing colours and moving reflections. Hence, reality appears to us in corresponding tints and shapes. The Vedanta proposes the famous example of the rope that we think to be a serpent. It is not rare that the representation we see in the mirror is grossly distorted by the imperfection of the latter: the concept reflects more the psychic and social conditionings in the mind of the thinking subject than the truth it is meant to represent. We are then sitting in Plato's famous cave, looking at our shadows on the wall of the cave instead of facing the bright daylight of truth outside of it. Patanjali says along the same lines: "The seer is sight itself but thought untainted, appears as if tainted through the vagaries of the intellect" *Aphorisms* II. 20.[1]

[1] An analogous argument is found, say, in Jacques Maritain's *Sept Lecons sur l'etre et les premiers principes de la raison speculative* (chez P. Tequi).

From the foregoing, it is evident that to know reality, beyond the fluctuations of our cognitive faculties, we had to find some ways to make our mind a more trustworthy instrument. As Patanjali puts it (opus cit. I.1): "When mind is controlled, Self stays in his natural condition". "Through chitta (human attention) you can contemplate the ultimate and when the ultimate is contemplated the chitta vanishes", echoes Shri Godpadacharya. When the doors of perception are cleansed as William Blake says, Reality reveals itself inside and outside the subject: Well! there is no inside or outside any more. There is Reality. But to enter the Kingdom of God that is the reality, one has to be born again to a new way of knowing. St. Paul said (*Corinthians* 13.12) "Now we see in a mirror dimly, but then face to face. Now I know in part: then I shall understand fully". Paul's "then" is the "now" of Sahaja Yoga.

After the Kundalini crosses the Ajnya chakra it brings the restlessness of the psychic activity under control. Then the Kundalini Energy spreads in the nervous tissue of the brain and clears it. The subject feels in his head a new quality of silence which dissolves thoughts, concepts, projections and any manifestations of the mental or emotional length waves which are the normal product of the standard mind. Ego and super-ego recede back from the temples and the radiation of the consciousness in the middle of the brain expands. Away with doxa......! episteme is dawning. Socrates can rejoice at last! What is left is whatever is.

> "When mind's activity is controlled, illumination results, mind reflects the nature of either the seer, the seen, or the seeing, as pure crystal reflects the colour of whatever is placed on it" (I.3.41) Patanjali. *Aphorisms*.

This is the state of the witness (sakshi swarup), which begins with thoughtless awareness. It cannot be enjoyed long if the Ajnya chakra is not fully opened and it cannot be enjoyed at all if the Ajnya chakra has not begun to open. This latter condition was unfortunately the one of many thinkers who evolved theories on God, Evolution and History. Thus these various theories were bound to reflect the distortions of the mind which projected them. It is not surprising, I suggest, to see how badly the concept of God has been variously distorted by a partial grasp of the truth.

Concepts about God which were not warranted by the underlying experience of the one Reality only too often provided a conceptual framework for man's foulest deeds. Instead of being a reflection of the sublime, formal religious doctrines have happened to befool people to such an extent that it looked sometimes like a bad joke turned into cold blooded murder. When mythical beliefs are legitimized by short-sighted rationality and strengthened through the mechanisms of social organisation, one might well witness the birth of a monster, a monster which is to devour many a human life: it is the holy war (the jihad) for the "true faith", the Nation, the victory of the proleteriat: God, of course, fades from the picture but not the legitimization of violence.

Give a truth to men, and see what they will do with it! It seems, alas, that half received truths are sometimes more dangerous than plain ignorance because they generate fanaticism and deeper mistakes. The various religions might well have manifested themselves as real flowers on the universal tree of religion. Cannot we perceive a basic unity underlying the different messages of Shri Rama and the Prophet Muhammad, Lord Buddha and Lord Mahavira? Are they not all expressions of the Holy Spirit? But people removed the flowers from the living tree and made the dead flowers their own property. "Religion" comes from the latin word "religare" which means to bind, to unite. What religion happens to be about could precisely be to unite the history of God and the story of man into a single poem to be sung within human consciousness. But historical world religions have not been very successful in their attempt to realise this end.

World religions are living parts of the mystical body of God's teachings to Mankind. But this body has been cut into pieces. Today, at the time of integration, the dead pieces lie apart... "Jesus is the only one!" "Muhammad is the last one"...while Lord Jesus and Muhammad are angry at the fanaticism of such followers. Contradictions in the scriptures and dogmatism go against the principle of Universality. But before feeling the vibrations from the Holy Spirit who could tell who is right or wrong? One could not feel God! Now, with Kundalini rising, we have seen that all the incarnations are aspects of one Being; the exclusion of one of them by the mind of the sadhaka causes hurdles in their integration as the corresponding chakra does not open. So a Christian has to take the adornation mantra for Muhammad, Lord Shiva, etc.

Fanatics are the hardest to crack. Most remarkably, the incarnation they are supposed to worship is angry with them. A dogmatic Catholic is stopped at the Ajnya chakra by Christ himself; a Muslim would have a problem with his void (adorned by the principle of the Primordial Master of whom Muhammad is an incarnation); and Hindus have trouble with their Nabhi chakra (adorned with Lord Vishnu). The deities are angry with the misidentification of the sadhaka. Lord Jesus said: "You will call me, Christ, Christ, but I will not recognize you".

Epistemology comes from the greek word "episteme": knowledge, that Socrates and Plato used to oppose to "doxa": Opinion. Epistemology deals with knowledge and the epistemological breakthrough with new ways of knowing. Now at last the world can be changed because the inner revolution endows man with the possibility of knowing Reality instead of elaborating opinions, concepts, representations of it. We know reality instead of relating imperfectly to it through conceptual representation. Our thoughts are forms; belonging exclusively to form is limitation. Beyond limitation is "what is". Knowing what is I can act rightly[2]. Let us consider now what the history of the concept of God has been. It might help us to understand the development of the world religions and to avoid further confusion.

We should firstly refer to the anthropological finding that social roles tend to be functionally structured. Let us consider a Polynesian or African primitive community. Despite the fact that any tribe might be differentiated from another by all kinds of idiosyncrasies, we can generally distinguish a pattern of social organisation reflecting the functional tasks the community has to perform in order to survive physically. The subsistance function involved agricultural work and hunting, the security function maintained a fighting force, etc. While the presence of hunters, warriors and peasants is easy to understand, one might wonder what functional imperative corresponds to the universally acknow-

---

[2]"If man has learned to see and know what really is, he will act in accordance with truth. Epistemology is in itself ethics and ethics is epistemology." Herbert Marcuse *One Dimensional Man*. Beacon Press. (Boston) p. 125.

ledged existence of the sorcerer, medicine man, wizard, etc. What role necessary to the survival of the communal organism does he perform, which could justify the privileged status he usually enjoys?

The wizard was the mediator between the forces which shaped the tribe's environment and his community and thus, he was the one who would orient the pattern of the community style of life and activity. Being in communication with the gods of the forest, the god of rain, etc., he would determine the appropriate time to launch hunting operations, crop raising and various other activities essential to the material life of the tribe. Between the common tribesmen who did not understand the powerful cosmic forces but who felt their impact and the cosmic forces themselves, the wizard stands as the one who provided the tribe with an understanding of its own position in the global ecology and this understanding conditioned the tribe's rhythm of life. As the wizard had annexed to his profit the monopoly of this knowledge, he was considered to be a pre-eminent member of the community, enjoying authority and status in the collective decision making power.

With the sharpening of man's conceptual ability the concept of God gradually evolved from the identification with the natural forces towards more personified and elaborate representations of the Divinity. This development was also made possible because a more sophisticated social organisation somewhat lessened the intensity of the human fight against nature for physical survival. It is also the time when the divine masters (Avatars, incarnations) enlightened mankind in more elaborate terms. But all the time, the concept of God performed the same vital function: it provided man with the criteria for identity and integration on which individual thought and social action could be grounded. In the same way that the individual looks in the mirror to see his face, societies looked to the concept of God to find their own image. Hence the History of Nations is deeply conditioned by their respective religions. Because of the worldly power gathered by the knower of religious matters, we soon witness in history the elaboration of sophisticated social mechanisms to control the monopoly of the interpretation of the Knowledge.

The concept of God which attributes meanings and defines purposes provides the mould in which social energies are to flow; it can be called teleological knowledge (from the Greek word

"Telos" meaning the goal), in the sense that it establishes the priorities to be reached. Because of this, the world religions soon tended to involve themselves in institutional build-up rather than inward spirituality. The spirit of the original religious teaching all too often vanished: the living perception of God was lacking but not the intellectual perception of the concept of God. The evolution of this latter and its influence contributed to shape the course of the human societies.

In the hierarchic agrarian civilisation of the past, the role of the primitive wizard was performed by a social class. This class enjoyed prestige and power because it retained the monopoly of knowledge over the concept of God. It retained also the consequent right to explain to man the sense of his destiny and how to act accordingly at the individual and collective level. The priests of Amon in the pharaonic Egypt, the Zoroastrian clergy in Sasanid Iran, the brahmins of pre-Mughal India, the Byzantine or Catholic Churches, played therefore a determinant role in the organisational pattern of the societies which supported them economically.

We could say that churches were to society what the mind is to the subject; an intermediary between the subject and reality which could neither be avoided or trusted. In the same way that the mind misrepresents reality and works on its own the churches and priests of all countries misrepresented God and worked on their own.

The monopoly of teleological knowledge implies a tremendous political power and hence history is filled with the struggle between social action and religious knowledge, the ruler and the knower; the ideal constellation would have been for a society to be ruled by the knower, the "King-Philosopher" of Plato's *Republic*, but those kings were a rare species who appeared infrequently on the stage of power: Janaka in Mithila, Rama in Ayodhya, Solon in Athens, Marcus Aurelius in Rome, and a couple of others.[3] More usually, the political ruler constantly tried to

---

[3] If one considers Reality to be exclusively the dialectic laws of Matter, then Mao Tse-tung represented in Peking the corresponding kind of king-philosopher. It should be mentioned that, in China the teleological function was traditionally a secular one: it was performed by the Confucean civil-servants and was later assumed by the guardians of "Mao Tse-tung thought."

incorporate in his royal prerogative the cognitive status and corresponding privilege of one who knows God. This is the rationale behind the conflict between the political and the religious power, the state and the church, the power which controls the monopoly of action and the one which controls the monopoly of knowledge. Sometimes the ruler won: this success is manifested, say, by the claim of the Roman Emperors from Augustus (63BC—14AD) onwards, to be at the same time Caesar and Pontifex Maximus, an attempt emulated by Henry VIII Tudor in the 16th Century, or by the Japanese Meiji Emperors heading the Shinto cult; not to mention various kinds of "Divine Right" monarchies from Louis XIV to the Chinese "Son of Heaven". From the time of Friedrich II Hohenstaufen (1194-1250 A.D.), Western medieval Christianity was split between Caesar (the "Holy" Roman German Emperor) and the Pontifex maximus (the Roman Pope) who both pretended to rule Christendom. The eventual result of the conflict was to be the eruption of Protestantism which broke the monopolistic political power of the first and the monopolistic religious power of the second.

In the modern secular world, the churches are dead for all practical purposes in the sense that, as a rule, they no longer shape the priorities of the individual and collective actions nor do they provide the criteria and means to identify man's relation with his physical environment and to act upon it: these functions are today performed by science and technology. With these faceless inheritors of the wizard the yawning gap between knowledge and action became more marked.

It is on the basis of these developments that 19th Century Western thought proclaimed the death of God but the real meaning of the above related evolution was overlooked.

The classes, groups and people in charge of the concept of God had operated without authorisation as the mediator of a higher knowledge. They worked on their own wordly goals instead of reflecting the knowledge they were supposed to communicate: the knowledge of God. All the while the substance of this knowledge departed from the concept which was to represent it. Hence when Positivist thinkers crushed the concept, they merely crushed an empty shell. God is well, alive, and, playfully enough, wonders: "Children, when are you going to grow?...".

In the 20th Century, the relation between church and state,

teleological knowledge and social action, seemed sometimes to be controlled by the new ideologies which appear to be the secular inheritors of the concept of God, proposing their own alternatives to the notion of "Divine Providence". Fascism, National-Socialism, Marxism, all tried to inherit the wizard's function, the monopoly of knowledge. Fascism and Nazism were so clumsy at it, that they would not survive. Meanwhile the priest-political commissars of the Stalinist New Rome persecuted dissenting thinkers according to the same logic which induced the medieval Catholic Church to burn mystic preachers; the monopoly of interpretation of the old and new bible (Judaic and Marxist-Leninist) has to be kept by the guardians of the true faith. It is the basis of their political power! Moscow inherited from Byzantium and Rome a spirited "anti-heretic policy"...Meanwhile, bureaucrats thought they were controlling knowledge for the state purpose, without seeing that technology (and the resulting militaro-industrial complex) was far from being under their control. God's knowledge is so subtle that science and technology, crept away from it.

The new "Churches" have not proved to be much more enlightening than the old ones in fact they have been much more repressive and bloody than churches ever were. Quite generally, the modern advanced society is no longer grounded in the Concept of God which still used to ensure some minimum of social virtues. They have been built up on materialist concepts which are the substitutes for the Divine Providence: the Marxist laws of historical dialectic, the Capitalist laws of wealth accumulation. Again, I must repeat, these laws represent only a partial, imperfect, perception of Reality and the societies which follow them suffer the consequent imperfections.

Distressing as they may sometimes appear, these developments were unavoidable. History has been made out of human actions which corresponded to the "tainted" cognitive faculties of man. When Socrates and Plato in the 4th Century BC were exhorting their fellow Athenians to re-organize society on the basis of knowledge of reality (episteme) rather than on the basis of opinions about it (doxa) they were in a sense talking in vain because they could not provide the concrete means to do so. Socrates did not raise Kundalini on the agora! The citizens could simply not understand what they were talking about and rather than following the Platonic approach, they turned to the notion of the Aristotelian City (polis) where the democratic decision comes out of the confrontation of several opinions. Who could blame them? Without cleansing Patanjali's mirror one cannot initiate qualitative changes within and outside of oneself. It is right that reformers were considered "Utopians" and "Idealists", that is, not realists, because they were not providing the concrete tools whereby people could directly relate to reality and initiate the consequent process of qualitative change.

In 1582 AD the Mughal emperor Akbar after having initiated a series of debates between representatives of Islam, Hinduism, Zoroastrianism and Roman Catholicism, promulgated a new religion; the Din-i-Ilabhi, "The Divine Religion" which would integrate and transcend all the existing religions...or so he hoped. Of course it could not work, it did not work; the essential knowledge was missing. The gross method of founding a religion on one's own opinion cannot of course reach the subtlest dimension of Reality. As HH Mataji puts it: "It is so very subtle that it is easier to lose it than to find it". Inspiration may come from the Universal Unconscious but the human receiver jams the message. He starts rationalizing, adds or subtracts, the subtlety is gone and the whole thing becomes an empty circus. Or in the words of HH Mataji: "The car that is not yet started, what's the use of driving it?".

The knowledge of God, so spontaneous and subtle, opens between two thoughts, in the space of thoughtlessness. Whenever the "theologians" made frantic attempts at comprehending the Divine, they missed this subtle space and often landed up in the collective supra-conscious or the collective subconscious. (Conceptual confusion went so far as the extreme of Tantrism in India which mixed up sex perversion with spiritual rebirth or the European Wars of Religion between Catholic and Protestant in which innocent people were tortured and murdered in the name of Lord Jesus Christ).

With Sahaja Yoga awareness, idealism and realism, mysticism and pragmatism are merged into one attitude of integrated understanding. One becomes aware of collective consciousness by various information received in the hands and the chakras even before the brahmarandra is fully pierced. We can know the condition of anybody's chakras. Relating these facts to the traditional paths presented by the past leaders of Mankind we repeat that the awareness of one's own chakras casts a clearer light on the earlier religious teachings.

As previously said, Kundalini moves from Mooladhara up to Sahasrara only if all the chakras open. These chakras represent the various aspects of the subject who has inherited them as the milestones of his evolutionary pilgrimage. They are also adorned with deities, some of them Incarnations who led Mankind through the various periods of its evolution in awareness.

Incarnations accentuated the Archetype (aspect of God) that they were representing and asserted their spiritual manifestation according to the problems of the time. For instance, at the time of Shri Rama, a model for kingship was needed. All the Incarnations of the Principle of the Primordial Master spoke against intoxicants which go against human awareness. Alcohol is one of them. Therefore Christ, who delivered another message, did not emphasize this point, which had already been made by Moses. Now, look at the story! Many monasteries of Christendom became expert producers of wines and spirits. How could Lord Jesus encourage alcohol which attacks consciousness? HH Mataji says that, in Hebrew, "wine" meant the juice of the grape and not the fermented stuff. The monastery sponsored drinking habits; the rectory became the ancestor of the pub. Doesn't this example nicely illustrate the peculiar human way we did justice to these Incarnations? The chakras' awareness reveals that the ingestion of alcohol disturbs the Nabhi chakra and one thus fully understands the Adi Guru's ban on alcohol which was to preserve this chakra. All the guidelines of moral conduct given by the past Incarnations were meant to keep the deities in the chakras auspiciously happy.

Kundalini's rising also provides the proof of the unity of the World's religions. For instance a Christian will have to recognise Shri Krishna if his Kundalini is to stay above his Vishuddhi chakra and, similarly, the Kundalini will not cross the Ajnya of an orthodox Hindu who would reject Lord Jesus Christ. This very case happened in a little town near Madras. An Hindu scholar was prostrated at the feet of HH Mataji and everything had worked smoothly upto the level of the Ajnya chakra.

There, nothing doing, the Kundalini would not cross despite HH Mataji pouring vibrations onto him. Then I told this gentleman: "You should recognize Lord Jesus Christ", he said, "I recognize that he is a Saint". But that was not enough; Lord Jesus is to be recognized as an incarnation. This he could not do and we advised him to prepare himself to this effect because without his acceptance of the Christ his own Kundalini would refuse to rise and the Ajnya would be kept closed. Lord Jesus, in the Ajnya chakra, is extremely sensitive and gets annoyed with narrow minded dogmatic Christians who refuse to recognize His Father Shri Krishna. He is also extremely particular about the protocol of his Mother. Lord Buddha, in the right temple, blocks the Ascent of those who invoke the letter of buddhist teachings to deny the spontaneity of self realisation.

There was also the funny case of a Sikh gentleman who was a disciple of Guru Nanak. Now Guru Nanak and the Prophet Muhammad are two incarnations of the one same Original Teacher, (The Adi Guru, Satguru, Dattatrya). This Sikh had to take the name of Muhammad, whom he did not recognise, before he could get his realisation; while a strict Muslim had to take the name of Guru Nanak. When one recalls how fiercely Sikhs and Muslims fought each other in previous centuries, the meaning of Kundalini's soothing and unifying action becomes apparent.

The ascent of the Kundalini in a subject can be followed by the Sahaja Yogis who are present; thanks to vibratory awareness the progression of the Kundalini is known to us: we feel in our hands in which chakra there is a problem and we can also feel it directly in our own chakra. If there is, say, a problem in the Vishuddhi chakra of the aspirant, very often, by focusing our combined energy on this chakra, we can clear it out and liberate the way. We also obtain the same result by worshipping the deity of the specific chakra. For instance, knowing that Lord Jesus resides in the Ajnya chakra we turn our attention to Him and ask Him for assistance and forgiveness. I remember one instance like this in Delhi. Our group was trying to raise the Kundalini of an old man but She again, would not cross the Ajnya chakra. In collective consciousness we could all feel the pressure on this chakra. HH Mataji then asked me to say the 'Lord's Prayer' taught by Lord Jesus. I did it. Immediately his Ajnya chakra was cleared, his Kundalini reached the Sahasrara, we felt our heads being relieved and we all shared the blissful intensity of the Grace pouring into him. I remember this experience quite well because, in my childhood, while I was in a Catholic boarding school, I had to repeat mechanically the Lord's Prayer every day as a lifeless ritual... and suddenly this very same prayer revealed its tremendous power in the midst of what traditionalist Christians would consider to be a 'Hindu' gathering. Those are God's playful ironies... The Lord's Prayer, HH Mataji says, is the mantra for the Ajnya chakra and only after realisation can it be fully operative.

The religions of this Kali Yuga have been limited by misunderstandings and fanaticism. The religion of Sattya Yuga will worship all the various aspects of the One God. It will spread the joy and the love that radiates from this exquisite pattern of Divine relationships. Furthermore, we will discover that human relationships and institutions are the reflection of this original pattern.

The religion of the Age of Truth will, above all, worship the boundless love and dazzling glory of His Holy Shakti. The worship of the Holy Spirit will bring about the one true, fully integrated world religion for all the deities are parts of Her Cosmic Being. While I am writing these lines, the deities in my own chakras manifest their happiness by propelling me into thoughtless awareness! They thus give me their endorsement for my uttering the truth.

Now, after realisation, we roar with laughter when we see how foolish we have been, how serious Dignitaries pontificate in the ecclesiastic circus. Sahaja Yoga makes you understand the stupidity of all the empty pomp and show of rituals and prayers.

Shonalika Varma who was hardly five years old and born realised, went with her parents to see a lama. When she saw everybody prostrating before him, her mild sweet nature suddenly turned into wrath. She planted herself before the lama and raising her little voice said : "What is this? By shaving your head and wearing this long robe you do not get entitled to this worship". Her parents were shocked and reprimanded the child, but she cooly turned round and replied: "This man is not even par (realised). Why do you touch his feet?"

Aradhana, another born-realised of about the same age, had gone with HH Mataji, who was the chief guest, to a programme celebrating Shri Ramana Maharshi's birthday. A saffron-robed monk, solemn and important-looking, who was representing a philanthropic institution, sat next to HH Mataji, After some time the child suddenly shouted: "Mataji, who is this man in a yellow maxi. He is giving tremendous heat to all of us". The non Sahaja

Yogis were very surprised at her disgust, but of course she was right.

In this Kali Yuga, HH Mataji says, if you want to know what were the teachings of an Incarnation you can safely find it out by assuming it was the opposite of what the followers are doing.

For instance, Christ was the model of purity; look at the sex morals in the Christian countries! He said to have nothing to do with dead spirits...but spiritualist churches are inviting UPIs. The vibrations of so many churches are spoiled by tombs and surrounding cemeteries. The Prophet Muhammad, the Primordial Master, warned us not to indulge in any intoxicant but Muslim poets have written books of praise on the virtues of Alcohol. The Sikhs, followers of the same Master in the form of Guru Nanak, were told not to smoke or drink. In London, they are the faithful worshippers of Scotch Whiskey but refuse to wear a helmet on a motorcycle because they feel it goes against their religion... Do you really think that the great Sat Guru Nanak Sahib incarnated to tell us not to wear helmets on motorcycles? And of course Sikhs smoke like the defunct chimneys of London's foggy industrial past.

Buddhists are busy believing in all kinds of foolish rituals and formal initiations while Buddha himself did not even believe in God. His followers are worshipping his teeth, hair and nails; without even feeling the vibrations of these things how can one know they are from the body of Buddha?

Mahavira preached non-violence. Many Jains, henceforth will not kill even one mosquito. In one particularly orthodox community a poor brahmin is paid to stay in a hut full of bugs so that the bugs and insects can feed on his blood. Did Mahavira preach to save animals and sacrifice human beings?

Sahaja Yogis know that the goal of all the World religions is the union between the jivan and the atma, the union between the atma and the paramatma; that is, the identification of the seeker with his Self and the merging of his Self into God. He witnesses the play of the dynamic Love of God like a flute.

Self-realisation and God-realisation are not time-differentiated logical sequences but they represent various types of spiritual actualisation which depend upon the spiritual potentiality of the subject. They might, or might not, occur simultaneously.

When the Kundalini, settled in the Sahasrara, unites with the Atman located in the heart chakra, the human consciousness has realised the supreme religion. It is the state of integration between the Atman and the Shakti (God and the Holy Spirit). This state also expresses the Unity between the unmanifested God (Parabrahma, Paramatma, Brahman) and God within man (the Atman, the Self) because it reflects the state of Unity which preceded the Original Distinction (the original apparent distinction takes place between the God Almighty and the Holy Spirit, Sadashiva and the Adi Shakti).

This Unity is expressed in the Word, Brahma Tattwa, the Aum and Amen which has incarnated as Lord Jesus, the Christ, the Son of God, Mahavishnu. Let us remember now what has been said in the older ages:

"In the beginning was the Word, and the Word was with God, and the Word was God. He was in the beginning with God; all things were made through him, and without him was not anything made that was made. In him was life, and the life was the light of men... The true light that enlightens every man was coming into the world. He was in the world and the world was made through him, yet the world knew him not."
—John. 1.

"Of that goal which all the Vedas declare, which is implicit in all penances, and in pursuit of which men lead lives of continence and service, of that will I briefly speak. It is Aum."
—*Katha Upanishad*

"The syllable Aum which is the imperishable Brahman is the universe. Whatsoever has existed, whatsoever exists, whatsoever shall exist hereafter is AUM. And whatsoever transcends past, present and future, that also is AUM. All this that we see without is Brahman. This Self, that is within is Brahman. This Self, which is one with AUM."
—*Mandukya Upanishad*

And to the angel of the Church in Laodicea write : "The words of the Amen, the faithful and true witness, the beginning of God's creation"   —John. *The Apocalypse 3.14.*

We can relate Christhood-the-Word-Aum to Sahaja Kundalini Yoga in exposing the symbolism contained in the sacred syllable.

"A"   Represents the Tamo guna of the Virata, the Primordial Being (desiring mood). At the cosmic level it is the Ishwara whose shakti is Mahakali. At the microcosmic level it is Ida nadi and the left side S.N.S. At the microscopic level it is the nucleus of the atom.

"U"   Represents the Rajo guna of the Primordial Being (activating mood). At the cosmic level it is the Hyranyagharba whose shakti is Mahasaraswati. At the microcosmic level it is Pingala Nadi and the right side sympathetic nervous system. At the microscopic level it is the electrons of the atom.

"M"   Represents the Sattwa guna of the Primordial Being (revelation mood) which evolves AUM to the level of the Primordial Being Himself, the Virata, whose shakti is Mahalaxshmi. At the microcosmic level it is the Sushumna and the parasympathetic nervous system. At the microscopic level it is the valency of the atom.

The Adi Kundalini (Holy Spirit in the form of the Primordial Kundalini) is said to be "trigunatmika" that is, containing the three gunas. What She does is to unite the A, the U and the M. Hence, at the Divine energetic level the Adi Kundalini generates the AUM which means, in personified terms, that the Adi Shakti is the Mother of the Son God.

AUM is a sound whose symbol is ॐ in the Devnagari script. The symbol actually represents the primordial movement of the Energy. Its manifestation as Chaitanya (wave of life force) can be felt through the parasympathetic nervous system after self realisation. This energy is at work everywhere and all the time but before realisation man cannot feel it.

We hope that the reader has followed this development and we wish to come back to a point we have considered at length, that is the cognitive faculties of the human being.

Man relates to representations about Reality and not Reality. These representations are opinions in the Platonic sense, that is pictures distorted by the mind's conditionings. To know reality implies then that the conditioning factors of the mind, that is the three gunas, can be overcome. Beyond the gunas, there is the Self: to know the Self is to know Reality. But the perennial question of the past metaphysical systems was the one stated in the *Brihadaranyaka Upanishad* : "By whom shall the knower be known?" How do the striving energies of the Chinese and Japanese Zen monks finally collapse in the stage of "Satori"? How can one master the intellect (the buddhi) so as to reach the "wisdom of the all reflecting mirror" symbolised in Mahayana Buddhism by the Boddhisatva Avalokitesvara? We should keep these questions in our mind while opening again the fourth gospel : when John says that the Word "gave power to become children of God" what did he mean? The *Prasna Upanishad* tells us "by meditating upon AUM, the wise man attains Brahman"; "AUM is Brahman. AUM is all. He who meditates on AUM attains Brahman" echoes the *Taittiriya Upanishad*. How to become a reborn child of God, how to know the All, how to meditate upon AUM?

The answer to these many questions is one and this answer is given by Sahaja Yoga. I mean, Sahaja Yoga is not a theory about the Answer. It does not propose for you just a new system of thought, just one more intellectual sedimentation on the fossil of the concept of God. No! It is the Answer itself. How does a human being become AUM?—By putting A, U and M together.—Who does in fact put A, U and M together?—the subject's Kundalini does it. How does the Kundalini manifest Herself? Through Sahaja Yoga.

As Adi Shakti the Almighty Sacred Mother created the AUM. As Shri Gauri She created Lord Ganesha. As Shri Parvati She created Lord Kartikeya. As Shri Radha She created Mahavishnu, who was born to Mother Mary as Lord Jesus. As HH Mataji Nirmala Devi She created a new race of Sahaja Yogis. She says that Sahaja Yogis have been created in the pattern of the Great Son God.

With a new devotion to the Divine Energy of the Adi Shakti, to the presence of the Holy Spirit within us, we can now understand the *Mandukya Upanishad*:

"The Self is AUM, the indivisible syllable. This syllable is unutterable and beyond mind. In it, the manifold universe disappears. It is the supreme good—One without a second. Whosoever knows AUM, the Self, becomes the Self".

This knowledge is now open to the common man. It is so fantastic... Imagine! Just by extending their hands in front of HH Mataji or Her photograph, people have felt the cool wind of the Life Force (Chaitanya Lahari). I don't know how to marvel at HH Mataji!

When people deal with the extraordinary, it has to be in the past or in the future but it cannot be coped with so easily when it's happening in the present. Well, let's see what's going to happen this time. I think men are much more open minded today than they used to be.

HH Mataji has disciples who are Catholics, Protestants, Marxists, Hindus, Sikhs, Zoroastrians, Buddhists, Jains, Muslims, etc. Disciples among Indians, English, Iranians, Latin Americans, Germans, French, Swiss, Russian, Australians, Japanese, Chinese, Americans, Malaysians, Algerians, etc. People from Poland, South Africa, Finland, Ghana, Brazil, New Zealand, Mauritius, Italy, Hungary, etc. Despite this variety in the type of Sahaja Yogis it has been noticed that they all have broken the bondage of fanaticism and blind faith, the artificial barriers of race, community or religions; perhaps they present an unmatched assortment of qualities. They have become peaceful, blissful, compassionate and powerful!

Sahaja Yoga discriminates between true and fake seekers with tremendous subtlety. There are a few people who do not feel the vibrations; if they humbly and ardently ask for it they always stand a chance of getting it. But some of them just conclude that Sahaja Yoga is false and fake. They exclude themselves from it.

For so many people, as HH Mataji says, "the blossom time has come". When a true seeker who has not damaged himself comes before HH Mataji, his Kundalini, out of joy, rises with tremendous force. If the seeker is wounded the curing process starts. Slowly but surely, through the opening of his own chakras, the subject who accepts the teachings of his experience opens himself to the knowledge of the Great Primordial Being (Virata) who manifests and integrates the various aspects of the One God. He enters intimate and living relationships with the various Deities and Incarnations who revealed the Virata's chakras. Sahaja Yogis have been seeing them in beatific visions, seeing also the previous Incarnations of HH Mataji.

The Divine Love has cast Her net and draws the human souls back to cosmic consciousness. We let ourselves be caught and sweetly admire the gracious perfection of our Mother's movement. We feel blessed by Her attention. We are proud of Her glory. We adore Her. We enjoy every minute of our ascent. And we share this joy in the oneness of collective consciousness. Collective consciousness is the net of Her Love. It is the Religion of the present time. In this consciousness, many, many of you, brothers and sisters, will become the joyous worshippers of the Divine Love and will bathe in the beauty of your Self.

I see the dawn of universal realisation in this mass happening, and this should put the right emphasis on the astonishing historical dimension of Sahaja Yoga. Let us just cast a glance at the past : take for instance the great Islam scholar Ghazzali (1058-1111) who infused mysticism into Sunni Orthodoxy : he did so on the basis of the direct experience of the mystic's relation to God. He was more successful than the German Dominican Friar Meister Eckhardt (1260-1327) who got into trouble with the Western ecclesiastical authorities for the same reason; Meister Eckhardt also claimed to have experienced the identity of his own Self with the ultimate reality; the contemporary mystical movement on Mount Athos, in the Byzantine Empire, was however approved by a council of the Orthodox Church in 1351. All these attempts at breaking through have been limited in their impact because as a rule, the seekers did not have the power to communicate the stage they had reached. But now, with Sahaja Yoga, individual realisation can be propagated to the community. Of course, when I am talking about mass realisation, I am still talking about a minority of people, but this minority will be important enough to play its part in history. Science fiction's freaks expect the new race to land in an armada of galactic cruisers, spaceships and other UFO's. But the great message of world religions was the fact that the new race is to be born within us! Verily I can say that I am witnessing the coming of a new race, collectively conscious, defined by its capacity of tapping the Divine, thus bridging the gap between Finite and Infinite.

I can only urge you to take advantage of Sahaja Yoga. For the chain reaction of destruction within society and within ourselves has already started. If we allow it to work out we are going to be destroyed from within through the slow death of our higher awareness. That is to say the Incarnation of the Destroyer, the Rider of the Apocalypse is already at work within. Destruction belongs to the natural process of evolution; the calyx of the flower drops as the fruit matures.

I am inviting all the seekers: You too become a child of the Holy Spirit. We, Sahaja Yogis, are your own in the sense that we are in the service of God. Our aim in this life is to enable all the genuine seekers of Reality to reach their destination, that is, to reach the Holy Spirit. Oh! You don't know! We are so eager for you to get the reward of your quest! Every time a seeker joins us, we rejoice and exult. Come and share the religion of God: in truth, consciounsess and bliss, our religion is "to be".

7

Evolution in consciousness

"The beginning of the Universe, when manifested, may be regarded as its Mother. When a man has found the Mother, he will know the children accordingly."
—Lao Tzu Tao Te Ching.

"Did you think that I had created you in vain and that you would never be recalled to Me?"
—*Koran 23.114.*

Utopia, comes from the Greek "eutopos", and means "the place of happiness". The utopia which is proposed to you is no more Thomas More's island in the middle of the sea: it is the thousand petalled chakra in the limbic area of your brain, bathing in the nectar of blissful consciousness. Many mysterious paintings by artists such as William Blake, have expressed their inner vision of the Sahasrara. This place of happiness can be reached by your ascending Kundalini. Hundreds of Sahaja Yogis can bear witness to the existence of this inward island of silent bliss. On the old sanskrit maps of the spiritual country the island was termed the land of *Sat Chit Ananda* where truth, consciousness, and bliss are integrated. If many people today decide to take the Sahaja boat to reach it, I can confidently predict that a new society will follow the new man. Such a happening seems necessary and obvious once we have localised its place in the plan of cosmic evolution. In The Philosophy of History G.W.F. Hegel attempted to conceptualise the working of the Adi Shakti; he considered universal history as a striving of the spirit for its self-actualisation:

"It may be said of universal history that it is the exhibition of spirit in the process of working out the knowledge of that which it is potentially" and "the principle of development involved also in the existence of a latent germ of being—a capacity of potentiality striving to realise itself. This formal conception finds actual existence in spirit: which has the history of the world as its theatre, its possession and the sphere of its realisation."[1]

The various steps of history are the necessary gradations "in the development of the one universal spirit, which through them elevates and completes itself to a self-comprehending totality".[2] This development is a process of self-manifestation : "What spirit is it has always been essentially ; distinctions are only the development of this essential nature. The life of the ever present spirit is a circle of progressive embodiments."[3]

This succession of embodiments leads to the purpose of Universal History: the self-recognition of Spirit within History "for Spirit, in its self-consciousness must become an object of contemplation to itself".[4] The understanding of History as an evolutionary process heading towards its fulfilment has been developed by many thinkers. One finds the notion of the spirit striving to actualise itself through nature (Purusha within Prakriti) in a variety of accounts e.g. Plato's "Daimon" (Demiurge), Hegel's "Weltgeist" (World Spirit), Bergson's "Elan Vital" (Vital force).

Schopenhauer, Herder, and Fichte led the German school of thought to develop an evolutionary approach to history and were in agreement with the oldest traditions. Indo-Aryan thought conceived of history as a tale of divine will-power so that cosmology, mythology and history are traditionally closely connected. In the Mediterranean basin, the perception of history as an evolution towards a fulfilment is a fundamental Judeo-Christian idea which has been developed in the modern times by thinkers as different as Leibnitz, Marx, Renan, and Teilhard de Chardin. But what is the longed for fulfilment to be? This was, and still is the matter in question.

The knowledge granted by HH Mataji Nirmala Devi reveals the precious value of the findings of the previous seekers. We can know to what extent they had received intuitions from the Universal Unconscious and developed true insight into the evolution-

[1] G. W. F. Hegel *The Philosophy of History* pg. 54. (New York 1956) Dover Publications.
[2] G. W. F. Hegel op. cit. pg. 78.
[3] G. W. F. Hegel op. cit pg. 79
[4] G. W. F. Hegel op. cit. pg. 53.

ary process. We also know where they made mistakes or why they did not recognise an Incarnation.

Evolution is Sahaj, HH Mataji tells us, it is the spontaneous living process of a seed turning into a tree. Hence the movement is natural, synchronised, effortless driving awareness from matter to life, from life to the human stage and from human to the superhuman stage. As far as this latter step is concerned, it is very necessary that evolution takes place with man's conscious participation. When the human will-power is connected with the Universal Unconscious by Sahaja Yoga it becomes the instrument of evolution. It spontaneously brings about, at an ever-accelerating pace, the actualisation of the purpose of creation. The whole movement is smooth, sahaj. Our Divine Mother says: "Someone has worked at the roots of the Creation, my children, to prepare the stage for your ascent and to lead you through your ascent. Why become worried or frantic? Just receive the Grace with an open heart."

Let us now try to grasp better the great miracle that our Mother is performing.

If, by the Creation, God went from the Infinite (Himself) to the Finite (the Creation), the Finite should be in a position to tend again towards the Infinite and to reach it. It is this proposition that all the major world religions (based on the original sayings of the authentic teachers) are committed to elucidating. Sahaja Yoga can elucidate these ancient teachings by demonstrating that they lead the way towards self-realisation. For the history of man has to merge with the history of God. We will not try here to prove the existence of what we identify by the word GOD. At the rational level, it is a task which has been performed (Aquinas) or played with (Pascal) with an ultimate establishment of failure (Kant). At this stage of the argument we proclaim with our experience that whatever God is, it exists, and we are only concerned with the way He operates... the way He operates being precisely what the field of Creation—Cosmos—History is about.

Of course, God is indeterminate. Therefore we have to use a metaphorical language in order to veil our present conceptual inability to grasp the transition from the indeterminate to the determinate, from the unmanifested to the manifested. The ultimate Reality (God, Parabrahman) goes through phases of manifestations. Non-manifestation followed by manifestation defines a cosmic cycle (kalpa). Thus innumerable cosmic cycles have already been generated before the present one which has been engineered for the purpose of the ascent of this human race. But what is the "purpose" of Creation? We can say that, in the Creation, God as a Witness (Sadashiva)[5] desires to enjoy an even more accurate reflection of Himself. So, God as an Actor (Adi Shakti, Holy Spirit or Divine Mother) starts evolving the Creation. The different combinations and permutations of energy generate different strata of existence; the material universe we know is one of them.

All these creations are nothing but various steps of the Adi Shakti's movements of self manifestation. Through Her creations, the Divine Mother evolves traits of Her nature from potentiality to actualisation. The operation of the Holy Spirit is precisely what Hegel was trying to grasp in his philosophy of history.

Let us now refer to HH Mataji's account of the Genesis.

In the first stratum of existence there exists only Sada Shiva and Adi Shakti. Further differentiation occurs through the operation of the threefold seed energies of Mahakali, Mahasaraswati and Mahalaxshmi. Thus AUM separates into A, U and M. First, the Adi Shakti, through the Mahakali power, creates the principle of the Son God; The Adi Shakti, in the form of Shri Gauri, generates Lord Ganesha, the highest expression of Divine Innocence, whose abode is the Adi Mooladhara chakra.[6] There he purifies and controls the cosmic energies and keeps in check those that the Virata produces at random: He watches the gates of Hell. He is the unincarnated Archetype of the Son God. Sahaja Yogis have a special and very sweet devotion to Lord Ganesha because He is the one to grant this crystalline quality of innocence whereby true wisdom develops. Also, with His blessings, our consciousness reaches the stage of loving adoration which expresses the truth of our relation to the Divine Mother, the Adi Shakti.

Through the radiance of Lord Ganesha, the whole creation is permeated by utter holiness and sanctity. The Holy Spirit then forms the body of the Great Primordial Being who will programme

---

[5]In the Muslim Call for Prayer (Adhan) God the Father is invoked in the aspect of His greatness (Allahu Akbar : God is most Great) and in the aspect of His unity (Ilaha illa Allah: there is no other deity but Allah). Hence it comprehends both Virata (Akbar) and Sadashiva (Ilaha). The Kaaba of Mecca could be said to be a Shiva Lingam.

[6]Lord Ganesha conveys all the information from the personality to the Kundalini who thus tapes all the memories from present and past lives.

the further course of cosmic evolution. The three seed energies form the three Adi nadis of the Virata.

The next manifestation of God is Lord Vishnu and his shakti Shri Laxshmi, in the Vaikuntha stage. He maintains the cohesion of the Universal drama and prevents the triumph of the evil forces. Lord Vishnu is the Messiah, the Saviour who has been identified by so many mythological traditions as He represents the aspect of the Almighty Father who sustains and guides the cosmic evolution. To this effect He incarnates in a human body to trigger on this planet Earth, the successive steps of consciousness; He began by leading the fishes out of the water and is expected, in His tenth incarnation, to lead mankind out of the gunas. In Him rests our confidence in Destiny and Self.

In the cosmic water of the Vaikuntha Lord Vishnu sleeps and is attended by Shri Laxshmi and other forms of God. Lord Brahmadeva and Shri Saraswati are dangling on the Adi Swadhistan chakra which is rotating and moving in the cosmic multi-dimensionality to create the forthcoming forms of life and matter. Shri Saraswati, goddess of knowledge and creativity, learning and arts has been, for instance, worshipped in Greece as Athene. Lord Brahma's poem of the material creation is the object of science. When our swadhistan chakra fully blossoms we begin to feel like the participating actors of cosmic creation.

On the Adi Anahata chakra Lord Shiva, as the heart of the Virata, represents the spiritual Infinity, the existence itself as Sadashiva within the Primordial Being. He never incarnates. He is the all compassionate one (Shankara, Karuna Sagara). When He ceases to forgive, the final destruction takes place: this is "tandava" the dance of Lord Shiva. In us Lord Shiva is the spirit, the SELF, God within us. He is the Atman, the radiating consciousness of divine existence which is one with the divine love (Sati, Parvati). In the human psyche Lord Shiva rules Ida Nadi and the emotional body. His conveyance is the bull Nandi who represents full self confidence within the subconscious realm. The Great God is assisted by the famous deity Bhairawa, the demon killer, the Archangel Saint Michael who is also represented in the form of the conveyance of the Goddess: the tiger.

When the light of the Atma grows within us one can feel the silence: neither desire nor pain is experienced. A cool feeling, as if emitted from an ice cold source is felt. Gradually all disturbing waves have been transformed and one starts emitting peace and love for others. Within the being, extremely soothing waves of love creep all over. When the heart is fully enlightened by the Spirit, existence itself becomes the feeling. In this "witness state" one realises Lord Shiva, fully awakened within the heart.

Lord Dattatrya (original Teacher, Adi Guru) who is also dwelling in the Vaikuntha, represents a personification of the innocence of Shri Brahmadeva, Shri Vishnu and Shri Shiva. To him goes all the filial veneration due to the benevolent and enlightened Master. He, like Lord Vishnu, takes a human form many times to guide mankind. Muslims, Jews, Taoists, Zoroastrians, Confucians, followers of Socrates, Sikhs, etc... are all following one and the same leader, the ADI GURU (Sadguru). We should understand the futility of the quarrel between polytheists, monotheists, the partisans of various Gods and of the Undifferentiated. Kabir sings:

"If God be within the mosque, then to whom does this world belong? If Ram be within the image which you find upon your pilgrimage, then who is there to know what happens without? Hari is in the East: Allah is in the West. Look within your heart, for there you will find both Karim and Ram. All the men and women of the world are his living forms. Kabir is the child of Allah and of Ram; He is my Guru; He is my Pir."[7]

The awakening of the Guru within a subject sprays unbending rays of authority and dignity.

In the stratum of existence that we know, the material Universe, (Bhavasagara—the Ocean of Illusion) the Holy Spirit has set up the stage of the cosmic drama that man is to perform. HH Mataji tells us:

In a span of time stretching over six thousand billion years matter was evolved (atomic structure, etc.) by the aspect of God that expresses the Creator: Lord Brahma-Saraswati on the Adi Swadhistan chakra of the Virata. In four thousand billion years the galaxies and the solar system materialised. Then the earth found

---

[7]*Poems of Kabir*. translated by Tagore. MacMillan Press (Madras 1973) pg. 64.

the planetary position and spatial type of motion which made possible the appearance of the biosphere; ultimately the tissue of the living cell was generated, which is revealed by the bio sciences. These last developments took place during 1.1 and 0.9 thousand billion years, respectively. Clearly someone has guided this process. According to the mathematical laws of probability, the time it look for man to appear on earth would hardly suffice to produce a unicellular being. With Her typical touch of humour our Divine Mother comments: "There has to be a very great juggler to do the trick."

As we said, the purpose of the cosmic play is the self-actualisation of Primordial Energy within the Creation. History is then the story of the evolution of Energy from gross matter to ever more subtle manifestations of consciousness, which reveal themselves through the human brain. The standard psychic state of the common man today (Homo sapiens) for instance, is the result of a very long progression; a very poem of creativity. The human brain is the culmination of almost three billion years of evolutionary history and represents the most complex—and still unknown—structure in creation. It has about eleven billion nerve cells or neurons, each of which is a sophisticated information-processing centre capable of taking split-second action. To enable you to read these words, millions of tiny electrical impulses flash to and from the vast neural network of your brain.

Thanks to this prodigious instrument, Man's consciousness gradually became itself the engine of evolutionary dynamism. He fulfilled a function which is perfomed at other bio levels through animal instinct, biological cycles, the laws of organically structured and inorganic matter.

Through the raising of this consciousness man increasingly became an active participant in the Creation. The extent of man's creative impact on his natural environment was dramatically increased by the technological discoveries of the Upper Paleolithic Age, some 70,000 years ago.

The raising of the head, at the completion of the animal stage, had given a different twist to the Vishuddhi Chakra which is placed at the basis of the neck. This movement gave rise to the ego which, inflating like a balloon, started pushing back the super-ego balloon. The ideal position for the evolutionary breakthrough happens to be when they balance each other in the centre. That is why many simple, innocent people in developing countries who have not yet developed their ego too much can settle smoothly in Sahaja Yoga.

When the shell of the ego and super-ego gets thicker, the link between the human conscious mind and the Universal Unconscious weakens. "Developed" people turn out to be completely covered and blinded by their ego. This of course explains why, in the (over) developed countries, a new born Sahaja Yogi takes quite some time to settle in the realised state.

In other words, while man's brain was becoming an increasingly sophisticated instrument, this instrument was not tuned to the wave lengths of the cosmic energy. That is why our stratum of existence has been called the ocean of illusion: without being connected to the Universal programme the human brain is working on its own, generating confusion or delusion: this aspect of the consciousness deluding itself has been called "maya".

Man's increasing power of thought and action made the more necessary for him to be provided with guidelines and criteria which his thought and action could follow, a process that we have already mentioned while presenting the concept of God. This is the juncture at which religion appears on earth.

We can say that the various world religions opened specific communication channels between the evolutionary programme and the earth where it is in the process of implementation. The great instructors of mankind (the Incarnations of God's different aspects), who launched these religions came from the Vaikuntha stage. The Incarnations can be categorized in four Archetypes: the Mother, the Father, the Guru and the Son.

- —Mother Incarnations come as a fully manifested single person or as the Shakti (power) of another Incarnation that is, the Mother of a Child Incarnation or the wife of a Father Incarnation.

- —Father Incarnations are the eight first incarnations of Lord Vishnu, the sustainer and guide of Evolution.

- —Guru Incarnations. The Primordial Master aspect of God has many a time guided Mankind through his many incarnations.

- —Son Incarnation. In the Vaikuntha stage, the forms of Lord Ganesha (left side) and Lord Kartikeya (right side) combine to become Mahavishnu who incarnates as Lord Jesus Christ.

The Child King will appear as Kalki, the culminating incarnation who integrates Lord Vishnu's killing power (samhara shakti) and Lord Shiva's destroying powers (vinasha). With altogether eleven destroying powers (Ekadesha Rudra), the Rider is going to destroy the world that has not accepted the higher evolution.

Let us remember that the seven Adi Chakras, set into motion by their respective deities, are the seven days of the Creation or, its seven evolutionary stages.

One of the oldest Incarnations recalled by the Indo-Vedic tradition is that of Shri Durga (see the Devi Mahatmyam or Shri Durga Saptasati). She is none other than the Shakti of Lord Shiva (Shri Parvati) who came to Nepal to repel an invasion of demons. They had conquered the conscious (cosmically located on this planet) and the supra-conscious realms. Shri Durga drove them from earth and threw them back into the subconscious. This cosmic struggle awakened the Heart Chakra of the Virata.

Another famous Incarnation worshipped in India, Indonesia and Thailand is that of Lord Rama. Shri Vishnu took his seventh incarnation 8,000 years ago as Lord Rama, the heir of the empire of Ayodhaya and he took for his wife the lotus-eyed daughter of King Janaka, Sita, who was the Incarnation of Shri Laxshmi. Their "love story" magnifies for ever the husband-wife relationship. The purpose of the Rama Avatara was manifold. Lord Vishnu has switched off his divine memory and, thinking himself to be a human being, he behaved in all aspects of life as a model for human behaviour.

As a King-Philosopher he enlightened human political institutions and geared them to the preservation of individual and collective dharma.

Lord Rama was a perfect son, a perfect husband, a perfect father and a perfect ruler. He was called "Maryada Purushottama" the best among all men who expresses the holy boundaries of the human culture.

I should like to open a parenthesis on the auspicious notion of Maryadas or boundaries. We already mentioned that, in order to master the art of being human, people must respect certain rules (boundaries, maryadas). These are rules of behaviour which keep open the communication channels with the Universal Unconscious. If we cross the boundaries, these channels are broken. Maryadas maintain auspiciousness in the human life.

Auspiciousness means the right thing, in the right circumstances, at the right time. A behaviour is auspicious when it is perfectly tuned to the cosmic waves of the Universal Unconscious. When behaviour, an institution, a painting or some music is fully auspicious in this subtle sense it reaches perfection.[8]

Lord Rama manifested auspiciousness in human relationships and wiped out those who were making fun of it. Through the battles recalled in *the Ramayana*, he slashed the overlordship of those demonic, egoistical and proud beings who had retained supranatural powers although already in a quasi-human form. In his wanderings throughout the sub-Asian peninsula (which at that time, had a different outline) Lord Rama also vibrated the earth and brought energetic mutations which favoured the rise of human consciousness. On the cosmic plane, Lord Rama resides on the right side of the Virata's heart where he more specifically controls the activity of the Adi Pingala Nadi, the supraconscious and its realms. He is assisted in this task by Lord Hanumana—Hermes, Mercury, Gabriel, the Messenger. In our mind Hanumana is the preconscious mind who brings to our consciousness the intuitions, hints from the Universal Unconscious. He also regulates brain activity, plays tricks with people's ego and holds it up to ridicule. When he recedes, the brain activity becomes uncontrollable.

Some of the names attributed to Shri Vishnu mean "the adorable Lord". His eighth incarnation as Lord Krishna, 6,000 years ago, beautifully illustrates the sweetness of the love that the Almighty Father has for His Creation. In the *Gita*, the Virata itself is shown to the baffled human eyes of Arjuna who contemplates the innumerable forms of the One. Lord Krishna opened a new horizon to the human understanding: the infinity of God's love and power. He also taught the human seeker to watch the play of the Adi Shakti as a witness, without being involved in the three gunas. However he did not provide mankind with the instrument to do so;

---

[8]The seven notes of the scale in the rhythm of auspiciousness are, of course, the seven chakras. To each chakra corresponds a cosmic vibration, a specific sound, colour, etc. So each chakra corresponds a specific day and planet. The science of Astrology is founded in these relationships. Superstitions are the degraded remnants of the ancient science of reading auspices, i.e. of interpreting vibrations.

the time was not yet ripe for that step. The human mind began preparing itself for the breakthrough. Lord Krishna awakened the Adi Vishuddhi Chakra of the Virata. He killed many demons who were opposing the evolutionary purpose. All the while, Lord Krishna played divine diplomacy with us, human beings. He tried to lead us towards higher consciousness despite our very limited understanding. His diplomacy always played for the well being of the Spirit (Hitta Karini).

For instance, Lord Krishna taught in the *Gita* to act but to leave the fruits of the actions at the Feet of the Lord (Karma Yoga). And to offer one's love to God, being fully one with Him (Bhakti Yoga). Both attitudes are beyond the capacity of human beings in the standard psychic state. By teaching Arjuna in this manner, Lord Krishna was merely pointing out to mankind the ineluctable necessity of the later advent of Sahaja Yoga in which Karma Yoga and Bhakti Yoga are spontaneously realised.

When the Vishuddhi Chakra blossoms, inward silence grows bigger; one develops a feeling of covering, encompassing the whole world, the whole Universe. Because Lord Krishna is awakened in the Chakra of the cervical plexus one can identify with His Shakti, the Viratangana, the all pervading power of greatness. Thus the mantra for this chakra is the Prophet Muhammad's call to Prayer: "Allah Akbar": God is most Great.

But if one takes the name of a deity before self-realisation, the unauthorised chanting annoys the deity. I know of a born-realized child who was trying to sleep in a room near a temple where so called devotees were endlessly chanting "Hare Rama, Hare Krishna". The child angrily got up, packed her blanket up and explained to the puzzled nanny: "God is so angry with this singing that He left the temple long ago. And now I am also going." Seekers who chant mantras without Divine authority can suffer from nose, ear or throat troubles. Cancer may spread to the areas controlled by the chakra's sixteen sub-plexuses.

The left side of the chakra, ruled by Shri Vishnumaya, Shri Krishna's sister, will be disturbed when the tongue utters blasphemies. UPI's can then enter the chakra and talk through this person. Vishuddhi possession aims at overcoming the subject's conscience; the victim can alternatively use a venomous language or become freezingly silent.

"The Saviour" is not the only aspect of God that visited Mankind in an incarnated form, for the Primordial Master "The Teacher" often visited us to guide our race on the central Path of Dharma. Lord Dattatrya led mankind through the void of the ocean of illusion. His location in our body similarly corresponds to the void between the parasympathetic vagus nerve and the solar plexus. He incarnated many times as Adinath, Janaka, Abraham, Moses, Zarathustra, Socrates, Confucius, Lao-Tzu, Muhammad, Guru Nanak, etc. His last incarnation manifested in the human form of Shri Sai Baba of Shirdi (died 15th October, 1918). Shri Sainath expressed himself in words that the reader can now better understand:

> "I am God. I am Mahalaxshmi. I speak the truth sitting as I do in the mosque. I am Vithoba. I am Ganapathi.[9] All offerings made to Ganapathi have reached me. I am Dattatrya. I am Laxmi Narayan. Why go for Ganga elsewhere? Hold your palm at my feet—here flows Ganga. I am Maruti."[10]

In this statement Shri Dattatrya clearly hints at the oneness of the Virata and at the flow of vibrations that we, ourselves, have experienced as coming from HH Mataji's Lotus Feet.

The Adi Shakti often incarnates as the daughter of the Primordial Master. For instance Shri Sita was the daughter of the King of Mithila, Rajah Janaka, the "royal saint". As the wife of Lord Rama she conceived the twins Lava and Kusha. Shri Sita later reincarnated as Muhammad's daughter Fatima and the two boys were again born to Her as Hassan and Hussein.

So through appointed seers, saints and prophets, through the coming of the Avatars themselves, the Holy Spirit provided mankind with divine guidance. She communicated the instructions that were necessary in order to follow the optimal path of evolution, evolution whose purpose was not discovered or understood by man. The message of these instructors (Satgurus) were meant to correspond to the level of conceptualisation of the societies of that time but were, above all, intended to stimulate it.

At first ancient societies used to perceive the Divine through

---

[9]Vithoba is Lord Vishnu. Ganapathi is Lord Ganesha.
[10]Quoted in *SAI BABA the Saint of Shirdi*. Mani Sahukar Somaiya Pub. (Bombay 1971) pg. 60.

the manifestation of Nature's powers: thunderbolt, sun, moon, rain, earth's fertility, etc. (The knowledge of the divine beings of the supraconscious heaven is attested by the Hindu, Greek, Iranian, Meso-Amerindian pantheons, etc.). Then the level of human understanding reached the knowledge of the existence of the divinities personifying the aspects of God in the Vaikuntha stage. This step in the history of religion is represented by the Hindu cosmology. The coming of Lord Buddha and Lord Mahavira expressed the rise of two exceptional beings who reached the status of Incarnations. Through their ascent the Holy Spirit implemented in the human awareness a better relation to Reality. Many other teachers, all over the world, worked for the same purpose and scholars today begin to recognise the historic pattern of their coming in time and space. For instance the philosopher Karl Jaspers calls "the Axis Age" the period between 600 and 480 BC, spanned by the lifetime of five great seers: the Iranian Zarathustra who operated in the Oxus-Jaxartes basin; the Judahite prophet Isaiah; Siddhartha Gautam, the Buddha (567-487) whose field of activity was present day Bihar; Confucius born in the Chinese state of Lu (551-479 BC); Pythagoras born on the Ionian offshore island Samos but who taught in the colonial Greek domain of Southern Italy. These five seers broke with the prevailing religious beliefs, trying to reform society and to lead their fellow human beings into new ways of deepened inward knowledge and righteous social behaviour.

The ninth incarnation of the Vishnu tatwa (that is the evolutionary principle of Lord Vishnu) manifested the teachings of the Saviour on the oecumenical scale of the five continents, whereas up to that time, his messages had been geographically confined. The creation of Lord Jesus Christ as Mahavishnu, the son of Shri Krishna, is foretold in Markandeya's *Devi Bhagavati*: constellations and galaxies of energy are roaring in each dust particle of his skin. Mother Mary, the incarnation of Mahalaxshmi, will see this cosmic giant of the divine forces, Her son, being hung on a cross to die. This is the most poignant and bewildering moment of the drama. We can only silently bow to the greatness of God's play. Opening the Ajnya Chakra of the Virata could not be done without killing the ego. Lord Jesus sacrificed Himself to be killed by the ego of the people. Once human beings killed Christ, the guilt of this horrid murder helped to subdue the ego of man.

However the symbol of Christianity should not be the cross but the resurrection. In Lord Jesus, the Father (Shri Vishnu, Shri Shiva) and the Son (Shri Ganesha, Shri Kartikeya) are one. The sacrifice of God for the sake of man permitted a very intense perception of God's love to mankind. At that time through Lord Krishna, man knew of the greatness of God but he did not know how to crucify his lower self to make his spiritual Self express itself. Through the resurrection of Christ human eyes witnessed the immortality of the Spirit (the Atman) within man. Thus His resurrection proved the sayings of His Father Shri Krishna in the *Bhagavad Gita*: "The spirit can not be destroyed. It is eternal." This opening of the Adi Ajnya Chakra of the Virata also began the last act of the great evolutionary drama.

Verily, the true guidelines of universal evolution are the steps of spiritual progress created by these Incarnations (Avatars) of God who come to teach man about his dharma (right evolutionary line, righteousness, virtue). Their action implemented the increase of the Spirit's awareness of itself in the material creation. However this progress cannot always be represented by a clearly ascending line: there were a lot of ups and downs! There is no point in insisting that religious teachers have been almost all equally misunderstood even by their closest disciples, followers, apostles. Arjuna did not show a better understanding of Shri Krishna than Peter did of Lord Jesus or Abu Bakr of Muhammad. The less God or his messenger were understood, the more the concept of God was developed and abused by the aforementioned institutionalized religions.

When the Divine Incarnation propounded the truth, the followers understood his message to be their own possession. After the death of the Incarnation, all too often the substance of the great teaching was lost and its empty form was called as religion. Now, as soon as one even thinks wrongly, the vibratory awareness reacts.

This is why we are confident that Sahaja Yoga will not turn into a dead Church. For a realised soul the deities are alive within; he becomes a recording and correcting instrument; a sensation of burning comes from the awakened reaction of the deities to any obstacles on the concerned chakras; the teachings of HH Mataji can be verified as they are directly built in to the central nervous system and this drastically reduces the chances of a realised soul making mistakes. As we have said before, religion becomes a daily living experience of the awareness. The inexpressible feeling of joy and peace that was experienced at the first breakthrough of the Kundalini gradually settles down as the witness stage develops.

The Indian Sahaja Yogis explain that the Kundalini rises at the first sight of HH Mataji (*Prathama Darshana*) as if she meets again Her primordial source, after having waited for so many yugas. In Her gushing welcome She pierces the Brahmarandra, granting rebirth. After this, the Kundalini falls to Her abode but She gradually comes back, to look after the reborn being, enriching and transforming him. Sahaja Yoga is a living religion which convinces you through the living proof of the Kundalini's manifestation. When it is properly established in a realised soul the subject can decode without difficulty the different sensations within the fingers, spine and brain. He reads the Universal Unconscious.

The New Age in which this possibility materialises for the masses now opens itself before us. This extremely bold statement asks for some kind of explanation. The material world we know around us corresponded to a specific stage of evolution and awareness, roughly the last six thousand years. Different evolutionary states were established in us before this modern one. As stated earlier, the overall structure of universal evolution is contained in the Great Primordial Being (Virata), the "programme" which came into existence before the creation of matter. It is the "seven stage programme of the cosmic pilgrimage". Each of these stages except the last one have been successively implemented. The stage of the present day Twentieth Century is known as *"Ghor Kaliyuga"* that is, the worst period of the Age of Darkness. It terminates the historical period between the manifestation of the sixth point (the Incarnation of Lord Jesus Christ) and the advent of the seventh one. We are quite near the completion of the cycle, in the very "last days" announced by many different scriptures.

HH Mataji once wondered: "People who accepted Christ were simple and uneducated fishermen, but priests and administrators rejected Him. Even today will people at the helm of affairs —bureaucrats, scientists, "intellectuals"—accept Sahaja Yoga?."

To overcome the ego is quite a challenge, no doubt, but I still hope that many will. Aren't there many wise thinkers who are expecting a breakthrough that would give evolution its real meaning?

If the matrix of intelligibility which gives an account for the evolutionary trend of history (and its subsequent morphology) is nothing but an ever expanding implementation of awareness within matter, we have found the Ariadne thread to interpret History. Our scheme of interpretation applied to the present day Gestalt of world societies (advanced, less developed, least developed) brings forward a pattern of meanings. To the advanced scientists this general picture unveils History as an integrated organism of bio-social eco-systems. But as these eco-systems are by now completely upset, many researchers are predicting that the breakdown of human societies appears to be a serious short-term probability.

The Sahaja Yogi, of course, is equipped to announce a most cheerful and hopeful news. His great message is this: Much before the doomsday's breakdown of cataclysmic proportions, an epistemological breakthrough will take place which is going to save most of humanity and transform accordingly the Gestalt of the Twenty-First Century.

Indeed the fulfilment of history is neither Hegel's State or Marx's communist Society, or the capitalist Millennium. According to the information I am presenting in this book, the new Age is the one in which man will undergo the most fundamental revolution of his not-so-long-history: he will, in his transfigured field of awareness, realise direct knowledge of God, Reality, which is the very purpose of Universal evolution. Or, in other words, God will witness His own divinity within and through the awareness of the twice born. It is within the human being that the self-actualisation process of the Divine within creation is fulfilled. Indeed, when we look at the human brain tissue with the aid of powerful scanning electron microscopes and when we see this fabulous neural complex of cathedral-caves, we are looking at the physical landscape in which Spirit is to actualise itself within matter. This moment is called the individual's self-realisation (samadhi). The whole drama is a grand poem of Divine Love.

The purpose of the creation is to offer to man—the chosen child of the Holy Spirit and crown of creation[11]—the highest

---

[11] Even the Devas have to take a human birth in order to reach the stage of God realisation.

possible achievement; the merging into divine awareness. Then the divine Self within man (Atman) which is the reflection of God Almighty, will know itself: the phenomenology of this tremendous process has been symbolized by the Archetype of the Son-Hero Saviour and by the myth of the Quest. The human seekers are the knights of the Grail. The "Lost Paradise" to be found again is Man's divine nature and the finding of it is the total Alchemical mutation that Medieval alchemists were hopelessly looking for in the philosophal stone. We are to become the *"Sakshi Swarup"*, the witness of the Divine Play. This new awareness generates a corresponding divine world: it is the Realm of Sacred Glory of which the great mystics of all religions had a glimpse in their "beatific vision"; it is the Kingdom of God promised to the children by Lord Jesus through the coming of the Holy Spirit. It is the pure land of the Boddhisattva Amithaba. HH Mataji says: "The children will be playing with the toy of Creation that God has created for them."

Self-realisation, enlightenment, (Samadhi, Nirvana), means firstly the merging of the individual human awareness with the Primordial Energy i.e. with the Mother; the Mother will gradually introduce the child to the Father as the Energy of God knows God; from a human standpoint the Almighty Father is utterly beyond man's cognitive reach and the Mother's grace is the indispensible mediator. This has been beautifully expressed by the place of the Virgin Mary in Christian theology.

Everything that has been generated by the Primordial Mother has to be perfect and holy. But complete freedom was granted; it was a necessary element of the perfecting process. Abusing this freedom, some created beings took to evil ways. These satanic forces could bring out of balance the lowest forms of energy (instinctual animality, subconscious libido) and they are especially aiming at the perversion of the human energies. It is in this respect that the Mother has been depicted as a hostile figure to these satanic forces because she intervenes to save Her Creation. This is why Coatlicue (meso-Amerindian Goddess) or Kali could be depicted in frightful traits. They are frightful for the satanic.

In the evolutionary process the hero's attention has been raised from the lowest to the highest forms of Energy. We must seek to free ourselves from the entanglements in the lowest forms of energy and, like St. George, kill this dragon. But one does not attain freedom by an outside show of asceticism. It is only through a genuine, inner struggle that we bring our attention to deeper stages of consciousness. The obstacles are there to overcome. The Mother wants Her child to grow. She is guided by Love. She is Love, Love and nothing but Love and thus She wants Her child to reach the very best, to enjoy what She has created for Her child.

The difficulties, fears, sufferings and death of the mythological records are indeed an essential part of the process of man's ascent; in order to resurrect to his divine Self through the Grace of the Mother, man has to die to his ego and super-ego; the process is agonizing enough, for the human psyche always threatens to be swallowed by the dragon-whale of the lowest involvements which would represent the regression of the psyche and the failure of the hero. But at this point, to quote Jung's pertinent remark, the Oedipus Complex is metamorphosized into a Jonah-whale complex: the fear is not of the incest but of the annihilation.

The Divine Mother gives the required sense of security and purity.

The awareness of the Divine is the highest stage of consciousness energy and it is granted by the Immaculate Mother. Shri Gauri's immaculate conception of Lord Ganesha and Mother Mary's immaculate conception of Lord Jesus manifests that the Divine Mother, the Immaculate,[12] grants spiritual rebirth to Her child.

Since man's consciousness awareness is to merge into the Divine Energy at the culmination of the cosmic drama one can truly say in this respect only, that the child has to re-enter the Mother's womb (*Kumbha*). This spiritual womb of our rebirth, or second birth, is nothing but the Mooladhara (not the chakra),

---

[12] Names are often given under the guidance of the Unconscious and, in this respect, HH Mataji's names are quite interesting. Nirmala is the sanskrit word for Immaculate. In Her childhood She was called Neera (Born from Water, Miriam, Marie). Her maiden name was Salve which reminds us of the ritual "Hail Mary" in Latin: "Salve regina coeli...". The Spanish speaking guests of HH Mataji in Colombia were surprised at this coincidence. After marriage, HH Mataji's name became Shrivastava. "Shri" means "the Goddess" (the Holy Spririt) and "Vastava" means "in reality". So, by a playful chance, Nirmala Devi Shrivastava reads "The Immaculate Goddess, the Holy Sprit in reality".

which is the house of the Kundalini.[13]

So, at last HH Mataji answers Hegel, Karl Marx and all those who waited for the culmination of History.

Human awareness is the medium and the field of the great mutation, the means whereby the Shakti-Spirit-Energy actualises itself in the human consciousness and hence, in World history; the cardinal point of this process within History can be described as follows: it is the possibility for a significant number of human beings, to develop the cognitive tools by which the union with Reality is to be achieved. This time has come. Self-consciously, quite a few men today are writing their history as the poem of the History of God. According to Henry Drummond's *The Ascent of Man* the meaning of history is given by what it moves towards, not by what it evolves out of. Similarly, the evolution which is beginning now, is an involution rather than evolution. It amounts to consciously rejoining the divinity that we came from. This involution can also be termed evolution in consciousness because we will participate in the process with our full awareness.

Whatever names we give to it, Copernician revolution of the psyche, Satori, Parousia, the happening of Self-realisation brings joy. "Oh! All this was a huge joke! Now I see..." In London some Sahaja Yogis just laughed aloud when they got their rebirth; "Oh! That was the thing!" Through tears of laughter and joy they gazed at the smiling eyes of HH Mataji realising the very fine humour of the hide and seek play.

Self-realisation represents the completion of the programme at the microcosmic level of the human individual. It represents, when implemented at the mass level, the completion of the programme at the cosmic level, that is, it triggers the awakening of the seventh chakra of the Virata. In this sense we can say that self-realisation manifests the fulfilment of history. In this same way we can say that the history of God and the history of man are two different versions of the same story. In concrete terms what all this means is that we can now enter into the cognitive realm for which we have been struggling for millennia; Sattya Yuga, the Golden Age, the Kingdom of Heaven, the Pure Land.

---

[13]The human womb in the woman and the prostate in man are the gross physiological manifestations of the subtle Mooladhara. Another word for the abode of the Kundalini is : Kulakunda.

Although these last statements may stir the scepticism of many a Western reader, there is evidence that the proposition of the New Age is as old as the Western consciousness itself. The expectation of the coming stage of fulfilment has been carefully printed in the human psyche by ages of eschatological expectations (*eschatos* in Greek means the last, that is, the last days) and it can be considered as a thematic unit pervading the mythological consciousness of quite different cultural traditions. It should be seriously considered if only because, as an archetype, this idea is a generator of psychical energy which has thoroughly conditioned —for the best and more often for the worst—the vagaries of European politics.[14] The announcement has been exploited to a maximum.

The eschatological scheme was usually revealed by an appointed doctrine (e.g. the seventh chapter of the Book of Daniel, the Sybilline Oracles (IV Century AD), Marx's *Kapital*, Nazi Rozenberg's *Myth of the Twentieth Century*) in the following way: The hosts of the Antichrist are about to win; but an elite of redeemers led by the Deliverer—Messiah successfully fights the last struggle leading to the new era. Following this belief the Maccabeans revolted against the Ptolemaic rule of Antiochus IV Epiphanos (165 BC). Constantine triumphed over Maxentius and inaugurated the Roman Christian Empire (IV Century AD). This same scheme led Godefroy de Bouillon to take Jerusalem, Frederick II Hohenstaufen to fight the Pope, Thomas Munzer to raise the German peasants against their lords. In modern times the new era would no longer be the second coming of Christ and the millennium but the highest phase of the Communist Society or the Nazi Third Reich. The hosts of the Antichrist had fought in the armies of Antiochus and Maxentius, the Moors and Saracens, the Church of Rome (Joachim dei Fiore), the clergy and medieval ruler (Munzer), the capitalists (Marx) while the redeemers were found in all sorts of chosen people, elected of Yahwe, crusaders or revolutionary vanguard of the proletariat. The last implementation of the scheme, forty years ago in Nazi Germany, has been its sardonic, satanic parody. The "hosts of the Antichrist", Jews, Bolshevicks and inferior races are overcome by the "Aryan redeemers" led by the "Deliverer" Adolf Hitler. The outburst of Nazi Satanism leading

---

[14]See Norman Cohn. *The Pursuit of the Millennium* (London 1957)

to World War II can be understood in the phenomenology of consciousness as the attempt of the forces of Evil to have man definitely forget the prospect of his own perfectibility that was announced by the eschatological scheme. After the horrors of that war it became hardly possible to think that the Golden Age was within man's reach. And yet it is, here and now.

The eschatological scheme has been provided for man by the Universal Unconscious, that is, the mind of the Virata, in order to announce the coming of the new era. In the *Kalki Purana* the tenth incarnation of Lord Vishnu brings an end to this Kali Yuga (Age of Darkness), this last period of the cosmic cycle when we developed our present level of cognitive capacities. In the four Gospels and the Book of Revelation to John the same event is prophesized, similarly leading to the Sattya Yuga, in the "heavenly Jerusalem". As usual this scheme has been distorted and exploited for political ends. My purpose is to now bring the eschatological sequence into its correct perspective, that is, to identify the actual happenings that the Universal Unconscious announced when it projected the eschatological scheme in the minds of the seers.

—*"The Doctrine"* is the doctrine of Sahaja Kundalini Yoga which was practised by the great ones such as Lord Buddha and Lord Mahavira and which is now revealed by the Grace of the Adi Shakti at the mass level of Sahaja Yoga; it is the doctrine of the spontaneous union.

—*"The hosts of the Antichrist"* are made out of the innumerable people whose psyche is overpowered by and identified with the forces of Evil (in the form of UPIs, satanic ego, etc.). They perpetuate and spread in societies those behaviours which lead away from the Sushumna channel of Perfectibility.

—*"The redeemers"* are made out of the community of the realised souls belonging to all nations, tongues, castes, etc. They have been redeemed by the Grace of their Kundalini and are now actively working at raising the Kundalini of their fellow human beings so that they also can be redeemed by their own Kundalini. We can consider the realised souls to be the redeemers to the extent that they are instrumental in this task of redemption.

—*"The Deliverer"* is Kalki, the tenth incarnation of Shri Vishnu; the returned King, who has been portrayed in both *the Apocalypse* and *the Kalki Purana*, as the destroyer riding a white horse. At the time of this writing, Lord Kalki has not yet been manifested and is still in a potential form in the brain of the Virata. He is already awakened in the brain of the Viratangana (the Shakti of the Virata) who has come in the form of HH Mataji. Hence, in all truth and for all practical purposes, HH Mataji Nirmala Devi is Shri Kalki. She is our hope. She is the Deliverer. She is salvation. She is the destination. No one else should be hoped for. When Shri Kalki will come in his fierce form, He will merely destroy.

—*"The last struggle"*. Strictly speaking the last struggle will accompany the coming of Shri Kalki and HH Mataji has not revealed anything about it yet. In a broader sense the last struggle has already begun. It is the attempt by HH Mataji and the realised souls to bring into this planet's biosphere the sattvic Divine vibrations of chaitanya. Every realised soul is an emitter of these divine vibrations and he is day and night fighting the negative vibrations in his environment.

—*"The new era"* is the Kingdom of Heaven brought onto this earth by the fact that human beings will participate in the divine, "heavenly" consciousness. There is no need here, or so I am suggesting, to predict the features of life on earth in the coming Sattya Yuga. The forthcoming change in society will be a product of the joint action of human and cosmic forces; there is just no way we can expect at this initial stage, to know what the process is going to be like. Also it is more meaningful to focus our attention on the present consciousness breakthrough which is the sine qua non condition for the advent of the new era.

By the Grace of HH Mataji there is one way in which this book can be very pertinently related to the history of the growth of your consciousness and thus to this eschatological climax of history.

AT THE BEGINNING OF THIS VOLUME THERE IS A PICTURE OF THE ADI SHAKTI IN THE FORM OF HER HOLINESS MATAJI NIRMALA DEVI. THE PICTURE OF THE ADI SHAKTI IS ENDOWED WITH THE POWER OF RADIATING THE VIBRATIONS OF CHAITANYA: THEY CAN GIVE REALISATION.

Now listen. Lord Jesus said we have to be born twice to enter the Kingdom; He said one has to be born of the Spirit; He said those born of the Spirit are like the wind, "he breathed on them, and said to them receive the Holy Spirit." (John 20.22.) Do you want to receive the breath of Christ? Do you want to receive the Holy Spirit? Are you asking for it?!

Chose a propitious hour, for instance early in the morning, a quiet room. Wash yourself; do not wear any shoes. In front of you put this book opened at the page of HH Mataji's picture and sit comfortably. Relax. HH Mataji says: "You have evolved from amoeba to the human stage spontaneously. Why should you worry about your coming evolution?" So, you do not have to strive to do anything. Just try to keep your mind quiet. Stretch your hands towards the picture, palms upwards. You might look at the Ajnya chakra of HH Mataji. Stay there for at least ten minutes.

Did you feel anything? A breeze or just a creeping sensation in the hands? An upward movement in your body? A sensation of well-being in the head? If you do not feel anything you should not feel upset. Be patient! As I said it took sometimes many days for HH Mataji to clear the chakras of some people. You should try again for twenty-one days every morning, with your feet in a basin of salt water. Afterwards, throw the water in the w.c. This will then offer each of the seven negatively charged chakras three times the chance to expell the negative vibrations into the salted water which works as an outlet.

This may sound fantastic and you may not do it. But remember, we are talking about God Almighty. Do you understand? Do you realise how fantastically dynamic His power is? His mere desire creates Universes! If you say that you believe in His powers, does your faith end up with Sunday mass, prayers at the Mosque or the study of the scriptures? Now the time has come to really know Him as the living true God. I would even suggest to you to ask an absolute question to the photograph: "Are you the Holy Spirit?" or "are you the Adi Shakti?" You may ask any absolute question such as "Is there God?" Amazingly enough, many have felt the breeze very strongly. It is the answer: "yes".

Some people whose Vishuddhi chakra is not all right do not feel the breeze but they feel relaxed and thoughtlessly aware. We have given HH Mataji's photograph to many patients suffering from incurable diseases: they did not even feel the breeze but have been cured.

Now, perhaps you understand why Moses and Muhammad forbade the making of images in the likeness of God. Unless and until the artist is a highly realised soul human creations cannot emit Divine vibrations. HH Mataji's photographs do; they raise our meditation and that is why it is right and good to handle them with due respect and worship.

You felt it? Isn't it great? Well, congratulations, Happy Birthday, Jai Mataji, Welcome! The next chapter is written for you.

8

After Self-realisation

Sahaja is spontaneity. It will always challenge any attempts to bring the free manifestation of divine energy into a humanly conceived system. This chapter is thus merely a collection of information, based on the experience gained by Sahaja Yogis. We are sharing this with you because we found out that many seekers coming to Sahaja Yoga with a heavily conditioned psyche need some time to cleanse their chakras and settle into the realised state.

But, first of all, it is fair to mention that some people do not need any further explanation. Along with the highly evolved souls, they feel the river Ganga rushing into their arms and body, filling each and every nerve with bliss. With closed eyes the growing silence in their being becomes light itself, while they are melting away, dissolving into a feeling of all-prevading greatness. When they open their eyes, having left behind time, space and illusions, they see the world around them, a spectacle, a play, a movement, offered to them for their enjoyment, to them, the Witness, the Self, the Child of God.

This same world that others see as a valley of tears has turned for them into the Kingdom of Heaven. We have heard and read recent descriptions of this state of grace by some of our elder brothers and sisters in Sahaja Yoga. They have described to us how they meditate on each chakra, how these chakras propel them into the various aspects of the cosmic consciousness and their letters are a song to the glory of the Paramchaitanyam Bhagavati Adi

Shakti Mataji Nirmala Devi. It might be premature to quote them here but they have asked me to call, on their behalf, the great poet Kabir.

"Kabir says: if you merge your life in the Ocean of Life, you will find your life in the Supreme Land of Bliss.
What a frenzy of ecstasy there is in every hour! And the worshipper is pressing out and drinking the essence of the hours: he lives in the life of Brahman.
I speak truth, for I have accepted truth in life; I am now attached to truth, I have swept all tinsel away."

Some of you may be self-realised from birth. We have a handful of born-realised people in our group. They have felt the breeze before and may be enjoying the witness state. But even the highest among them has to recognise HH Mataji Nirmala Devi, otherwise the vibrations start reducing. As a matter of fact some born-realised are not perfect and can be less receptive than a genuine seeker. All of them must come and learn all the secrets of Sahaja Yoga so that they can fulfil their realised state. As Christ said: "the light is not to be put under the bushel."[1]

However the experience of self-realisation of many people will be rather similar to that which most Sahaja Yogis went through. You feel a gentle breeze coming into your hands and this wind leads you into thoughtless awareness. You have crossed the gate of the Kingdom. Your ability to maintain yourself in it depends, among other things, upon the strength of your Mooladhara chakra and upon the width of the opening of your Ajnya chakra, which determines the state of the chitta (mental activity). The ego is still around. Moreover the complete past history of the seeker plays its part.

Many non-realised seekers think that self-realisation is the end of the road; but when we get our rebirth we start realising that it is in fact the beginning of life. Indeed the piercing of the Brahmarandra is at the same time, the end of the "old man" and the birth of the "new Adam". In this new life one should first of all

---

[1] We found out that many born-realised who came to us were suffering from arthritis. This is because, HH Mataji says, they have not used their spiritual power.

understand the value of the subtle plane of reality in which one has been born. Sometimes, when there are UPIs in the awareness, the seeker might not fully register the experience. Some just touch realisation and lose it again. Some feel their vibrations but, after a few days, start doubting the evidence of their own experience. Some question its value and meaning...

Spiritual rebirth is such a subtle happening that it should be received with a proper understanding. For instance, if a country achieves freedom without a struggle, its citizens will not understand the value of freedom. Rebirth, the freedom of Self, is granted by the Holy Spirit without any need for us to struggle and thus some new born seekers do not quite realise the priceless value of this spiritual freedom; they do not understand the greatness of the happening. The Holy Spirit is granting us an en-masse, effortless, "Jet Kundalini" realisation for the time has come for Her to manifest before the coming of the Apocalyptic Rider. After our realisation we should be keen to maintain it: the fight against misidentifications will enable us to establish the newly found freedom of the Self.

The vibrations are the subtle Chaitanya emitted by the Self. The twice born receives and emits them. The light of Self, which is translucid awareness, is kindled by Kundalini but we should keep the flame glowing; stormy waves might again blow from the ego and super-ego. I cannot become the keeper of the sacred flame without understanding and respecting the value of my rebirth. In this connection I should like again to refer to my own experience.

My case was very bad indeed. When I first met HH Mataji my mind was running wildly like a mad horse. In my seeking I had neglected my health and had developed serious liver troubles. I had become so dry and cerebral that I wanted to sort out everything through my brain. This poor thing—my brain—was not unlike a jingling piano player which was creating its own music thus greatly helping to increase the general frantic condition. I was dancing to that music in a rather clownish fashion, but around me no one could enjoy the show because all my friends were intellectuals too and about as thoroughly half-mad as myself.

By the time I met HH Mataji my search had reached its limit. I realised that I was living in a society that paid no heed to Dharma in a culture that excited my baser self and my ego alike. I was a bit puzzled to realise how "Kolossal" this one could be.

As I have already described, with my self-realisation I felt thoughtless awareness, peace and bliss. But my Vishuddhi chakra being in jeopardy, I could not feel the vibrations very clearly. My mind was in a turmoil. My ascent took the form of a slow moving drama; perhaps I had to record its various acts. Other Sahaja Yogis were much faster than me. HH Mataji never lost Her patience with me. She looked after me as if I really was a lost sheep. This time gave me an opportunity to clearly see the extent of the wasteland that we, westerners, have created within ourselves. I now knew that I belonged to a clan which is self-destroying, merrily frisking about the spacious, appealing, garlanded highway to Hell. Proud drunkards and sex addicts, pompous intellectuals which have made out of their brains a dumping ground of sterile ideas. I felt that it may be an impossible task to put this derailed, artificial society back on the right track again. This hopelessness would depress me and I could not allow myself to enjoy the bliss of the Self while the rest of my brothers and sisters were drawing each other towards Hell. My mind would know peace for a short while and be again dragged into turmoil and anxiety. Maybe I was just caught in the collective mess. Anyway, we now understand that, when we get self-realisation, we are not at the level of spiritual purity in which the past masters received the experience. Hence it is much more difficult for us to maintain the realised stage. Fortunately there are many Sahaja Yoga techniques which can help us.

What makes the present moment of history so dramatic is that, when the time has come to get self-realisation, the seekers are hardly in a condition to receive and keep it. HH Mataji often says that most of the ancient saints have reincarnated in the West. They get their realisation very quickly. While in developing countries where the attention is plagued by material problems the process is much slower. But the establishment of the realised state in the ego-dominated western mind is very slow. We have acknowledged mentally that matter cannot give joy, but while reaching this conclusion, we have overblown our ego. Moreover, to outwit the ego we took to extreme left-side behaviour: sex, alcohol, and drugs. These frantic extremes have created the tense, unsteady, nervous western personality.[2] To add to the chaos the false gurus have ruin-

---

[2] As Lord Ganesha controls the pineal body, the sin against innocence affects the pineal gland causing loss of attention, concentration and memory.

ed the chakras of so many seekers. That is why my Kundalini, though piercing the Brahmarandra and bestowing self-realisation, was again dragged back into the physical, emotional, mental and spiritual ditches of my being.

In India, people take time to get self-realisation because they are seeking materialism and only too often try to follow western life styles without realising what a dead-end our society has reached. But once they get self-realisation it establishes itself and these people often mature faster. They are helped by the fact that their native culture is based on Dharma and not on indulgence in baser pleasures. HH Mataji sighs: "One has the *chana*[3] (seeking) but does not have the teeth (innocence). The other has the teeth, but no chana."

Past experiments tell us that many people after a while slip out of the state of thoughtless awareness. Some of the new born Sahajis were upset by this. They found themselves again in their usual psychic environment (which might have been confusion)... After a few days they registered that the vibrations were no longer so strong while they were still confronting problems in their physical and social environment. A few of them were then assailed by doubts on the meaning of the experience of vibrations. If such is the case, I should explain clearly that there is strictly nothing to worry about but that one has to clearly understand one's own position.

Let us say you have felt the vibrations. This is the certificate of self-realisation that no one can sign but yourself: either you feel it or you don't. If you do, it indicates that the membrane at the top of your head has been opened by the Kundalini; usually it is a pinpoint like opening. We can say that, by Her Grace, the Adi Shakti has lifted your Kundalini above your Sahasrara, granting you self-realisation. However depending upon the condition of the chakras and the nadis, your Kundalini will not settle in the Sahasrara, but instead will return to Her abode in the triangular bone at the bottom of the spine. Then thoughtless awareness is disturbed and vibrations weakened.

There is no use in feeling frustrated in having been in the Kingdom and then to be out of it again. It would just throw you into the super-ego (lack of self-confidence, guilt, despair, etc.,)

---

[3] Chick peas.

and start a vicious circle of super-ego/ego. Just try to see where you slipped. Follow up Sahaja Yoga cleansing practices, and the realised state can be regained. For there are indeed major differences between a weakened condition and the non-realised state:

—Once the Kundalini has risen, She begins working on Her own to clear the chakras and nadis. One can feel Her sweetly tingling on the shoulder, rising in the spine or in the brain.
—The Kundalini knows the newly opened way to the Sahasrara and thus can ascend again.
—Through the subtle opening of the Brahmarandra one is connected with the all pervading subtle divine energy. It is the wind of the Holy Ghost that works to regenerate one's health (physical, emotional, mental).
—Through self-realisation one acquires specific Divine powers yet absolutely unknown. One should now learn how to use them in order to overcome difficulties and to settle into the realised state of the Witness.

We can say that, having received self-realisation by the grace of HH Mataji, now one has the capacity (and so the responsibility) to give realisation to one's self time and again, whenever needed. It is the choice of one's own sovereign freedom to decide to do so.

Self-realisation immediately starts a new machinery in the being; one feels the chakras in the fingertips, the spine or the brain; various organs and parts of the body record the problems to be corrected. One can correct one's own chakras and those of others. The first pressure I felt was of my puffed-up ego; it extended from the back of my left ear, up to the right side of the forehead. I could move it with the movement of my hands which were emitting vibrations. As the ego reduced I felt another pressure swelling in the right side of my brain: the super-ego. By giving vibrations, both of them were reduced towards the roots of the ears and I could feel the space of the limbic area between them. Thoughtless awareness spread from this space (*Vilamba*). As the Kundalini opened the Brahmarandra, the top of the head emitted a hot, then gradually cooler breeze; vibrations manifested instantly. Other Sahaja Yogis who were present in the room could feel them coming from my body. Then I learned the methods for raising and tying up the Kundalini. After some time, even a weak person like me could stabilize the realised state. I am only one among many examples which show that, with patience and determination (*sankalpa*), a wounded seeker can settle into the realised state. It is worth emphasizing this for it has also been shown that one can altogether lose one's vibrations.

You see, the Self is very sensitive. The catches on the chakras are indicating what is bad for our being. But the freedom to choose between good and bad is still intact. If one takes alcohol after self-realisation one feels pain in the Nabhi. But if the indication is deliberately ignored the vibratory awareness vanishes and one still has a good chance of becoming a first class drunkard. The moment of realisation has brought us on the central channel of Sushumna, the path of Dharma. In order to consolidate our position on this narrow channel and to firmly stand the lateral waves of the ida and pingala energies we help ourselves tremendously by respecting dharma. As a matter of fact, if we do not, we are quickly reminded by all kinds of signals that we are on the wrong track: bad vibrations, like tingling pressures, headaches, burning feelings, etc.

The vibrations indicate and gradually correct the physical, emotional and mental problems but they can be lost if one does not pay genuine attention to them, thus insulting the dignity of the Self's manifestation. I have lost...and regained, my vibrations many times, learning to shift my attention from gross and trivial matters. For quite some time after realisation my attention was still dragged to silly things but I could clearly see that, what used to be natural to me was in fact silly. By seeing the inside of my mind I came to discover good old UPI's crouching there trying to play tricks. I can also see them with my naked eye against the sunlight. In the practice of Sahaja Yoga I learnt how to identify them and drive them away. Many of us thus see our own Dark side and also cleanse it! HH Mataji says in Her very sweet way: "Unless and until there is light in the room how will you know what is wrong in it. Without light how can you cleanse the place or put it in a proper shape? So first is Self-realisation!" In the old days cleansing was first and self-realisation last. With the Sahaja Yoga of the modern time self-realisation is first and cleansing follows.

In other words, through enlightenment one can see the rubbish of evil within oneself. One wants to get rid of it. And that can be done; HH Mataji remarks: "Animals can lie in a stinking mud without being in the least disturbed. But human awareness would not bear it: it is a fact that bad smells are repulsive to human beings; we need not rationalise to understand this. But evil is not repulsive to human beings for they do not have the awareness of the realised state. After realisation you become aware of evil and the body shows the repulsion."

To the super-human awareness evil loses all its attractive powers. Gradually the former "temptations" are perceived as disagreeable, absurd or hideous aggressions. No point in feeling guilty, crying or brooding; we just face ourselves and get rid of it. We remove the attention from the objects in which it used to be helplessly engrossed. After realisation there is still a good deal of rubbish in us; but it is probably good that we can, for some time, see Evil face to face and see how repulsive and destructive it is. As the witness stage spreads in the consciousness, Evil cannot hurt us. The deep and thorough transformation of the Being is not, by any chance, a light affair that can be carried out overnight. It takes time to mature. Yet, when I look back at the transformation that HH Mataji has brought into my life, I am puzzled at the swiftness of Her movement and, above all, grateful for the depth of the dimension in which She operates and transforms. The Kundalini will not suffer one spot of the being to be left uncleansed. Sahaja Yoga takes root in a person who is genuine; despite a weak constitution such a seeker can establish his own self-realisation.

Self-realisation expresses the birth into a new life but the awareness and habits of the old one linger on for some time. For instance the human personality which has evolved from the animal stage still contains animal elements in its structure; it retains traces of its animal past. Furthermore, if a human baby stays with animals from his early childhood, he might forget his human nature. In any case, a baby has to grow up before being a fully developed person although from birth he is called a human being. In the same way a twice born is called "realised" from the moment of the opening of the fontanel membrane. But he has to grow and mature.

It's very simple, isn't it? Yet some people do not understand that much. They come to Sahaja Yoga programmes expecting that Sahaja Yogis should be perfect right away. They themselves of course should get a thundering realisation and be seated at the right hand of God the Father with all the angels of Heaven at their feet to give them transcendental experiences, sometimes a better job or the perfect wife... A few hippies who are as much misidentified with their long hair as executives are with their three-pieces suits, feel that long hair establishes their superior asceticism and behave with the consequent authority. A brain-washed Catholic preaches his gospel while burning everybody's Ajnya. A hatha yogi is not interested in self-realisation: the goal of his life is to suspend breathing, etc., etc.

Sahaja Yoga causes pure humour. Many seekers who come to the programmes with long faces are not able to control their laughter. We just laugh at the absurdities of modern life, at the idiocy of the behaviour considered normal in the contemporary culture. After realisation "the stupid joke is over" and we start watching it around us as a comic drama. Old involvements drop from us; we undergo a gradual but complete change.

The respective chakras have organic relationships with five seed-elements that the Vedas and classical astrology identify as earth, water, fire, air and ether. These seed-elements manifest the right-side cosmic vibrations which, in the material world, express themselves in the material elements of the earth, water, fire, etc. After realisation one can identify with the subtler principle of AUM within them; our relationship with the elements is thus transformed.

Let us take the example of the earth element (Mooladhara chakra, part of the Nabhi and of the Swadhistan), which expresses itself in MATTER. All our habits of comfort, behaviour, relationships manifest the grip of matter over us. After realisation priorities start changing.

I must say that renouncing those old habits which are detrimental to awareness becomes surprisingly easy once the fruits of the awareness joy are tasted. Other pleasures, in comparison seem quite tasteless and just fade away by themselves. Desires and the quest for satisfaction are now pursued on the line of the Sushumna, a tree which has many a delicious fruit. A supremely savoury one is desirelessness. Matter loses its possession value; the myth drops away. We enjoy something for sheer enjoyment's sake and not because the feeling of ownership gratifies the ego. The vanity fair of social showing off, exhibiting all the symbols of material wealth (My dresses, My car, My house, My antiques, etc.) is at the most perceived as an amusing but empty circus. We no longer seek short-lived satisfactions or phoney security through material accumulation. This aspect of materialism completely loses its flavour. The brain of a materialist is a flea market, a junk shop full of unnecessary envy, worries and desires; self realisation sweeps it out. And when the brain is cleared, one tastes the freedom of the spirit. Political independence and economic self-sufficiency cannot give any idea of what it feels like to be really free, to be free within oneself. Spiritual freedom is absolute; all the loads and the worries carried by the psyche dissolve. Surroundings have no power over us; we are masters of our lives.

The change of priorities of course transforms the criteria of judgement. One spontaneously develops a feeling for pure aesthetics; that is, in arts and in people as well, we can see holy, genuine beauty and, as we perceive it outside, we feel it inside also. Inversely we cannot stand the obscenity or vulgarity which all too often pollutes contemporary arts. And if a person is ugly and rotten inside, make up and artificial manners cannot hide it. For Sahaja aesthetics very much depend on vibrations.

Dead matter does not emit chaitanya vibrations but, when arranged in an ideal pattern which creates beauty, it starts emitting; we then perceive beauty as joy in the awareness! Beauty in behaviour is enjoyed in the same way; we relish our own virtues and those of others: innocence, generosity, dignity, modesty, friendship, etc. Misidentifications of the kind: "I am a hippie, a manager, a marxist," etc., are left behind like the snake's old skin. They do not catch the attention either: the junk shop has been cleansed. Attention flows to the Kundalini, the chakras and the genuine beauty. Human relationships are much more spontaneous and relaxed; social life changes for the best. We, at last, discover what it means to enjoy one another in the beautiful fullness of innocence.

Perfection emits perfect vibrations: we feel it as a cool breeze entering through the fingers, overflowing into the complete palm of the hand. Imperfect vibrations produce localised sensations in the hands, a feeling of tingling or a mild current in the fingers. Bad vibrations, or rather anti-vibrations, cause heat in the hands or the body, pressure, heaviness; tight feelings in the head, pain, shaking betrays the presence of UPI's. Various states of well-being correspond to these vibrations.

We are not involved in our body, its 'fitness' or appearance, but we respect it very much. It is indeed the temple with the seven tabernacles, the material sheath of the Atma, the vehicle through which the Divine awareness visits its creation. We keep it clean, neat and healthy.

We can cure ourselves and others with vibrations. For instance I cured my bad liver by application of my hand while taking vibrations from HH Mataji's photograph. My physical condition has improved so much that I really feel that I have a new body: no troubles, no doctors!

Every realised soul can develop and use his powers to cure people of various diseases. In an article on *Health and Sahaja Yoga* Gavin Brown writes:

> "Cancer, paralysis, organic malfunctions of all kinds, are cured, as has repeatedly been documented, not only by HH Mataji in person but by many of Her disciples who have achieved self-realisation by Her Grace. HH Mataji has often said that Yoga is the only cure for cancer."

The curing process relies on vibration therapy. I have witnessed many cases in which cures have been achieved. People who were condemned to death by doctors have been saved by Sahaja Yoga. But I must warn very frankly that the patient can fall back into his previous condition if he maintains behaviour which is incompatible with Sahaja dharma. A patient has to follow the diet! And why should the Kundalini cure someone who is not interested in Self-realisation? Kundalini heals the body because it is the temple where God is going to be enshrined. Thus Sahaja Yogis have no great interest in curing for its own sake; curing should merely be a by-product of Self-realisation.

Another astonishing property of Chaitanya vibrations is that they affect organic matter. For the first time we can give something to Nature. In the history of our race we have plundered and polluted Mother Earth in all possible ways. But now we can give her vibrations. At the Rahuri Agricultural University in Maharashtra, Mr. M. B. Dhumal and Professor M. V. Chavan have conducted irrigation experiments with vibrated water. The vibrated fields gave much higher yields than the fields irrigated by non-vibrated water.

The change in our relationship to matter is so subtle and deep that innocence, the essence of matter, starts blossoming within us.

At the same time we are much better off in all the concrete, daily aspects of our material life. We feel as if the angels are helping us. I recall here the case of Djamel, a friend from Algeria. For months he tried to be admitted to a post graduate school in London. Despite his good qualifications he had no success. A few days before going back to Algeria he paid a farewell visit to HH Mataji. She asked:

—"Djamel, when are you leaving?
—On Sunday.
—Why don't you leave on Tuesday?
—All right Mother."

On Monday he decided to drop in at the London Polytechnic. The registrar of the school told him: "You are admitted. When do you want to start your course?"

Matter entails life and death. Death is a form of matter's mutation. After realisation we understand death better. We know that:"nobody dies" and that the realm of the dead should not be allowed to interfere with that of the living. That is why we help people to get rid of UPI's. In this respect we discovered that some places and people are very uncongenial and we had to learn how to deal with antivibrations. The exercise is not always an easy one but we should realise that these bad vibrations are radiating anyway, whether we consciously feel them or not. Before self-realisation bad vibrations make one feel uneasy, nervous, physically upset, etc. By feeling them we can do something about them: In feeling a burning in one of our chakras we are already working out the energetic antidote against that negativity. The amelioration of the vibrations of the environment will also make us feel better. Let us not begin though by helping people who are emotionally very close to us because we are most likely to catch too much from them. We will be in a much better shape to assist them once we have gained some know-how through Sahaja Yoga praxis.

Once realised, by virtue of the organic relationship between the chakras and the elements, the forces of nature become our allied. For instance:

—Sitting on Mother Earth and also looking at the earth clears the chitta affected by Mooladhara chakra problems.

—Bathing one's feet in a river or the sea helps the clearing of the three lower chakras.

—Looking at HH Mataji's picture through a flame clears the Manipura and the Ajnya.

—Looking at the sky (air) helps clear the Vishuddhi and the Ajnya.

These are nothing but very simple and elementary tricks which stimulate our own creativity in drawing energetic support from the environment. The underlying principle is that, in order to leave you, bad vibrations are likely to need a support, an outlet. Little UPI is not going to leave if I don't give it a motorbike. This conveyance can be the elements, an insect, etc.

There are countless permutations and combinations of Chaitanya vibrations and matter. I hope that a Sahaja Yogi more competent than myself will expose some of the essential relationships between Sahaja Yoga and the physical, bio-chemical and medical sciences. For our purpose here it is enough for us to realise that Sahaja Yoga opens a comprehensive science of (physical, psychic, spiritual) man where anybody can be a doctor through praxis...to realise that we are one element of this cosmic ecology in which we can now consciously play our own music...to realise that it is in our "here and now" environment that we can start the dance.

We gradually discovered after our second birth that the vibrations are the second oxygen. We can feel the vibrations from the sun (which are cool) the moon, the sea, the sky, the trees, some temples, churches, etc., but, clearly, the strongest vibrations of all spring from Her Holiness Mataji Nirmala Devi or from Her picture.

The simplest meditation therefore is to sit in front of HH Mataji's photograph, with the palms of your hands upwards, everyday for some time, preferably at dawn. Through meditation I learned how to stay on the back of my mind-horse. The capacity of watching the mind became evident from the very beginning as I could see my ego and laugh at it. The great reward of meditation is to be able to develop the blissful quality of inward silence.

In deep attention, the one who meditates and the object of attention become one. So in meditating on the respective deities of the seven chakras we are expanding within ourselves the respective qualities of the deities. Meditating on the Mooladhara chakra we "become" the purity of Lord Ganesha. When our attention is tuned to Shri Brahmadeva in the Swadhistan chakra we gradually feel that everything in the Cosmos is pulsating, throbbing, arranging to create angles of beauty, order and harmony; we are one with it. At the Nabhi chakra level we enter into the subtle of the subtlest; we perceive the subtle Dharma in everything and everyone and we realise we are the instruments of Lord Vishnu; we feel part and parcel of His goodness and justice. In words and deeds we support others in their Dharma. At the feet of Dattatrya the Adi Guru the attention is enlightened by the majestic authority of the Truth. Through the blossoming of the Heart chakra we melt away in the joy of all pervading security and love. At the Vishuddhi chakra the awesome greatness of God may be experienced; the sadhaka is blessed by a deepening of collective consciousness. We know somebody simply by putting our attention there: our fingers and chakras immediately record the condition of this person.

When we reach the Ajnya chakra the eyes are closed. One may see the OM kara but ultimately silence as light is seen. We feel protected and enlightened, seeing through the darkness of ignorance without hesitation or fear, without hunger or hankering, fully resurrected.

The Divine Mother is the quintessence of truth, existence and bliss. When we keep our attention on Her we keep it on the Self which is of that same nature. When we meditate on HH Mataji in relation to the seven chakras we start experiencing that our seven selves are indeed part of the deities and that the deities are one with HH Mataji. Meditation on this identity opens the deeper stage of doubtless awareness. As we try to mediatate on HH Mataji's Kundalini we really get lost like a drop in the Ocean; we are absolutely silent. Joy starts pouring down like rain drops. Verily the Adi Shakti is described as *"Achintrya"*: "The one about whom one cannot think." Oh God of Glory! God of Love! God of Joy! What a feast Thou hast prepared for Thy children.

The flow of vibrations increases through the utterance of mantras. In Sanskrit *"manana"* means to meditate; a mantra is that which is uttered in the meditation: it is the phonetisation of vibrations into a specific sound, message and meaning. When a realised soul utters a specific mantra he mediates spiritual energy for the specific purpose to which the mantra relates. With the fullest possible devotion and attention we appeal to the deities of the seven chakras, beginning with the Mooladhara and ending at the Sahasrara. We thus ascend on the path of the Kundalini, raising our attention from one chakra to the other, invoking the successive names of the deities concerned. The mantra is at the same time the password at the gate of the palace (the chakra) and the salutation to the King (the deity). Sahaja Yoga has developed a full science of mantras. They are tremendously powerful and dissolve the obstacles on the path of the Kundalini because they awaken the deities and propitiate them to purify our psychosomatic instrument.

Meditation cannot be effective without full attention. Before realisation our attention is not under our control, like water draining off a cracked container, flowing into various external objects, restlessly carrying us away from our Self. Many of us were aware of this waste of energy but did not know what to do about it.

After realisation our attention deepens. The progress relies very much upon the time devoted to meditation, the conformity to dharma and last but by no means least upon the faith in Sahaja Yoga. "*Shradha* (Faith)," HH Mataji says, "is not blind faith but faith with enlightenment and verification; you must have faith!"

In this way, many Sahaja Yogis have automatically developed a considerable Self-control. The power of the consecrated attention can be compared to an invisible laser-beam which one aims at any part of the body to blast away bad vibrations. Let us say you meditate in front of HH Mataji's picture and you feel a burning in the right hand little finger which corresponds to the right side of the heart chakra; you send your attention to the right chest and after a matter of seconds the burning disappears, indicating that your energy has blasted away the "bad vibrations", UPI, etc.

—For instance, we are in front of HH Mataji's picture and we feel a burning in the right thumb. The sensation indicates that there is a tension on the right side sympathetic channel on the Swadhistan chakra whose right side is thus constricted. The problem can be due to over-activity of the right S.N.S. such as too much work pressure; too much physical activity; too much mental activity, etc. If the right thumb shakes it means we are possessed by a supraconscious entity. (This can be due to asahaja meditation, past attempts at controlling the mind or the body, etc.) We then put our right hand towards the picture of HH Mataji and the left hand on the right of the Swadhistan so that we directly channel the energy to where it is in special demand. After some time the burning disappears. The sensation is also felt directly in the body: one proceeds in the same way.

—We can raise our own Kundalini with our own hands by an ascending movement of our palms along the Sushumna; one can do it three times once for each of the nadis. It works better in the presence of HH Mataji or Her photograph.

—You can balance the nadis and the psyche. If I feel too agitated, restless or over-active, I raise, with my right hand, the Mahakali Energy of the Ida Nadi channel by an ascending movement along the left side of my spine, up to the Sahasrara. I do so because my state of mind indicates that this energy is lacking while the Mahasaraswati Energy of the Pingala Nadi is being overly used. I push down the latter by a descending movement with my hand along the right side of the spine. The fingers are directed towards the body as they work as energy transmitters. The right hand is always used because it represents the determination of the conscious being. Also, if one feels depressed or apathetic one can raise the energy in the Pingala Nadi and push down the Ida Nadi. We really feel that we are actually bringing ourselves into balance, nearer the equilibrium point.

—When they are in a proper shape the chakras are whirling wheels of energy, in the horizontal plane, rotating clockwise in their respective places of the body and sending forth the vibrations of the deities who preside over them; the Kundalini gushes in them to supply the energy. When we feel a tension or a pain in a chakra we can stimulate the rotation of the chakra. With the right hand we draw circles around the corresponding place of the body clockwise in front and anti-clockwise if we do it on our back, depending upon where we feel the obstacle. We feel the chakra being cleared. Sometimes the obstruction is a UPI and we hunt it down moving to another chakra ascending or descending a nadi, until finally it is expelled, occasionally through the Sahasrara.

The impact of these gestures which emit vibrations depends of course upon the level of awareness—energy that you can transmit with your hand. If there are many physical and psychic malfunctions, the process will take more time and the vibrations will be weaker. The force of the vibrations depends upon the force of the Kundalini at the Sahasrara and before ascending there the Kundalini dwells in the places of the body where there are obstructions (that is why, by the way, you can sometimes see with the naked eye the Kundalini throbbing at the level of a chakra because it is fighting the obstacle there). But whatever the condition of our energy may be these gestures have an impact even when we can not feel it. We realise the truth of this statement when our perceptivity increases.

The mind is our horse. If it is allowed to roam about in the attractive grasslands or to wander in the woods it will take us there; if it knows that we genuinely want our salvation it is our conveyance and, ultimately, when we reach the door (Ajnya chakra) of our ascent it stays at the door and leaves us in thoughtless awareness.

It is never too early to gather together whatever attention power one has to help one's spiritual Self. But how to do it? Buddha has said that when one attempts to control the mind one finds it frisking about like a fish thrown out of the water. The shastras and the puranas have compared the mind to a crazy monkey stung by a bee. Furthermore all practices of mind control support the identification with the ego and not with the Self.

Thoughts come from the past (super-ego) and the future (ego) into the present (conscious mind); the space of the present (*Vilamba*) is very small...and there only can peace of mind be found. Because of linguistic and conceptual developments the conscious mind of the modern man is constantly flooded by thought waves. When a thought reaches its end the attention jumps on to one of the many thoughts which are queuing up at the borders of the conscious mind; they want to capture our attention at the very second the previous thought ends.

With the entry of the Kundalini into the limbic region (Sahasrara) the space between two thoughts very much widens. The attention is carried above the lateral flow of thought waves like a lotus emerging from muddy waters into the fresh openness of the limbic region; the vertical ascent of the attention brings you into the everlasting present. Of course, after self-realisation, the sea of thought waves can rise again, but if one remembers the first experience of self-realisation in which the Vilamba has been felt, it is possible to recreate again the space of thoughtless awareness. This space widens spontaneously in the presence of HH Mataji; Her *darshan* (physical presence) silences the psychic agitation.

Thoughtless awareness gradually settles down in the Sahaja Yogi. Meanwhile, to watch one's mind gives a good training. HH Mataji says "Be watchful at the beginning of a thought because you never can catch its end". We should be able to watch the images, thoughts and moods which flow through our mind without being caught and involved in them. This becomes much easier with Sahaja Yoga because we can rest on the Sushumna dimension that the Kundalini has prepared for us. This is the stand point and the watch point, the steadfast boat on the moving sea of the psychic waves transmitted from the ego and the superego. Once we are realised when we say "NOW", we can climb back into the boat, that is rejoin thoughtless awareness. After some time, when the thought waves settle down, we begin to see images or short visions... they emerge from the subconscious and the supraconscious and can, sometimes, look very pleasant, fascinating or even clestial; they test the witnessing power of our thoughtlessness; we should deny them and refuse to get involved: the goal is the Self and its Reality : *"Twamekam Sharenyam Twamekam Warenyam"* "Only You are to be sought and are to be surrendered to".

By learning to witness mental and emotional waves we not only develop the vitally important witnessing power; we evolve a very deep and subtle understanding of people's moods and motivations; and above all we can merge into collective consciousness.

In collective consciousness we are aware of each other although there might be thousands of miles between us; simply receiving a letter from another Sahaja Yogi can uplift the energy. HH Mataji often remarked: "God's telecommunication department is very dynamic". Collective meditation is the first experience of sharing the intensity of the Kingdom of God. One of the greatest blessings that God can grant us is to meet, to live with, to be surrounded by other Sahaja Yogis. The community of the self-realised (the Buddhist "*sangha*") definitely assists each individual's progress. There is a certain "divine arithmetic" of numbers in Sahaja Yoga; seven Sahaja Yogis or more transmit more energy. The mere increase in the number of the realised souls is strengthening everybody's awareness. It is a cosmic, minute and automatic process.

If my Vishuddhi chakra is obstructed you will feel it in your throat; if you are emotionally disturbed we will have to soothe your heart chakra. The collectivity of the Sahaja Yogis nearly fits the words of the Prophet Muhammad:

"All Muslims are as one person. If a man complaineth of a pain in his head, his whole body complaineth; and if his eye complaineth, his whole body complaineth."

At this stage, we could bring a subtle, integrated perspective into the enquiries of contemporary scientists and in the teachings of Lord Jesus Christ who announced the advent of the Holy Spirit.

In the last chapter of *Supernature*, Lyall Watson, the biologist, speaks like a prophet:

"We are indeed larvae, eating our way through earth's resources in a mindless, caterpillar fashion, but I believe that the imago is already beginning to stir within. When the climate is right, it will break out not as some sort of supercomputer but as an organic being that will embody all of Supernature and look back on technology as a childhood toy".[4]

These lines express the expectations of the imminent advent of a collective being. This collectivity is also at the core of a solemn promise which has been made a long time ago:

"In that day you will know that I am in my Father and you in me and I in you" John 14.20. "And I will make it known that the love with which thou has loved me may be in them and I in them." John 17.26.

[4] Lyall Watson *Supernature* (Hodder and Stoughton Pub.) 1973 p. 312

We, the Sahaja Yogis, have jumped into collective consciousness. Vibratory awareness is the breath of the Holy Spirit that carries the sublime dialogue between God and his new born child, the Sahaja Yogis. These vibrations are also being emitted through our being; of this we have no doubts! Furthermore the awakening of the Kundalini, traditionally described as the most difficult feat ever performed, has become a child's play for the Sahaja Yogis.

It is such great fun. Trekking in the high valleys of Nepal, I gave awakening to Tamang children just by playing with them. Walking in a city's street with my attention in my Sahasrara I can help the people around me by putting my attention on them; I know their problems, which chakra is caught up, which mantra can help them. When I meet some of my realised friends, my whole body is bubbling with joy...we are swimming like happy ducklings in the Ocean of the Cosmic Mother's love. Of course when I go into the city, to the office, etc., I catch all kinds of vibrations but gradually I handle them all right. I have also been able to give realisation to a few people. It is a very deep fulfilment; a great joy. The highest possible form of creativity (Swadhistan chakra) expresses itself in the power of transforming others.

It is most amazing that, despite my weak constitution, I could raise the Kundalini of many people from the very first day of my realisation. I have not heard of anyone so far who has been granted such power by his guru, not to mention the complete knowledge of how to use it. I could raise the Kundalini by moving my own hands! In other words, the power of the Self, the vibrations, had started manifesting through my gestures and attention. HH Mataji gave each of us such tremendous powers and knowledge so freely and willingly. What generosity and what patience! Does She conceive us, the Immaculate, Nirmala, in Her Sacred Heart and raise us to the promised second birth through Her Sahasrara by which a new collective Being is born? She looks so human and so simple. But how is it that thousands have seen the pulsating Kundalini of the seekers who touch Her feet? And thousands feel the wind of the Holy Spirit just from Her picture! Is She not the Incarnation of the Holy Spirit that the Kingdom of Collective Consciousness could open to Mankind? And what a Kingdom! Through our spiritual rebirth we enter into a state which is dynamic, not static. For some it is a slow, for many a fast moving ascent. The crowding thoughts which represent the sedimentation of the experience of others (through books, school, etc.) within our awareness disband and we start experiencing the Self. While scientists and researchers talk of exploring the outer space and colonizing the galaxy, a new kind of scientists have discovered the Sushumna secret path to the inner space. Thoughtless awareness leads to doubtless awareness in which the union of the Self with the great Primordial Being (the Cosmic Virata) is ever more deeply experienced through collective consciousness; the Yogi lives in a state of cosmic communion.

With the complete Self-realisation the full witness state is established, which is the aspect of God the Almighty that human beings can experience. Great souls live in a state of desirelessness, with powers over the elements and drenched in bliss.

The state of God realisation is the highest condition that a human being can achieve and so far only Buddha and Mahavira have reached it. Until God realisation one receives God's blessings by asking for it. With God realisation, the Self is empowered by God's powers. Karmas (actions) become automatically *punyas* (spiritually meritorious actions): whatever one does is an act of divinity; this is why Shri Krishna's Maha Kali's *samhara shakti* (destroying power) is fully justified. God realised souls and Incarnations take God's laws into their own hands. They administer His Kingdom.

9

Tantrism as an expression of evil

Imagine someone sitting on a crocodile mistaking it for a log. But suddenly he notices that the innocent log is in fact a deadly beast. And then the beast starts moving. He is really frightened. He shouts frantically. But his people around don't pay any attention and relax on their logs, enjoying the torpor of the leisurely river.

Imagine someone who lives with his friends on the first floor of a house. One day he goes in the basement and finds out that the foundations are absolutely shaky, full of cracks and fissures. The house might collapse any time. Half panicked he rushes upstairs to warn his friends. But they laugh at him: "There isn't even a spot on these flower paper walls; this house is perfectly safe; you are mad."

These examples hardly illustrate my condition when I discovered how the forces of Evil have been able to spread unnoticed. How they permeate modern norms and criteria of references, how they condition the behaviour of huge crowds of innocent people. I was shocked! I was frightened! Yet, HH Mataji told me to expose the truth. So, in this chapter, I want to take you with me in the basement of the house of men to show you the threat to our race. It is a threat to our body, mind, awareness and evolution. Its essence must be denounced now.

"Tantra" means a technique to handle a mechanism, while "Yantra" means the mechanism. The mechanism for the union of the human attention with God is called "Kundalini Yantra", and the knowers of the corresponding technique, "Tantra", are tantrikas, who should really be the Sahaja yogis. But in fact, the historical manifestation of tantrism often comes to mean just the opposite of the awakening of the Kundalini. Some so called tantrika confused spiritual, enlightenment with sexual perversions, indulged in black magic, spread violence and terror. In the modern times, the forces of Darkness are expressing themselves in new ways but along the same lines. Hence, in this chapter, we will use the terms "Tantrism" and "tantrika" to cover these various asahaja (anti-God, anti evolution) behaviours. Let us begin by exposing the original mistake: the confusion between Kundalini awakening and the sex act.

Sex is at the core of nature's song of life. God, HH Mataji says, has given sex to men and woman to be enjoyed fully in the institution of marriage which is a most important and sacred source of human happiness. First comes the encounter, the shyness, the romance, the sweet play. And then the beautiful poem of union, intimate and tender; it is a music spelling delicate notes of pleasure, joy and thoughtlessness. The love between husband and wife has to expand into deep state of oneness and the blissful intensity of sex[1] has to play its full part. This relationship has to be respected

[1] How does sex pleasure relate to the chakra system? The Mooladhra chakra, located at the base of the trunk, "where the body is sewed", is the only one outside the spine or the cranial box. When there is sexual activity, Lord Ganesha or Sushumna (Parasypathetic) innocently releases one millionth of Pranava (Divine Energy). This happens in every chakra wherever there is need for Pranava. The only difference is that the Mooladhra chakra is outside the spine and hence one feels the Pranava's effect for a short time, while in the other chakras, one does not feel it. Before realisation, we cannot enjoy the experience of intensity through the other chakras and we, of course, indentify intensity of a sensation with sex. When Pranava is felt the curiosity for this joy is aroused. In the state of complete realisation the limbic area in the brain is filled with Pranava. So, fully realised souls are all the time drenched in complete bliss for the Pranava flows in their Sahasrara from its very source, "Sadashiva".

The real dimension of sex is easy to understand. It is a result of the Mooladhara chakra's activity. The dharma of any chakra is to be respected. As far as the Mooladhara chakra is concerned this means enjoying sex in the privacy of married life. Then Shri Ganesha is pleased: sex is a spontaneous, joy giving parasympathetic activity. But if the God is insulted he receds and sex can lead to frustration, addiction or exhaustion because it has become a disconnected sympathetic activity. While men with a spontaneous sexuality are still happily potent at the age of seventy.

by the entire community: "Where the women lead a respectable life and are revered there resides the play of the Gods." If sex is made cheap and vulgar, it will disturb our awareness. If it is presented as a tool for spiritual enlightenment it can ruin our chance of evolution.

The mother of every individual, who is to grant his spiritual rebirth, is his Kundalini. She has only this one child.

It is very important to note again that she is placed in the triangular sacral bone (Mooladhara) above the centre which controls sex. In that centre, the Mooladhara chakra, Lord Ganesha, the child of the virgin, the personification of Divine Innocence, is guarding the protocol of the chastity of the Mother (Kundalini).

The subtle Mooladhara centre mainifests the gross pelvic plexus, and four sub-plexuses: The Mooladhara centre has four petals. The subtle petals manifest the gross four sub-plexuses which control and supply the vital energy (pranava) to the various organs as shown below.

4 *Petals* : 1. Inferior haemorrhoidal—Rectum
2. Vesical —Urinary bladder, vasculae seminalis, vas deferens
3. Prostatic —Genitals, prostate gland
4. Uterine —Uterus, fallopian tubes vasculae seminalis, vas deferens

At the time of Kundalini awakening the attention completely recedes from sex. One becomes like a child and, in this respect, the Freudian perception of childhood is completely refuted by Sahaja Yoga. A baby does not suck his fingers according to sexual drive but, very often, according to which chakra is obstructed. This spontaneous perceptibility of the vibratory environment becomes obvious in the case of born realised children.[2] Christ said that one has to be a child to enter the Kingdom of God and HH Mataji's greatest advisers are children. She calls them the vice chancellors of the Sahaja Yoga University.

[2]If someone smokes the child sucks the index finger (Vishuddhi chakra). If the father or mother has a stomach problem he sucks the middle finger (Nabhi chakra). Realised children know which chakra is caught; they shoot at people with their index finger when they see UPI's hovering around them they relieve people of their problems in all possible ways; they often play with water to relieve themselves from the burnings caused by surrounding anti-vibrations.

The fact that the palace of the virgin queen Kundalini (Mooladhara) is set above the guarding post of the Mooladhara chakra indicates that human beings are already programmed for evolution in such a manner that sex plays no part in it. But its missuse can be a direct challenge to this evolution. As previously described, a human being is a cell of the vast cosmic organism, the Virata. The cells are maintained in a proper pattern of relationships through family ties. The satanic forces have understood that to endanger the cells, they have to break this vital pattern. Therefore they concentrated their attack on the family, and their weapon to this effect is degradation through sex.

Their thoroughly devilish trick was to present sex degradation as a tool for spiritual rgowth; the blasphemy kills the cell's chances of evolution by spoiling the mother Kundalini. Such is the frightening secret of the old story of tantric occultism.

The roots of the darker side of tantrism are as ancient as the awareness of religion, and they have prospered in all the countries from time to time. In India the phenomenon came into full force during the years AD 900 to 1400. The compulsive religion imposed by Emperor Ashoka, the artificial, extreme austerity of Jain ascetics created an atmosphere of repressed sexuality which paved the way for the spreading of tantrism. Around the Sixth Century, absurd monastic ways of life of the three official religions, Hinduism, Buddhism and Jainism transformed the people into coloourless stereotypes of prudery. Although these religions believed in the middle path of righteousness and in marriage, the sex life, even in ordinary families, was extremely suppressed.

All the so-called religious elite believed that celibacy was the only way to salvation. In the same way, Christian methods of sex repression paved the way in the West for the propagation of Freudian ideas whose public acceptance ultimately led to the destructive permissiveness of the Western society.

Buddhism and Jainism preached complete renunciation, and among Hindus, Brahmacharya (celibacy) even after marriage was accepted as the only way to God. Even today, in all these religious sects, many young people take to unnatural celibacy. The temperate householders were looked down upon by the monks and ascetics who were supposed to have renounced the world. Those who had never gained any satisfaction from their phoney renunciation gradually gave up their forest dwellings, sought power as advisers to the rulers, and became the propagators of tantrism. The kings were licentious and permissive and gave royal support to their ministers. After a period in which the normal desires of human beings had been suppressed by "religious" artificiality, a strong reaction spread in the form of a public acceptance of tantrism. However this acceptance was mixed with fear for the common folk were really afraid of the tantrikas. They had become experts in witchcraft and could kill at a distance by controlling spirit possession. Violence very early on became an integral part of tantrism beside the accomplished arts of persuasion and enticement.

From the very beginning of tantrism, tantrikas proved to be the undisputed masters of mystification and mass conditioning. First they took over the world of Art, which was the most powerful medium of the ancient civilizations.

They befooled the simple, innocent craftsmen (*shilpakaras*) by convincing arguments. In Nepal, they told the artists that the Goddess of Thunderbolt is a virgin; so to keep her away from a temple, one has to decorate its walls and roofing with obscene eroticas. Another ingenious argument they gave is that we have to leave our passions and lust outside the temple, and hence all that is bad in us must be carved on the outer walls of the temple. Very clever indeed... Later on, all that is outside crawled inside. Yet the craftsmen who built these temples under the compulsion of tantrika ministers managed to play down this forced display of eroticism. The temple of Konarak is the exception to the rule, for the chief architect was himself a tantrika of the worst kind; hence the sculptures of the temple exhibit the naked dance of vulgarity. In the temples of Khajuraho, they put in full view the healthy joyous, divine figures of Gods and Goddesses; erotic groups are not within easy reach of the eye. Many Indians visit these temples without even being aware of the erotics but the foreign tourists, wildly run around looking for them. Similarly enough, in Nepal you have to search for obscene statues, which are usually carved near the roof. Of course, tourists equipped with cameras and zooms overcome this difficulty... and in Nepal just as in India local villagers watch them with contempt. For, despite all the efforts of the tantrikas, villagers found difficult to accept the aesthetics of vulgarity and the profanation of their Gods. Mostly foreigners pay attention to tantric art, and all the related books and postcards are printed for them. I have yet to meet an Indian householder who has read the Kama Sootra.

Yet, up until the Fifteenth Century, the ruling class of Hindu kingdoms, from North to South, from East to West, was completely brainwashed by the intellectual feats of our clever tantrikas. Competitions were held to reward erotic art. Secret sects, horrid rituals mushroomed here and there. Public festivals spread the tantric hold over the masses. In North India songs, language, and humour became gross and vulgar; jokes revolved around sex; relationships—even between brother and sister, adolescents and grand mothers—lost their joy giving innocence. The awareness regressed into sex, drugs, wine and violence.

Maharashtra and the southern states resisted Tantrism and, gradually, tantrikas lost the control they had gained over the pattern of life of ordinary people in Punjab, Bengal, Uttar Pradesh, Assam, and Bihar. But the adharmic wave had started. A Muslim Nawab having three-hundred and sixty-five keeps ruled over a territory which had been part of the empire of the great one who had magnified the one man-one wife relationship: Lord Rama. People who were formerly religious were driven into the very opposite of innocence and purity. A licentious and permissive attitude towards life created a society where women were dominated, insulted, and treated by men as objects of possession and cruel enjoyment. Children and youngsters lost respect for their mothers and were fascinated by glamorous courtesans. Prostitutes became wealthy, successful, socially important and were worshipped instead of the self-sacrificing, devoted housewife (Gruha Laxshmi) who brings auspiciousness to the family. This attack on womanhood clearly shows that Tantrism expresses the absolute negation of the family and of everything India stands for because it is a direct satanic challenge to the Great Goddess of holiness who is at the core of the Hindu family and worship. That is why many great saints such as Guru Goraknath, Gyaneswar, Kabir, Nanak, Basova, incarnated in India to oppose the tantrikas.

How could one deliver such a devastating blow to human dignity?

The demonic forces had first to remove the attention of the Divine from the area where Satan, the collective principle of Evil, wanted to operate. To this effect they devised a thousand methods to insult the gods in their own temples. The idea is to perform something extremely ugly in a place or condition which is blessed by the presence of the Divine. For instance profane a temple; proclaim ascetism, holiness, love and insult it by "free" sex; talk about ideal values and practise just the opposite. The Divine Presence or attention recedes, disappears, and in the vacuum thus created negativity can operate.

The trick can be better understood through the following example:

Centuries ago, the tantrikas discovered that when a blasphemy is committed in a holy place, the awareness of the Divine recedes from that place. For example Kali (Durga or Mahakali) is the goddess who presides over the left side of the Virata. In some very sacred temples of Mother Kali, they performed horrid ceremonies (ritual orgies, even murders) by which they pretended to be worshipping the Goddess. They would debauch young virgins in the temple of the Virgins, (Shri Gauri, Shri Ganesha). Although they were punished in one way or another, they adamantly carried on with the filthiest sins. In many sects the corruption of virgins became a ritual. The priests themselves enjoyed the brides before the husband. The most cruel practices were adopted: small children were sacrificed and the statues of the deities bathed in blood. Lamas buried them alive in the walls of the temple. Tantrikas used the bones and skulls of murdered men and women as their wine glasses. Most of them shared sex among themselves and some who were extreme celibates satisfied their baser instincts by killing innocent victims. Acts of extreme sex sadism (aghori) were performed in the presence of the Holy Mother Kali. Her attention withdrew from such profaned temples and the lower spirits of the subconscious, no longer kept in check by Her attention, invaded those temples at the bidding of the tantrikas. The common religious folk were told that spirit possession was the will of the Goddess. Or even worse, many said that the Goddess herself was incarnating. Even today, during the Nauratri festival, when the Mother Goddess is worshipped in Her temples, the tantrikas work out their methods of displeasing Her. In the day time the temple is flooded with a horde of lepers, beggars, hideous maid servants who get possessed. They start humming "hum hum" and go on swinging round and round. Some sing loudly, some tear their clothes off. The simple people who visit the temple believe that the

Goddess has entered into these clownish women. They give them flowers and money and, with great faith, put red powder (kum kum) on their foreheads as a token of worship[3].

Tantrikas work on the same principle as described before to spoil the nadis and the chakras of those who are seeking. They are aware that, in the centres of the spinal chord, there are deities seated who represent the different aspects of God. So they do whatever is possible to insult the divinity within man. If the seeker falls into the tantrika traps, the attention of God Almighty, who is watching through the Deities, ultimately recedes. The satanic guru then introduces a spirit in the chakra. (This is called "initiation"). After that, the unfortunate seeker confuses the symptoms and effects of spirit possession with awakening and spiritual growth. Sometimes they used "asanas" for the sex act, and controlled the semen, which they regarded as the nectar of life. Kabir has lashed them right and left; he reminds us that, "the nectar of life flows at the Lotus Feet of the Divine". One cannot understand to what limits of stupidity these dissatisfied, repressed ascetics have gone to express their hidden desires.

Over a few centuries, tantric writers managed to defile the authentic tradition of Kundalini Yoga. They attributed ambiguous, erotic meanings to the spiritual vocabulary which expresses states of consciousness. It is just very sad that modern intellectuals have stirred such an interest in these twisted writings. Moreover ancient books on the art of sex love for the married couple were spoiled through the introduction of various perversions.

The whole language of cosmology and mythology becomes charged with sexual connotations. In tantric texts, Mircea Eliade notices, "... we find ourselves in a universe of analogies and double meanings. In this 'intentional language' any erotic phenomenon can express a Hatha-Yogic exercise or a stage of meditation just

---

[3]These possessed women can exhibit miraculous powers or tell the future. They prophesize and impress people by the knowledge they have of their life: they can "help" to solve material or personal relationships but HH Mataji says: "only stupid and blind people can be befooled and have interest in them. Why not ask a simple question: What is the interest of God in telling you the number of the winner in the next horse race? What interest does He have in these material things? If He has to give, He will give something of supreme importance, our Self-realisation".

as any symbol, any 'state of holiness' can be given an erotic meaning"[4].

In the ambiguous allegories of the tantrikas, the lingam (Existence) and the yoni (Power), the vajra (Thunderbolt, Self) and the padma (Lotus, Sahasrara) become symbols for the sex organs; the *bodhicitta* (Enlightened consciousness), the *amrit* (Divine Nectar pouring down from the Sahasrara) are said to be the human sperm; the *bhaga* (cosmic matrix) of Bhagawati is a human womb, etc., etc., etc. Ancient sacrifices such as the Ashvamedha or the Yagna (fire ceremony) are profaned by sexual interpretations and obscene pantomimes. The great incarnations are profaned and insulted: the Divine Love (prema) between Shri Radha and Shri Krishna is reduced to an adulterous passion (*parakaya rati*) and the Bengalese Courts of Love[5] consequently make fun of conjugal love (*svakiya*). Buddhism undergoes the same disfiguration as Vishnuism. In the *Cina-cara-sara-tantra*, Buddha is "surrounded by a thousand mistresses in erotic ecstasy". Tantrism has become a sort of parallel world, a satanic shift of meanings in which all values are turned upside down[6].

The fire of Tantrism spread wildly through human societies and left behind confused priorities and disturbed awareness. This can be credited to human weaknesses but now, through vibratory awareness, one realises that tantrika sorcerers work through UPIs. Power obsessed and sex hungry, the tantrikas tried to exploit human beings in all aspects of human life, to connect evey human endeavour with sex activity and to reduce human awareness to the animal one.

In tantric India, as well as in other parts of the world, fertility cults were established. They overpowered a large number of kingdoms. Tantrikas have always been more interested in the urban crowd, especially the rich and the powerful. Many intellectuals and artists accepted tantrism as a part of cultural life. Art turned away from holiness and aesthetics extolled the flowers of

---

[4]Mircea Eliade. "*Yoga Immortality and Freedom*" p. 252.

[5]In Bengal they used to hold poetic competitions or tournaments with love as the subject.

[6]HH Mataji says:"If someone becomes blind in the month of sawan (rainy season) he sees everything green".

hell[7]. The victims of Tantrism were also good orators and writers, and the tantrikas used them to produce obscene lite rature describing how one reaches God through sex. Their books filled the libraries of the kings and they were given land and properties as a reward for creating pornography. In the process, tantrikas committed the ultimate blasphemy of insulting the Kundalini which is the sadhakas' mother and the manifestation of the Holy Virgin aspect of the Adi Shakti. The *Kularwana Tantra* (V. III-12) tells that "the true sexual union is the union of *Parashakti* (Kundalini) with *Atman*." In the tantric sacrifices of mahavrata, to effect the coincidentia oppositorum – the union of opposites—between ida and pingala nadis, a chaste young man (brahmacarin) had to unite with a prostitute (*pumscali*)! These practices were justified by clever theories of transphysical sex sublimation.

When one visits a new house, one should enter through the gate and not through the back door. Alas this is precisely how 19th and 20th Century western archaeologists and tourists discovered India. Their contact with the Hindu civilization was spoiled by the excessive interest they had in tantrism. They could not see, may be, that sex cult spoils sex love and that fertility cults destroy fertility. As so many westerners today seem to be worshipping the modern forms of such cults we could wonder whether their attitude is helping the drop of the birth ratio in the postindustrial societies. Foreign tourists queue to photograph the eroticas of Khajuraho and Konarak, foreign seekers easily become the prey of the modern tantrikas disguised as gurus, and intellectuals have completely misunderstood the spontaneous (sahaja) and holy (pawitra) nature of Kundalini Yoga. Actually, the bulk of the literature on Kundalini presents as "Kundalini awakening" the symptoms of the sympathetic nervous system, excited and exhausted by the activity which mishandles the Kundalini: (asahaja activity).

Arthur Avalon tells us (*The Serpent Power*) that the awakening of the Kundalini arouses an intense heat and its progress through the chakras is manifested by the lower parts of the body becoming as cold as a corpse, while the part through which the Kundalini is passing is burning hot. The Buddhist tantras speak

---

[7] We should rather speak of hell's "publicity department" that is, the apparent attractiveness of vices. Hell itself does exist. Its horror has been meticulously described by Lord Mahavira.

of "the great fire". Other texts quoted by Lama Kazi Dewa Samdup and W.Y. Evans-Wens (*Tibetan Yoga and Secret Doctrines*) attribute this heat to the transmutation of sexual energies. All these explanations are nothing but tantric rationalizations to cover up tantric amateurism and spiritual naivety. What actually happens can be described as follows:

Sahaja Yogis have seen the pulsation of the Kundalini at the base of the spine (Mooladhara). But tantrikas confuse the (Mooladhara chakra (abode of Shri Ganesha) with the Mooladhara (abode of His mother Kundalini). When the Mooladhara chakra that controls the sex is excited for Kundalini awakening, Lord Ganesha gets angry and he pours out his wrath that is felt as the "great fire" or the "inner heat" (in Tibetan gtum-mo).[8] As the pelvic plexus is connected with the left and right side sympathetic nervous system, the wrath of Shri Ganesha spreads through the SNS, causing overactivity and chain reactions.

The symptoms can be of various types: some people go into trance, start dancing or shouting, jump like frogs and suffer tremendous heat. In mass hypnosis they can take off all their clothes. Sometimes they get blisters on their bodies and feel as though they have been bitten by a thousand scorpions. Genital activity increases. Apprentice sorcerers in Kundalini Yoga are most eager to share their experiences with us. We can read in a magazine devoted to (pseudo) Kundalini experiments the following account of Kundalini "awakening":

"My mind was *hyper*-hyperactive as I tried to understand what was taking place. Physically, I went through a variety

---

[8]Shamans and sorcerers sought mastery over the inner fire. Perfected Kirlian photographic apparatus registers the heat of the SNS as an increase in the brightness of the corona. Lyall Watson reports such experiments ("*The Romeo Error*" p. 163): Increase in brightness was shown after the subject had taken a drink of alcohol, or with marijuana, transcendental meditation, psycho-kinesis, acupuncture and spiritual healing. It is totally overlooked that the increase in the brilliance of the aura indicates a short circuit in the "overloaded SNS; it is nothing but a red light warning signal pointing out an artificial excitment of the SNS which is exhausting the limited pranava (vital energy). The problem with Kirlian photography is one of interpretation. After some years of practice with vibratory awareness we can make out when the increased brightness of the halo around the palm of a spiritual healer indicates the presence of a UPI. Only a few healers are born-realised. Tantrikas can also cure diseases through UPIs but the long term result is the wreckage of the nervous system.

of symptoms, including anorexia, headaches, trembling, fever with alternate chills, nausea and dizziness. Emotionally, I went up and down the keyboard of euphoria, joy, bewilderment, anxiety, depression and the familiar despair. I was at times deluded and often disorientated. On one occasion, I actually believed that I had died. Such peace! I was almost disappointed to realise I hadn't. I was afraid to leave my apartment for fear someone would notice my schizophrenic-like behaviour. I gazed into a mirror and observed a "wild" look..."

Burning overactivity of the SNS is similarly reported as Kundalini awakening by an "authority" on the subject. He describes his experience as follows (*Yoga Today* April 1978);

"The heat grew every moment, causing such unbearable pain that I writhed and twisted from side to side while streams of cold perspiration poured down my face and limbs. But still the heat increased and soon it seemed as if innumerable red-hot pins were coursing through my body, scorching and blistering the organs and tissues like flying sparks. Suffering the most excruciating torture, I clenched my hands and bit my lips to stop myself from leaping out of bed and crying at the top of my voice. The throbbing of my heart grew more and more terrific, acquiring such a spasmodic violence that I thought that it must either stop beating or burst. Flesh and blood could not stand such strain without giving way any moment."

What an attractive, heavenly experience of spiritual liberation! After reading this, one really feels a deep yearning to be born again!...

Such symptoms take place because of the novice and/or sinful handling of the Kundalini Yantra by an unauthorised person. Cancer, which is caused by overactivity of the SNS can also manifest similar pain. How can a sane man believe in self-realisation through tortures? The Kundalini is the spiritual mother of the seeker. She patiently waited through all the lives of the seeker for the moment of spontaneous salvation, and would never torture her only child. As David Baxter puts it ("sahaja yoga" in *Yoga*

Today November 1978) "Pain is caused by idiotic attempts to raise Kundalini. If she is planted in us by the Divine would He want Her ascent to be painful? Her rising is completely soothing and relaxing." Kundalini rising can only be the supremely pleasant experience that we have already described. It is an inside happening, silent, majestic, blissful.

In a non-realised being, the conscious mind is not aware of itself because it oscillates between the past and the future. We are constantly riding the waves of thoughts. When an individual thought ends, for a split-second the mind is devoid of thoughts and in touch with the present. But immediately the vacuum is, so to speak, bombarded by thoughts from the ego and the super-ego, and a new thought carries our consciousness outside. The inward happening of Kundalini rising sucks the attention inside. The space of thoughtlessness (*Vilamba*) increases and later, ego and super-ego deflate and recede into pingala and ida nadis. First the Kundalini showers the cooling divine power onto the lower plate of the brain (*Moordha*); one feels very relaxed and a bit sleepy; the cool, soothing feeling later on trickles down ida and pingala; no fire, no tortures, no gesticulations. Already when the Kundalini crosses the Vishuddhi chakra, very often the face starts changing, becoming mild, radiant and divine. Little children get their realisation very easily and usually go off to sleep: no spiritual preparation, no exercises were required... a smile of HH Mataji did it!

This is precisely the trouble with Sahaja! It is just too simple to be true. You know, people have their own ideas. They have sorted out what should happen when one meets Reality: one has to jump like a frog or shiver like an epileptic. One is blinded by a great light. One has to pay money for it (you can use credit cards). One has to go to church and sing together—it feels so nice. One has to disturb the traffic in Oxford Street, faithfully hopping and shouting God's name. One has to shave one's head. One has to wear orange clothes. One has to worship a little fat boy who is the "satguru" and who sits on a throne two stories above the bent heads of the crowds; one has to buy many Rolls-Royces for the fat little boy. One has to enlist inmeditation classes; a good bank account opens for you the hierarchy of transcendance. One has to prostrate oneself flat on the ground before the great lama from Tibet on the marble floor one has prepared for the great lama (very expensive). You do it one thousand times! And as the lama told you to fast before this auspicious day, you are sure to remember the experience.

Maybe the tantrikas appeal to the ego of the seekers by letting them believe that they can buy, gain, achieve their own self-realisation. This myth of efforts and strivings of course attracts the ego: "I" can do it, "I" can pay for it, "I" can achieve it. Of course this attitude works on the sympathetic system and the seeker starts progressing on the lateral channels, ida nadi on the left, pingala nadi on the right. They eventually experience new phenomena of awareness and interpret them as an evolution of their consciousness. But as HH Mataji says, "Whatever is unknown needs not be Divine and whatever is written needs not be scriptures"; UPI's and drugs give experiences but they take you away from the inner space of the Self.

Unguided seekers will not be likely to fall into the clutches of the tantrikas if they understand one simple thing. Any new phenomenon of consciousness does not mean progress; it might express regression and self-destruction. Any special power exhibited by anyone does not mean Divine Power; it might express a spirit's power, the power of the Dead. Actually if you try to reach your yantra in a naive or unauthorised way before self-realisation, you are bound to damage it. It is like trying to get a car moving without switching on the ignition.

"The seed has to sprout in its own delicate, spontaneous way," HH Mataji explains, "You should not touch its germinating power before it has sprouted"; nor should anyone else. Alas, believe me, evil is very much at work in the world today. Before going to a guru, be careful, use your common sense and the whole tantric scene will appear to you as a huge joke. There is a Yogi and a Baba, a Rishi, a Guru, a Swami and a Bhagawan. All holy people as the names show. They are heading different spiritual movements but they have one thing in common: female devotees are running their baths, and they live on OPM (other people's money); they are the parasites of the society. This and everything else is of course perfectly all right: they are so perfectly divine that whatever they are doing, they cannot sin. That is why, perhaps, they never explain their techniques...

When disciples from tantrika gurus come to us to be cured, they emit the same kind of burning vibrations as those emitted by the patients from a mental hospital; in the presence of HH Mataji they may start shaking. This suggests the extent of the damage done to their awareness system.

Isn't it time to stop this nonsense and to denounce the formidable mystification which is taking place under the new forms of tantrism?

HH Mataji Nirmala Devi openly proclaims that the false prophets of the last days announced in the Christian scriptures are very ancient demons. Men such as Ravana, Mahisasura, Narakasura, Madhu, Kaitabha, Raktabija, and women such as Putana, Surpanakha, etc., who are reviving in modern times the age-old satanic abuse of tantrism. In the same way that Hitler turned the swastika of Lord Ganesha in the sense of hatred and destruction, these Satans are using all the human knowledge of Tantra and Yantra to destroy the atmosphere and conditions of our spiritual evolution. They have no soul, no conscience, and no feelings. They want power, money, women, and in the process of getting these, they commit the greatest crime of spoiling the Kundalini of others. Today's sorcerers and fornicators are leading the armies of Antichrist. But if everybody is fake around there must be somewhere, someone who is genuine; there cannot be copies without an original Model. This book is written so that you get your chance to know that the Model has come to reveal itself and to denounce the deceivers and imposters.

Let us now expose some of the techniques they use to finish off the spiritual potential of their victims.

First we should briefly summarize the pattern of the strata of consciousness that surrounds our conscious mind, in order to explain how a UPI can penetrate into a human aura. On the left hand side of the human personality, beyond the Ida Nadi, the collective subconscious stores the people who die with too much conditioning. On the right hand side, the collective supraconscious, beyond the Pingala Nadi, stores the dead spirits who have been working physically or mentally and have been overly busy with planning activities and ambitions. In both these areas there are seven strata which are occupied by different types of spirits of dead people. Dissatisfied, demonic, depraved spirits dwell in the lowest strata. Under the lower area of the body *i.e.* below the excretory organs is the "hell". The normal people exist in the higher strata closer to the Sushumna path, while the realised souls exist in the area of the Super Consciousness i.e. the higher areas above the head (Brahmarandhra).

The lower area of the human personality is exposed to the various types of hell. If the attention gets lost there, a person may exhaust all his holiness and be thrown into hell by Lord Ganesha. This person will pass through various lives of horrible existence.

In these lives it might be very difficult to improve for it is easier to fall than to rise.

If one casually lets one's attention drift in these lowest strata it can be caught, attached and trapped there. Hence it is very important that we begin to realise how sexual promiscuity outside of marriage can expose us to the aggression of hell within ourselves. It is really time to open our eyes. In a brave and thoroughly documented book which has just been published, Graham Heath destroys the myths of the permissive society "with its emphasis on early or casual sex".[9] Sexual permissiveness attacks emotional security, character consolidation, social values and behaviour. Its consequences on families, children and the way babies are treated is disastrous. The threat to health has only recently appeared in its full, frightening magnitude. The link with criminal assaults becomes statistically apparent. In the chaotic state of affairs which arises when the marriage institution is not respected we lose the maturity to love; G. Heath wonders: "Are we in the process of destroying that maturity in those who do possess it, and preventing its emergence in the adults of tomorrow?". His penetrating study shows how "an odd coalition of sexual revolutionaries, prestigious researchers and enterprising businessmen" have managed, in one generation, to threaten the very future of our culture and civilisation.

Mr. G. Heath is in fact denouncing the left side tantrika attacks on the West. We should simply add to his findings that the sexually promiscuous tantrika life style ruins the attention, the chakras and the chances of spiritual rebirth. This more subtle destruction does not appear in the statistics related to pregnancy in the young, to abortion, venereal disease and divorce. Only an introduction to Sahaja Yoga could reveal the full extent of the wreckage.

[9] *The Illusory Freedom. The intellectual origins and social consequences of the sexual revolution.* H. Heath. (William Heineman Medical Books Ltd.) London 1978.

The tantrikas have acquired, through occult practices and black magic, the ability to control spirits. They draw UPI's from the collective subconscious and supraconscious, and innoculate the psyche of the victim so that the attention gets more and more attracted towards the lower area of the personality.

Through black magic (*smashan vidya, preta vidya*) hordes of depraved spirits are overpowered. These spirits are generally of two kinds. Those who had lived an extremely austere life suppressing all natural, temperate lifestyles and those who used their wealth, high position or power for indulgences. Such spirits are eager to accept the tantrika's control and they enjoy their unfulfilled desires by entering into someone's body. They become UPI. Among the human beings, weak minds and dominating minds are the first to be controlled by the corresponding type of spirits. When this phenomenon spreads, the tantrika can control mass suggestion or mass hypnosis through the UPI's they hold under bondage.

Vamacaris (tantrikas using the power of the subconscious) went to the extremes of horror in ritual cruelty (sex murder). On the other end of the tantric scope, some of the supraconscious people propounded vegetarianism and fasting to weaken the sadhaka and do not act through sex organs.

Let us now review further details of the occult practices.

(i) Spoiling the Mooladhara chakra. They encourage meditation on sex and/or the Mooladhara chakra. They draw the consciousness into sex. They even sometimes introduce UPIs into the genitals by direct physical contact. In the beginning Lord Ganesha multiplies warnings and signs of displeasure. (To a clairvoyant, Lord Ganesha might appear in the Mooladhara chakra which looks like burning iron; waves of heat pass on the sympathetic system, etc.) If the sex act is performed in the name of spiritual liberation, Kundalini does not come into play at all, but freezes down. Ultimately Kundalini and Lord Ganesha disappear, like any reflection disappears from a mirror which has become too dirty, or has been broken.

(ii) Spoiling the Ajnya chakra. They ask the seeker to close his eyes. They touch the Ajnya chakra, the eyelids or the point between the eyebrows. As they screw the UPI into the Ajnya chakra it gets short-circuited and the victim sees a spark, a flash, or a bright light. He might see shapes and colours. Sometimes an eye may appear. This is the eye of Lord Jesus Christ who warns the seeker but then he disappears. Later on the subject may see the third eye of Lord Shiva burning red indicating his temper. Ultimately the subject crosses the boundaries of the conscious mind; he can see spirits, horrid creatures and, in some cases, develop siddhis[10] (powers such as materialisation, levitation, etc.) all brought forth by the dead spirits.

Smartly enough tantrikas attack the seats of the Son God within man (Mooladhara and Ajnya) because he is the Keeper and Guardian of the Holy Mother Kundalini. And there are countless practices of sorcery. Contaminated food, so called presents from the saint (prasad), brings the UPI to the Nabhi chakra. Talismans and necklaces attack the heart and the Vishuddhi chakras, etc., etc. Direct contact is not even necessary. For instance they often use symbols or names. HH Mataji says that tantrikas manipulate symbols of the tantra (mechanism). Through the strivings of the sympathetic nervous system, after much effort and practice, their attention can move on the rim of the chakra. Thus they can picture chakras correctly or they may distort the pattern, forms, colours of the living chakras in the human body. Both ways are unauthorised; (unauthorised representations by a non-realised soul emit anti-vibrations).

These symbols work as signboards for the UPI under their control. They are so to say planted at the borders of the conscious mind to call the powers of the Dead. These designs, pictures, statues, are the airfields where the UPIs land when they erupt from the subconscious and supraconscious realms. When the attention of the human being is drawn into the symbol, the UPI enters it.

Giving mantras is a favourite ruse of the fake gurus (mantrikas). Do you want to know the trick? They give the disciple a "secret mantra" which is the name of a deity: Rama, Krishna, Aim

---

[10]Traditional Scriptures warn not to be attracted by siddhis which very often are the powers of spirits. Even hypnosis or ESP (extra sensory perception) express a temporary spirit enticement. Some spirits are known as "Karnapishachas" meaning: the spirit who tells in the ear.

(Mahakali) Rim (Mahalaxshmi) Klim (Mahasaraswati) Chamunda, etc. They give these same names to the UPIs they control. When the disciple goes on and on chanting the name, the deity is disturbed by the unauthorised calling; it gets annoyed and disappears from the chakra as it does from a temple or place of worship. Then these spirits which are controlled by the tantrikas enter into the psyche. (The Vishuddhi chakra is always affected by the effort of chanting). As the disciple goes on calling the UPI it nicely settles down in the vacant area of the body (a chakra, a nadi, an organ, a nerve, etc.).

Though some of the disciples who are basically good people feel very much shaken up in the beginning, they do not interpret correctly their healthy distrust, the protests of the physical organism or their feeling of unease. They are befooled by clever theories which teach you to face these symptoms as a spiritual challenge. Followers spur themselves to greater efforts by which they only further destroy their balance and insult the divine. Ultimately when things come to the worst the disciples of a satanic teacher are completely drained of their divinity and holiness. The protecting deity of Lord Ganesha and Lord Jesus Christ disappear from their respective centres. Thus the gates of hell can open out and their attention takes them to doom. The dead entities from other realms enter through ida and pingala nadis and overpower the subject's conscious mind. They are brain-washed and never question the tantrika "guru". They may lose their sense of decency and denounce the morals of human life. Reasoning, critical sense and discrimination are gone; some of them can turn into sex obsessed rapists or murderers. They kill and think they are doing God's work. Spirit enticement has finished the human awareness in them. The shape is of a human being but, inside a monster is born out of the putrefaction.

Tantrikas can use spirits from the right side (*savya margi*) and from the left side (*wama margi*). When the awareness moves over to the left of the Ida Nadi it passes into the subconscious. One can again develop animal faculties (acute sense of smell, sight, hearing). Some people, propelled by drugs or alcohol can further regress to a state of vegetal torpor. These experiences signal a regression into the past as vegetal and animal stages are part of mankind's biological build up. The thin border between individual and collective subconscious is easily crossed; we enter the field of intoxication and trances, African, Polynesian and Amerindian sorcery, voodoo, shamanism and occult initiations. Through the powers of the dead sorcerers might kill somebody at a distance. History exhibits cases of mass murders which have been ordered by sorcerers and carried out through spirit possession. At the command of his master a spirit can materialise things (*bhanmati*) carry somebody (levitation) or speak through mediums, palmists, etc. These practices are common among aboriginals (in India: aghoris, nagas, kapalikas). They also kill people secretly, indirectly, by a method known as "*Hanana*" or "*Maran*".

Initially the human psyche very much resists the invasion from the Dead (collective subconscious). In order to break this resistance the sorcerers operate in a thoroughly clever, organised, and co-ordinated fashion. They can use brainwashing "meditation" techniques. Or they draw the human consciousness into drugs, alcohol and perverted sex. When this is done the introduction of a UPI is for them a child's game.

With the right side movement of the attention through the ego one enters the supraconscious and later, the collective supraconscious. Making any effort moves the attention on to the right side. This happens even when one does too much worshipping or too many rituals or too much meticulous observation of asceticism. This movement is stimulated by contact with so called invisible masters (realised souls cannot be contacted), mushrooms, LSD, etc. Supraconscious mood seeks control, mastery and domination. Such people are extremely clever egoists and full of pseudo-knowledge (knowledge information and not knowledge awareness). They often take to extreme abstinences and austerities which excite the pingala nadi.

Savya margis can be hatha yogis, fakirs, raja yogis and cover a whole range of spiritual exhibitionists. They seek the admiration and worship of the crowds and show off with healing powers or unusual physical abilities (such as fasting, controlling breath for three or four days, etc.). Tantrikas who use supraconscious spirits may or may not use sex but work mainly on the nabhi and ajnya chakras. They are very successful at building big organisations and collecting money because supraconscious spirits turn their disciples into over-active, very efficient organisers, planners and operators.

The spirits from the right side could be say, dead generals, businessmen or administrators who, at the time of death, did not quite resign themselves to leave the chairman's seat. They are busybodies hovering around still trying to express themselves, to influence human affairs. These UPIs are very egotistical and when they enter into the ego of the disciple they make him more dynamic and "creative". But these entities are feeding on the energy of the subject and his organism cannot go on bearing them for ever. After a couple of years victims start rattling like junky cars.

Tantrika sorcerers know which spirits to put in which people; they first send forth their hosts of entities to gather information about the history and the character of the human being who comes to them. This invisible network of spies finds out the potential victims: hypocrites, licentious, selfindulgent, the naive and the rich... UPIs can also be removed and replaced. It is a 24 hour flying circus, occult and satanic, which crushes people while doctors, psychologists and other scientists refuse to "believe in spirits"... But they don't believe in Lord Jesus Christ either who put the spirits into the pigs. They go on prescribing little tablets, three times a day with a glass of water, to people sinking into neurosis and paranoia. In a few years of Sahaja Yoga activities we have been able to record hundreds of cases of patients who were alcoholics, drug addicts, psychopaths, schizophrenics, etc., having been cured. Most of them were supposed to be incurable patients; and most of them were possessed.

Because of the interference with the sympathetic system tantrikas can suffer from cancer, leprosy, diabetes and venereal diseases. They die miserably; but this part of the story is never told.

So the Japanese tourist climbs his telescopic ladder to take a close up shot of the erotic statues on the walls of the Nepali temple. Maybe he thinks he is climbing the ladder to heaven? A Nepali peasant, in the neighbouring field turns towards his wife who looks at the scene with a shy mocking face. I ask my servant to translate what they say. He does it graciously. "The foreign sahib on the ladder is a savage, an idiot and a buffoon."

In Delhi I interviewed many politicians and civil servants, asking their opinions on tantrism and sexoyogic practices. They corroborated what I had found out in my extensive trips through India: the immense majority of Indians are neither aware nor interested in tantrism. At the most they see it as a dark page of their history which called forth the wrath of God in the form of foreign invasions. Tantric kingdoms collapsed within a few centuries and their temples were buried under the earth. But Westerners excavated them and revived interest in tantrism. A comment of a very senior Indian bureaucrat was as follows: "How can you ever believe that sex is connected with spirituality? Then, if you do, why do you put rapists in jail? You should worship them as saints. But even in licentious and degenerated societies can we meet anyone who is obsessed by sex and, at the same time, leads a balanced and happy life. Is such a man respected by anybody?." Indeed, despite the craze of "liberation", we do not yet erect statues to commemorate a nymphomaniac, a great syphilitic or a top alcoholic.

In the true Hindu and Christian traditions the joy giving charm of sex is enjoyed in the privacy and sanctity of marriage. Tantric stories about Krishna leelas (the play of Krishna) had no other purpose but to attack the marriage institution. Tantric artists even depicted Shri Ganesha having sex with his mother Gauri, a blasphemy akin to showing Christ with his mother!... This horrid statue caused Sahaja Yogis to vomit for days together. Of course, for the time being, there are very few Sahaja Yogis but they are related to the Absolute. In this world of confusion, their reactions provide criteria to judge what is right and what is wrong.

Under the leadership of HH Mataji, Sahaja Yogis are daily repelling the onslaught of the forces of Darkness. We could give you countless examples. During her stay in London HH Mataji was dealing with an American boy who had been involved in experiences of meditation. He had recently been driven by an urge to kill his parents and, when he realised the horror of it he attempted to commit suicide. He sought refuge at HH Mataji's feet as his very last hope. The mantra given to this boy was "shringa". As this is the name of a great ancient sage HH Mataji was surprised at the self-destructive drive of this unfortunate boy and went into meditation to see what was the matter. She then saw a very ugly demonic figure with one single horn in the forehead and realised at once that shringa also means unicorn. This devil was then overpowered and answered HH Mataji's questions. He told Her that the sorcerer at the head of the meditation organisation controls many devils like him; they need more UPIs in their ranks to spread the occult empire because it is difficult for them to enter into human beings. So, when they drive people to suicide, the departing spirit of the victim is very easily brought under the sorcerer's control and joins the ranks of his UPI army.

London, May 1978. Another boy involved in the same type of worldwide organisation is trying to get relief from pains and headaches. His girlfriend weeps and sobs; the other evening she saw a horrid devil, half-buffalo, half-lion, trying to get out of her friend. Then a round bubble appeared and pushed this devil back into him. She was very scared and did not know what to do. But we did...

Tantrism is an ideology that flourished through some of India's perverted pseudo yogis who could not achieve any spiritual growth and had been discarded by their own gurus. But tantrism as a life style appeals so cleverly to our weaknesses that it became a universal feature of this Kali Yuga. Ritual prostitution existed in Egypt, the middle eastern and meso American empires. Courtesans became the centre of court life and social entertainment in Alexandria Rome, Kyoto, Paris, etc. De facto, tantrism became a part of the Chinese, Greek, Roman cultures. It dominated the erotic art and literature of Japan (the Edo period 1603-1867) and of 18th Century Europe[11]. It flourished in the decadent Berlin of the 1920s and, after the war, in all classes of the European Society. When obscenity seeks the endorsement of aesthetics it is called "eroticism". When sex researchers such as Freud, Wilhelm Reich of Alfred Kinsey enlighten us we are told to seek inspiration from the "natural" behaviour of some captive male apes and monkeys! And when money comes into the game, pornography floods the cities.

But what are we doing to our homes, families and children?

Dr. Alex Comfort writes: "There is a pattern of mother-and-father relationship which is virtually essential as a nest for normal child development."[12] While Margaret Mead points out that women "may be said to be mothers unless they are taught to deny their child-bearing qualities."[13] Now tantrikas are out to destroy these vitally important relationships. Through arts, science and media they have launched a "big operation of behavioural engineer-

---

[11] A most demonic tantrika operated in 18th Century France as the writer Marquis de Sade. Another one, Rasputin, brought the doom of the Romanov imperial dynasty. He has incarnated today as a "spiritual master" preaching sex liberation.

[12] A. Comfort *Sex and Society* pg. 85.

[13] M. Mead *Male and Female* pg. 192.

ing."[14] Women are taught to replace the joys of maternal love by instant erotic gratification. The trend is reflected in the monotonous increase of divorce statistics.

Historically tantrism flourishes best in a bustling, money-conscious, entertainment-hungry, sex-mad urban consumer society where surplus money and leisure time are available. In this city the population is fluctuating, unstable, traditions are given up, power is corrupt, vice perfected and made commercially profitable. It is a pleasure-bent merry-go-round in which not many remember that all such societies have in the past been brutally destroyed by invasions, wars, revolutions, epidemics or natural catastrophes.

In the modern city the courtesan and the playboy are set up to be models of behaviour. The media worship them! A woman who loses her sense of chastity becomes "attractive"—that is, she develops an effective power to attract and subdue a man's attention, no matter how powerful he is. The "playboy" type of man has been immortalised by Mozart's "don Giovanni" and very finely analysed in Kierkegaard's *Diary of a Seducer* or Choderlos de Laclos' "*Les Liasons dangeureuses*". Women are passing pretexts for his sensual and aesthetic pleasure. Both the courtesan and playboy centre their amorous life on the gratification of their own ego. They pick up lovers, enjoy them and throw them away. They are trying to liberate themselves from their own conscience; sin is "holy" or "natural". But as they play with feelings, emotions and sex they cross the boundaries of ida nadi. What happens then? The UPIs are invited from the collective subconscious and become the invisible participants in the amorous game; they enjoy it and gradually dominate the human actors. The possessed being becomes a vehicle for spoiling another human consciousness. Sexual promiscuity[15] spreads further. The consequence of this snowball effect cannot be stressed enough: "sex has become more meaningless as it is more available," says Dr. Rollo May in *Love and Will* (p. 14) and, in consequence, love has come to seem 'tremendously elusive, if not an outright illusion". The immediate consequence of promiscuity and of the damage brought to the unity of the married couple not only

---

[14] G. Heath. op. cit. pg.

[15] Among these consequences it is worth mentioning here that "promiscuous sexual behaviour, be it in the male or the female, is intimately associated with the development of cervical cancer". Dr. A. Singer: *Sexual Promiscuity and Cervical Cancer*. pg. 4. See also Rotkin in *Cancer Research* (1973) pg. 33, 1353, 1367.

disturbs the potential for happiness and fulfilment of both partners: it exerts a disastrous impact on children and adolescents who find themselves floating in an emotionally meaningless world.[16] The long term consequence for society can be tentatively put in Unwin's words: "any society is free to choose either to display great energy or to enjoy sexual freedom: the evidence is that it cannot do both for more than one generation"; *Sex and Culture* (p.412.) The truth of the matter is that the occult powers are bent on destroying the Christian civilisation. To this day, the way their theories have been widely accepted prove that they are immensely successful. Have our cities truly become "Babylon the great, mother of harlots and prostitution?"

There was much more to Tantrism than erotic friezes. It was in fact the penetration axis of an all out satanic strategy which aimed at preventing mankind from reaching its evolutionay destination; it did quite well indeed...Today, people influenced by the occult forces and even those who spread their dominion are totally unaware of what is really going on. Satan is a collective principle which works through us unnoticed. Crocodile? Which crocodile? ...Let us now review how it all happened in the West.

The terrible conflicts of this century shattered man's sense of moral values and faith in God. During the two World Wars huge numbers of people died a brutal, cruel death. Their spirits could not be appeased and many of them stayed among us, forming an invisible film of frustrated and revengeful awareness around the conscious mind. Some of them swelled the battalions of the UPI reserve army of the sorcerers.

In this uncongenial atmosphere evolved souls do not often take their birth and animals start incarnating in the human realm (demographic explosion). These newcomers to the human race have not developed their sense of dharma in previous lives and

---

[16] The following quote summarizes changes in the total health situation of adolescents in England during the past ten years, "Socio medical problems of pregnancy, abortion, sexually transmitted disease, drug addiction, alcohol abuse, alienation and homelessness have shown significant increases in the past decade...Disturbed behaviour originating in childhood may be exacerbated in adolescence, and the prevalence of psychiatric disorders rises. There is a relatively high incidence of suicide, attempted or successful, among older adolescents".

1975 Report of the Chief Medical Officer. Quoted in Unwin's *Sex and Culture*.

they easily fall into the spider web of the tantric collective consciousness that tantrikas have patiently woven.[17]

The weaving of the web within the human collective consciousness has been the brain-child of the spider sorcerers and they completed it in the last 20 years. For Satan the problem was to create an atmosphere in which man forsakes his dharma negating God without noticing it. Many brilliant minds unknowingly prepared the web. Tantrika ideologues sometimes came as atheist theoreticians, scientists, psychologists. Sigmund Freud was among them.

Freudian psychologists who studied and treated pathological cases and possessed patients came to the conclusion that the suppression of sex urges creates conflicts and inhibitions. They preached the liberation of the UPI in the subconscious. This trend of thought led them to discard all the past religious teachings of temperance and piety. Attention was focused on incest, that is the blasphemous insult against Shri Ganesha and Shri Gauri. Of course Jung opposed Freud; he exhorted us to become aware of our cosmic self (collective consciousness within the Virata), thus bridging the gap between psychology and religion. In his old age Jung shone with peace and serenity; Freud, after having led a very unhappy life got cancer of the jaw and died miserably. Never mind! Western thought followed Freud and not Jung. This illustrates again one factor which explains the success of de facto Tantrism; human beings eagerly take to theories which justify their lower drives. And the more so in an industrially developed society where our weaknesses are exploited to earn money.

When this conceptual groundwork is done tantrikas influence image makers; they penetrate the world of newspapers, show business, media, arts and publicity. They can be movie makers, actresses, writers,...Modern media technology directly helps them to spread their demonic vibrations all over the world.

Take the example of pornography in the form of films, books and magazines. In which way does this filth affect society? "Edinburgh criminologist Professor F.H. McClintock has noted that group sexual attacks, including gang rape, involving young people are increasing, and he suggests that the commercialization of sex

---

[17] When the atmosphere is no longer congenial for animals to enter the human stage the rate of birth drops automatically for evolved human souls are in limited numbers.

and violence in the media and in pornography may be much more closely associated with the increase in violent sex crime than some leaders of public opinion would have the public believe".[18] Students of the Marquis de Sade tortured and killed a ten year old boy[19]. A sixteen year old boy convicted for the sexual murder of a woman was an avid reader of pornographic publication[20]. In the trial of a man found guilty of six rapes it was found that the criminal was obsessed with sex films: "He would watch a film then go out and rape" (Cambridge Evening News 3 October, 1975). This short statement illustrates perfectly the tantrika sequence: the UPI enters through the media into the human consciousness, overpowers the subject and spreads Satan's kingdom[21].

Sexual violence is the extreme, undisguised result of the tantrika trend; it shows tantrism in its naked horror. But tantrikas seldom expose themselves so openly. They prefer to act under the camouflage of liberation, fondly courting public opinion for endorsement and legitimacy. They propagate ideas and lifestyles which wreck in very subtle ways the morality of human beings. As the commandments of religion are no more accepted who can challenge them? Cinemas, books, magazines, advertisements, pictures, shows, songs can infuse the tantric poison into collective consciousness: the bomb is dropped through the media; its shell breaks into the head of the subject; the psychic nerve gas spreads unnoticed in the awareness system. It shatters the wisdom and finishes off the discrimination in two gasps. It gets rid of the conscience[22]. The

[18]G. Heath *The Illusory Freedom* op. cit. pg. 56.
[19]H. Johnson *On Iniquity* pg. 32.
[20]G. Heath *The Illusory Freedom* pg. 39.
[21]In England and Wales rape has increased by over a hundred per cent in the ten years following the liberation of pornography. The annual average figure for 1976 indicates that, every day three women are raped. The statistics for the London Metropolitan Police area indicate an increase of almost 200 per cent between 1963 and 1973. (*The Illusory Freedom* appendix 3).
[22]A tantrika view of the conscience could be perceived in the words that Shakespeare put in the mouth of the second murderer in Richard III:
"I'll not meddle with it; it is a dangerous thing: it makes a man a coward: a man cannot steal, but it accuseth him; he cannot swear, but it checks him; he cannot lie with his neighbour's wife, but it detects him: it is a blushing shamefaced spirit that mutinies in a man's bosom: it fills one full of obstacles: it made me once restore a purse of gold, that by chance I found; it beggars any man that keeps it: it is turned out of all towns and cities for a dangerous thing; and every man that means to live well endeavours to trust himself and live without it".
Shakespeare. *Richard III*. Act 1:4

sense of shame and decency which separates us from animals (all too often) vanishes. The masses follow the slogan of liberation. Are we letting hell loose on this fair earth?

You must probably be as shocked as we were when the whole picture revealed itself to us. We were dismayed at the extent of our society's self-destruction. I, personally, was horrified. But today we know that the Divine protection is more than a match to Satan's challenge. And when we can see the problem it is already more than half solved. We ought to seek God's protection. What we mostly need, at this stage, is some humility.

In their limited findings psychologists dealt extensively with the super-ego while the ego, unchecked, covers the brain of the Westerners. Without our knowledge we became ego-orientated. We negated God and demons and lost perception of what is sinful and what is Godly. We used sex for the expression of our ego. Industries cashed in on human weaknesses, money supported vices and production flooded the markets with superfluous goods which further drew attention into artificiality[23]. In the name of this model of development we pretend to rule, guide and inspire the so-called developing countries! In the meantime all limits (mariada) which define human dharma are rejected. As a result society breaks: destroying families, bringing about juvenile delinquency, abortions battered babies and, through alcohol, drugs and sex, a powerful swing back into super-ego, onward into the tantric web.

In this respect it is particularly sad that the hippies—who were supposedly seeking a more spiritual fulfilment—proved to be the most powerful social force to spread the liberated life style. They rejected parental authority and threw away all the hitherto accepted norms of behaviour: drugs, communal sex, social parasitism became objects of eager experiments; hippies carried the western ego to its last extremities. They just undertook whatever they

---

[23] The popular craze for a suntan in the West is an interesting example in which industrial profit making, tantric stratagem and media power spread at mass level a pattern of behaviour harmful to the subject. Over exposure to the sun's rays causes fast ageing of the skin, eventually leukemia, breast cancer and brain damage. We know through Sahaja Yoga that it affects the pingala nadi and the liver. But somehow the image of the suntanned, quasi naked, "attractive" women or men goes into the brain of people. So creams and lotions are sold and competition goes on for exhibiting fast tanning. Body consciousness hangs pervading over the crowded beaches; expectations are created; peace of mind is disturbed.

pleased, not minding in the least about breaking away from society. A flower cannot blossom if it is cut away from the tree and yet the 'flower children' pretended they could do just that.

The spiders, mean and watchful, were crouching in the centre of the web. In the Nineteen-sixties they rushed out! Tantrika sorcerers started all possible kinds of religious movements, spiritual organisations, etc. The human beings already threatened by entities pushed the UPI's Trojan horse within the walls of the human city: parapsychological societies and spiritualist churches which, in fact, are inviting UPIs, mushroomed everywhere. Money flew in as rich converts were particularly sought after. This occult invasion is of course aimed at those human beings which are more likely to break into the super human awareness of the Kingdom of God : the seekers.

Quite a few people today are aware of the coalition between the forces of the dead, the fornicators and the sorcerers. They are afraid of the false prophets and some of them hesitate to approach HH Mataji, fearing to be hurt again. This is the precise reason for which the Lieutenants of Satan come as spiritual leaders: to prevent the children from finding their Divine Mother. Shoudn't we expose them?

I remember HH Mataji was once speaking about the satanic forces. Among the seekers gathered around Her you can see happy smiles and beaming faces; many seekers have gone through powerful experiences and know that what she says is absolutely true. But some of the newcomers are shocked: one of them protests: "Our guru says that everything is divine, everything is good." HH Mataji replies: "Will the satanic forces speak against themselves? Will the thieves say that one should lock the house? They will always say that everything is fine. Keep all open for them to enter and loot you." While we are all laughing aloud I remember that Lord Jesus said the same thing:

> "Every Kingdom divided against itself is brought to desolation: and every city or house divided against itself shall not stand: and if Satan cast out Satan he is divided against himself; how shall then his Kingdom stand." Luke 12.25

The greatest cunning of the Devil manifests in making people believe that he does not exist. The past instructors of mankind tell us that he does; and HH Mataji gives the same warning. Now choose for yourself: on which side is HH Mataji? Where do YOU stand?

The followers of the false prophets and sorcerers mentioned in St. John's Apocalypse can still get realisation but it is more difficult. If they are identified with their "guru" we are definitely wasting our energy in trying to help them. Besides the UPI put into them by their masters will try to bother us. HH Mataji says: "First let us begin by reaching those who have not badly overloaded themselves." The vibratory impact of collectivity will increase with the growth of our number and, at a later stage, we will demystify those who have turned the Temple of God into a "spiritual" market place.

I accept that I am very slow to settle into the realised state. But this makes me feel very concerned for all those who commit the same mistakes because of spiritual naivety. At one point in my life, in my ignorance, I bowed to a wrong teacher, to a false prophet.

HH Mataji says that She does not want to hear about the "sins" we have committed. Sometimes She asks people to write their story in a letter that She tears up without reading; I heard Her saying: "What sin can you commit that I cannot devour. You know, the Devi's love is like the bottom of the Ocean; no matter how big the Ocean is, its bottom is always bigger".

The time has come for us to change before the coming of Lord Kalki which embodies the destroying power of the Adi Shakti. HH Mataji is working very hard, day in and day out to give us the chance of redemption.

I must say it: there is a cosmic struggle going on. Before realisation only the dullness of my awareness prevented me from perceiving how it affected my environment. Now I see it while realising also that the psyche and the environment are in constant osmosis[24]. In this struggle a choice has to be made and the alterna-

---

[24]"There are many intuitions in American science fiction which are unconsciously hinting at some aspect of the actual cosmic struggle. The hero, usually, is the one who has mastered higher awareness like Paul MuadDib in F. Herbert's *Dune*. Man can be ruled by emotional and mental control (cf: thema of psychic intrusion) in Asimov's *Second Foundation*. Children are merging into a collectively conscious being (cf the coming of Kalki) in A. Clarke's *Childhood's end*. See also the thema of R. Bach's *Jonathan Livingstone Seagull*.

tives are dramatically stressed by some of St. John's last statements:

> "Blessed are those who wash their robes that they may have the right to the tree of life and that they may enter the city by the gates. Outside are the dogs and sorcerers and fornicators and murderers and idolaters and everyone who loves and practises falsehood".—John, *Revelation 22.14*.

I have not said it; I am just quoting an out of fashion author who wrote before the modern intelligentsia discovered "tolerance". But what I say now is this: At this juncture of history it does not matter that much what we decide to tolerate or reject. The only question which actually matters (and which is, I may suggest, a deadly serious one) is the question: what is tolerable to Lord Kalki.

Certainly this chapter has a bitter taste to it. If one sees its implications and fails to focus on the good news of Sahaja Yoga it could prove to be frankly frightening. Many a clever mind will thus prefer to sneer, laugh and make fun of it. I don't like writing about UPIs Satan or doom. But it is my duty to tell you the truth before the next coming of the Apocalyptic Destroyer.

Did the Western elites ever understand the forces which shape mankind's destiny? Let us give but one example of their short sightedness in dealing with a specifically satanic outburst of right side tantrism (the unauthorised exploitation of the sun channel's energy).

London 1939. Crowds are massed outside the Prime Minister's residence at 10 Downing Street to cheer him on his return from the Munich Conference with the French Daladier and the German Fuehrer and Chancellor Adolf Hitler. Neville Chamberlain appears at a window, flourishes the agreement with Hitler and exults: "My friends...there has come back from Germany peace with honour. I believe it is peace for our time" Six years later after a titanic war the allied troops discovered the inhuman horror of the concentration camps: Dachau, Auchwitz, Buchenwald. The whole world was dumbfounded as the Nuremberg trial exposed Nazi atrocities. How can such things happen? How could a highly civilised country such as Germany become the instrument of the Nazi Beast? The Western mind, in its ignorance of the occult powers of Evil, never quite managed to understand these agonising pages of European history.

The first definition of Tantrism we proposed, "a blasphemous, sex focused ideology" refers more specifically to left side tantrism and the occult invasion from the collective subconscious. Right side tantrism does not focus so much on sex but moves the occult worlds for the sake of power and domination; it paves the way for the invasion from the collective supraconscious. Often left and right attacks combine, alternate and react to each other; thus works the satanic pliers.

The relationships between occultism and Nazism have been established by many writers and historians.

Adolf Hitler, born in Braunau on Inn, a well known centre of spiritualism, became himself a medium for right side UPIs.[25] Karl Haushoffer, Hitler's mentor, exhibited clairvoyant powers as a general in the First World War and was in close contact with the Tibetan tantric sects which were working on pingala nadi. The dark mystic of the Nazis centred around the Thule Group and the Black Order of the initiated SS. The core of the Nazi secret doctrine was to prepare a superior race of supermen which would welcome on earth the Luciferian advent of the outside powers that are the supraconscious demons. For this purpose the Third Reich was to spread its dominion as far as Gobi and Tibet. This is why Hitler committed the fatal strategic mistake of opening a second front against Russia.

Hitler himself was an ascetic, vegetarian right side tantrika. Saintly austeriy, such as Buddha's, spreads universal love while supraconscious austerity results in relentless brutality. During the first phase of his career Hitler used the supraconscious powers for his political ascenta nd military success. But soon he was overpowered. The UPIs used him and the Black Order for their own purpose. Insane cruelty was introduced through their sadistic domination.

When the forces of evil attack mankind from the supraconscious area they operate through the ego and thus cannot be detected until it is too late. For the ego has become a brilliant master of deceit, ruse and camouflage. That is why Hitler could befool Hindenburg, Chamberlain and many others.

[25] See Pauwels, Bergier *Le Matin des Magiciens* (Gallimard 1960) pg. 434.

If European leaders had been even slightly aware of Tantrism and its methods, World War II could not have taken place because they would have understood in time the magnitude of the Nazi threat. For Sahaja Yogis it is extremely easy to make out the tantric stratagems of Hitler and his clique.

To begin with the Nazi's use of Lord Ganesha's swastika exhibits the typical trick of insulting the Divine through the blasphemous use of a divine symbol. The attention of Lord Ganesha who watches the gates of Hell recedes and UPI armies gather around the Nazi crowd. The Wagnerian decorum, the SS swearing-in at the stroke of midnight, all the image devices mounted by Goebels were aimed at enticing the masses.

At the crucial moment of the great popular rallies, Hitler would appear equipped with a full battery of hypnotist UPIs swarming in his ugly little figure. There he performed and in his characteristically shrewd words onlookers would be, "swept into the tremendous stream of hypnotic intoxication."[26] Torrents of UPIs would flow through him into the hysterical crowd.

Mass hypnotism is the classic right side gateway to mob politics and war; Hitler enticed individuals with the same mastery. Benito Mussolini who was himself rather disturbed on both pingala and ida nadi used to refer to Hitler as "this little clown". But the Duce was soon totally overpowered by the magnetism of the Fuehrer; the ascetic tantrika had accumulated more psychic powers than the licentious fascist leader.

A whole book would be required to elaborate on the intimate relationships between tantrism and the atrocities of World War II. My purpose here is merely to warn Western intellectual statesmen and politicians not to commit the same mistakes as their fathers; we can no longer afford to ignore the forces of Evil.

UPIs are more dangerous than ever because the sorcerers have now incarnated to lead them. Satan has raised his banner. In Russia, where research institutes are intensively busy with parapsychological research, could UPI dominated individuals take control of the formidable Soviet military arsenal? Can a conjunction of UPIs and machines destroy the human race? In the permissive West and in Japan, maybe in the whole world,

---

[26]Robert T. Elson, *Prelude to Wars*. (Time Life Books 1977) pg. 122

tantrism has firmly settled in an incredible variety of forms. The nucleus of society, the family, is destroyed. With left side UPIs tantrism swelled into hard core pornography, etc. Right side UPIs account for thousands of daily upsurges of brutality and murderous violence. Some African dictators are demons. Many terrorists are reincarnated Nazis and Fascists.

Could you not read the whole story of possession written on the grimacing face of Charles Manson, this bloody butcher, instigator of ritual crimes? The 1969 Beverley Hills massacre took place in the pure Kapalika tantric line of human sacrifices. Where sex and violence meet, the left and right side tantrism complete Satan's circle.

Of course all the responsible citizens of the human Civitas want to stop demonic trends but are they equipped to repell the onslaught of the occult powers?

Governments could pass and enforce laws which cleanse the media, eradicate vice and protect the family. But all this is not enough! We have to discover ourselves and our surroundings. Only the divine phenomenon of en masse realisation will wipe out the psychic chaos created by these reincarnated demons.

All the demonic forces have clubbed together and the anti-God campaign has been launched with unprecedented ruthlessness. Those who, in their freedom, decide to choose God's side should now gather together. Everything that has been written in this book points to the amazing fact that, wherever we are in the world today, we can spread the Kingdom of God around us through the beautiful oneness of a joint human undertaking. This is the full implication of the power to raise Kundalinis which the Holy Spirit has granted to each Sahaja Yogi. If you choose to join us in this grand "rescue operation" you will soon experience that the collective undertaking will also greatly strengthen your faith. After all, you are being contacted by this book at the very beginning of a fantastic historical process in which you are now invited to participate although your immediate environment does not know anything about it. The paradox of this situation will sometimes stir up your incredulity. Whenever possible, the best way to deal with this situation is to give yourself proof that your environment can also participate in your new experience. After your self-realisation you will be able to do so by raising Kundalinis. Actually so many of us in this lifetime have taken a human birth for this very purpose! Let us put ourselves in a proper shape again so that we can be the instruments of the Holy Spirit. This world can be redeemed; let us try to understand our luck: we are called upon to invite onto this planet, innocence knowledge, joy and love. We should give ourselves credit and accept that we are worthy of this task. We have to use in all ways possible the power we have to spread realisation NOW.

10

Collective salvation before the coming of the Rider

Dreams are sometimes the messengers of the Unconscious. I should like to mention a dream that Dr. Rustum Burjorjee had just before meeting HH Mataji:

> "I am fighting with a horrible large evil strong-man. Then I heard the sound of a hunting horn and a lot of animals rushed out of the nearby forest. And after the animals came men dressed in scarlet and gold clothes leading white hounds, with birds and doves and there came men and women all dressed in scarlet and gold, riding white horses. And finally there came a very beautiful woman also dressed in scarlet and gold, riding a white horse and wearing a large diamond shaped ruby on the left ring finger. Behind her a magnificent stag with golden antlers, shining in the sun, breaks out of the forest; then came the King. He is invisible and is surrounded by four men who form a square. Behind him comes a riderless white horse which is his. He has yet to manifest and ride it. And by then I knew that Evil no longer had a chance".

The relationship between this white horse, announced by millennial scriptures, the blossoming of Sahaja Yoga and the great advent of HH Mataji is at the same time intimate and formidable.

Now, at this concluding stage of my humble, yet vital, pronouncement on Sahaja Yoga, let us again review a few facts.

A saint known as Baba Jagannath from Ambarnath made publicly a surprising confession; his own Guru, who is living in the Himalayas, had told him that the Adi Shakti Herself would cure his Ajnya chakra. So he waited for HH Mataji...who corrected the chakra in no time. Mrs Schaeffer, the wife of a wealthy American businessman, visited a very much respected age old saint near Rangoon. He told her about HH Mataji saying: "She is the Mother of the Universe". Madhu Dhave, an Indian gentleman living in New York, was told by a great sage of Kerala that the Adi Shakti has incarnated in the form of Her Holiness Shri Mataji Nirmala Devi. This guru had not even seen or met HH Mataji.

It is very confusing in the beginning to even think about it. I could not bring myself to believe that a Divine Being could incarnate in such an unassuming, simple personality. Then I started thinking about all the other Incarnations. They were all very human and yet, Shri Rama and Shri Krishna were recognised by simple folk who were not realised souls. These people really seem to have been more sensitive to the subtle Divine than we, modern materialists, possibly could be. Think of the ego-orientated, stupid fools ideologues (Pharisees and priests) and administrators (Romans,) who did not recognise Lord Jesus. Are we, by chance, the reincarnated Romans of those days?[1] Are we going to repeat their brilliant performance?

I started seeing myself, seeing my kinsmen, the intellectuals who guide the ego-orientated countries. We do not want the truth! We do not want to face it. We do not want to give up our self-appointed churches, our crowns, our mental games and our myths. We never did, never will. Because we are cowards: as a result of our own dominating nature we are afraid to be dominated; we project our own ego's puffiness in our idea of God and thus we do not want to recognise Him. Intellectuals have written so many

---

[1] One day HH Mataji referred to the way in which the past Incarnations (Socrates, Zoroaster, Muhammad, Sainath, Christ, etc.) have been persecuted. She said: "Imagine someone who is born at the tenth storey of a building and all the other people are born on the ground floor. How can they understand each other and communicate? My father told me: Nirmala, unless and until you give them en-masse realisation they will not believe there is a second storey to this building."

books! They have built a huge sand castle of "*Avidya*": false knowledge. How can they know their misidentifications, how can they get rid of all the irrelevant beliefs they have lived with? Why should they accept anything that does not support their own theories? I know it is very, very hard. I have gone through it.

Even after self-realisation, many western Sahaja Yogis cannot stop their mind games...[2] I just hope they are not going to take as much time as I did to overcome confusion. But now I can no longer go on with falsehood nor can I bear to see so many seekers misguided, for I know that salvation lies in accepting the truth.

The Great Incarnation of the Present Time has not incarnated in the West. It is too bad for those who thought that God is a white Anglo-Saxon Protestant. But She incarnated in a Christian family to experience how far we had gone in our narrow-minded religious dogmatism.

As we said, according to Sanskrit scriptures, there are four types of Incarnations: the Father, the Mother, the Son and the Primordial Master. The Holy Spirit has acted mostly as the potential power, helping the male Incarnations. But sometimes the Holy Spirit incarnates all alone. These incarnations of the Adi Shakti as Shri Durga, Kartyayani, etc., have been recorded by the Hindu tradition.

The last Incarnation of the Vishnu Principle of evolution is Shri Kalki, the rider. But the Incarnation of the Holy Spirit has to come on this earth to convince us of God's power and to give salvation. After all, God Almighty has to save the flowers of His Creation through His power of love before the manifestation of His destroying power. The wheat is being separated from the tares.

The modern times are the worst kind, no doubt, because the sensitivity to the Divine has practically vanished. So many devils (Rakshasas) have taken birth to take full advantage of the

---

[2] Games of doubts, games of self-pity, games of the ego. Lord Krishna is the Lord of the Play and when we indulge in playing games the Vishuddhi chakra is caught. Immediate consequences are: blurred sensitivity and awareness. We see this happening every day among us here in London. Many people come to the programmes and then fizzle out. They escape: "She is too pure, too great for us. We are so soiled. We are unworthy of God's Love. Let us perish". HH Mataji sometimes weeps with anguish : "The Ocean of Sin cannot be greater than the heart of your Lord who loves you. He can drink all the poison. Come back".

present confusion. But, as Kali told Nala, this is also the time in which the true seekers will get their self-realisation.

Yesterday there were 5,000 Sahaja Yogis. Today there are perhaps 50,000 and how many tomorrow? No doubt this miraculous phenomenon has been triggered by HH Mataji. We have witnessed Her great powers. We have received Her knowledge. We have verified it. We have experienced it. Among us are doctors, scientists, psychologists, lawyers, gardeners, artists, engineers, bureaucrats. We all understand the language of vibrations which HH Mataji has decoded for us.

She told Doctor G. Adler, President of the Association of Jungian Psychologists, one day: "I have come to give a mouth to the Unconscious".

Actually many people who have not been in direct contact with HH Mataji can feel the vibrations. Some of them might be born realised. Furthermore, since Her birth, our Divine Mother has granted countless "long distance" awakening and realisation. But the people who merely feel the vibrations do not know about the working out, meaning, monitoring of the energy. They cannot, go deep into it. The decoding system of Sahaja Yoga which is HH Mataji's gracious gift to Mankind works out with an amazing accuracy. Sahaja Yogis can interpret the messages brought to their attention by physical sensations and they can answer back! They can also operate the energy according to the needs of the moment.

But, above all, each and every Sahaja Yogi who has risen in his awareness can bear witness to a great truth. When we have asked "who is HH Mataji?" we have been blessed by a deep, dignified and respectful silence. When we have asked "is She the Divine Mother?" our vibrations become extremely strong and joy pours over our being like a gentle waterfall. And we get drenched in the beauty of living in blissful timelessness. We have recognized Her. We bow to the Truth. We worship Her Advent.

Can you now read the tale of the World's oldest legends?

There is a big show going on. Its title: "The play of recognition". Planet earth is the stage, with a resplendent variety of decorations and accessories. There are nice guys and bad guys playing various roles. And there is, of course, the figure of the hero. The mother of the hero sweetly engineered the whole play for her child's triumph. But he does not know it. He is a bit freaked out. He has good and bad days. He fought in Shri Rama's army to conquer Lanka. He sought Shri Krishna's guidance "tell me clearly what to do, I am confused". He, like Lord Jesus, was delivered to the wicked, but was not overcome by wickedness. Tough time! Down to the nineteen-eighties. By the way, do you know what I am talking about? Do you know who I am talking about? Actually, it is about somebody you might not know. I am talking about ourselves. About us and no one else. Us! Do you know? Please! Wake up! Let us not escape it. That's what they wanted to tell us all these seers, angels, prophets and madmen. They wanted to tell us "you are the heir to the Kingdom". Then, of course, smart as we are, we stoned them.

The seekers of truth is the child-hero who must undergo the pilgrimage towards the city of the Self! The Father is the conscious one, the witness, knower of the field (*Kshetragyna*). The Mother is the Unconscious and thoughtlessness is the space where they meet. If the conscious and the unconscious are not in some kind of balance the Father turned supraconscious punishes you (e.g. the eagle devouring Prometheus' liver, the sun burning Icarus' wings) or the Mother turned subconscious swallows you (the whale of Jonah). To balance the energy and tune in with the Divine is the supreme art of life. This art is spontaneously mastered through the blessing of Sahaja Yoga.

When you have travelled on the Sushumna path you cross the gate of the Ajnya Chakra. This is the resurrection of the Divine in you which was previously buried in the three gunas. Then the attention is raised towards the Holy City of the limbic area: you reach the sanctum sanctorum of the Sahasrara. The subsequent meeting of the Kundalini Shakti with the Atman, at the Brahmarandra, expands the individual consciousness into the cosmic union with the Universal Unconscious. This union blasts away human dimensionalities. Each and every one of us bears within ourselves the limit that mankind as a collective entity is called upon to cross. Those who become aware of this, set themselves up as cosmic actors. Those who were poets will now write the supreme poem. Those who were artist will erect the magisterial work and those who were knights, fight the last struggle. The limit crossed, the Kingdom opens which is bathing in the zenithal splendour of God.

At the same time as I name the path I ought to mention the foes. Alas, today they are formidable, the more so because they are invisible and very cunning. Without seeing them you cannot deal with them and without dealing with them, you cannot see them because of clouded awareness. This is the vicious circle that somehow must be broken. But can you do it? Let me now propose very humbly a new approach which could be of some use for understanding the status of the last quarter of this century.

Refer to the myth of Icarus: the modern man has developed his psyche and his society in climbing the sun line, that is by using the Rajoguna energy of the right side of the Virata. When the point of balance was lost, this ascent led man towards the extremes; the excessive involvement in the Rajoguna triggered the reaction process whereby the activity of the psyche tilted towards and shifted to the Tamoguna, that is, slipped into the collective subconscious. The moment of the collapse, the fall of Icarus, took place during the period stretching between the two World Wars. Where does Icarus fall?—in the sea. Now, it is out of this very sea that issues forth the Beast of the Apocalypse.

Those who expect St. John's prophecy to be fulfilled through the thrilling appearance of some exotic marine creature landing on Malibu beach or Rio's Copacabana are very much misled. As systematically documented by Jungian psychoanalysis, the sea is most often the symbol for (what Jung called) the Unconscious and what we call, in this instance, the collective subconscious. The beast to devour the psyche might well come from the nether regions of the collective subconscious. Now the Beast has reached the firm ground and starts walking on it boasting and blaspheming. This means that once it has invaded the subconscious of many a fellow-man's psyche, it goes on overpowering the conscious side of his psyche. The consequent hypothesis is that the Beast is something akin to a satanic collective UPI, a case of collective possession which issues from the subconscious libido and which is accepted, rationalized and magnified by the mental side of the overpowered human mind. I will not name the Beast, the false prophets or the foul spirits. But you have been warned: the sorcerers, thanks to their command over the UPIs,[3] are presently

---

[3] To repeat only a few instances; they can order a UPI to carry someone and then the subject will exhibit a capacity of flying in the air. They give their followers mantras to repeat which are nothing but names of UPIs. They put UPIs in food and give it to followers to eat. They introduce UPIs into your chakras by touching them, etc.

manipulating the irruption of the sub and supraconscious into the human psyche. While assuring for themselves a psychic overlordship on the minds of their followers they condemn them to a regression, to a bad deviation from the evolutionary process that is prepared for the ascent of Man.

The scenery of the struggle is fairly easy to describe. There is a multitude of people who are not bothered. They are very superficial, ignorant of everything that matters and especially ignorant of that ignorance. Eventually they think they are successful in life, and line up on the side of what they think to be the stronger party. These are the tamasic or half-baked rajasic temperaments. They are extremely conditioned; they follow the trend. In this Kali Yuga they, obviously, tend to take to adharma, that is, unholy life.

This is the crowd around the actors although these people can be in command of high social positions, be successful, wealthy, etc., etc. They can also be the innocents of the Third World's deprived strata who are paying for the mistakes of others: these may be very ordinary souls, slaughtered animals who have taken their birth in the human stage. They are blind to the truth for they have not yet developed their human perceptivity.

Then you have the purely rajasic temperaments. This party has moved matter and agitated quite a bit of thought for the last centuries. They wanted to assert the worth of their existence and, meanwhile, they have brought society to its present stage. They are not happy about it but, by now, the more agitation they generate, the greater the confusion they produce: they are caught in the entropic net. When their frantic research leads them away from dharma they are the prey to the satanic forces and become themselves dangerous. On top of it all, of course, let us not forget that the money making machinery works at its best through the exploitation of the human weaknesses. The cosy, comfortable dissolution of our awareness into vice is encouraged in all possible ways; it takes place through a smooth series of happenings which, though destroying the subtle consciousness, are pleasurable to the baser self. When the sorcerers and the machinery combine, who can resist them?

The sattvic elements generate balance and wisdom. They try to keep to righteousness but, in the prevailing mess, they become extremely frustrated and lonely because they cannot bear the injustice and misery of a human society where the majority of relationships are reduced to sex, money and power games.

Now, of course, each of us is a mixture of those three types depending upon the pattern of movements of energy on Pingala, Ida and Sushumna nadi. When the energy operates mainly through one channel we evolve the corresponding temperament. As it is, as we are, we have to face the sorcerers of Satan.

There is, in this present time, in the earth's biosphere, a collection of perfectly satanic personalities. They are challenging God. Unlike ourselves, they know the show, they know God but they have completely cut themselves off from Him, the source of joy and bliss. In this condition existence for them is a burden, they know it, and the only way they can get a relief from existence is to provoke the final destruction of the whole creation, that is, to provoke the dance of Sadashiva. For them nothingness is salvation. To this effect, they are now spreading on this earth as many sins, blasphemies and abominations as possible. They can do so because they control the UPIs.

There are also many on this earth who are the future Sahaja Yogis, the children of HH Mataji, the children of God, but who do not know it yet. They seek the taste of the joy of truth and love, in the blissful existence of the Self. They hope for the destruction of wickedness. Searching for them are today's Sahaja Yogis who have been enlightened by HH Mataji. They are eager to spread self-realisation as much and as fast as possible because they know that the time is short.

The time is indeed short to completely awaken oneself to reality and then, to awaken others to it. In the West, HH Mataji said once, salvation is a salvage operation. It does indeed sometimes look like a crash rescue operation... we have to work very hard to spread the message of our emancipation. Let us get out of the satanic net because Shri Kalki will come in his destructive mood and will wipe out wickedness. Those who would still be identified with it, who cling to falsehood, will have a bad time.

Can we say at this stage what will be the outcome? The destruction of wickedness or the destruction of the Universe? The colossal alternative is between the dance of Sadashiva and the ride of Shri Kalki.

To be sure, Shri Kalki has been duly announced by the ancient scriptures. He will come, it was said, at the end of Kali

Yuga; virtue will have vanished, there will be famine, wars and criminal rulers. Women bear too many children.[4] The Brahmins would have lost the knowledge and have only the white thread to distinguish them. Substance and real worth have departed from everything. The sacred rites are gone. The earth is worshipped for its minerals only. Men and women live together without being married, bound by sensuality only. In the *Devi Purana,* the description of Kali Yuga is very vivid. It says that in these days people will eat from steel plates, women will dress like men and men like women. The description of the degenerated modern urban societies is surprisingly correct. Similarly, Lord Jesus announced that his second coming will take place amidst a widespread condition of sin on earth. The sequence can of course be related to the image of the lotus in Hindu mysticism. The flower of purity grows in the mud (Pankaya): the alchemy of the Divine Grace transforms the sinner into a saint. Yet, despite the insurance of the writing of the past, we have no hard guarantee that the play will culminate in the hoped for happy end. The very notion of cosmic play, to begin with, refutes the deterministic paradigm and the consequent traditions of religious (Calvin) or chemical (Monod) necessity. It implies the dynamic dialectic of change and necessity that frames the rule of evolution at the molecular,[5] human and cosmic levels. The probability that the seventh chakra of the Virata will completely open to bring forth the advent of Shri Kalki is serious. The alternative implying the total and final destruction of this Universe, is by no means excluded: if man as a whole, in his adharma, crosses the point of no return after which it is no longer possible for him to recognize God, the cosmic play of Creation will have lost its meaning. In the final dance (Tandava), God Almighty calls His Power back to Himself and thus all the worlds dissolve into nothingness. But HH Mataji has, comfor-

---

[4]Actually as so many young mothers in the West are unworthy of this name, many souls are reluctant to take their birth in such an atmosphere, detrimental to the family and the child. The birth rate is already now sharply dropping to the great dismay of the manpower resources planners.

[5]See *Das Spiel: Naturgesetze Steuern den Zufall* by Manfred Eigen and R. Winkler Piper (Munchen and Zurich 1975). This monograph proposes a dynamic vision of physical chemistry and molecular biology which sharply contrasts with the mechanistic and deterministic atmosphere of J. Monod's *Chance and Necessity.* (Editions du Seuil 1970).

tingly enough, told us: "Now I can see that Tandava is averted by the creation of so many Sahaja Yogis. If the wind blows and one sari is firmly tied to the tree of truth, then all the saries tied together to the first one will not be blown away." She declares Herself to be very pleased to see so many people getting realisation in Sahaja Yoga. She says: "I have never achieved that much before." For the first time in history so many human beings are recognising the truth of a Divine Incarnation.

That is why—or so it seems—man is holding the key role in the last act of his salvation. Again, "Sahaja Yoga is the salvaging operation before the last sorting out by Lord Kalki".

Let us now refer to St. John's vision of Shri Kalki:

"Then I saw heaven opened, and behold, a white horse. He who sat upon it is called Faithful and True, and in righteousness he judges and makes war. His eyes are like a flame of fire and on his head are many diadems; and he has a name inscribed that no one knows but himself. He is clad in a robe dipped in blood, and the name by which he is called is The Word of God. And the armies of heaven, arrayed in fine linen, white and pure, followed him on white horses. From his mouth issues a sharp sword with which to smite the nations and he will rule them with a rod of iron; he will tread the wine press of the fury of the wrath of God the Almighty. On his robe and on his thigh he has a name inscribed, King of kings and Lord of lords".—Revelation of St. John 19.11.

St. John's attention is struck firstly by the horse and then by Shri Kalki. This sequence is not without significance and we should now relate the horse of Shri Kalki to what was previously exposed.

We have said that the cosmic-microcosmic relation, the link between the Cosmic evolution and the human microcosmic evolution consists in the fact that the seven point programme of the Virata is built in each and every human being as the psychosomatic and spiritual instrument of self-realisation. We have also mentioned that self-realisation is the opening of the seventh chakra.

The implications of this happening are as follows:

—On the microcosmic level the opening of the seventh chakra at the individual level represents "the" synthesis of self-realisation.

It is firstly the integration of all the different elements[6] of the human person.

—It is also the synthesis between the Human and the Divine, the Finite and the Infinite, the overcoming of the Limit.

—On the cosmic level the opening of the seventh chakra of a great number of people represents the opening of the seventh chakra of the Virata.

—The relation between Epistemology and History, the link between knowledge and evolution is the fact that, when a sufficient number of human beings will have expanded their level of awareness to the dimension of self-realisation, the seventh point of the cosmic programme will be implemented.

Put in more scholarly terms, evolution of history and phenomenology of consciousness are merging together because their respective fields have been brought together by the advent of this ultimate happening; the Holy Spirit manifesting the deity whose abode is the seventh chakra of the Virata. Shri Kalki is the redeemer and the destroyer, the white rider of the Christian and Hindu eschatologies. His coming is actualised by Sahaja Yoga's implementation of collective consciousness on earth.

THE COLLECTIVE CONSCIOUSNESS OF THE REALISED SOULS IS THE HORSE OF SHRI KALKI. And now I must again tell you: please, understand your importance: *by building up the collective consciousness of the realised beings you are preparing the cosmic horse of the returning King.*

In HH Mataji's amazing plan of redemption mankind is to be saved through man's participation. Without this participation, Shri Kalki will not come and Sadashiva will rise up and dance Tandava for the final destruction. Is it what we want? No! We want the Kingdom of God, His love and His justice. We want to know our divine parents and our divine Self. We want the Golden Age. Perhaps you are scared by St. John's frightful description of the Rider. But the destroyer of the wicked is the saviour of the innocent. Yes, we have committed many sins but this need not mean we are wicked; we have been misled, confused. Let us *now* renounce our noxious behaviour. The wicked ones will, anyway, laugh at my warnings and sin until the very last moment.

---

[6] A human being is a system of energy-awareness (mandala) made out of the auras of the five elements (koshas), the various chakras, etc.

The wicked ones are basically of two kinds: those who are innately wicked and others who take to wickedness. The first lot is doomed to the lowest pits of hell. The second type may be saved by Sahaja Yoga. But the nadis are weak, the chakras drained off and the awareness spoiled. "God's power can destroy Evil but what is to be done when Evil has entered into the awareness of the seeker?"

Only we can answer this question by siding with righteousness and holiness and asking for self-realisation.

I certainly would not wish the condition of "the lake of Sulphur" (Apocalypse) on anybody, wicked as he may be but then, please try to take seriously the warnings of one who, for the time being, is a lone voice, seemingly isolated among the noises of the modern world, making strange utterances and predictions. Why do you need to believe me? Signs, wonders, miracles? Just ask for the vibrations and thoughtless awareness; this is the medium through which everything else will be revealed. The other signs will not convince anyone anyway. We are surrounded by rumours of wars, the majority of the world population is starving, there is widespread immorality, violence, pollution, climatic threats, people are and will remain blind to these. It is now that the chance is given to us to return to God the place in our life that is His due. If we are not actively seeking His truth now we will be among the five foolish maidens who were waiting for the bridegroom; as he was delayed they fell asleep. When he came there was no oil left in their lamps and they did not enter with him into the house. When Shri Kalki manifests, we should be ready.

> "But take heed to yourselves lest your hearts be weighed down with dissipation and drunkenness and cares of this life, and that day come upon you suddenly like a snare; for it will come upon the face of the whole earth. But watch at all times praying that you may have strength to escape all these things that will take place and to stand before the Son of Man".
>
> Luke 21.3.4.

Lord Jesus Christ, Mahavishnu, has all the eleven rudras (destroying powers) of Lord Shiva. But He uses only one power: forgiveness. You know that He warned us: the sin against the Holy Spirit will not be forgiven. At the very second Lord Jesus ceases to forgive, He becomes Shri Kalki. Up to that point, we have all latitude to repent, to be forgiven, to improve and purify ourselves: the worst sinner has his chance. At that point, that's it.

The Rider is the destroyer. That was made perfectly clear in the Gospels and the Kalki Purana. When He will come, He will neither argue or listen neither save or forgive. We should clearly understand one thing: HH Mataji is the Saviour because She is the compassionate One to grant us emancipation before the coming of Shri Kalki. She is the Comforter that Christ has promised. Therefore all our attention should be on Her, on the Now, and on self-realisation that She grants. Shri Kalki is not to be expected now. We are not ready for Him. He is the beloved and most obedient son of HH Mataji. He listens to Her and delays His coming because the Divine Mother wants us to get our realisation first.

Indeed the Kundalini is the Mother of our second birth which is the identification with the Self. Kundalini is concretely manifested through Sahaja Yoga. Which was brought to us by HH Mataji Nirmala Devi. The new man and the new world find their origin in one Divine Incarnation who became flesh and is dwelling among us full of grace and truth unknown to the world and yet redeeming it.

The second birth of the Spirit, collective emancipation, all this has been promised. We, Sahaja Yogis from the five continents bear witness to the truth and divinity of HH Mataji's message. We very ordinary human beings, do feel the vibrations of the Holy Spirit and the new consciousness.

If you are seeking Reality, if you are seeking God, come and get it NOW. It is here for you. We beg you: do not delay.

You can contact Sahaja Yogis at the following addresses:

Sahaja Yoga c/o—A/203 Giriraj Apts, Mandapeshwar Road,
              Borivli (W), BOMBAY, 400092 India

25, Carlisle Mansions, Carlisle Place, LONDON S.W.1
              United Kingdom

Now, brothers and sisters of the scattered flock, where do we stand? Many of us are drawn into a mess. All right. It will not be that easy to get out of these quicksands of adharmic behaviour in which we have been sinking. We might well have to suffer. But there is one thing we should never forget: we now know that the Divine Love of HH Mataji is greater than any sin. Let us take refuge in Her and we will be safe. The surrender to HH Mataji will tune the psyche on to the frequency of the Universal Unconscious and Shri Kalki, as the brain of the Virata, is nothing but the personification of this Universal Unconscious. This is the secret rule which will grant you the mastery of cosmic horsemanship.

Part Five

THE DIVINE MOTHER

"Behold the Mother"
John 19.27

"You are verily that which cannot be uttered specifically"

Shri Brahmadeva to the Devi
in the *Devi Mahatmayam or Shri Durga-Saptasati*

Whatever has been said about self-realization suggests that it is a very difficult thing to achieve. Awakening of Kundalini is supposed to involve a tremendous task of cleansing, taking lives after lives of dedicated efforts. But for HH Mataji it is just a play. It can happen in a moment.

Jagannath Baba, came down from the Himalayas for one of HH Mataji's programmes. Somewhat sceptical, he was arguing with the disciples while waiting for HH Mataji to make Her appearance on the dais. As soon as HH Mataji entered the hall, he prostrated completely (*ashtanga namaskar*) at Her feet, calling Her "Adi Maya, Adi Maya". Later on he told the disciples that as soon as HH Mataji had entered the hall, suddenly he saw everybody's Kundalini rise, like the children in class standing up for the teacher. It was an unprecedented happening.

I who write these lines am also so very fortunate to have been blessed by such a unique, unprecedented spiritual personality. Now I am enjoying the play which She has created.

When I got my realization and when the vibrations started flowing from my being She taught me how to use this new vibratory awareness. "Ask any absolute question" She suggested. The first question "Is there God?" was answered, to my great surprise, by a tremendous flow of vibrations coming in my fingers and palms. I asked many such questions and was blessed by clear answers; the answer "yes" comes as an increase in vibrations. I asked is such and such guru a realized soul?" The answer "No" came as a burning on the finger tips. Sometimes the whole hand felt very hot and heavy.

I realised that this vibratory awareness was establishing a rapport, an actual dialogue with the Divine. What an amazing attainment! I got answers to various questions, even questions pertaining to my own relatives and friends. Other Sahaja yogis, small children who are born realised, were getting the same answers.

The experience was more than convincing. HH Mataji used to illustrate it in the following terms:

> "You all are like a computer assembled, organized, and fitted through your evolution, reaching at last the stage in which you are ready to be plugged into the mains. When the Kundalini gets connected with the Universal Unconscious, you can have a direct communication with Reality".

After all, if the Universal Unconscious has to speak to Mankind there are basically two ways. It can communicate in dreams, symbols, intuitions; and it can incarnate as a human being to bring into full light everything that was unknown and unexplained, thus switching on a continuous "communication current".

To be sure, past incarnations have clearly spoken about Truth, Knowledge and about the fact that their actualisation would supervene at a later stage of history. For instance, in St. John's Gospel we can find the following quotations from Lord Jesus:

> "These things I have spoken to you while I am still with you. But the Counsellor, the Holy Spirit whom the Father will send in my name, he will teach you all things, and bring you remembrance of all that I have said to you.. and now I have told you before it takes place so that when it does take place you may believe."—John 14.25

> "It is to your advantage that I go away, for if I do not go away, the Counsellor will not come to you: but if I go, I will send him to you. And when he comes, he will convince the world concerning sin and righteousness and judgement... I have yet many things to say to you but you cannot bear them now".—John 16.7

These statements suggest that Lord Jesus could not convince the human beings in contemporary Galilee. Why? Because they had not yet reached the level of evolution in which they would be ready for vibratory awareness. Of course the Holy Spirit did inspire the Apostles but that was not yet the fulfilment of Lord Jesus' promise. Indeed the sinful condition of the world in the past centuries makes it quite clear that it has not yet been convinced "concerning sin, righteousness and judgement". And the modern man does not care.

HH Mataji has described and explained all the debated aspects of the teachings of past Incarnations. We proved Her sayings with vibratory awareness.

It is only now that the full meaning of the Evangelist's words can be understood for She has completed the Christian message. We, at last, fully understand the life of Lord Jesus Christ.[1] He kept referring to His Divine Mother as the Holy Spirit because in the Galilee of that time no one was supposed to know the true nature of the Virgin Mary. Lord Jesus was the Son of the Adi Shakti who incarnated in the Mahalaxshmi form as the Virgin Mary. He would not have tolerated the satanic forces at work in Galilee turning their attention towards His beloved Mother. Any attack on Her would have triggered Universal destruction. So He kept the secret. But announced the coming of "the Spirit of Truth who proceeds from the Father" and who will bear witness to Him.

It is at this juncture that I wish to mention ancient scriptures, half forgotten under the dust of the millenia... Indeed, when confronted with the surprising experiences we are now having in the last part of the twentieth century, these writings are unveiling a fresh meaning that is of practical use to us. For instance, to the extent to which they reveal the aspects of what they call "the Divine Mother", they also provide clues as to how to recognise Her in case She were to take a human birth as She is reported to do.

We can refer to the collection of mantras known as *Shri Lalita Sahasranama*. Among the thousand names of the Devi, let us con-

---

[1] HH Mataji says: "After His Assumption, Christ descended on this earth in a hidden place while the Holy Spirit (Mary) stayed back to inspire the faith of the early Christians. After Her assumption She joined Her Son and they lived together for many years in Kashmere . They are buried there."

sider the following; Her hundred and tenth name is "Kundalini". It means that She resides in each individual in a potential state, coiled like a serpent at the bottom of the spine. She is also "Sahasra dalapadmastha" (528) that is, residing on the thousand petalled lotus at the top of the brain. The relationship between these positions is exposed by Her numerous names which remind us that She confers the bliss of liberation to her devotees: *Mokshadaini, Muktidaini, Pashahantrini, Mukti-Pradasani, Bhavaragny-Kutharika,* etc. She grants the spiritual birth to Her child by ascending, as the uncoiled Kundalini, to the Sahasrara. But when and how is the Kundalini to rise? This question is answered in another text. In the *Devi Bhagavat Puran,* Shri Markandeya tells us that you can recognise the Shakti by the fact that the Kundalini of the seekers (*Bhakta*) rises in Her presence. She is the one who raises Kundalini at a glance: In this holy scripture the Devi tells to Himalaya: "There is no difference between me and Kundalini. Sahasrara is the only complete and very best goal of yoga. When Shiva and Shakti are united the amrit is flowing and feeding the deities of the chakras".[2]

A non-realized reader cannot make much out of Shri Markandeya's writings. But, after our rebirth in Sahaja Yoga, we have been able to check all the above points. They are all correct and coherent. In the presence of HH Mataji thousands of Sahaja yogis have seen the pulsating of the Kundalini and have also seen Her movement upward with their naked eyes.

As we now move to other ancient scriptures let us not be blinded by "religious" parochialism. A mind overly conditioned by the fatherly connotation of the Judaeo-Christian tradition will, at first, have some difficulty at the conception of the Divine in the feminine form of the Mother. And yet, the cult of the Motherhood of God, from time immemorial, has been attested by archaeological evidence from all quarters of the globe. It seems that it is the Indian subcontinent which presents us with the most elaborate expressions of this worship.

According to Advaita Vedanta Ultimate Reality is formless undifferentiated consciousness (*Nirguna*). This condition, which is

---

[2]*The Devi Bhagavat Puran* Kalyan edit. (January 1960) p. 412 (free translation).

THE DIVINE MOTHER

at the same time Absolute Being and Absolute Nothingness[3] cannot be conceived of. Through eons of ages, it goes through alternate phases of potentiality and manifestation. The alternation of this cosmic rhythm has been called: "the respiration of Brahma". When the ultimate reality rests in its latent phase, the Unmanifested, it is contained in "IT". In the activating phase of its manifestation, the "IT" becomes "HE" and "HER"; HH Mataji says that the first step of the Creation takes place when God separates itself into Himself as a witness and Herself as His power. One aspect is Sadashiva (The Primordial Existent and Witness, God the Almighty, the Father, the Purusha); the other is His power, the Adi Shakti, (the Primordial Energy of Divine Love, the Divine Mother, the Prakriti).[4] Thus the Mother is Primordial Energy. The relation between the Shakti and God has been admirably expressed by Shri Seeta, rebuking Ravana in Lanka's Asoka park: "As the sun's brightness belongs in separably to the sun so do I belong to Rama". The Creation, spiritual and material, springs from the Divine Mother, the Holy Spirit of the Christian tradition. She creates various strata of existence, among which this phenomenal universe. As this Primordial Energy of the ultimate is the genitrix of everything we experience, She is worshipped as the Sacred Mother. We read in the first sutras of *the Kama-Kalavilasa*:

> "Victory to Her the Primordial Power, the seed from which Sprouts hereafter the entire creation, static and kinetic universes, the eternal, the incomparable, who is of the nature of Her own bliss, and who manifests as a mirror to His (Shiva) self".

The Samaya Mata recalls that the distinction between He and Her is only an apparent one: "There is no Shiva without Shakti nor is there any Shakti without Shiva. There is no distinction between them just as there is none between the moon and the shining". The Shakti combines in Her person both the manifestation of the Universal Existence (male form) and the Universal

---

[3] In Mahayana buddhism "tathata" (suchness) and "sunyata" (emptiness) are interchangeable notions.
[4] Purusha and Prakriti represent the apparent opposition between the Father-Spirit and the Mother-Nature.

Energy (female form). She is thus identified with the One. The actualisation of this primordial unity within the disciple is the object of the Shakti worship. She is the central object of worship because She is the manifested dimension of the Ultimate. She is the Great One who bridges the gap between the Infinity and the Finite; only through Her compassionate mediation can the finite human being regain Infinity. And that is indeed the very blessing that She wants to graciously bestow on Her children.

> "Thyself, with a view to manifesting Thyself in the form of the Universe, inwardly assumest the form of Consciousness and Bliss".—Shri Shankaracharya, *Saundarya Lahari* 35

Let us again remember that the Holy Spirit, as the Primordial Energy, is the Christian mysterious symbol for the Mother.

We ought to mention, that in the apocryphal Acts of Saint Thomas, the Holy Spirit is (rightly) invoked as "hidden Mother", "Mother of all life". These statements should help us to recognise the true wisdom of the early gnostics and Syrian fathers who grasped something of the identity (Holy Spirit = Mother = Energy). The esoteric perception certainly casts a new light on the intriguing dialogue between Lord Jesus Christ and Nicodemus:

> "Truly, Truly, I say to you unless one is born anew, he cannot see the Kingdom of God. Nicodemus said to him, "how can a man be born when he is old? Can he enter a second time into his mother's womb and be born?" Jesus answered "Truly truly, I say to you, unless one is born of water and the Spirit he cannot enter the Kingdom of God"—John 3.3.

The necessity to return to the Divine Mother in order to become a New Adam, a second born, a Divine Child has been asserted by Lord Jesus. It is time that those western seekers who have engaged themselves in intellectual pursuits use their intellect to discover the Unity of the message of the various mythologies and religions; they had better realize the greatness of the Christian promise and the value of the other world religions. HH Mataji has brilliantly exposed these teachings in a new light which also illuminates other religious traditions and contemporary science. It is time for us to discover that the true object of Knowledge is integration. All the great religions are one. This is revealed by actualization when our own integration takes place through rebirth.

Although the Great Goddess (Adi Shakti) is "Truly forlmess" (see *the Devipurana*) She has been worshipped through millenia in countless aspects and forms.[5] The three great aspects through which She is channelling Her own power are Mahalaxshmi, Mahasaraswati, Mahakali. She is also known to have taken various incarnated forms (*avata:as*).

It is thus described in the Scriptures that She is the Primordial Power, the utterly Holy. It is certainly not easy for the western reader to face the very serious hypothesis that She can take human form. To talk about it is even more difficult. This field of reality only underlines the limitations of ideas and words.

It is only in the holy silence of collective consciousness after achieving self-realization that anything can be revealed about Her. She is supreme, beyond praise, beyond words and certainly beyond anything that can be written. And yet the purpose of this book— an introduction to Sahaja Yoga—cannot be fulfilled without paying due homage to the absolutely unique personality of the Mother who can trigger the super human step in the dynamic process of evolution. After all, the validity of Sahaja Yoga rests upon the authenticity of the teacher who revealed it. And who is great enough to perform such a grand task? Hence in this pitiful time of false prophets and commercialised gurus listen to the TRUTH. When the thieves and the robbers are transvestite as saints, teachers and yogic masters, when traditional religions have only too often sunk into lifeless conformism, or economic activities, when words such as 'Divine', 'God', 'Holy Spirit' sound almost futile, when the honest seeker is left alone, seemingly abandoned between the stupid and the perverted, at this time I have to tell you: awaken your mind to the prospect that the Divine Mother is manifesting in the

---

[5]Historically, we find reference to a Mother Goddess in the earliest stage of the Indus civilisation. She was worshipped in the cities of Mohenjo-Daro and Harrappa. With the later Vedic Aryans, Mother Goddess was worshipped as Usas, Prithvi (Earth) and Aranyni in the *Rig Veda* and Shri Gayatri in *Yajur Veda* and as Shri Mahalaxhmi, Durga and Jagadamba in other Vedas. In the *Upanishads*, She appears as Uma and Heimavat. In *Puranas* She was worshipped as Shri Lalita and Kali and in *Agamas* and *Tantras* as Shri Mahakali, Tripura Sundari and Rajajeswari. In *Tantras* the left hand ritual (Vamachara) and the right hand ritual (Samayachara) are mentioned as belonging to shaktism.

present time. Of course truth is beyond belief and disbelief; it can be experienced only in doubtless awareness because that is where truth belongs. However to those of us who have not yet experienced we may say a few things:

She is the teacher who displays a total mastery over the ultimate knowledge and who at the same time also provides the disciple with the possibility of experimentally verifying the authenticity of this teaching; She is the teacher who transforms the disciple's awareness into a new dimension instead of merely teaching him... Such a teacher can only open a new cycle of knowledge in which science, philosophy and spirituality will be synthesized in one integrated understanding. You naturally wonder: who can this teacher be?

There is a way to get the answer and HH Mataji usually expresses it in the following image:

> "Nothing is easier than turning on the light in a room. You just press the switch button. But there is a big mechanism that works it out: wires, power houses and the whole process of scientific discovery which mastered the use of electricity; there is a long history behind the discovery of electricity. In the same way, there is a great dynamic organisation that works out Self-realization; let us first switch on our lamps and in their light we can understand the mechanism much better".

So HH Mataji invites you to first get your realization and then see for yourself. But we, Her disciples, would like to tell you a bit more about Her.

Modern psychoanalysis emphasizes the fact that dreams carry important messages from the Unconscious. Countless people who were about to meet HH Mataji were visited by premonitory dreams. Rustum, an Oxbridge educated doctor in psychology recalls many of them. The night before meeting HH Mataji he had the following dream.

> "Act One. I am quarrelling with a friend in great despair. (This friend represents a vital part of myself I cannot integrate).
> Act Two. I am asked to give evidence in a court case against

this friend. The proceedings are interrupted by the arrival of the Queen. The trial comes to an end.
Act Three. I meet an Indian woman, of about 45 or 50 years, dressed in a red and gold saree who teaches me how to dance. We dance facing each other and I experience a tremendous sense of liberation.
Act Four. I am reunited with my friend who has become a hero and I am healing him."

Premonitions manifest in the wakeful state also. Before meeting HH Mataji, Sheila used to take a daisy for support of her meditation (Daisy is the Christian first name of HH Mataji). She remembers taking hours to draw, with great care, the picture of an Indian woman she had never seen. On top of it all she used to go "incredibly high" while driving her car past the house where HH Mataji was granting self-realisation: "I did not understand what was happening. Driving down that bit of Marylebone Road I just used to get tuned into a different dimension. Better than a joint. Perceptions were more acute: magnified sounds, brighter colours. I was ridiculously happy, elated."

"On my way to the Sahaja Yoga programme in Caxton Hall," James tells us, "I felt sort of mellowing down inside and the head becoming very clear and light. I told myself 'wow this is the big thing' and hurried up."

When one travels in the non-dimensional space of consciousness there are no ready-made maps to tell the traveller which road to choose and which one to avoid. It is relatively easy to make a mistake which can spoil a whole life. The safest rule is to trust only in one's own experience but even then some experiences are misleading. The only way I can help the reader is to propose my rational approach as a possible way for him to explore. And I can help him in gaining some confidence in this exploration by giving him facts.

> —In India, great yogis came out of the forests and they did prophesy about HH Mataji. For instance, Gargangar Giri Maharaj whose Ashram is near Kolhapur said that, at the time of HH Mataji's birth he saw the complete Shri Chakra[6]

---

[6]The Shri Chakra can be described as the instrument of the power of the Holy Spirit.

coming down upon earth. He says that She is the Adi Shakti Herself...! and that he does not understand why She is giving realization to people who do not deserve it; it took him thousands of years to achieve this state that She is granting to disciples in a matter of minutes.

—Innumerable people have had visions about HH Mataji. A little group of London Sahaja Yogis were meditating in front of HH Mataji. Suddenly one of us left the room. When we asked him why, later on, he said that he had been aware of thousands of white-clad beings around us and that he had been scared by their might.

—In Buenos-Aires a lady who had no knowledge of the Indian mythology began describing Shri Laxshmi in the Vaikuntha stage, lost in ecstasy in front of HH Mataji. March 1976: HH Mataji is sitting in my garden in Katmandu, gazing toward the sky. I am sitting nearby. I am looking at Her. Suddenly the lines of the garden around HH Mataji are melting away. I realise that all the lines are dissolving and only one presence remains which imposes itself onto my attention; my gaze abandons the vanishing garden and again I look at HH Mataji. And I see the figure of a man or rather, of a God, a face of unsurpassable greatness, light blue in complexion, radiating with a beauty and majesty for which there is no name. I am bewildered, adoring, subjugated. Yes, it is You, I have already seen You, I remember this Godhead...and then I bend towards the ground because I feel my eyes are not pure enough to look at Him. When I look at Her again, everything is normal. I tell Her what happened. She says simply: "It was Shri Krishna".

—In various instances HH Mataji has publicly exhibited a command over cosmic forces such as atmospheric conditions, sea, etc. HH Mataji says that cancer can be cured only by Sahaja Yoga. In various places of India there are records of cases of cancer which have been cured by HH Mataji. These records, I understand, are authenticated by medical reports of established doctors. Many kinds of diseases have been healed by the Sahaja Yogis themselves in

Bombay, Delhi, etc.[7]

—People who are followers of certain pseudo "gurus", when exposed to Her darshan (physical presence) begin shaking and shivering in front of Her. So do patients from lunatic asylums. Yet She has the power to soothe them with great compassion and understanding.

—Merely by looking at Her, people have improved their eyesight. By touching Her Ajnya Chakra we have felt thoughtless awareness; touching the Chakras in Her back, even through Her coat, we feel throbbing in our fingers; stretching out our hands towards Her we feel the breeze; looking at Her we get the coolness; listening to Her we feel something rising within our spine.

Hundreds of people have eye-witnessed the breathing of the Kundalini on the bent back of somebody prostrated at Her feet. They saw it pulsating at the triangular bone and in different chakras. This happens only when the subject is at the feet of HH Mataji or when he faces Her.

We have heard and seen that, when she says a mantra, the pulsation reacts to it and moves its way along the spine. When She puts Her hand over someone's head, we can see the dilation of the subject's pupils and feel with our hand the pulsation on the top of his brain. After a while, we can feel a column of hot or cold breeze coming out of the area of the fontenale membrane.

By singing the praises of Devi Durga or the Litanies of the Virgin Mary in front of HH Mataji the vibrations have sometimes increased so much that our hands have become ice cold. On these occasions we also went into very deep contemplation.

What is all this about? Who is HH Mataji?

HH Mataji Nirmala Devi was born the day of the spring equinox, the 21st March 1923, at twelve o' clock in Chindwara,

---

[7]Aubrey Menen, author of *The New Mystics*, reports such cases of cure. But he spent very little time with HH Mataji, gathered only a few facts and the image he offers of HH Mataji's spiritual activity is extremely superficial. He does not even mention Sahaja Yoga!

in the exact centre of India.[8] She chose to take birth in an Indian Christian family. Her forefathers were the great "Shalivahan" emperors from Rahuri-Nandgaon. HH Mataji's father was a very high realized soul, the guru who introduced Her to the workings of modern men. He was a man of great character and honour, a great model of accomplished human behaviour. His generosity and integrity were universally respected and he eventually became a prominent figure in the Freedom movement and the only Christian member of the then Central Legislative Assembly. This intellectual giant knew many languages and had full mastery over at least eleven of them. He knew the whole of the Bhagavad Gita by heart and translated the Koran into Hindi. He was familiar with almost all aspects of the arts, literature and science. And yet he always behaved with great simplicity and modesty.

HH Mataji's mother, a well-educated lady holding an honours degree in mathematics, strictly upheld the values of personal and social dharma. It is said that she never told a lie during her lifetime and would not tolerate any compromise with falsehood. She educated her children with firmness and loving care and managed domestic affairs with aristocratic dignity. Always showing a heart-felt concern for the well-being of all the dependents of this very wealthy but sacrificing household, she was the mother of young and old alike.

While she was pregnant, HH Mataji's mother felt all of a sudden, an intense desire to see a tiger or a lion in the open. No one could draw her mind from it. It was an obsession. One day a rajah from the neighbourhood invited her husband to join in a big hunt for a formidable man-eater tiger. So, he reluctantly accepted to take his wife with him. The next day, they were both sitting with a strange feeling of expectation in the jungle watch-tower (*Machan*). The night came and the surroundings were bathed in

[8] At this moment, taking into consideration the local time, the Sun was exactly on the Meridian in full glory, and being in the zero degree of Aries and the 30th degree of Pisces, it made a rajayogo (astral configuration of prominence and power). The rising sign is cancer with the ascendant in the 9th degree. It is strongly aspected by five planets (Jupiter, Mercury, Uranus, Mars and the Moon, while it is occupied by Pluto which itself forms grand trines with three of the five planets and sextiles with the other two). The Ascendant in Cancer indicates the Universal Mother while Jupiter strongly aspected in the fifth house makes Her a World Teacher. The combinations of the planets in the angles of the chart indicate unprecedented spiritual powers.

the glow of the full moon. After some time a thick silence descended upon them, and, suddenly, a huge tiger emerged from the undergrowth. At this sight the mother felt elated and bubbling with joy. She entreated her husband not to kill the majestic beast. He yielded, asking smilingly: "Is it the Goddess Durga who will be born to you?"[9] After that evening the tiger vanished without a trace.

When HH Mataji was born, She was spotlessly clean as if bathed in scented water. Looking with awe at the smiling and radiant baby the grandmother exclaimed: "She is Nishkalanka![10]" The mother had delivered the baby without the slightest pain and was able to resume her household duties immediately. Since Nishkalanka is a boy's name HH Mataji was named "Nirmala", (immaculate).

On Easter Monday, the miraculous child was baptized amidst general rejoicing. On the way back home, the coachman lost control of the horses; something had frightened them and they reared so violently that the whole coach collapsed! Everybody was desperately anxious for the life of the baby. HH Mataji was found under a heap of the coach's wreckage and a couple of plump ladies-in-waiting unhurt and smiling as ever.

Nirmala spent a very happy childhood and, of course, was the darling of everybody. Even today people remember what a lovely adorable little girl she was. All the animals and birds were her friends but, sometimes, she would really frighten the maids of the house for even snakes would come in her hands to be caressed. Also they would often find her alone in a remote corner of the house, her face beaming with inward joy, lost in meditation. But most of the time she was bursting with energy and used to inspire her playmates in drama, songs and dances. When she played the role of Shri Krishna, at the age of seven, huge crowds were enraptured by the sweetness and vividness of her play; a feeling of spontaneous and total identification with the deities emanated from the grace of her acting. She very early exhibited an exquisite

---

[9]The vehicle of the Goddess Durga, the Mother of the World, is said to be a lion or a tiger.

[10]In *the Shri Lalita Sahasranama* as translated by C. Suryanarayana Murthy, (Bhavan's Book Bombay 1975) the 153 rd name of the goddess is Nishkalanka, meaning, "faultless brilliance". The tenth Avatar of Vishnu, the Incarnation to come is known as "Kalki"; it is the short form of the world 'Nishkalanka'.

taste for music and the arts, an innate enjoyment of all the many forms of beauty. She loved everything that was genuine, natural, and used to go to school barefoot in order to feel the earth. Her father laughingly told a new driver who had to pick her up after school: "It is easy to recognise my daughter. She is the girl who carries her shoes (chappals) in her hands."

During holidays the young Nirmala often went to Mahatma Ghandi's ashram. The Mahatma used to call her "Nepali" in reference to her half-Indian, half-Mongolian features.[11] She participated in all the activities of the ashram and one can see how her shining presence silently inspired Ghandiji. Most of the themes of the Mahatma: balanced production, social dharma, simplicity, integration of all religions were a prefiguration of "Sahaja culture".

When the time came to go to the University, Nirmala chose to study medicine: She wanted to know how far the human knowledge had gone. A few weeks ago in London, I personally met an old professor of medicine who had been her teacher. He still remembered her very well and recalled with a touch of pride, that she had been his extremely obedient and brightest student. Fortunately I met some of Her school mates and college friends. I was really struck by the tremendous respect and love they all have for Her.

After the struggle for national independence the young woman married Mr. Chandika Prasad Shrivastava, who was to become a prominent member of the Indian Administrative Service. Later on he was elected as the head of one of the specialized agencies of the United Nations system. Her in-laws contend that, "Verily, She has been a Griha Laxshmi; ever since She came to the house, grace and wealth has flowed in the Shrivastava family." All her relations sing her praises. It is impossible to describe how much She cares for her family and how much her relatives adore her.

Despite the fact that She is a prestigious spiritual leader, worshipped by thousands all over the world, HH Mataji has always been extremely respectful and obedient to Her husband. She goes out of her way to support his official life and would even give up a spiritual function arranged in Her honour if he so requires. Many

---

[11]The Goddess is known to be the daughter of the Himalayas and is reputed to have taken Her birth in Nepal. Years later, a physiognomist compared the proportions of HH Mataji's face with those of the Devi as described in an ancient book. They were perfectly matched. This man prostrated himself at Her feet.

of Mr. Shrivastava's friends say that they have never heard or seen such an ideal wife and I am amazed at the mildness with which she takes all the brunt of married life. Indeed, her husband is so very busy that she is often lonely. But she never complains about anything and she goes on, happily caring and labouring for her household. She remarked once: "It is not necessary to spend long hours together but to deeply enjoy the few short moments of togetherness." This is one of the ways She manifests—in Her own life—Her great concern for the upholding of ideal familial relationships. The importance of the family is indeed a paramount aspect of her spiritual teachings and Her own life tells the same story. HH Mataji Nirmala Devi is a wife, mother and grandmother. She devotes Her time to Her family life, social obligations and to Sahaja yoga in a full and profound way; God knows how she does it! HH Mataji's two daughters share the loving attention of their mother with thousands of disciples who claim a different, but very real type of dependence. HH Mataji has raised their Kundalini, granting them the second birth of integrated awareness. Yet, She never neglects Her household, children or grandchildren. Actually, She adores playing with them. And She extends Her exquisite motherly touch to everybody She cares for. While Her husband was the Chairman of the Shipping Corporation of India, the employees would say that "She is precious, like a mother to us. Because of Her we always felt we were all family members."

Those who know Her from childhood remember Her very clearly and love Her very dearly. All Her relations from parent's side and from Her husband's side come all the way from far off distances when they know about Her programmes. They have told us so many stories about Her sweetness, love, modesty and generosity. They all believe that She is a Goddess and there are some who said that they had recognized Her from Her very early age.

HH Mataji's husband, an extremely intelligent gentleman, rationally acknowledges the fact that the knowledge of a divine personality can never be taken for granted; although he is aware that his wife is quite an extraordinary woman, he confesses that to this day, he does not know who She really is. This example should teach patience to those Sahaja Yogis who would like to have revealed to them, at once, the full manifestation of the glory of God. With great admiration, Mr C.P Shrivastava spoke of his wife to a group of Indian Sahaja Yogis who were interviewing him a few years ago:

> "Ever since we have lived together constantly. Nirmala has been a dedicated wife, standing rock-like in periods of difficulties and crises which always recur in everyone's life. Her attributes are numerous, but I would mention only a few of them. First and foremost in her straightforwardness: her innocence. She cannot sometimes understand the tortuous ways of others. Her heart is full of genuine compassion for the poor, the needy; the afflicted. She cannot bear the sight of hungry children—tears flow out of her eyes. She is generous in the extreme and gives away her belongings to others with sincere pleasure. She is not attached at all to any material possessions. Her personal requirements are minimal and her personal expenditure almost nil.
>
> In her personal habits also she is most remarkable. She can live in any surroundings and feels no discomfort, no hardship. She eats with equal relish whatever is cooked for her meals, whether it is cooked badly or well"

It is very typical of HH Mataji's very liberal style that she never asked her husband to take to Sahaja Yoga. Her daughters told us that She never put any restrictions on them and educated them in complete freedom. But She did expect everybody to lead a very dharmic life; there would be no alcohol, gambling, etc. in the house.

We have never heard HH Mataji saying anything harsh. In Her company one really forgets that there is also an aspect of God which is wrathful! Because she is so mild and sweet it is very easy for inconsiderate visitors to show complacency and presumptuousness. Even when some of us had gone more than half way towards the gates of hell She would say, "If you are dirty you are not the dirt. The Divine can and will cleanse you" and "hate the sin but not the sinner". She has always been open to discussions, patiently listening to our foolish arguments and even asks many times: "I do not understand the ways of human beings. You had better enlighten me". The truth of the matter being of course that She knows about us much more and much deeper than we do. "Patience" is really a key word when it comes to presenting HH Mataji's character. Sometimes we just cannot understand the extent to which She bears the rudeness and arrogance of some people.

Her patient handling of all kinds of problems shows the neutralizing capacity of love expressed from an integrated, balanced standpoint. One story is typical. A husband and wife came to HH Mataji for advice. They told Her that they were unhappy together. HH Mataji spoke first to the wife, and told her "the wife has to bear because she is *'Dhara'*, the one who bears." The husband took up the theme, saying "that is true, I tell my wife to bear whatever I am". So HH Mataji turned then to the husband. "Why do you want to be renowned as an oppressive man" She asked, smiling, "would you not like to be a lover to your wife? I think your childhood must have been very harsh, that is why you do not know the art of love."

Of course, when needed, HH Mataji can act to show temper. She does so to assist those who endanger their spiritual growth by their own foolishness. For instance, it happened once in 1972 when the first group of Indian disciples gathered together at Bordi, north of Bombay. HH Mataji had worked on them during two years and nobody could get self-realization. Then, at the Bordi programme, Chandubhai, a Gujarati gentleman got it. Some of the disciples were murmuring among themselves, "Why did Mataji give realization to one Gujarati and not to Marathis?" When She heard about it She was really amazed at their stupidity and scolded them nicely. The next day, propelled by this burst of Her correcting energy, many of them got their self-realization. Indeed, it is written that, whatever the Goddess does, She does it for the well-being of the spirit.

One of Her remarkable qualities mentioned by everyone, is that though She is from an aristocratic and rich family and Her husband is a very highly placed officer, She is extremely mild, humble and kind. She gets up early every morning and quietly does the household work by Herself I have been told that, when She was building a huge house for Her husband in Lucknow, She cooked Herself for the fifty labourers. As they brought all their relatives, altogether 200 people came for this lunch. It proved to be a very abundant meal, for the workers families took a lot of food back home! She is extremely good at all these little practical activities that one would have thought to be below the threshold the attention of a spiritual personality. She is a charming housewife and a superb cook! Many times we have witnessed the manifestation of Her Annapurna aspects. Recently we went for a Sahaja Yoga programme and dinner at the house of some Maharastran ladies living in London. Again, After the meal they were surprised that though there was a large crowd, still there was an excess of food remaining after all had eaten their fill. They asked HH Mataji, "How is it that we cooked for twelve, yet at least twentyfive have eaten and still so much is over?" HH Mataji laughed; indeed, for Her control over the elements seems to be inherent. Certainly, whenever She is going out for any kind of programme we know that it is no use listening to the weather forecast—it will always reflect Her mood rather than the predictions of the meteorologists. When She took a short vacation in May the sunshine exceeded all records; but when She expressed concern over the excess of sunbathing and sinful behaviour in the name of holidays, the summer weather was wet and cloudy. The whole pattern of British weather seems to have been modified since Her arrival in London—as any gardener will confirm! In the same way, Her subtle influence is reflected in little happenings like the ones described, which appear miraculous to the participants and which gladden the hearts of those who experience them.

We have noticed that Her adaptability is super-human: She can sleep on a rock in the open; we saw Her at a programme, sitting in the same chair for nine hours and walk away fresh and relaxed. Her asceticism is perfect like Rajah Janaka's who lived like a saint in his royal palace. We never heard Her complaining about material surroundings, lack of comfort or petty problems. Yet she understands ours and comforts us. Whatever the environment may be this satisfied nature radiates a queenlike majesty.

Once in India She stopped at the derelict hut of a very poor woman and thoroughly enjoyed a little meal offered in a dirty pot. Later on some of Her disciples asked why She spent so much time with this beggar; She answered with pain in Her voice, "Oh my children, do not talk like that for she is the widow of one of my dearest sons." Later they learnt from the villagers that the departed husband was a devotee of the Goddess (*Devi bhakta*). Another time, She visited a Saint and sat on the bare ground of his cave. As the attendants protested She asked with a smile: "Why can't I sit on the floor. I am in the palace of a King."

In Her behaviour with people HH Mataji is completely open and straightforward. With elderly men She is respectful but with much younger boys and girls She laughs and jokes; She is so interesting, so full of wit and humour! Our greatest delight is to sit for hours just enjoying Her company. With men She maintains a proper, dignified distance. She is affectionate with ladies and extremely free with little girls. In all these manifold aspects of Her moods, She can be said to be the embodiment of correctness and modesty. And She answers the greeting of the devas, "To the being who abides in all beings in the form of Lajja (bashful modesty)."

If HH Mataji chooses to denounce a false prophet She does so with forceful determination and imperious authority. But deep down She weeps and is thoroughly unhappy. "If they would only take your money I would not mind that much, but they spoil your Kundalini and rob you of your right to be reborn. The fulfilment of creation, God's realization of his will is challenged by these fools. They do not know what they will have to pay."

In public meetings She always talks with the greatest frankness, whenever it is needed, not fearing nor minding in the least attacking established ways of life, beliefs and dogmas when She finds them so very detrimental to the spiritual progress of Her children: "I am not here to seek votes but to tell you the truth." Many people have been convinced by Her outspoken courage and determination. But, sometimes we get worried for Her safety: She replies with a reassuring smile, "Love is much more powerful than all the hatred of the world". She added once with a childlike laughter, "Do not worry, no crucifixion in this lifetime". Some eminent people warned Her that She may be killed by the thugs of a false guru. She said, "This time the drama is going to be different. Why are you afraid? Have you not seen how evil people shake before me?"

Entire volumes of books would not be enough to tell you how we discovered a super-human perfection in someone who is human par excellence. One of the least expected and yet most delightful traits we discovered in HH Mataji is a prodigious sense of humour. We sit on the floor around Her for hours together, giggling, laughing and enjoying Her subtle jokes and sparkling wit. She often says She cannot remain serious for more than ten minutes. HH Mataji's depth is unfathomable, no doubt, but this depth is bubbling with joy. What a delight and a privilege to witness Her play! The most trivial incident creates a tale of wisdom, a poem of beauty; playfully, effortlessly, HH Mataji answers a question in the depth of our mind and opens a precious little corner of our heart. She creates pure aesthetic moments out of nothing with the thread of Her very fine humour. She weaves the flow of hours, hearts, minds and happenings in an exquisite and refined tapestry. What a play!

One day HH Mataji expressed the wish to visit the abode of a great sage, high on a hill. This guru was known for his mastery over the elements.

"Mother why do you want to climb this hill just to see this man?" asked the disciples. "Just check the vibrations." From the top of the hill came cool vibrations and the Sahaja yogis recognised at once that the guru was a man of God. As HH Mataji began climbing, torrential rain started pouring down and She was completely drenched. One could see the silhouette of the guru frantically gesticulating, trying to stop the rain. When the Devi reached the place the saint lamented: "This wretched rain always used to obey me but this time I could not stop it. Mother, why have you taken away my powers?" Mataji smiled: "You have purchased a saree for me. Now I will have to wear it." The saint melted away with love. He had also understood that the water dripping from the Devi's saree was vibrating, that is, blessing his retreat.

Before meeting HH Mataji I did not imagine that the Divine is so full of humour. Humour is effervescent in Her daily miracles, curing, lectures and meetings. I just don't know how to do justice to this joyous trait of Her inimitable style.

Often the play is a game of hide and seek. It is the game the Devi played with the seekers for thousands of years: "I am like the mother bird who takes her little ones out of the nest to teach them how to fly. She flies away, hides behind a tree and calls them. The children rush toward her, but she flies behind a further tree and calls them again."

Hiding is, of course, the consummate art of Mayadevi, the Goddess of illusion. A lady told us she knew Mrs. C.P Shrivastava for the last twenty years. She met her mostly at diplomatic parties and receptions. She knew a very quiet and dignified lady who would hardly speak, and was stunned to discover HH Mataji at a spiritual function, a forceful outspoken leader, superbly articulate, playfully mastering rhetoric art and full of deep insights. She could not understand how a person of such talents and intelligence could patiently hide herself behind the personality of the silent housewife, all the time graciously listening to the superfluous and bombastic talk of half drunk people.

If such patience is at all possible it is because the Goddess is the embodiment of perfect humility. "Why should we be proud of our qualities? Are we proud of having a nose in the middle of our face?" She never publicly claimed to be the Adi Shakti. "Christ said I am the path, I am the truth, I am the life. And human beings crucified him for it. This time they will have to find for themselves". But we can assure you: those who want to find it are greatly helped to do so.

Whatever HH Mataji is doing She does it with full involvement, full detachment. There is no way She or Her behaviour can be categorized. Yes, we can say a few things: She radiates boundless love, peace of eternity, profound wisdom, majestic modesty and absolutely childlike innocence. She is Knowledge that is beyond human knowledge. She is nobility, generosity, selflessness, simplicity. And yet, when these words are not rediscovered through the inward quality of the purified consciousness they hardly tell anything of the plenitude that HH Mataji expresses in any of Her actions. She is always absolutely relaxed, and whatever She does is perfect. When She plays with her grandchildren, Aradhana, Sonalika, Anand or Anupama, when She looks at the design of a carving, when She deals with us, when She addresses a meeting, when She grants Realization, She is fully present in Her action, more than anyone could be and yet, She is never contained in that action: Her presence, intense as it may be, is never exhausted by being there. She is totally human and totally super-human; to comprehend HH Mataji is an absolute impossibility for people fond of rational identification (I know what I am talking about); we just go nuts, up and down, left and right, and we do not find anything. But in the surrendered silence of thoughtless awareness we can know something. That the drop dissolves in the ocean. Kabir says: "When I am drenched in your Grace why should I speak". Nanaka says, "Oh seeker, unless and until you have found yourself, how can you recognize the illusion?"

Worldly people in India who had the opportunity to come in contact with HH Mataji have been struck by many various traits of Her character but the words which come most often, as we said, are innocence, compassion and simplicity. HH Mataji appears to many as a very lovable and compassionate lady but some people may not go beyond these first impressions. Now with Sahaja Yoga a new perception asserts itself. A whole book would not be enough to recall the truly extraordinary experiences and visions that have marked the relationship between HH Mataji and the Sahaja Yogis. Disciples of all races, religions and creeds, in India, USA, Africa, Europe, etc., have recognized specific aspects of HH Mataji's divine nature. They have not only seen Her in the Vaikuntha stage but in the human manifestation of Her previous incarnations as Shri Seeta, Shri Radha or Mother Mary. Many of them are able to relate to Her in the terms of awareness which express some of Her powers. Many ordinary people today are rediscovering the meaning of the ancient hymns and scriptures. HH Mataji moves the angles of awareness in such a powerful way that one can feel in the brain the movement of the pressure and its release. She does it by moving one finger, uttering a mantra, and mostly, perhaps, just by the quality of Her meditation (*dhyana yoga*). The head feels lighter and one jumps into the various dimensions of the collective (cosmic) consciousness.

HH Mataji has introduced to us the complete science of mantra. When She speaks a mantra She says it in the form: "Aham Sakshat" (Adi Shakti, Jagadamba, Adi Guru, etc—according to the significance of the mantra for a particular blockage); it means "I am the very embodiment of" (the Primordial Power, the Mother of the universe, the Primordial Master, etc.). While we, when we say the same mantras express them in the form "Twamewa Sakshat..." meaning You are indeed that deity or divine aspect. To explain the whole science (*mantra shastra*) would require another book. But this distinction is an essential feature which embodies an important truth; and the efficacy of the mantras spoken in this way according to who is the speaker illustrates in a very practical way how "the truth shall set you free", i.e. liberate you from the bondage of catches on the chakras.

The subtle control over the perceived environment which starts to manifest after self-realization, raises all kinds of questions and uncertainties. Gradually these are answered, soothed, neutralised.

Confidence comes with experience. Sometimes the experiences are very practical ones. That HH Mataji does, in Her Adi Shakti aspect, control the drama—of this we are no longer in doubt. That is the benefit of our experiences. But the actors are left with their freedom. It is an extremely subtle relationship, in which we have to learn how we can rely on our divine parents.

In The Gita, Lord Krishna says to the disciple Arjuna, "*Yoga kshema vahamyam*"—I look after (lit: carry) your yoga (realization) and your kshema (material well being). After self-realization through Sahaja Yoga all of us have greatly benefited in our well being (kshema). It has happened in so many miraculous ways to each one of us that it is impossible to describe. The changes start manifesting as soon as one gets realization.

Regis, a postgraduate physics student, had been offered a job in Libya. His research was completed but he had not had his doctoral thesis finally typed and bound according to the regulations. He came to HH Mataji with his work and told Her "whatever happens I don't mind, I shall take the job, only bless what I have written! HH Mataji put Her hand on the pile of typescript for a few seconds and said "take it". The next day Regis telephoned to say the examiners had waived formalities and awarded him his doctorate.

HH Mataji is a Mother. In the smile of Her eyes, in the caress of Her voice, motherhood vibrates in the fullness of love, tenderness and sweetness. She showers Her blessings on the disciples with endless generosity. Even on the material level of day to day life, yogis are invariably better off: Health improves dramatically. Hippies who were squatting in a comatose condition return to the University and get the highest marks. This Farmer makes a bumper harvest. A secretary gets the job she was dreaming about. You find the absolute car, the best available flat, the perfect business partner. Buses are waiting for you. Friends show up at the doorstep when one feels like seeing them. It is slightly embarrassing mentioning these things, but they keep happening. My brother had to appear before the examining professor to defend his thesis in Law. He had to face this crucial examination in extremely difficult conditions. I gave him bandans. Our two sisters and myself prayed to HH Mataji. The examination turned out to be a miraculous success. More recently, a friend got a very highly paid assignment in Saudi Arabia. He thanked Mataji, but told Her he would miss having Her darshan in London. A few days later the contract was cancelled and he got another assignment in London and for the same salary! It is as if all the angels are busy relieving us from the petty troubles of the worldly life so that we can give our attention to what really matters.

But it should be clear that HH Mataji has not come on this earth merely to act as a marriage counsellor and job agency. In Her generosity She promises us that whatever we ask Mother will give, provided it is not harmful. But, She says, be wise: ask for the supreme.

The supreme is beyond thought, beyond desire, beyond preconceived ideas and concepts, which are limited. Children do not have so many problems in this respect.

All four of HH Mataji's grandchildren are born realized souls of a very high spiritual quality. From them we have learned many things in Sahaja Yoga, though their ages are only 7, 6, 4 and 2 years. The eldest grand-daughter Aradhana told us that they love to sleep with their grandmother, because a very cool soothing breeze flows through Her nose. The children freely hit each other and the Sahaja Yogis, but they never raise a hand to their "Nani". "One does not beat a Goddess" says Anand, the grandson. Every day the children love to place their head on their grandmother's feet; they have done this without prompting since a very early age. Whenever disciples come to the house, the grandchildren immediately come to assist HH Mataji to give realization, raise the kundalini, clear the chakras. As soon as the job is done they return to their play without further ado. This is their spontaneous way of expressing their devotion to HH Mataji.

Whatever we write about HH Mataji must seem fantastic and perhaps unbelievable. But these happenings have occurred in the lives of thousands of people who have met Her. Finally, it is easier to accept than to disbelieve. The pressure to acknowledge the truth mounts up until all the doubts simply dissolve in loving joyful acceptance. It is a miraculous dynamic power in HH Mataji which works out all these miracles. The key to understanding and enjoying this power as one's own, is the acceptance that She is unique, universal, supreme. We found it hard to believe, to accept, to conceive of as possible. But then we found that the joy of acknowledging this truth is overwhelming. When we realize that She is the Primordial Mother, with all Her powers integrated in one personality—we realize that what we see manifesting in all these ways is Her own innate play. With this acceptance, all the parts of the puzzle fall into place, the mystery is solved, the quest is over, and we sing aloud with happy laughter, and blissful understanding.

Instead of disbelieving what we tell you at the very beginning of Her wondrous story, try to believe that She is Adi Shakti. It will help you much more to understand the magic of such a great happening as Her Advent.

Some people are helped to understand the nature of the Devi through the descriptions written by the great saints of the past— which at last take on a real meaning.

"Salutations again and again to the Devi who in all beings is termed as consciousness"
"To the Devi who abides in all beings in the form of pure intelligence"
"To the Devi who abides in all beings in the form of power..."
The Devi Mahatmayam—17-19; 20-22; 32-34

Words, whose meanings were totally hidden open themselves in the ecstasy of awareness.

"Blessed are the few that serve Thee, the flood of Consciousness and Bliss, having, as Thy abode, the mattress of Paramshiva, laid on the couch of the (multi-triangular) form of Shiva, in the mansion built of Cintamani stones, attached to the pleasure garden of Nipa trees, in the isle of gems, surrounded by an avenue of Kalpa trees and situated amidst the ocean of nectar."
Shri Shankaracharya *Saundarya Lahari* : 8.

In many instances, the first meeting with HH Mataji produces a decisive impression. Arneau, a law student from Switzerland, came to London to see HH Mataji; back home a few days later, he wrote to Her:

"I do not fully realize yet the huge blessing that has been bestowed upon me: I have been able to see You, to talk to You and, above all, to become a realized being! I feel as if

I went through a wonderful dream and, as I begin to wake up, I realized that this dream was reality. I know with all my heart, with all my soul and with all my spirit that you are Love par excellence, that You have given me a means to find happiness through the vibrations that you emit from your being. However, I am aware that now it is my responsibility to establish in me through meditation, this same happiness, calm and joy that was with me in London. Saturday evening, here in Geneva, I meditated on your picture and then went out to eat in a restaurant. I was alone and I was smiling because of too much happiness. People thought that I was crazy or drunk. Yes, I was crazy and drunk with joy and I knew that this joy came from you."

Mr B G Pradhan, an advocate to the Bombay High Court, was with HH Mataji during Her 1972 trip to the USA. He noted down a few experiences of people who came to HH Mataji:

Mrs Joyce A Vernon of Cortland, Ohio State. Professor in Food Technology Department, Ohio University. She had never visited India or heard anything about Shri Rama and Shri Seeta, or read any book on Hindu religion.

When her Ajnya Chakra opened she told our Divine Mother Mataji and others who were there in these words:

"Mataji, I see you going in a plain dress along with two young men, and the whole town, as it were, following you, and I am also trying to follow you and join you, but the two young men are no allowing me to join you where you are going, and oh! it is terrible to witness that sight as if you are discarding me from your being, and the whole crowd which is following you is in a dejected mood. It is terrible, it is terrible. I can't bear that sight." So saying, she began to weep and embraced and hugged our Mataji, and with great difficulty Mataji consoled her. Our Mataji, then told me "Pradhan, you might be knowing that she is giving the description of Rama, Seeta and Laxshmana leaving Ayodhya for 'Vanvas.' (Exile in the forest). Her description exactly tallied. I then explained to her the whole incident in its true perspective, and she was surprised, to know that our Mataji was then in the form of Seeta, now reborn."

Mrs Janice Hoover of Youngtown in Ohio State. When her Ajnya Chakra opened, she narrated what she saw in these words:

"Mataji, I see you sitting in a hut. I can see you through the door of the hut. I am seeing that you are not taking any food. I therefore take a brass dish with some eatables in it and request you, Mataji, to eat the eatables, but you refused to take anything. I repeated this for three days, but you did not respond to my request, and I found you sitting in a dejected mood and I could see a man with a white beard sitting in that hut." (She saw Mataji as Seeta living in Valmiki Rishi's Ashram). She had never visited India, nor did she know anything about the Ramayana.

Mr Joseph Lord of Akron, Ohio State. He is a Mechanical Engineer at Akron. He is about 55 years old, and now a Minister of the Church:

When his Ajnya Chakra was opened, he narrated the following incidents:

"Mataji, I see a bright boy of about 6 or 7 years old and he has got four or five playmates of his age and I am one of them. We formed a pyramid, climbing one above the other, and the bright boy was on the top, and he caught hold of a pot hanging under the ceiling, and he brought it down and we all boys ate the butter-like thing which was in the pot. In the meanwhile, a lady came and she got annoyed and brought a long piece of cloth and tied all of us to a pole. Thereafter, Mataji well dressed in gold embroidered blue Sari with a golden border, and having a belt studded with pearls, etc., came there and requested that lady to untie the piece of cloth and leave us as we were innocent. Accordingly, that lady obeyed you and left us free."
(He saw Mataji in the form of Radha).

These visual experiences can go along with powerful phenomena of the consciousness. Such was my vision of HH Mataji as the Goddess Durga in which I felt the blissful shower of the Kundalini. One month after her realization, a young woman, mother of two realized children, wrote to me:

"That evening when I came back from work, I was very tired and my back was aching. I laid down on my bed with my hands and my head towards the picture of HH Mataji. I felt the breeze coming in my hands. After some time the pain vanished and I became completely peaceful and relaxed. I lay there for a while, then sat up and turned towards the picture. I was perfectly thoughtless and silent. Then it all began. I saw rays of white and blue light spreading from the picture into the whole room, and also through my body. I felt a creeping sensation in my head, golden wreaths were now oozing out and whirling around the picture. I felt as if the top of my head had started to melt and I hear myself muttering: Oh my God! Oh my God! There was a great bliss pouring into me and as I was still staring at the picture I saw the sacred heart of our Lord Jesus and a picture of the Buddha sitting in meditation. Tears of joy were pouring down my cheeks. I did not know what it was and was very moved; I walked away to do some work in the kitchen. The peace was with me. When I came back into my room I sat in front of the picture with stretched hands. The light and the whole thing came again.
That night I slept very well. When I woke up in the morning and looked out of the window everything glittered with a dazzling whiteness. Snow had fallen during the night and the sun was shining."

Usually, HH Mataji does not encourage visions because, She says, they divert the attention, either towards the collective supra conscious or the collective sub-conscious while one has to be in the present. The anchorage of Self-realization is to merge in the truth of the self, to taste its blissful, joy giving intensity. People with a supraconscious leaning or a background in hallucinatory drugs sometimes cannot avoid seeing things.

Such has been the case of Patrick when he saw HH Mataji for the first time; he could see vibrations as many coloured sparks shooting at people from the top of HH Mataji's head. He describes one of the visions he had a few years ago:

"HH Mataji is working on my chakras. She asks me to hold my breath. Then something seems to grow in HH Mataji;

it comes out of Her physical shape and stands over me. It is difficult to describe what the apparition looks like because, although totally familiar, it is really outside the human dimensions, like a sort of universal personality or archetype; am I looking at the Virgin Mary? The whole place fills with light. Mataji dissolves in the light."

I remember HH Mataji, after a programme at Caxton Hall, London, raising the Kundalini of a hippie lost in visions and admonishing him: "Don't look at all these forms. See me now, as I am in the Present!" There are so many miraculous happenings in the lives of the Sahaja Yogis that I don't even mention here Indian Sahaja yogis. Their stories would cover volumes. Thousands of cases of cure by Sahaja yoga have concretely demonstrated the dynamic properties of Chaitanya vibrations.

In Kuala Lumpur, five hundred people came to HH Mataji for curing various diseases. She feels the only way she can handle this big gathering is to ask for the help of Mother Earth (*Bhoomi Devi*). She made everybody stand barefoot on the ground, and while vibrating them, pray Mother Earth to absorb their load; the earth sucks the antivibrations and people start feeling the relief; many of them feel the breeze in their hands. I have myself witnessed many cases of cure. In Bombay, a man brings to HH Mataji his son who had become addicted to hashish. HH Mataji grants him a session of vibrations therapy. The next day both are back. They tell us that, for the first time for ages, the boy spent the night in peaceful sleep, and never again craved for hashish. The same type of instant recovery manifested in London where an alcoholic was brought to the programme by his desperate wife. He stopped drinking overnight. I have seen myself a man who suffers from arthritis coming to HH Mataji walking on crutches and leaping away freely half an hour later. Yesterday, a girl told me that, while shaking hands with HH Mataji, she felt a tremendous power rushing from her hand into her whole being, etc., Such miracles are happening literally everyday.

As a human individual HH Mataji is an extremely kind and sensitive lady who extends her tender motherly love to all sentient beings; the relationship of a Sahaja Yogi to the human person of HH Mataji is thus very intimate and expresses the manifold nuances of the delicacy and purity of love. It is the love of a child for his mother but is also the love of the human soul for the spiritual reality of which it is itself a part. Hence the relationship to HH Mataji, as far as I experience it, is unique in being at the same time very human and personal while representing also a deep, holy, intimate relationship to my own awareness.

When going deep into meditation, I have found that there is no perception of "I", the creature, and You, the creator, or any feeling for the individual Gregoire. What I perceive without thought is "existence." Whether it is a man or God which is existing in me is a question that I do not consider, because, at that level, it has lost its relevance. If "I", is my ego and super-ego then I can say that I cease to exist. If "I" is my Self I can say I begin to exist. At any rate "who am I", "what is Sahaja Yoga", "who is Mataji", are questions which are melting together into the silence of one consciousness. Indeed, it is said that She is Chitkala[12] (that part in us which is the Art of pure consciousness). And in that consciousness, we can realize why it is that She is called Ananda Kalika, that is: dwelling in everybody as the bud of all bliss and enjoyment.[13]

Oh Sacred Mother! You are the supreme artist! When we turn towards You, our faces shine with joyful beauty. O Devi! You are the Great Alchemist. When your love pulsates for us we feel in our heart the stone turning into a spotless diamond.

One of the factors which makes it very difficult for a human being to recognize a Divine Incarnation (and to distinguish the genuine from the fake) springs from the fact that the human conceptions regarding the Divine have always been cloaked in a mythical haze. As a matter of fact, when the humble dimension of our daily life is not open to the divine we tend to exile the latter to a far-off domain of mythical expectations. Also religion becomes for us an isolated set of activities to be performed between business and family life. If, however, there is a God or Divinity, should it not pervade our daily life? Should He not relate to us by taking a human birth in a very human way? The sad logic of sin is that, the more wrongly we behave, the less we are in a position to perceive our own divine nature and then we cannot conceive that God

---

[12] See *the Padma Purana* and *the Shri Lalita Sahasranama*

[13] See the other names expressing the Devi as Bliss itself: Madhumati, Yogananda, Brahmananda, Saccidananda, Satyananda.

considers us as his Own children and wishes to deal with us accordingly. God is our Father and our Mother. Has the Mother taken form this time? If so, it certainly is an extremely human one.

"Only You, Mother, could incarnate in this Kali Yuga" exclaimed Ramakrishna. In the ancient *Nala Damayanti Purana* Kali explains to Nala the importance of Kali Yuga, the modern times. When the worst of all times (Ghor Kali Yuga) will torture Mother Earth, the Adi Shakti will incarnate and grant salvation to the saintly seekers who are now seeking God, secluded in thick jungles, steep valleys and inaccessible mountains. They will be reborn in Kali Yuga as normal worldly people, ordinary householders. She will then give birth to a new race. Glory to Her. Her coming in Her complete, integrated form, should truly represent the most formidable event of World History. HH Mataji did once say, in a very deep meditative mood, "To grant you salvation, my children, I have come with all of my powers." Later on she said that this should not be told to people who doubt Sahaja Yoga, and that we should bear this in mind when telling people. Even if She is confronted with the question of Her true nature in a direct way by someone hostile or doubting, She very intelligently avoids it. But we do not feel the same restraints. Oh! Let us all rejoice!

> "O Queen of the Universe, you protect the Universe. As the Self of the Universe, you support the Universe. You are the (goddess) worthy to be adored by the Lord of the Universe. Those who bow in devotion to you themselves become the refuge of the Universe."
>
> The devas to the Devi in the *Devi-Mahatmyam or Shri Durga-Saptasati*.

Many people will not believe this to be possible. They will wonder "how can HH Mataji give mass self-realization when it took so many lives for the great saints to reach it?" This question can only arise in the mind of somebody who is not familiar with the nature of the Divine Mother. After all She is the para-Shakti, the power beyond all powers. And it has been clearly said in the Sri-Lalita Sahasranama that She is "Sobhana-Sulabha-gatih" (683rd name): the easiest path to self-realization. She is

"Ksipra Prasadini": the One who showers grace on Her devotees very quickly.

For a very simple and innocent heart, the recognition of an Incarnation is quicker than for an adult and his loaded psyche. I recall the case of a twelve year old Greek boy who met HH Mataji in London. His uncle asked him whether he would recognize HH Mataji as the Adi Shakti. He said "yes" and when HH Mataji asked him why he answered: "I get more breeze from you than any other images of God. Whenever I think of you, I get vibrations and you are the highest because when I take your name the vibrations of every image increase."

Somebody doubted this but the child firmly repeated "whenever I take Her name a fountain of cold breeze comes from the centre of my palm and goes to my fingers." This boy was wondering how HH Mataji had come to this earth!

You, who are reading these lines now please, try to accept that something infinitely important was unknown to you until this day and that it is unveiled to you now.

You who read these lines in the Twenty-first Century (or whatever it will be called) please forgive me for not singing Her Praise, for not extolling Her. But, you see, in 1976, I wrote these lines for people who did not know anything and I wanted to introduce Her Advent without shocking them to much. How could I tell them who She is? Pray, forgive me.

Sometimes one wonders how come that so much freedom is enjoyed in HH Mataji's presence? So many of the Sahaja Yogis have been, once upon a time, involved in a spiritual movement. There, one would hardly see the guru or talk to him; the servility of his followers make the scenery of the show. The poor disciples exhaust themselves at his service and give him time, money, properties and wife. And the explanation by which he justifies all their problems is, "You have to suffer for your karma", or some such nonsense.

Now, interestingly enough, in the presence of HH Mataji, the same seekers often start arguing. It looks as if they are no more enticed and can express themselves again. Some of them quibble and raise all kinds of captious objections and can even become frankly rude. Sometimes we just can't bear it. But She says:' 'What can they take away from me? They are to be saved. So, I really have to mother them." She never loses her temper, sweetly answers and tries to soothe them. While talking we know Her attention is on the awakening of their Kundalini. But there are limits to what HH Mataji can do: Realization, She avers has its own protocol: "You have to ask for it. I can cook for you. But can I eat and enjoy for you?"

One day a boy started vehemently arguing as soon as She asked "please extend your hands towards me." In collective consciousness, we felt that his throat centre was badly disturbed. He went on misbehaving although he saw an American gentleman being cured and his own friend declared feeling the cool breeze HH Mataji's last remark was: "I am at least happy that you felt free to talk to me because this shows that Sahaja Yoga respects your freedom." We all felt very sad about this incident and she consoled us.

"My children, you must know I am beyond insults and pain. Do you know that when Christ was crucified he was a witness to his pain? He can never be humiliated. But these people are under the pressure of the satanic forces. We have to save them. Do you want them to go to hell?"

I recall another instance in which an acupuncturist follower of Lao Tzu became very disagreeably aggressive when HH Mataji moved her hand around his aura. She told him in a quiet and persuasive tone:

"How can you telephone with a disconnected line? You cannot follow Tao. You have to become Tao. You have to be realized otherwise all spiritual practices and gestures are tomfooleries. All your acupuncture will just activate the sympathetic nervous system. If you try to handle your machinery without establishing the connection with the source of its power, the para-sympathetic system, you will spoil it. When Lao Tzu was alive, how many believed in him and how many opposed him? Why do you believe in Lao Tzu? Because he is no more and you can handle him instead of him handling you. Once he is dead you are using him and following dead rituals. Today, Lao Tzu is dead and Mataji is living. So many people feel the divine breeze in their fingers. My child, how long are you going to cheat yourself? Why not know your own powers?"

It may not be an easy matter to recognize a divine incarnation, especially not the present one who seems to have come as 'Mahamaya', that is, 'the Great Illusion.' But we find this difficulty mentioned in all the scriptures. Both Shri Krishna and Lord Jesus made it very clear that they also presented an opportunity for the sinners to further sink into sin: people would not recognize them but would misbehave with them. HH Mataji never acts harshly or uses abusive language. She goes on tolerating. But, at the end, her attention recedes from someone who does not behave himself. So, perhaps I should suggest the following to those who refuse the possibility given by Sahaja Yoga of recognizing the Divine Mother. As long as you do not know who HH Mataji is try to keep the sound attitude that intellectual fairness requires; "What I don't know, I don't know." Without the experimental data provided by Sahaja Yoga's vibratory awareness the recognition of the Divine Mother is rather unlikely. Sahaja Yogis can themselves peep through the veils of Maya (illusion, delusion and ignorance). But as far as the true nature of HH Mataji is concerned, no one is entitled to expect to be introduced to the heart of this sacred mystery at once.

Yet, our chances of recognizing the truth are infinitely better than in any of our previous lives. First, we could, for a change, use our brains in a meaningful way. If it is true that the Quest of Mankind has been the quest for a higher consciousness; if it is true that the break into this new consciousness is a matter of survival for the human species; if it is true that now is the time that is ripe for such a decisive evolutionary step... the historical happening of a divine incarnation which brings about the fulfilment of the potentials of human consciousness appears to be a logical necessity.

Taking into account the considerable metabolic changes that en masse Kundalini raising will provoke in the cosmos, should we be surprised that the highest expression of God itself is initiating it? Should we be surprised that such a powerful incarnation is cloaking its true nature in a very human appearance? Who could today bear a direct knowledge of its divine effulgence? Why should we wonder that the happening occurs at a time of wickedness and perils as announced in the scriptures of various religions? Would the Western world not accept the Mother along with the Father and the Son? When regional civilisations will, at last, overcome cultural provincialism, more and more people will realize the living unity of the various religious traditions. They will also realize that the pattern of meaning of the religious message, when brought into perspective with the contemporary state of thought and society appears to be very consistent with the information I am now sharing with you; thousands of people all over the world have been self-realized by the raising of the Kundalini. Apart from en masse realization, this rising is in itself the proof that the Divine Mother has come. Indeed, as we said, the authorized scriptures describe the process of liberation and resulting bliss as nothing but Her own moods of consciousness.[14]

I believe our intellect can take us to the shores of the Sea of Truth. It is a sea of Divine vibrations, and today, by our Divine Mother's grace, we can dissolve in it. At the time of all other incarnations the Shri Chakra did not descend on this earth. In other words, it was not possible to feel the Divine vibrations at the mass level. It is only after HH Mataji's birth that the all pervading power has been activated on this earth by the Shri Chakra. The whole planet was covered by Divine vibrations. That is to say the Kingdom of God started in this world. Great numbers of people entered the pilgrimage of the spiritual quest. Many, all over the world, must have felt the breath of the Holy Spirit. However, they might not have understood what these vibrations are, how to retain them and link them with deeper stages of awareness. They might not know what or who is the Source of the Divine light. Actually, there are some bornrealized who do not know their own powers. Now, how could one tell them and explain to the general public what the problem is? Had HH Mataji claimed that She is the source, nobody would have believed it. They would have just made fun of it.[15] So first she took twelve people as Her disciples. She

---

[14] "Thou are diverting Thyself in secrecy with Thy Lord, in the thousand-petalled Lotus, having pierced through the Earth situated in the Mooladhara, the Water in the Manipura, the Fire abiding in the Swadhistana, the Air in the Heart, the Ether above (the Vishuddhi) and Manas between the eyebrows (Ajna) and thus broken into the entire Kula Path.
Having in-filled the pathway of the Nadis with the streaming shower of nectar flowing from Thy pair of feet, having resumed Thy own position from out of the resplendent lunar regions, and Thyself assuming the form of a serpent of three and a half coils, sleepest Thou in the hollow of the Kulakunda."
Shri Shankaracharya *Saundarya-Lahari* 9.10.

[15] Satya Yuga can only blossom with the recognition of the true Incarnation.

worked on their chakras one by one, showed them all the various stages of Kundalini awakening and, after two years, granted them self-realisation. Then, gradually, she chose more people. When they reached fifty-one, she started an en-mass self-realization movement. Those fifty-one could explain through knowledge and experience, what the true nature of HH Mataji really is. More people started verifying through vibratory awareness the truth of HH Mataji's supreme, cosmic personality. Experiments and visions precipitated. Those who accepted Her as the Incarnation of the Adi Shakti on the basis of these experiences were blessed with very deep contemplative sensitivity and doubtless awareness (Nirvikalpa samadhi). Some of the Sahaja Yogis are performing wonders and miracles, curing people and giving self-realisation. It is just not possible to write about all of these happenings in this book. There are already publications issued in India and more books will be coming forward.

Today, people can see with the naked eye Kundalini's throbbing and rising, they see people cured, completely transformed after getting self-realization. The powers of the Self manifest into the power of the Collective Consciousness. If, after all that, the people are not going to accept the Holy Spirit, how can their folly be forgiven? Lord Jesus made adamantly clear that the blasphemy against the Holy Spirit will NOT be forgiven.

We can better acknowledge now the deeper meaning of the incarnation of Jesus Christ in relation with the Holy Trinity. According to HH Mataji's teachings, the Father aspect of God had been manifested by Lord Krishna, who had awakened the fifth chakra of the Virata through his own incarnation recalled in the Mahabharatha. By His incarnation in Galilee, Lord Jesus awakened the sixth chakra of the Virata. By His crucifixion on Golgotha Lord Jesus Christ crucified Himself on the ego and the super-ego of the Virata; by his resurrection He opened the cosmic possibility for mankind to resurrect into the divine consciousness. Buddhahood or Christhood are states of the perfect mastery over the movements of the intellect (Buddhi). The supreme master of the Buddhi is Lord Jesus; his cosmic location is within the Ajnya Chakra of the Virata. In each and every one of us, Lord Jesus Christ is the Lord of the Ajnya Chakra, the narrow gate that the Kundalini has to cross before reaching the heavenly kingdom of the Sahasrara.[16] As aforementioned this is revealed by vibratory awareness. I know that, as long as my Ajnya Chakra is not fully cleared and open, I cannot settle into thoughtless awareness. At this point of the body which corresponds to the crossing of the optic nerves, ida nadi and pingala nadi cross each other. There, in the Ajnya Chakra, the Christ controls the pineal and pituitary glands and can overcome the influence of the left and right side sympathetic nervous system over the psyche (ego and super ego). Hence, at the level of both cosmic and individual development, the incarnation of the Son opened the way for the advent of the Mother, the Holy Spirit. It is indeed fit that we mention the Father and the Son in the chapter dedicated to the Divine Mother. For, no one else could bring onto this earth the third incarnation of the Holy Trinity. As this incarnation represents knowledge, awareness and integration it also brings about the full revelation of the previous teachers' messages. Lord Jesus said: "But when the Counsellor comes, whom I shall send to you from the Father, the spirit of truth, who proceeds from the Father, he will bear witness to me"; John 15-16. We all feel that the vibrations which are emitted by HH Mataji and perceived through Sahaja Yoga are indeed the cognitive instrument which reveals that Lord Jesus expressed the resurrected life of the Spirit which is issuing from the three gunas (and the three nadis, within the body) as the AUM, the Word, the Amen. They are the fantastic blessing bestowed upon us by the enlightening love of the Holy Spirit.

In order to recapitulate what we have been saying in a theological manner, we can summarize as follows the respective natures of the three persons of the Holy Trinity.

The FATHER: The Almighty Allah is not personified. He is utterly beyond our reach but not beyond the Mother's. He is expressed as the Adi-Bindu, the primordial existence who is witnessing the play of His own power. God-the-Father is called in Sanskrit Sadashiva. He is the supreme witness who manifested his fatherly dimension to Mankind through the Krishna Avatar of Shri Vishnu. From the time of Krishna's incarnation, Mankind became able to

---

[16]"I am the door, if any one enters by me he will be saved and will go in and out and find pasture." John 10-7
Indeed, Lord Jesus said, "I am the way, and the truth, and the light". But He did not say, "I am the destination". The destination is the Sahasrara, that is, the Holy Spirit.

conceive of the greatness of one ultimate God who encompasses everything (the Virata aspect of Lord Krishna).[17]

The MOTHER: The Adi Shakti is the Power of God the Almighty, the Primordial Energy; the Christian tradition invokes Her as 'Holy Spirit', by whom the unmanifested ultimate Reality, becomes manifested. She forms the 'Adi Valaya' the original elliptic movement of cosmic energy which creates the AUM and the myriads of Universes. She is the supreme power of Divine Love who is to bring Her children back to their Father.

The SON: The Son is the embodiment of AUM, the breath of life, the manifestation of the conjunction of the Divine Existence and the Divine Energy through whom the Universe has been evolved from the Adi Shakti and through whom it is to return to Her. This supreme union of contemplation and power manifested itself as Lord Jesus Christ, Mahavishnu the ninth incarnation of Shri Vishnu. From the time of the Lord Jesus' incarnation Mankind became better aware of the necessity to crucify one's lower nature (ego and super-ego) for the sake of the Self.

The Holy Trinity of the Adi Bindu, the Adi Valaya and the AUM represents a given level of God's manifestation. A further elaboration of this manifestation corresponds to the stage of the Virata, the great Primordial Being who manifests the main aspects of God through the Holy Spirit. If we refer HH Mataji to the first stage of revelation-creation, can She be the Adi Shakti, the energy of God? If we refer Her to the Vaikuntha stage of the Virata, can She be the Viratangana, the energy of Virata? If we refer Her to previous incarnations, is She their Shakti as Radha, Seeta, the Virgin Mary, etc.? If we refer to Her as HH Mataji, we know that she is the Mother of Sahaja Yogis. And if we refer to Her as Mrs C P Shrivastava, She is a lady, who, compassionate or distinguished as She may be, will not retain our attention. How to make out the puzzle?

In the classical Greek play the term 'prosopon' means the mask hiding the face of the actor who is performing on the stage. The latin word 'persona' comes from this Greek etymology and so

---

[17]Before the apparition of the God of the Jewish people, YAHWE, JEHOWA, the Pharaoh Akhenakon (1367-1350 B.C.) fought the Egyptian pantheon of the Theban priesthood and tried to introduce the cult of the one Father god, the solar-disc Aton. He might have been the first to manifest Shri Krishna's influence on the Mediterranean shores.

does the word 'person'. I want to tell you that the person who introduced us to Sahaja Yoga will, in this life time of Hers, extend Her Divine Love to many of us. She has come to fulfil the age-long quest of the genuine seekers of Reality.

You who have reached this delicate and crucial point in the book, try not to be too upset. Of course, an intellectual will be aware that he cannot know whether I am pointing out the right track, or not, whether I am talking of awareness or auto-suggestion whether I am clinging to reality or inflated representations. "Is he really witnessing the modest beginning of an historical process? "Is he projecting wishful thinking and expectations?" Many people are seeing a pattern of meanings where there are only unrelated events; how could you tell?

How can you know whether I speak the truth or not? They said, "Lo, here is the Lord" but it was His opponent. Many people also have declared listen! the stones are singing". But it was just the wind...I agree. In the Crusade of Children, thousands of children of all parts of medieval Europe rushed towards the seashore; they walked into the sea thinking the sea would open itself and lead them to Jerusalem. But the sea did not open. Poor kids, they went back home. In those days I would have thought of freighting a ship or I would have stayed at home.

I should offer you some sort of Pascalian gamble "let's admit that God exists"...proposed Blaise Pascal to the 17th Century libertine. My proposal to you is: "Let's admit that HH Mataji Nirmala Devi is the avatar of the Adi Shakti..." so then?

Let me put it in slightly different terms. Either HH Mataji is "That", or She is not. If She is not, you had better forget Sahaja Yoga. If She is, however, you should try to get in closer contact with Sahaja Yoga.,

> —The negative hypothesis means that the author of this book is one of those preachers that are so numerous today i.e., either somebody trying to fool you, or somebody fooled by his teacher. To be introduced to the knowledge of such a fantastic event, you have to take a few (apparent) risks and you won't solve the question anyway by wondering about it.
> —The positive hypothesis means that the One who is the Most High has come and is working for our salvation. It

means that the twentieth century break-through of awareness has been correctly identified by this book. It means the opening of Sattya Yuga, the golden age. The positive hypothesis implies that we might now reach the end of our lives-long quests and that our real ascent begins.

I know you hardly believe this to be possible. But when did God conform to our expectations? When did the established priests and doctors recognise a divine incarnation? Let us try to be a bit smarter this time. Instead of crucifying the Avatar and worshipping him afterwards let us try to worship right away. Now I hope that many of you will open their attention and intelligence to the possibility that, once more, the Divine Power has taken a human body, at the time which was prescribed and in the form which was not expected. And above all, I hope that you will be able to experience the truth by yourself. Let me pray to Her, the Glorious One, in the words of the ancient gods:

"O Queen of all, you who exist in the form of all,
And possess every might, save us from illusion, O Devi".

I realize how shocking it might be to read this chapter. Traditionalist, conformist people will anathemize me as a blasphemer. Self righteous rationalists will call me a madman. And yet, I am willingly writing for them also, I am writing for everybody. I am not to decide, who has ears and who can hear! Truth is carried by its own power and will reach the hearts of the genuine seekers. There is not a word in this chapter which is not true.

How can one relate to the fact that HH Mataji could buy a sweater in a department store and be in the Vaikuntha stage at the same time? Our reason has difficulty in understanding this because it has been trained in the logic of discrimination (a legacy of the Ionian thought, Aristotelian categories and bivalent logic) and not in the logic of integration (the principle of immanence and of analogy). Our hearts do not easily open up to the Divine because they have been hurt by the evil of Kali Yuga. At the present time we can get nearer to the Divine through the path which the Divine has prepared for this purpose and, today, this path is the opening of Sushumna by Sahaja Yoga. Of course, we remain free to try any paths we like but common sense should tell us here that the mere strivings of the intellect will not lead us very far.

THE DIVINE MOTHER

I have not really described to the reader what our own relation with HH Mataji is because there are feelings I do not know how to express in words. At any rate, this book is an attempt at explaining, not a devotional song. If I were to express anything about HH Mataji, I would try to sing or to write a poem, or, most probably I would prefer to keep silent. Silence expresses more. Basically, I just feel like a child who has found an extremely loving mother, who is very powerful. I have also said that I have seen much much more in HH Mataji than the human person. In the perceived dimension, another dimension opens itself and in this latter another one, a dimension within a dimension, within a dimension...an endless opening towards infinity, infinity playing within itself. And yet HH Mataji is beyond whatever I have perceived.

I feel as if HH Mataji came as the great illusion, the Mahamaya: the All powerful sacred Mother of the Universe has come into this world which is her own creation but the world knows her not. Delusion and confusion are, after all, the necessary elements of the great play of recognition. It takes some time to learn the rules of the game but it is a beautiful game to get into.

There is one cardinal principle to win at this game, a principle which has been exposed by Shri Krishna, Lord Jesus, the Prophet Muhammad and all the great seers, a principle which is clearly explained by HH Mataji in relation to the spontaneous working of the autonomous nervous system. This principle is "SURRENDER". This word challenges our ego and our conditionings. But let us surrender them to our wisdom. In more specific terms we can say that it is a surrender to Self, i.e., surrender to God. It is the disposition of our psyche which is most likely to bring our attention into that equilibrium which suits the working of the parasympathetic nervous system. Surrender implies that one gives up the strivings which project the psyche's energy into the sympathetic nervous system (ida and pingala). This surrender implies an enlightened, conscious decision because in God's cosmic plan the freedom to surrender is left to Man. We are free to tell the Holy Spirit: "I want what Thou wantest." Surrender is also the very disposition by which we keep ourselves connected with the Universal Unconscious in the same way, say, that a surfer surrenders himself to the wave in order to ride it. After realization, it is surrendering which maintains the attention within the central path of awareness. We can understand that our ego and super-ego do not reach reality and thus accept that "I do not know but let me know". Surrendering to God does not mean that we give Him anything. What can the drop of the "I" give to the Ocean of Divine Compassion? We just have to allow the boundaries of the drop to dissolve into the Ocean. We lose a limited personality to become the great one. That is why all the great religions, without exception, emphasize the necessity of surrender; Hinduism, Buddhism, Christianity, Islam present in different terms the same imperative.

In many religious traditions, there have been two main pillars to frame the gate of surrender, these are 'faith' and 'renunciation'.

I must say that many people in my generation always had a sustained dislike for these two theological leit-motives. In the priests' mouths, faith sounded very much like "I don't know what is going on but let's hope for a happy end". An attitude which, along with the existentialists, we did not find very respectable. It seemed to be the blind alternative to a knowledge one feared to be frightful: "let's hope that truth is nice because if it is not, we had better not know it". Also we felt: "what is human knowledge worth if it cannot reach God; knowledge, not faith is the way!"

By now I know that faith is not what the common use of the word made it sound like. Oh no! In our heart resides the Atman, the Self, the Ishwara, the Purusha. Glory to Him! Faith in God is our way to relate to Him, our way to affirm to Him, "You are" in our daily life, our way to assert Him although still being under the veils of Maya. To get the Sun's rays, a flower has to turn towards the Sun. That is what faith is about. When rightly directed, faith is the power which introduces knowledge to its object: reality.

Thanks to Sahaja Yoga, I also realize how futile it was to think that we could "reach God"; the mere striving to do so cannot, ultimately, awaken the energy of the para-sympathetic nervous system because striving itself uses up the energy of the sympathetic Maybe we can say that nobody is big enough to be the chamberlain of God. The Divine has to introduce us to itself. The Ocean has to comprehend the drop of water and not vice-versa. Hence the incarnation of the Great One who came as the master of the Kundalini.

I always wondered about the fact that, whenever Incarnations came on this earth, they were never recognized. They were not only denied but insulted, exiled, stoned, crucified or poisoned. Of course, after their death, they are duly exalted! Is it that they were then fully recognized? By no means! They were worshipped after their death, for a past Incarnation can be better handled and manoeuvered by the human ego. In their name money could be raised and power abused. Whereas Lord Jesus Christ lived in complete poverty and Shri Krishna as an ordinary cowherd boy, their followers accumulate in their names estates and possessions, and enjoy them. That is why, may be, in HH Mataji Nirmala Deviji's incarnation, something was to happen by which we could avoid committing such mistakes. This something has to be a practical tool of knowledge by which we can recognize the incarnation during Her lifetime. The instrument of recognition is, of course, the vibratory awareness, or, in other words, the Divine breath of the Holy Spirit.

Through vibrations, we can enter into contact with the deities of the various chakras. We have experienced it on many occasions.

We go deep into thoughtlessness (dhyana) and, with full attention, we ask questions on the chakras. For instance we ask Shri Rama and Shri Seeta on the right side heart chakra: "Did you come in the form of HH Mataji"? The answer, "Yes" comes instantaneously in the form of an increase of cold vibrations in our hands. If we are treating a heart patient, such questions asked to Shri Shiva or Shri Durga, very often bring a release of the pressure on the patient's heart that we were feeling in collective consciousness. We have asked the deities of all chakras, "Is HH Mataji the Adi Shakti?' We have asked the Original Adi Guru, in the region of the Void: "Are you within HH Mataji?" We have asked Shri Krishna on the Vishuddhi Chakra: "Is She the Virata?" We have asked on the Sahasrara : "Is HH Mataji the collective incarnation?" Everytime that we were deep enough in dhyana to be connected with the deities (devatas) the answer "Yes" has been given by increased vibrations and deepening awareness. When She is praised as the supreme Holy Spirit the devotees are blessed with tremendous vibrations. This is a fact! It is a scientifically established truth for it can be experienced and the experience is also communicable! The process is so minutely subtle and automatic...as HH Mataji says, our subjective instrument (tantra) has become a computer connected with the Cosmic Programme.

The nature of HH Mataji, the one who has granted us the Yoga of Spontaneous Union, can only be approached through these experiences, when the Yogi has already reached the level of the Sahasrara. But even non-realized seekers are provided with overwhelming evidence: Who can perform such a feat as, say, the following one? In a small town in Andhra Pradesh we visited a school. Eight hundred boys and girls had been assembled and welcomed us with songs and cheers. HH Mataji delivered a short speech and, at the end of it, asked everybody to stretch their hands towards her. They did it. After a couple of minutes HH Mataji asked, "those who feel a cool breeze coming in their hands should raise the hand." Some eight hundred hands raised at once; everybody was radiant and smiling. This stupendous happening has been witnessed by hundreds of non-Sahaja Yogis, local teachers, doctors, lawyers, parents, etc.; when we (Sahaja Yogis) stretched our hands towards them, we received forceful waves of vibrations which propelled us into dhyana in no time.

Thus, Sahaja Yogis have been able to develop a living faith in HH Mataji. It is faith enlightened by experience and verification. We have been convinced!

The other aspect of surrender, "Renunciation", did not attract us either in the least; what is the point of renouncing? This beautiful world around us is here to be tasted, to be enjoyed, life is to be relished like a precious nectar.

Well, I still agree with this. And the supreme, adorable paradox is that only renunciation makes it possible. To renounce means to renounce appearance in order to enjoy reality; to reject the fake for the genuine. It is the capacity of the enlightened wisdom to understand that cravings and possessions do not lead to happiness. This is what Shri Kirshna told us in the Bhagavad Gita. It is what Lord Jesus preached. It is the way of Muhammad, of the Buddha and the Mahavira. Through the blessing of HH Mataji the common Man of today, can, at last, make their wisdom his own.

The matter is simple to understand. I have only one capacity of attention and if I want to invest it into the real, I have to withdraw it from the appearance. Attention is usually invested in appearances, such as material accumulation, possession, ego trips, etc., leading to the kind of social interactions that we know only too well. Such is the case because those matters are felt to be sources of satisfaction. There is, of course, a little problem here. If I have no hint that reality is more enjoyable than appearances, I am not going to make any move towards it. The cycle of reincarnations enables us to obtain hints about higher strata of existence and higher satisfactions. We are successively provided with moments of thoughtless awareness (in enjoying beauty of love), with flashes of intuition which enlighten us. We are provided with different kinds of inward experiences which point the way towards the supremely enjoyable state of bliss. It is as if the screen of delusion (*Maya*) is removed and the Divine within us remembers itself.

When, through thoughtless awareness, we become aware of our act of existing, existence itself brings supreme satisfaction and joy. Then flowers, trees, rivers, clouds, smiles, friends are fully enjoyed, everything concurs with our happiness, the world is pulsating around us. In discovering it, in seeing it, we feel this pulse singing the song of our own joy. We can stretch our hands, call, "Mother"!...and feel the Divine Grace pouring within us. This is the kingdom which opens itself within through my as yet limited knowledge of the most sacred incarnation of HH Mataji Nirmala Devi. When this dimension has begun revealing itself, you do not find any great interest in the objects of attention which are supposed to bring pleasure and satisfaction, you have renounced them without even noticing it.

After all, what do we mean by satisfaction? What are we looking for? What are we hunting through the whirlwinds of successive rebirths? The answer is simple: it is INTENSITY. It is intensity that we are running after because it is the essence of any real satisfaction. We are steadily trying to improve our general capacity of perception to be able to absorb an ever growing level of intensity. Intensity can be clear like a child's laugh, intimate like physical union, vibrating like a starlight at night, serene like the silence of love. I do not know what intensity is. I suppose it is the way we perceive the emanations of the Holy Spirit. It is certainly also a plaything for Maya to confuse and delude Man who has been searching for it in the drums of war, in furious passions, in psychedelic escapes, etc. Again "Renunciation" is the psychological attitude by which we free ourselves from lower involvements in order to be receptive to those which are higher (i.e. nearer to Ourselves). If we put our attention at the feet of the Adi Shakti, if we understand a little more of HH Mataji's cosmic personality, we will certainly have found the way to propel our psychic energy towards the Sahasrara.

So faith and renunciation are truly vital aspects of surrender and surrender means nothing but our Self accepting and recognizing its own divinity. Maybe we should invent new words.[18]

The relation between surrender and spiritual growth can be better understood through the tool of vibratory awareness. We have found out that a chakra cannot open itself fully if the subject does not surrender to the deity who presides over this chakra. The last chakra is the abode of the Holy Spirit and of Kalki. Without surrendering to the Holy Spirit this chakra cannot be enlightened and Kalki will not settle in it. Such a surrender is not based on an austere discipline of mystical exercises[19] but on witnessing and acknowledging an inward experience. The apparent difficulty to recognize HH Mataji vanishes on the grounds of those experiences. Yet, at every stage, a humble heart is very necessary to approach this formidable incarnation because it cloaks itself in the veils of the fathomless illusion it generates (*Maya*). Why is an all loving Mother so elusive? Why is the path steep and the gate of the Ajnya Chakra so narrow?

It is true that HH Mataji will do everything which is in Her power to give the spiritual birth of the Sahasrara to as many people as possible. But this power is, in a way, self-limited by the rules of the game that the Adi Shakti Herself laid down at the beginning of time. As far as human beings are concerned, the rule of the game is freedom. Only a free and conscious being can participate in the higher synthesis of awareness. He has made himself fit for this evolution by making free choices, confronting difficult decisions, being involved in the three gunas and yet not being totally overpowered by them. The stage of his psychic life, although open to contradictions, has not been captured by the poles of this contradiction, (ego and super-ego). The delicate task that HH Mataji

---

[18] But should we not re-invent a language?! They have taken the word "real" and made out of it an advertisement for Coca-Cola. They have taken the word "love" and drawn it in a pornographic sewage. They have taken the word "freedom" and put it in the grave. They have taken the "word God" better not say what they did with it! It is time to communicate in the collective consciousness. Mallarme said: "rendez un son plus pur aux mots de la tribut" we will baptize the words anew.

[19] Traditions such as the Sufi, the Zen or the Jesuit were meant to bring the subject's psyche into the right balance. Quite a few Zen masters reached realization.

is performing in this lifetime of Hers can thus be described as follows:

She invites free beings to freely choose the path of higher evolution. If she were to induce them to do so by exhibiting supernatural powers or by triggering right away the supra human consciousness within the subject, the latter, overpowered by the experience, would have lost his freedom to reject it. And freedom is truly the essence, the dharma of the human condition which is respected by God. Up to the very last step of the evolutionary process. HH Mataji says that "the purpose of emancipation is to introduce the Kingdom of God to the human awareness. The responsibility of every individual is to accept Him in full freedom. The object of Sahaja Yoga is complete liberation.[20] Hence nothing can be done arbitrarily by Adi Shakti. The only thing I can do is to lead you and guide you to awaken your Divinity in full freedom".

The plants have no choice; the angels know God. But we, human beings, have the privilege to discover Him. If the purpose of creation is God's self-recognition in creation through the field of the human awareness, such a purpose is reached only when this awareness has made itself ready for it through the trials and achievements of its own freedom. If God was to so wish, He could grant Divine awareness to a stone, but the participation of the stone would have been nil and the evolutionary purpose not fulfilled. Freedom gives Man a chance to participate, to say yes or no, to perform in the cosmic drama of recognition the part given to the creation. It is all a play, don't you see?

It is the cosmic play of Joy. It can be actually felt and experienced that HH Mataji is Brahmatmaikya-swarupini (672nd name of the Devi) that is, She is the union of Atman and Brahman, of the individual soul with the Cosmic soul. In this union collective consciousness is manifested. Thus, when HH Mataji moves Her right hand on the palm of Her left hand we can feel the movement in the Sahasrara; when a devotee in India presented HH Mataji with beautiful roses many Sahaja yogis in London felt at this very time a strong rose fragrance, etc., etc. The full actualization of the cosmic union is the great culmination of bliss that can be reached

---

[20]cf. "Universal History exhibits the gradation in the development of that principle whose substantial purport is the Consciousness of Freedom". G W F Hegel *The Philosophy of History*.
(Dover Books) New York 1956 p. 56

by the integrated consciousness when the seventh chakra is fully awakened.

The sacred lineage of the satgurus and the Divine Incarnations of the past, have led us to the condition of awareness in which the promised rebirth can take place. It is happening now. The Devi Herself is leading us through the great fulfilment of our collective seeking.

One important fact should, at last, be emphasized. HH Mataji is a mother and a guru. This makes Her mission quite delicate as She sometimes points out: Because a mother hates to scourge her child and the child takes all kinds of liberties with her. Whereas the guru has sometimes to scourge and punish and the disciple has to always show him utter respect. The unique personality of HH Mataji, however, beautifully integrates these two aspects. And the Sahaja yogi, while feeling that he is Her blessed child, also understands that you evoke the blessings of the guru by paying him all respect. The importance of the guru was very clearly stated by the Scriptures: —

> "By the grace of the Sat Guru
> The Teacher true
> The seekers attain salvation
> While living with wife and children
> As Householders."[21]

We can also refer to the *Subhagyodayam* of Shri Godespadacharya:

> "Only through the grace of the guru can the Kundalini, which is the giving source of the ultimate fortune, be risen. Then you will be in the service of your guru and he will open this path to eternity. In the Sahasrara there is a moon and it pours nectar drop by drop. The yogi enjoys that nectar which fulfills him totally. He leads his life on earth in a complete Sahaja balanced manner and he is not disturbed by anything, not even siddhis. As sun and moon are in the sky without any bondage in the same way he crosses this existence on earth and does good for everyone."[22]

[21]*Guru Baba Nanak* B P L Bedi (New Light Publishers). p. 98
[22]*Subhagyodayam* Shri Godespadacharya (Yogshri Peeth Trust) Rishikesh 1973. 52nd Verse. p. 195 (Free translation).

I, a seeker who accumulated so many mistakes, an obviously imperfect Sahaja yogi, I experienced the rain of nectar! I also felt the celestial breath. We raise kundalinis. We grant self-realisation. How is it possible?

HH Mataji behaves in an absolutely human way, just like you and me. Yet She is above frustration, above complaining, expecting, resenting. Above jealously, melancholy, pettiness, possessiveness, temptation, boredom, anger, secretiveness, vanity. She is above intrigue and falsehood, tensions or indulgences, above all those moods and games into which we so commonly indulge. She does not know any doubt or fear of any kind. She does not take anything from us. But She goes on giving. She is the giver of peace. She is the giver of joy and awareness. She is the giver of the Divine breath which melts into the stream of bliss. She is the giver of knowledge: knowledge of God, the Almighty, of the Divine Incarnations, of the Kundalini. She commands all the mantras. And we know that the most powerful of all mantras is the mere uttering of Her name: OM SHRI MATAJI NIRMALA MA. You can try it yourself with due respect while meditating in front of the picture.

She is the giver of boons, the bestower of material prosperity and success. She blesses us with firmness, faith and security. She clears our nadis and chakras, destroys our bonds, washes our sins away and grants true liberation. She is the essence of sweetness, the heart of supreme generosity. A simple gesture, Her mere touch opens the Kingdom of God. It does! We have all witnessed endless sequences of miraculous happenings!

She loves Her devotees as Her children. She cares so much about us! Unattached and untroubled, without any anxiety or selfishness, in Her intense compassion, She works days and nights for our salvation. It is for us only that She developed a spontaneous, effortless method which is at the same time an inner yoga and a collective yoga. Pure, bashfully modest, of faultless brilliance in the midst of the worst problems of our modern life, She stands and saves the world.

When all the Divine forces were helpless to eradicate wickedness She emerged for the Divine purpose of revealing Sahaja yoga. She is the giver of freedom. How are we going to respond to Her Advent? What will we do?

Are we going to stick to our ignorance and arrogance? Are we trying to compute, analyse or judge Her? Can we ignore Her Advent? Are we going to deny it? Or are we, at last, surrendering to our wisdom so as to enter in the Kingdom of our Father that She wants us to enjoy?

Oh, beloved, sacred Mother, kneeling, with folded hands, bowed head, I urge You! Forgive us, we are vain, ignorant, full of the noises of empty knowledge. We just do not know anything about You who were so eagerly sought by the knowledge of the sages of yore; can we at least recall their sayings?

> "There is a thing inherent and natural,
> Which existed before heaven and earth.
> Motionless and fathomless,
> It stands alone and never changes;
> It pervades everywhere and never becomes exhausted
> It may be regarded as the Mother of the Universe
> I do not know its name
> If I am forced to give it a name
> I call it Tao, and I name it as supreme".
>   —Tao Te Ching[23]

The time has come to name Thee: Aum jai, Shri Maharajni, Shri Maha pujya, Shri Mahadevi!

Thou art verily the Power beyond all powers, the power of God the Almighty. Oh supremest One! Thou art the Great Incarnation. Let it be announced. Because Thou granted us the knowledge through which we can utter these sacred words, the Age which opens is the one of Thy Revelation. Almighty Sacred Mother I prostrate myself at Thy Feet. From these Feet spread the cosmic rays that generated the whole Universe. This is the greatest of all times because we can behold Thee in the human flesh. Glory to Thee. Aum. Amen.

> In the name of all the true prophets and in the name of all the saints
> In the name of Sadashiva

---

[23]Tao Te Ching in the translation of Chiu Ta-Kao. Unwin publishers (London 1972) p. 37.

In the name of Lord Rama
In the name of Lord Krishna
In the name of Lord Jesus
In the name of Allah, the Merciful, the Compassionate
We, Sahaja Yogis from the five continents
Bear witness to the truth,
To the fact,
That Her Holiness Mataji Nirmala Devi is the Incarnation of
The Holy Spirit.
Aum Shanti Shanti Shanti

It is very difficult to write these lines. For many of you at the very outset will not like to face the truth which is the greatest and most important in the history of our creation. Some of you reading these fantastic statements may feel that they are altogether too much to believe, that they are the ravings of another deluded soul who has found his panacea but lost his intelligence in the process. I can do nothing if you are not prepeared to face the truth with me and to be reassured by my experience. I can only say that it is by honest and genuine experience, and in spite of difficulty to believe, that I have been convinced. Many of us are now convinced completely; for some, reading this book will never be necessary—for them acceptance is easy because the truth is self-evident.

But for all of us it seems that time is short. These are times of very crucial emergency. Our greatest concern is that if we do not recognize the Advent in these self destroying modern times, we will be responsible for the gravest mistake. To maintain self-realization one has to recognize HH Mataji Nirmala Devi, who is the embodiment of all the Deities.

And without self-realization we are not complete, nor do we understand the eternal truths:

—that God Almighty is the Doer and the Enjoyer.
—that the all-pervading Divine Power of Love manifests all that is His will and performs all acts, which in our ignorance (Ego) we think we are doing.
—that mankind has to be saved so that this Creation may be saved.
—that Self-realization is the fulfilment of our evolution and

thus God realizes his joy of communicating His love to His Creation.

In this first introduction to Western people, we understand, it may not be tactful to announce HER Advent. But there is no other way. Now is the time for the truth to be.

Part Six

THE OLDEST QUEST

"Seeking is the path, my dear one, and the Almighty God confers light when there is the earnestness of seeking as a beggar at His door."

—Satguru Baba Nanak.

Those who have already been convinced about Sahaja yoga, either through intuition, experience or instant recognition, can quietly close the book at this page. This last part of the book, I reckon, is rather heavy. I have the slight feeling I played monkey games with the monkeys : a lot of arguments and dignified quotes, hiding myself behind Plato's beard and Hegel's humourless prose. Yet it has been written for those who wish to relate Sahaja yoga to a mental set-up, to the history of the human seeking. Indeed, for many intellectuals, the revelation of Sahaja yoga comes as a great surprise, out of the blue. They find difficult to establish a bridge of understanding between the contemporary state of world affairs and the manifestation of Sahaja yoga. But, after my realisation, I could see how, in fact, Sahaja yoga answers the human research and stirrings of the past centuries. I could see the thread of the Quest leading straight to it.

# 11

The philosophical roots of the ideology of development

1. *Presentation of the topic*

Development today, as a phenomenon as well as an ideology, is a product of the West. As an ideology, it remains mostly implicit and unformulated but can be considered an all-embracing "Weltanschauung" which establishes the first basic assumptions of all decision-making processes. The idea of development is the most important factor in the contemporary history of civilisation because it includes the cultural, psychological, economic, social and political parameters. It conditions the conflicts of international relations (East-West, North-South) as well as underlines those of the individual pysche (action versus contemplation). It affects the life of the individual and of the collectivity. Furthermore it transcends the borders of the Western world and regulates the activity of the whole planet. At this point, we are witnessing the spread of a typically Western world view daily confronting the conceptions of other ancient civilisations : Islamic, Buddhist, Hindu, etc... Thus one of the relevant questions about the future of mankind appears to be "what sort of synthesis between these different civilisations is possible?" Is any synthesis possible at all, and, if so, could the politics of development become the vehicle for a new form of integrated world-civilisation?

All the while, it has become apparent that the development model of the last decades has largely been a failure. Although development is largely identified with economic growth, economic growth does not mean automatic social development. Increase in the per capita income or in the gross national product does not prevent social disruptions. The modernisation of society in the so called developed world does not mean any genuine achievement of human qualities by its members. Values are artificial; relationships mechanical. The outside development is not connected with the human substance. We are becoming aware that man himself has to be changed if society is to evolve. Indeed, development implies individual spiritual development as well as collective social development. Both of them are linked and the relationship between the two can be shown by answering the question : why did development occur as a result of the Western civilisation and not, say the Eastern one?[1]

Now, this question is such a broad and complex one that we need some introduction to the way we intend to deal with it.

By definition, a study of civilisation implies the study of an almost unlimited number of variables. There are, roughly, two ways to proceed with a cross-cultural approach in a comparative analysis. One can isolate and follow one or a few variables : geopolitics, technology, literacy, economics; the danger here lies in boldly extrapolating from the particular to the general, and in considering one's field of study as the single causal explanation of the whole. The other method is to consider, as far as possible, the ensemble of the variables and to build a model based on quantitative data. The danger here consists in being inevitably incomplete and incapable of inducing historical meanings.

Both methods run into a major difficulty: how to discover the right link in the cause and effect process? Indeed the very way of asking the "why" implies a choice which has to be careful. To quote Max Weber's statement :

> "Why did not the scientific, the artistic, the political or the economic development there (China or India) enter upon that path of rationalisation which is peculiar to the Occident? For in all the above cases it is a question of the specific and

---

[1] In the specific model of Japan development the Western input also played a key role in triggering the Meiji revolution.

peculiar rationalism of the Western culture".[2]

It is all right to orient the debate in this sense as long as one does not start from the generally granted premise that Western culture is more rational than the Eastern one. This would be totally misleading because it does not consider the fact that Oriental civilisations were more "rational" than the Western one in the realm which mattered to them : the mystical path. Siddhartha Gautama, Lao-Tzu or Adi Shankaracharya may have been more "rational" (clear, systematic, efficient, etc.) than, for instance, Meister Eckhardt, John of the Cross or Theresa of Avila.

This leads us to our first methodological remark: in a comparison between A and B, one must not judge B according to the criteria of A. This point was made clear by the German historical school, especially with Herder's notion of "Volksgeist": each people has a genuinely original spirit.

But then, if one cannot use the standard of A or B which are by definition historically linked, on which standards could one possibly rely for our comparative analysis? The answer is that one has to find out if there exists a common criterion for A and B and to start from there. The search for the common criterion, for the lowest common denominator, leads to a second methodological remark : in a comparative study of civilisation, the study of the philosophical variable has a logical priority over the others because it deals with the basic common element : Man as he "is" and as he "ought to be". In short, to deal with the possibility of improving man (the perfectibility of man)[3] amounts to dealing with the space between Man and God. To have a certain conception of the ultimate reality implies having a corresponding perception of the human condition. This perception doubtlessly influences the general orientation of a civilisation. Man influences history by the very notion he has of God, himself, and history. In the different manner in which the Western and Eastern minds approach the common problem of human destiny we find some opportunities to understand why two different civilisations setup different general criteria

[2]Max Weber: *The Protestant Ethic and the Spirit of Capitalism* (The Scribner Library) page 25
[3]For a distinguished historical account of the topic see John Passmore *The Perfectibility of Man* Gerald Duckworth & Co. (London 1970)

of behaviours, why the one evolved an ideology of development and the other did not.[4] And ultimately we will try to answer the great question : what are the conditions required to ensure a successful synthesis of the Eastern and Western cultures.

Hence we will follow the first method we mentioned previously: We will follow a single variable but will not try to derive the larger picture from it. This variable is the different conception of the perfectibility of man in Western and Indian philosophy. This topic is central to both philosophy and development. I choose India as the element of comparison because, following most orientalists, I found the Indian contribution to be decisive in the evolution of Asian thought.

2. *The basic notions*

Let us have a short glance at Indian thought. It would be a bad neologism to speak of Indian philosophy. Indian philotheism would be a more appropriate term since, for an Indian seeker, the aim is not so much to love wisdom as to love and realize "God". Trying to define what is Indian thought appears to be a difficult task because of the confusing wealth of various mythological traditions. This pluralism can be explained by the absence of any dogmatic church, in the catholic sense. The free competition of religious ideas and experimentation coexisted with some great schools of thought which never reached a monpoolistic status of the Christian church under the Roman Empire. Rulers such as Ashoka or Jain ministers who tried to spread their powers in organizing religion ultimately failed. The establishment of four Peethas by the successors of Adi Shankaracharya has not been a significant event in the history of Hindu religion.

Thanks to the stimulus of competitive conditions, Indian religious enquiry reached a very high level in both speculative thought and concrete experimentation. Furthermore because of a monsoon-tied agriculture, the mass of peasants remained acutely aware that their fate depended upon forces beyond human control. In this environment, the teachings of the great spiritual models found a fertile ground. Maybe the common denominator of all

---

[4]We cannot say, of course, that the East did not evolve a genuine philosophical reflection on social development. But a thought such as, say, Gandhi's has yet to prove that it can guide society on the path of material development.

the Indian scriptures (Vedas, Sutras, Puranas, Upanishads, Dhammapada, etc...) could be suggested in T.A. Raman's words:

> "The cornerstone of the Hindu faith may be taken to be the belief in a World soul, or rather, a soul of all the Universe, Paramatma, the Supreme, the one reality of which all individual souls are parts. Defining the purpose of life as self-realisation, which means harmonizing one's individual soul with the Infinite, the philosophers...examined rationally every means to realize this end, the beatitude of being merged in the Supreme".[5]

Self-realisation through union is the key-word of the Indian religious experience that we find with various expressions in all schools: Vedantist, Advaitist, Buddhist, Jainist, etc...Union (in Sanskrit, "Yoga") introduces us to an important notion to be defined: the mystical path.

For a westerner, the word mysticism is mostly connected with the notion of irrationality, sweet madness, unnatural and extraordinary phenomena. It is fundamentally important to free our brains from these cliches: six millenia of Asian experimentation in the "mystical" realm and major pages in the history of world civilisations cannot be merely based upon fancies, dreams, hallucinations. In the Indian spiritual pursuit it was conceived that you cannot perceive the unlimited with the limited human mind. They knew what the greatest of the ancient Greeks also came to discover: whenever the human mind gets closer to reality it drops human made concepts and merges with the truth. They knew that, when the decision making instrument is not sensitive to the Absolute, decisions are relative and imperfect: the intellect goes on compromising with falsehood to please the ego's vested interests.

In order to see the implications of the mystical experience, let us define the word "metaphysics".

"Meta" in ancient Greek means beyond. Metaphysics appears to be what is beyond physics. Physics, in its philosophical sense, means our three dimensional world: time, space, causality.

Our mind, in its intellectual process, evolves within physics. Reasoning, analysis, science belong to the third dimension. The

---

[5] T.A. Raman *Report on India* (Oxford 1943) page 21.

fourth dimension, infinity, cannot therefore be reached or grasped by any intellectual activity. Insofar as it is "metaphysical" a being is out of the mind's control. But it is not out of man's reach. Karl Jaspers writes about the Buddha's doctrine :

> "There is only one means of liberation; to transcend ignorance by knowledge. But nothing can be changed by insight into particulars here and there. It is only the fundamental state of vision in which we see the whole that transforms and saves."[6]

Beyond the simple verbal concept (vitarka-vikara) the direct contemplation (dhyana) leads us to the domain of spiritual union. Sri Ramana Maharishi said: "Yoga is the suppression of the vritti (modifications of the thinking principle). Then the seer abides in himself". It will be remembered that Aquinas defined as a condition of perfection the removal of "whatever hinders the mind's affection from turning wholly to God." The space generated by the mental activity of the subject is the ego; the space that the emotional side of the psyche evolves is the super-ego. Once these psychic spaces are overcome, the attention of the subject merges into the metaphysical dimension of Self or Soul. Nothing is left but the pure "I am That" awareness. Through this trip into the fourth dimension, the yogi is united with the whole cosmos as well as with himself :

> "The seer Vamadeva realising Brahman, knew that himself was the self of mankind as well as of the Sun. Therefore, know also, whoever realizes Brahman knows that he himself is the Self in all creatures".
> —*Bhihadaranyaka Upanishad*

Metaphysics, for the ancient Greeks, was the knowledge of that primordial reality beyond physics, which sustains the world of physics. But it should be emphasized here that knowledge-mutation is a realisation which takes place far beyond metaphysical speculations. For these also depend upon the human per-

---

[6] Karl Jaspers *The Great Philosophers* (Harvest books) Vol. 1 page 26.

ception of the Absolute, or God, and this perception is limited. The human awareness cannot comprehend reality through the intellect's striving; it has to evolve to the point of self awareness. In that realm the human mind gets connected with the Absolute; there is no contradiction, no compromise and no wrong decisions.

The mystical path consists in overcoming the brain's usual performance in order to attain higher stages of consciousness beyond the three-dimensional world. Modern science is not yet in a condition to explain such experiences but it has lately reached a point where researchers have begun to perceive the direction of their work, especially in the field of the neuro-endocrinology of the brain and other researches in psycho-somatic medicine: Is there any kind of "genetic message" in the human seed that brings forth the consciousness mutation? If the process is an evolutionary one, what kind of energy operates the connection of the human attention with a higher level of awareness? Increasing references are being made to Kundalini-yoga: the yoga which awakens the residual consciousness within man. Various publications today[7] are expressing the first astonishment of modern researchers in front of a realm that great saints have been exploring empirically for millenia and which can be expressed in secular terms as the world of maximization of energies. Many Westerners today are considering with a new interest the ancestral spiritual "know-how" developed in India and are beginning to understand how these investigations were of central importance in the elaboration of the Asiatic world. The influence of the great spiritual masters was based upon a deep knowledge of the psycho-somatic integration of human and super-human energies together with their ability to present this knowledge in a coherent theology. Indeed, they deeply determined the way Asiatics considered

---

[7]For instance the brain's unkown continent was the major theme of a rather naive article entitled "Boom Time on the Psychic Frontier" (*Time*, March 4th, 1974):

"In Washington, the Defence Department's Advanced Research Projects Agency assigns a team to investigate seemingly authentic psychic phenomena at the Stanford Research Institute...The Menninger Foundation in Topeka, Kansas, reports incontrovertible proof that subjects trained by biofeedback can control their blood circulation and lower the temperature of the parts of their bodies at will... The ancient yogic mythic skills suddenly seem within the grasp of everyone".

human destiny and thereby the way they considered what should be done about it.

Of course, people familiar with the condition of contemporary India could disagree with my presentation of India as a spiritual country. But let it be emphasized that the India I am mentioning is the India of Sri Rama and the yogin Vashista. In the last millenia the Indian subcontinent has been invaded so many times (Greeks, Huns, Iranians, Afghans, Muslims, British) that, no doubt the original values have been shattered. In the prevailing insecurity saints had to withdraw into the jungles and the social system based on spiritual values could not survive. Actually we can probably trace the origin of Hindu decadence back to the period described in the Mahabharata, about 6,000 years ago. Yet the movements of historic trends should not prevent us from perceiving the spiritual substance of the Hindu civilisation. When we leave urban India and go to the villages we find that this substance is still very much alive.

3. *The evolution of Western thought*

Whereas in the Indian beliefs a godlike perfectibility is within the possibility of man, the evolution of Ideas in Western civilisations ends at the opposite conclusion. Paul Valery once said that the Occident was the outcome of Greek philosophy, Christianity and Roman Law. The first two elements are of major concern for the understanding of our argument.

The Olympic pantheon of Homeric Greece corresponded to a purely anthropomorphic view of the divinity which reflected the motivations of the warrior society of that time. Hence Xenophane used to lament:

> "Homer and Hesiod have ascribed to the Gods everything that is a shame and a reproach amongst men, stealing and committing adultery and deceiving each other".[8]

This stage in the history of religion indeed represented a very limited and distorted perception of those superior beings that were called Gods or Devas.

---

[8] Xenophane in G. S. Krik and J.E. Raven: *The Presocratic Philosophers* (Cambridge, 1957) page 33.

With the end of the heroic age during the VI Century B.C. and the development of urban and political entities, we can witness in the plays of Aeschylus a moralisation of the divinity. Furthermore, in their quest for metaphysical perfection, the pre-Socratic philosophers were led towards an impersonal conception of the divinity and thus, completely dismantled the Olympian religion. The "Boundless" of Anaximander starts looking very much like the Hindu *"Brahman Tatwa;"* Aristotle sums up: "of the Boundless there is no beginning...but this seems to be the beginning of the other things, and to surround all things and steer all... And this is the divine for it is immortal and indestructible"[9]. Parmenides carried the investigation further with his famous "Being". "One way is left to speak of Being", Parmenides concluded, "that it is" and "it was not in the past, nor shall be, since it is now, all at once, one, continuous"[10].

As early as the 5th Century B.C., Parmenideanism was a culminating point in the history of ideas. As the 20th Century French Thomist Jacques Maritain stated:

"The metaphysical intuition of Being is that very intuition that our human intellect can experience at the peak of its intellectuality" (My translation).[11] But Parmenides made his thought felt mostly by Plato's conception of the "One". "The One neither is one nor is at all... It cannot have a name or be spoken of, nor can there be any knowledge or perception or opinion of it. It is not named or spoken of, not an object of opinion or of knowledge, not perceived by any creature."[12]

This "reductio and absurdum" was to create the difficulties of Platonic mysticism: how was it possible to be united with this unfathomable One? Indeed, by that time, Greek seekers were very much involved in the experimental explorations, that is, they were not so much concerned with speculations about the highest "One" but rather with the question of how to attain it. Now I should

---

[9] Aristotle *Physics*, 20367

[10] Parmenides in G. S. Krik and J. E. Raven, Op. Cit. page 243, 347

[11] "L'intuition metaphysique de L'etre est l'intuition par excellence dont notre intelligence humaine est capable a la cime de son intellectualite". Jacques Maritain. Sept Lessons sur l'etre et les premiers principes de la raison speculative (Pierre Tequi) p. 68.

[12] Plato. *Republic* Book VI, p. 494 A. Today Sahaja yogis know that what Socrates called the eternal forms of truth and beauty are in fact the deities.

say straight away that during my period of studies, I felt this latter attitude to be the right one. For quite some time I had been frustrated to see that many of my teachers, many of the thinkers of the past are satisfied by merely understanding the possibilities of human evolution. But understanding was not good enough for me. Becoming—not understanding—is the point! I kept trying to find out whether anyone had given the key to that becoming.

In Empedocles' 5th Century poem entitled "Purifications" the view prevails that the proper home of men is among the Gods. The human soul is involved in cycles of transmigration from which it can escape by purifications. We are far from Pindar's "mortal things suit mortal beasts" and from the powerful Greek tradition that the attempt to equal the Gods (*hubris*) is the greatest sin. For Pythagoras purification was the contemplation of orderly perfection. This brings us back to Plato.

Socrates, through his disciple Plato, can be considered as the key figure of Western philosophy before the Semitic contribution.

He exposed a synthesis between the speculative and experimental approach to the "First things" and drew from it a complete social and political philosophy. Never before Socrates and Plato and never after them have Western and Eastern philosophies been closer in their perception of the nature of the ultimate reality.

Let us skim very rapidly the Platonic formulation:—

—On the speculative level, Plato described in *the Republic* the form of the good as "the cause of all that is right and beautiful in all things" (Book VII, 517C). Therefore it will be identified with the supreme beauty of *the Symposium* and with the "One" of Plato's *Parmenides*. The way is paved once and for all for the Thomist ontological equation of the Real: BEING=GOOD=BEAUTIFUL =TRUE which is analogous to the Indian description of the Whole (*Brahman*).

—On the practical level, Plato states in the *Phaedo* that the soul freeing itself from "the body" by acquiring "knowledge" can reach eternal reality and "remains ever constant and changeless with the unchanging because of her contact with things similarly immutable" (Phaedo, 79.cd). For Philosophers "lovers of that reality which always is", to know means to love what is known. Through love (in Indian mysticism: Bhakti yoga) and knowledge (Jnana yoga) the philosopher's soul contemplates the form of the good and, indeed, becomes the good, i.e. perfect.

As a conclusion to Platonic ideas (and Aristotle's in the Nichomachean ethic) one can say that there is a divine element in man which can be actualized by contemplation. Since contemplation is the highest goal in life, the ideal Platonic society will be ruled by a philosopher-king and philosophers who devote themselves to contemplation. Since "the multitude cannot be philosophical" below the level of "philosophical goodness" we find the "civic goodness" of laborious and socially-minded people who have no prospects of joining "the company of God".

Interestingly enough, the Hindu caste system prefigures exactly the Platonic picture of the society where the upper class (*Brahmins*) devoted to contemplation preceded the second hierarchic class (*Kshatriya*s: warriors and civil servants) devoted to action. (The two other classes according to the laws of of Manu are the *Vaishyas* or merchants and the *Sudras* or manual workers). The saints were held in high esteem. The Kshatriyas were protecting them and sought their advice. (For instance, the term "*mantrana*" meaning in Sanskrit "the advice to the King" comes from the verb "*manana*"; to contemplate. And so does the term "*mantri*" minister). The advice to the King was sought from the depths of contemplation. The royal adviser had mastered meditation. The class sytem which offered pre-eminence to the saints also represented a judicious system of political check and balance. The separation of knowledge, power and money prevented the despotism of the wicked. We will explain later on why the primacy of contemplation over action as a behavioural value led to the immobilism of the Eastern Civilisations.

The arrival on the grecko-roman scene of Hebraic concepts caused a tremendous crisis in the philosophy of the West.

The Semitic God was a providential and personal God, father of His elected people. By definition a "Persona" has a form and one form excludes another: the metaphysical union with a formally personal God is an impossibility. Hence on the practical level, Man's path towards Godlike perfection is drastically cut off. On the speculative level, quite logically, if man cannot move towards God it means that he cannot discover anything about Him: knowledge is to be found in a sacred Book (the Torah, the Bible or, later on, the Koran) which is the exclusive and complete source of Revelation. Unfortunately, this is the very spirit in which the Hebrew followers of Christ, though wellmotivated, transmitted and distorted the teachings of their Master who had spent half His life fighting against formal conformism to the Scriptures. As a result, the narrow limitation of "biblical space" was to act as a permanent restraint on Christian (as on Muslim) speculations. The right attitude was no longer the experimentation but the belief, not the seeking enquiry but the dogmatic obedience. "If you will enter into life, keep the commandments" Matthew, 19.20. Clement of Alexandria claims that Man "could not be saved in any other way but by believing."[13] Alas, that was a well meaning bad mistake! Believing in God increasingly came to mean believing in a book and in the people in charge of its interpretation whereas experiencing God had meant depending upon one's own quest for the Truth. The pathetic mistake of turning Jesus against Socrates produced centuries of Christian contradictions and the ultimate break between spirituality and society. Despite all efforts one can read between the lines of the Gospel "Ye must be reborn", which indicates that Socrates and Christ said the same things. We have seen that Socrates holds some ideas about Man and God which were substantially akin to those presented in the classics of Indian thought. But Plato did not go as far as the Hindu seers who discovered through contemplation that the Soul was a part of God, indeed God itself (The Atman). The Platonic contemplative soul was "like" the form but did not merge in it. Hence, the basic problem of the God-Man relation was not solved in a metaphysically satisfying way. That is why platonic philosophy could not defend its position in front of this Christian theology which was nursed in the Augustinian cradle.

The ideal conception of the aristotelian city (polis) was based on the union of morality and politics which promotes the best regime: But, for Augustine, the city of God is the realm of the absolute, the city of man the realm of the relative. Man, corrupted by sin, cannot relate to the city of God except through the mediation of the church which provides both political and spiritual guidance. Hence the christians were prevented from seeking moral goodness in political institutions and truth in personal seeking. The political consequences of this human made concept of the relation between God and Man find their most powerful expres-

---

[13]Clement of Alexandria Exhortation to the Greeks trans G.W. Butterworth (London 1919) p. 191.

sion in the theory of Niccolo Machiavelli: "as politics and morality have nothing in common, to ignore morality is good politics!" The metaphysical consequences of the same concept splits the human from the Divine, the concept from the spirit and introduced in Western thought a dualist transcendency which explains why, later on, attention would be focused on contradictions and not on synthesis. Metaphysics were to be cut off from the immediate concrete actuality and from any experimental realisation because it now belonged to the city of God which was beyond man's reach. On those premises Western theology built up further confusions.

"Since" as Aquinas put it "no name is predicted univocally of God and of creatures" (*Summa Theologica* pt. 1, 913, a 5) man separated from the perfect evolves hopelessly in the realm of imperfection. The cause of this was to be found in the "original sin". But how could an Almighty and providential Father let man commit such an irremediable sin? If, as the Bible suggests, History is providentially determined how can man be responsible for sin, and if, as the Bible suggests, man is responsible for Sin and therefore punished, how can history be providentially determined? What is its purpose? How can Providence and Evil be reconciled?

"God, the Author of all creatures but not of their defects, created man good" Augustine wrote in the *City of God* "but man corrupt by choice and condemned by justice has produced a progeny which is both corrupt and condemned". The answer tells us that man has enough free will to choose evil and to be punished for this choice. But then, argued the Neo-Platonists the Gnostics and the Pelagians, man should have corresponding freewill to choose the good, i.e. to carry on his perfectibility. However Jewish thought rejected the possibility of the spiritual research of man. The Jewish faith consists of accepting a revelation which has been granted once and for all. This revelation commands adherence and not enquiry. That reaction proceeded logically from an antropomorphic conception of "God" and the lack of metaphysical categories which prevented the disponibility towards any sensible kind of "*Unio mystica*".

The Council of Orange in 529 and the Council of Quierzy-sur-Oise in 853 asserted the official view: "To those who are saved, salvation is a gift of God; but those who perish are lost through their own fault."[14] That is it! The statement was to remain the position of the Church: Man has not enough free will to overcome the predestinated necessity of his doom. Of course when the doctors and priests of the Council said "a gift of God" they meant "a gift of the Church". They also meant that Man is doomed unless and until the Church (and not God) saves him. Once more a human institution was pretending to represent the Divine realm in order to rule the wordly one better. All the while the enquiry of the seekers was discouraged.

Christianity, however hellenized, remains a Hebrew religion; Tertullian exclaims in *De Praescriptione*: "What is there in common between Athens and Jerusalem, between the Academic and the Church?. . .For us, we have no need for curiosity after Jesus Christ, nor for investigations after the Gospel."

The answer of orthodox theology to the curious, all too curious Western mind was to anathemize its attempt to solve the contradictions in which it was enmeshed by that very orthodoxy. The Church was telling Man that he was basically depraved while requiring from him a moral behaviour. The official doctrine had of course to live with this contradiction, that can be expressed as Kant did:

> "The consequence of the depravation of man is the denial of all moral worth in man... for he (the depraved man) would then be supposed unable ever to improve himself, which cannot be reconciled with the idea of man, who, as such, as a moral being can never lose every inclination toward what is good."[15]

Indeed the impact of Judeo-Christian ideas on Greek philosophy produced an intellectual framework where speculative enquiries were doomed to be debated hopelessly within the predefined space of dogmatically contradictory issues.

With the rise of its political and economic power under the Roman Empire, the Church had the means to defend its ideological monopoly with great force. It had however a hard time doing

---

[14]quoted in H. Daniel Rops: The Church in the Seventeenth Century. Trans J. Buckingham (London 1963) p. 341.
[15]Emmannel Kant, *Metaphysics of Morals* Part 2, "Doctrine of Virtue".

so because the contradictory content of the dogma was a perpetual invitation to divergent speculative enterprises and an endless source of ideological controversies. From the bloody quarrel of the Byzantine Empire to the Jansenist-Molinist conflict of the 17th Century—not to mention the wars of religion—we have witnessed different attacks on the established doctrine, centring on the same issue: what are the relations between Man and God?

In short, since the "speculative space" of Catholic and Orthodox dogmatism framed the debate in fundamentally contradictory terms, this latter was doomed to failure. And the failure of enquiry went along with the respect for the established institutions and the acceptance of religious doctrines. The situation, pregnant with ideological conflicts, gave birth to different trends that I reduce, very roughly, to three main positions.

1. *The Dogmatists.* Up to this date, the Catholic church cloaks its doctrinal contradictions in the purple of dogma, trying to reconcile in the subtle "distinguo" of Aquinas, the numerous conflicts which never ceased within itself. Among them should be mentioned the irreducible incompatibility between free will and necessity which the Thomist synthesis tries to hide. When endowed with ideological monopoly and temporal power, the Church acted as a restraint as well as a catalyst on the two following streams.

2. *The Marginals.* A constant but very diversified current of thought claimed the possibility for Man to achieve in this life an individual—and sometimes Godlike—perfection. And therefore, in the choice between necessity and free will, these people generally advocated free will. The spirit of free speculative enquiry and of spiritual experimentation akin to the Indian and Greek tradition is the main common denominator between completely different types of spiritual experiences. We find there the Gnostic with Dyonisius the Aeropagite, the neo-Platonic thought with Plotinus, Pico della Mirandola and the 18th Century Cambridge school. We find the Christian mystics on the border of heresy with Meister Eckhardt, John of the Cross, Teresa of Avila. The "heretical" mystics with the Anabaptists, the Cathars, the Brethren of the Free Spirit etc... The 16th Century Spanish "illuminists" persecuted by the Inquisition of the Dominican Melchior Cano. In quite another direction we find some mighty free thinkers like Erasmus, Spinoza, Goethe or Nietzsche. This list is by no means complete but is intended to show the persistency of a tendency wich reap-

peared in the late sixties of the present century. A significant portion of the Western Youth then engaged itself in various types of research in the field of consciousness. However important this current may be in the history of Western ideas, these people are marginals because up to this date they never managed to ground a durable, viable, social and political unit and therefore define themselves by opposition with the existing units.

3. *The Reformists.* The category of the reformists laid down the philosophical assumptions underlying the ideology of development. Like the dogmatists they did not believe in the possibility of Man to reach individual perfection. But unlike the dogmatists, in the choice between free will and necessity, they generally emphasized necessity with an important corresponding development in their perception of the perfectibility of man. Man could reach the level of perfection appropriate to his condition by adopting a certain behaviour subjected to and participating in the general law of Necessity. Thus was introduced the notion of "task perfection" in the realm of action versus the old conception of "becoming perfection" in the reality of contemplation. And where, of its very nature, the contemplative ideal promoted an individualistic view of human destiny and evolved corresponding values, the active ideal fostered the social dimension of human fate and developed a set of values oriented toward social achievements. This current, springing from Aristotle, took, of course, different expressions (Renaissance, Reformation). At the time when a still religious perception of the world identified necessity with providence (God's action in the world) the Reformation flourished with William of Ockham, Luther, Calvin and Zwingli. Reinhold Niebuhr and Karl Barth are the contemporary representatives of this trend. However religion became increasingly marginal among people's concerns. As perfection lies not in becoming something but in doing something, the emphasis of speculation shifted from spiritual to material pursuits. This turning point of Western thought took the following form.

With the secularisation of the Providence-necessity and the replacement of transcendental necessity (necessity from above) by immanent necessity (the necessity from within which is the philosophical element involved in the concept of legitimacy of J.J. Rousseau's Social Contract) there appears historical necessity with Burke, Herder, Hegel and Karl Marx. As a mental category it is, to a large extent, nothing but a transposition to the worldly plane of the traditional Judeo-Christian belief in Providence.[16]

For the enlightened philosophers of the 18th Century it was of major importance to reconcile the confidence in Man's possibilities and free will that they were advocating with the belief in a secularized necessity. Indeed, to advocate free will only, to believe in a pure "laissez faire, laissez-passer" world view would have meant to advocate the indeterminancy of history. And this, translated into moral terms, implies that man has no guarantee to reach "the good". As we can see in Kant's interpretation of Rousseau's second discourse as a vindication of providence German philosophers avoided the indeterminacy of history by defining historical necessity as the necessity of good.

By this means we arrive at the secular synthesis of necessity and free will which has proven to be the most formidable archetype of contemporary thought. The idea is that through the selfish and contradictory strivings of his free will, man, in fact, unknowingly implements the higher evolutionary plan of a superior necessity. This necessity which had been the Christian Providence became Herder's "golden chain of improvement", Fichte's "World-Plan" as well as Kant's "purpose of nature" and Darwin's "natural selection". It evolved from the dialectic actualisation of Hegel's "World Spirit" through Karl Marx, Engels and Lenin into "the historical Law of dialectic materialism" which provides the cornerstone of Mao Tse Tung's thought. Amusingly enough, we find the same optimistic confidence in the magical property of necessity in the bible of the capitalist mode of production; we read in Adam Smith's *The Wealth of Nations*:

"When the entrepreneur intends only his own gain...he is... led by an invisible hand to promote an end which was not a part of his intention...By pursuing his own interest, he fre-

---

[16]"The idea of History precisely like modern political/economy could appear to have emerged through a modification of the traditional belief in Providence... secularization is the temporalization of the spiritual or of the eternal. It is the attempt to integrate the eternal in temporal context."
Leo Straus. *Natural Right and History* The University of Chicago Press (Chicago 1955). p. 551.

quently promotes that of society more effectually than when he really intends to promote it"[17].

Such a thinking was of course a mighty incentive to accumulate material possessions with a self-righteous and quiet conscience. It is a truism to say that, in the history of civilisation the image of good and what should be done in order to reach it was tightly linked with that civilisation's concept of the Divine. Locke, in order to sanctify the concept of private property[18] was telling us in *The Treatise* that the true ground of morality can only be the will and law of God. In other words, different concepts of God generate different ways for the civilisations to prescribe a set of rules and this in turn evolves different patterns of behaviour. The sequence remained operative after the secularization of theological concepts into the modern realms of the philosophy of history and political economy. The Jewish religious tradition of a providential order found new expressions in historical (Herder, Burke, Kant, Hegel) and economic (Malthus, Ricardo, Smith, Marx) necessity. Through various formulations the same basic idea remains. From the Book of Ezekiel to the October Revolution each generation claimed to be charged with the unique mission of bringing history to its preordained consummation. In the process, the second coming of Christ and the millenium of the Kingdom of God faded away in favour of the materialist millenium of the marxist and capitalist societies.

God is, was and will be what He is, but anyone can use His name for wordly purposes. This has been amply demonstrated by the history of political philosophy.

4. *A comparison between the Eastern and Western perception of Man's perfection*

I am the first to admit that I have made some gross simplifications in order not to lose myself in the History of ideas. However, these simplifications do not undermine the logic or value of the argument that may now be presented.

---

[17] Adam Smith *The Wealth of Nations*, Book IV. p. 12

[18] Be it mentioned, en passant, such has not always been the Christian position. St. Ambrose of Milan tells us "The Lord God specially wanted this earth to be the common possession of all, and to provide fruits for all; but avarice produced the rights of property".

We saw that, because of particular, historical conditions, India evolved a high level of both abstract metaphysical speculations and practical techniques of contemplation which form the core of the Indian civilisation. This level of religious knowledge permitted the Indian value system to consider man's Godlike perfection as within the realm of practical possibilities. In the Brahmanic and Buddhist world-view there is no split between the Divine and earthly cities, but one single cosmic city. For this very reason, within this unique city, the Indian seeker was rather inclined towards Divine goals than towards earthly ones. Whereas, in Western thought, the Divine city is the realm of cause, the earthly city the realm of effects. But it is not possible to connect the effect with the cause since dualist transcendency established an abyss between the first which is Infinite and the second which is Finite. The consequence is the alienation of man who is separated from his cause, who is separated from the possibility of understanding himself and the universe. The link between the two cities is not the mystical path but the belief in established creeds and doctrines.

Practical mystical experiments were forbidden by the ruling class of priests in contradiction to what happened in India. Thus it is not surprising that where India developed a system of values based on individual self-realisation, Western countries developed a system based on social values and collective realisations. The material and not the spiritual realm was indeed the only one where the Western seeker could hope to achieve something after having escaped from the theological schizophrenia of the two cities; the West opted for the earthly city.

The secular attempt of the Western mind to domesticate thought and matter can probably be traced back to the 15th Century Renaissance. By lowering the standards of human goals, the new type of Westerner got rid of the claim to metaphysical perfection. Leonardo da Vinci noticed: "the supreme happiness would be the greatest cause of misery and the perfection of wisdom an opportunity for madness"[19] (The painter of the Mona Lisa was at the same time a technological seer who, prophetically enough alas, was also designing helicopters and tanks).

In exhorting his fellow Florentines to value more the fate of their city than the salvation of their own soul, Machiavelli

[19]Leonardo da Vinci *Carnets Gallimard* Vol. II p. 61 (my translation)

split politics from morality and freed political action from moral principles. Indeed we can say with Leo Strauss that:

> "In modern Western philosophy, there came into being a new type of theory of metaphysics, having as its highest theme human action and its product rather than the whole, which is in no way the object of human action."[20]

Consequently, the modern emphasis on incremental perfection, improvement, as opposed to the characteristic Grecko-Hindu yearning for eternity, rested on the new creed that Goethe laid down in Faust: "In the beginning was the Act."[21]

Since action implies movement, task-perfectibility implies progress; like Darwin, Spencer tells us that progress is not an accident but a necessity. Now, going back to action, we see that by its very nature, action calls for reaction, interaction i.e. social intercourse and collective dimensions. While Western thought enquired within the realm of action and society, Indian thought pursued its search into the realm of contemplative consciousness. In the East the most respected form of power would not be the might of the Machiavellian prince but the wisdom of the detached saint. (*Stitha projnya*).

Let us conclude in Platonic terms: Indian civilization promoted the superior "philosophical goodness" and Western civilization the inferior "civic goodness." But when the highest goal was only attainable for a small group of individuals, the contemplative elite, the lower goal was within the reach of a large stratum of the population: the social-minded dynamic elite. The latter seeking different ways of reaching perfection by social action, evolved a task-perfectibility concept leading to unlimited improvement. When this concept was applied to the economic parameter we obtained the philosophical assumption underlying the contemporary ideology of development.

Now, it is easy to imagine the criticism that this point could raise and that could be formulated as follows: "let us admit that the different perceptions of Man's perfectibility in Eastern and Wes-

---

[20] Leo Strauss *Natural Right and History* (op cit) p. 320
[21] "Mir hilft der Geist! auf Einmal seh' ich Rat
Und schreibe Getrost: Am Anfang war die Tat" Goethe *Faust* (Aubier) p. 41

tern thought correspond to your description : it is far from obvious that such concepts have any effect upon political and economical conditions". This remark would revive the old debate on the relationship between ideas and facts in history and compel us to go further into argumentation; after having described what the variable is—the perfectibility of Man—we should explain how it works by jumping into the field of psychology.

5. *Spiritual libido*

The question is a concrete and specific one: "Through which channel will the influence of this variable exert itself on Man's behaviour?"

One can tentatively summarize the answer as follows: the perfectibility of Man is the very ideal or archetype which mobilizes the energy of the spiritual libido.[22] This latter, through the conditioning ego of the human psyche, exerts a determinating impact on human action.

By archetype we imply the notion developed by Jungian psychology: Man receives from the collective unconscious some ideal models which strike his consciousness in the form of powerful intuitions. These archetypal manifestations are so effective they determine the mould channels along which human energies may flow.[23] In this respect, the role played by the idea of the perfectibility of Man is easy to understand: Every choice, every action implies for the subject an idea of the better and of the worse. Perfectibility means that one tries to move in order to realise the former and avoid the latter. An idea of the better or of the worse implies an image of the Good. This image is normative because it defines a set of principles liable to bring about the Good. By this very normative dimension, the archetype of perfectibility is pres-

[22] The word is used here in its latin Pascalian and not in its Freudian meaning. It expresses a basic and intense desire or passion.

[23] As Bertrand de Jouvenel point out, Man can be tamed by images. In the *Critique of Pure Reason* Kant logically noticed that ideals "form the basis of the possible perfection of certain actions" and "although we cannot concede to these ideals objective reality (existence)...they supply reason with a standard which is indispensible to it, providing it...with a concept of God which is entirely complete in its kind, thereby enabling it to estimate and to measure the degree and the defects of the uncomplete". One could add: influencing what should be done about it. See E. Kant. *The Critique of Pure Reason* trans. K. Smith (London 1950) p. 486.

criptive because norms are understood as committing people to certain behaviours and forbidding others.

By spiritual libido, we understand the desire of a man to be an active part of a supra-human task. The desire to be endowed by one's activity in a kind of "superior dimension" has its roots deeply imbedded in the unconscious of the human psyche. It can be understood as a way of overcoming the mind's doubts and fears by offering to the subject a feeling of union with powerful forces, a feeling of strength and security. By dedicating his force to a goal which transcends the narrow limits of his ego, the subject seeks to find at the same time the justification of his destiny and a kind of immortality. The subject moved by the spiritual libido aspires to be the chosen instrument of Necessity.[24] It is true to say that self-interest guides the human being, but it is even more true that self-interest very often, after passing through different phases of trial and error, takes refuge in a psychological mechanism of identification with goals going far beyond the subject's ego. The remaining task however is to evolve a dimension of consciousness which permits discrimination between goals within this suprapersonal realm.

Present historians, very aware of the particular features of the modern capitalist era, tend to identify social and political structures with economic concerns. As I said, by perceiving the determinating function of the economic infrastructure, these people often forget other elements. In fact, the above-mentioned psychological relationship plays a major role in evolution. This mechanism provides us with the rationale underlying the claim (of Plato, Kant and Hegel) that "models", "ideals" and "ideas" influence history.

Spiritual libido took two different historical forms and this difference, established the gap between Asian (Indian and Far Eastern) civilization and Western civilization.

In India, because of the level of experimental and speculative enquiry in spiritual matters, spiritual libido was rather directed towards spiritual ends and appeared therefore in its individual expression. The purified individuals could indeed cleanse the

---

[21]See the Hegelian concept of the "Hero": "Such are all great historical men—whose own particular aims involve those large issues which are the will of the World-Spirit". G.W.F. Hegel *The Philosophy of History* Dover publication New York 1956) p. 30.

"Doors of Perception"[25] and eventually reach the highest goal: mukti (liberation) which grants the realisation of Brahman or Nirvana. The consequence, during the last centuries, is the cultural depreciation of collective and social values. And we must not forget that Indian society was organized more around its culture which was based on inner human values than around its economics. Thus it is not surprising that Indian civilization, encouraging individual self-realization and diminishing the value of social achievement, would relatively depreciate politics, positive law and economics which are typically social concerns, in favour of metaphysics and religion which are there understood as the path of individual perfection. Nor is it surprising that the spiritual libido being withdrawn from worldly things and mundane goals, Indians did not have either the ideological background nor the available human energies to develop an economic growth-oriented society. The Indian Buddhist monks who travelled over three-quarters of the Asian continent built-up a certain Asian cultural homogeneity along those principles.

In the Western world, because of the philosophical evolution that has been described above, spiritual libido was not allowed an individual spiritual realization: it appeared thus in its collective expression. The main consequence is a decisive maximization of energies on the level of the individual as well as on the level of the mass, which found its main historical expression in both messianic imperialism and the ideology of economic growth. In both of these cases the subject enjoyed the comforting feeling of being the instrument of providence or of its secular substitute.

Firstly, on the political level, a psychological study of the ideological nature of any imperialist expansion (Roman, Muslim, British...(would reveal the existence of the above-mentioned unconscious identification of the tool (eg. British soldier) with the goal (spreading of the British "civilizing mission"). Just read R. Kipling'! It is not an accident if cultural messianism and religious wars are characteristic of the two religions (Muslim and Christian) which discouraged mystical achievements (of course Sufi mys-

---

[25]The title of Aldous Huxley's main book on drug-taking is *The Doors of Perception.*

His epigraph is from William Blake: "If the doors of perception were cleansed, everything would appear to man as it is: infinite."

ticism shows the depth of mystical Islam but let us not forget that Sufism revolted against official Islam). The libido sought its satisfaction in deeds rather than in ecstatic contemplation.

Secondly, the other main historical expression of spiritual libido as applied to secular goals is the ideology of economic growth. This appears to be the logical outcome of our argument. As we said before, the Western attitude to the economic realm is the result of the secularization of typically Christian concepts and attitudes: Necessity, in the Christian world, was successively understood as God's Providence (Augustine, Aquinas, Calvin), the laws of history (Herder, Savigny, Kant), and the mechanism of economics (Malthus, Ricardo, Smith, Marx). In all these cases, the neutrality of the ethical judgement with regard to the defect of the process of Necessity (the theological problem of Evil, the historical problem of War, the economic problem of social costs and pollution) is made possible only by an a priori optimism about the End: 1 - the second coming of Christ, 2 - the Kantian universal state, the Hegelian Prussian state, the Marxist highest stage of communist society, 3 - the assumption of an ever-expanding growth.[26]

In order to bring about the chosen End, the historical actor has to comply with a very specific type of behaviour that Max Weber[27] sees emerging from Christian asceticism and that Freud calls self-repression.

Asceticism consisted of not following the petty egotistical tendencies which could work against the flow of necessity. Hence positively expressed, the ascetic does what necessity requires him to do: the ascetic fasts and the capitalist saves in order to conform to their perception of theological or economic necessity.

This idea of working with necessity is another way of defining spiritual libido, properly restated as the will to be the instrument of necessity. This concept involves what Weber calls the idea of the calling. Once necessity is identified with economic mechanisms

---

[26] The end of the capitalist society is not at all a goal but an unlimited process without any perception of its result. "Incrementalism" rests on a very inconsistent theoretical basis.

[27] "One of the fundamental elements of the spirit of modern capitalism, and not only of that but of all modern culture: rational conduct on the basis of the calling was born...from the spirit of Christian asceticism" Max Weber *The Protestant Ethic and the Spirit of Capitalism* (the Scribner Library) p. 180.

which are supposed to be working towards a happy end, the process of economic growth rests on powerful ideological assumptions capable of mobilizing and stimulating human energies.

The stimulation of human energies as well as Weber's mention of Christian asceticism leads us to the Freudian theory that civilisation inevitably rests on repression. The delay of instinctual gratification (consumption) made possible by scarcity lays down the foundation of civilization (saving, investment). Indeed, it seems true that the typical 19th Century lower class Protestant Englishman, with his values of social discipline and saving, presents the personality structure which is to be found in every period of economic development: personal self-repression generating social dynamism. All successful cases of development give an example of a dominant ideology which forces the worker to work and obey. The Shintoist nation cult in Japan or Marxism in China help the worker to internalise the coercion, that is to accept self-repression in favour of production. The Communist party worker is bent by the same ideal as the medieval Cistercian monk: to live in conformity with the "higher order" through selflessness. The difference, is that, economic production and not contemplative meditation is the prescribed behaviour to reach this goal.

If we extend the Freudian analysis to our specific argument, we could conclude as follows: Energy is undetermined, neutral, powerful. Let us consider "spiritual libido" as an undetermined and potentially very high state of human energy. In the Indian world, such energy found its determination in being directed towards highest individual "satisfaction". In the West we found another determination: this energy was individually repressed and directed towards collective achievements. A powerful climb of pingala nadi had started.

I could everyday witness the consequences of this latter trend. Of course, looking at the sophisticated chaos of the modern society I did not think much of the West's faith in Action. In Switzerland or in the USA life is basically reduced to work. Even outside of working hours everything has become a kind of task. If we do not perform, we do not enjoy. We do not know how to do without doing. As the thinker had been tricked so has the doer.—Becoming- not doing- is the point. Many of my friends agreed with this but we did not know how to become that.

6. *The condition for the synthesis*

Would it be possible to propose a model of social, collective development based on inner dharmic values? A model in which the spiritual libido satisfies both personal and collective achievements?

The advent of such a system was the life goal of Gandhi. The Mahatma was no dreamer but a very practical man who knew the true needs of India. He proposed a model of development based on communal village development, adequate rural technology, integrated farming and land use practices, participation of the masses. A practical, comprehensive education system would teach the principles of individual and collective development. He foresaw a society where production and consumption would be balanced; the artificial values of mechanical industrialisation would be disregarded and Dharma respected. Those who do not see the relevance of Gandhi's ideas fail to consider that many of them have been successfully borrowed by Mao Tse-Tung and that China exhibits today the major case of successful development in the Third World. However Gandhi's ideas of integrated rural development could be implemented only in China, thanks to Mao's ideological monopoly enforced by state coercion. Because of this coercion the value of inner individual development vanished. Thus the above raised question has not been answered. In a way, China without coercion would be the model of Gandhian development. But can it work? Gandhi himself never had a chance to put his system into practice. After his tragic murder he was dutifully worshipped...and betrayed by the Indian bureaucrats. They represented a poisoned gift left over by the British civil service: because of their managerial background they could not take the Mahatma seriously. A westernised politician, Jawaharlal Nehru took the power and tried to enforce the Western model of development. Gandhi and his ideas were put on the shelf.

What I described as Western values, social dynamism and economic production are by now pretty much spread all over the world. Under both, capitalist and Marxist labels, it is called "development". Meanwhile, the spiritual values of the East are fascinating a growing portion of the Western intelligentsia. Thus we should be able to look forward to reaching a kind of synthesis. Yet we seem to head towards chaos and not towards harmony. The West has failed to promote the "civic goodness": material affluence does not prevent social alienation. The East has failed to promote the "philosophical goodness": the religions are dead or turned into myths, the number of saints is dwindling, the Eastern youth tends to be atheist and is fascinated by electronic gadgets. While the West is now exploring the avenues of spiritual self-realization the East is committing itself to material collective realizations. The West is importing fake gurus from the East and the East is importing industrial pollution from the West. In the post-industrial evolution of the advanced countries, society tends to be drawn into the quicksand of consumption: people refuse any more personal repression for production. But alas, the withdrawal from social dynamism is not always coupled with individual self-realization. This reflection could be a sound comment on the present crisis of civilisation in the West. In the developing societies religions have become disfigured by misunderstandings, and superstitions. The great masters of the past did not have such a lasting impact on society. Most contemporary "religious leaders" are fake and corrupted. Hence in Asian countries the old native values of human perfectibility are abandoned in favour of a collective commitment to the modernisation. But this tremendous development effort is generating more problems than it can cope with: higher birth rates, inflation, urban slums, etc... In the midst of the general confusion, the United Nations system is trying to promote a concept of development which is involving both, individual and social gratification. Can this be done?

In this study of the background of the ideology of development, we have encountered some basic philosophical problems and contradictions: the relation between man and God, free will and necessity, action and contemplation, individual and society. Of course, both terms of the above mentioned relationships exist in both Western and Eastern philosophies but it is also true that in each case one term is more dominant and therefore determines the general evolution of the whole conceptual apparatus. Hence the practical synthesis between these various contradictions could also mean the possibility to integrate Western and Eastern cultures in a new world civilisation. This would be the achievement of the millenial quest of mankind for the primordial things and the right society.

We have said that the way Man has understood his potential for improvement has ultimately generated the world as it is today.

Hence, if we want to evolve beyond the present state of confusion in world affairs, it is very necessary to evolve a new understanding of this potential. Such an understanding could be stimulated by the following suggestions.

The West has developed what the East was lacking and vice versa. Both civilisation models are one-sided. Hence the spiritual libido carried Man towards the extreme instead of keeping him on the central path of balance between spiritual and material involvement. In the West, the extreme of collective and social dynamism has been responsible for religious wars, colonial imperialism, totalitarian regimes and a socially irrelevant concept of economic growth. In the East, the extreme of individual mysticism has been responsible for spiritual egoism, the degeneration of the caste system and social immobilism.

Thus a successful model of development would imply that human energies can exert themselves towards both individual spiritual and collective material realisations. This is the old Platonic problem: how can one promote at the same time philosophical and civic goodness? The solution of the king-philosopher proposed in *the Republic* (which proved to be unrealistic) rested on the assumption that "the multitude cannot be philosophical". But it is precisely because the collectivity could not reach the good that appeared this split between the city of God and the city of Man (Augustine and the Catholic Church), between morality and politics (Machiavelli, Hobbes), the split of the human identity between the individual soul and the social being (J. J. Rousseau). Societies have evolved on the basis of these contradictions. In order to truly change society for the better, these contradictions must be overcome in a way which can be historically implemented. Now, it is not possible to have an impact on history without having an impact on the masses.

Thus the theoretical answer to our riddle is straightforward. The synthesis between morality and politics, individual and society, contemplation and action implies that SPIRITUAL REALIZATION BECOMES A COLLECTIVE PHENOMENON.

A couple of self-realized souls such as Plato or one of the rishis of the Upanishad cannot have a concrete and lasting enough impact on society. These higher beings are telling us "become one with Thy highest Self" but they do not tell us how to become that, here and now!

Unless and until spiritual self-realization becomes an immediate and practical possibility for a significant number of individuals there will not be any way to promote at the same time civic and philosophical goodness, collective and individual development. Collective spiritual realization would trigger the integration of the city of God and the city of Man. Only then would the individual self-realization evolve immediate positive effects on the collectivity because the happening would have repercussions in the social dimension. Only then would collective development avoid the usual oppressive and alienating consequences for the individual because it would be conducted through enlightened beings. Once the human freedom is thus freed from ignorance it will know how to evolve in time with necessity. Actually, such a community of self-realized people would itself become the instrument of Evolution. Millions of seekers, the very cream of Mankind, throughout continents and millenia, have strived to actualise this very ideal. Fantastic human energies have been mobilized to that effect. Today, the historical conditions have evolved to such an extent that the perennial questions are stated in the global terms of world development. The key to the new development model we are proposing is that the synthesis between action and contemplation is within the reach of the multitude. We can easily see that this is the necessary condition for the spiritual libido to avoid the extremes of human behaviour, and to maintain itself on the central path of the synthesis. The longed-for golden age or satya yuga may well be the synthesis between the material and the spiritual millenium. At any rate, while we are wondering, history is at work; energy is working its way towards destruction or integration. It cannot be stopped!

Between our utopia of integrated development and reality only one question is left pending : How can this happen? How can mass realization become actual? How can it be triggered here and now?

12

The great dilemma

1. *The perceived contradiction between the Finite and the Infinite*

If we look at modern literature we might endeavour to follow a common thread going through it. For instance, the great Russian writers (Dostoyevsky, Tourgeniev, Tolstoy) have been obsessed by the same problems that have moved Hoelderlin and Albert Camus or led Herbert Marcuse to advocate "the great Refusal": it is the problem of the existence of evil and of the human existential contradiction. Thomas Aquinas had written, seven hundred years ago: "The minimum knowledge of the highest things that can be acquired is more desirable than the most certain knowledge we have of lesser things" (my translation).[1] Obviously with the passing of centuries, this beautiful optimism faded away. Modern man, if he is at all reflecting upon his own destiny is much more likely to say with Kierkegaard: "Fear comes from the fact that Man not only has possibilities, but Man is pure possibility".

What is it that has thus shattered the modern thinkers? Looking for this answer, let us consider the various philosophies. Soon we will discover that there seems to be a constant theme underlying different historical systems of thought, to such an extent that these systems differ in their historical manifestations but not in their fundamental premises. This common theme is so rooted in

[1] "Minimum quod potest haberi de cognitione rerum altissimum desirabilius-est quam certissima cognitio quae habetur de minimus rebus" (Summa Theologica 1 qu. 1a 5).

whatever is the human condition that it appears to have influenced in a trans-historical way how man thinks about himself and how he acts accordingly.

Furthermore, when we turn our attention towards the various provinces of philosophy (i.e. cosmology, epistemology, ontology, political philosophy) the same theme emerges again. When thoroughly investigated, these provinces boil down to an essential contradiction, a primordial dilemma which, under different conceptual manifestations, reveals a fundamental structural identity. This great dilemma is nothing but the intellect's perception of the contradictory relationship between the Finite and the Infinite. These words awaken, within the modern psyche, connotations of two entirely incompatible dimensions, two mutually exclusive strata of existence. To speak of a synthesis between the two sounds like a contradiction in terms, a mathematical impossibility.

For the human understanding, the primordial contradiction lies in the fact that the Infinite (absolute, universal, necessary, "Cosmic") manifests itself to men through the Finite (relative, particular, free, "microcosmic"). The Infinite is at the same time revealed and concealed by its very manifestations (the Indian notion of Maya, the Christian notion of Mystery).

"Why bother?" could one wonder—The trouble is that Man's consciousness iself participates in the elusive play by which the Infinite appears within the Finite. Therefore mind's self-consciousness will be acutely aware that the human condition is defined by a fundamental contradiction there is something boundless within the ego-bound man. "Man is neither angel nor beast" said Blaise Pascal; but it is difficult to act, live or think being a "Neither nor". The French poet Paul Valery sighs "Man is too particular, his soul is too universal"[2], yet to be human is nothing but to endure this contradiction without being able to escape it.

The problem can be exposed by an example. We observe that, in order to exist as a human being, the child has to quit the mother's womb and the state of cosmic unity he was enjoying there. The necessity to be separated in order to exist expresses the essential feature of the microcosmic, finite dimension. The essence of a new form (be it a being, a thought or a word) is at the same time manifested causality and limitation. The specificity of the form

---

[2]"L'Homme est chose trop particulière, l'ame trop générale."

structurally entails a negation: "*omnis determinatio negatio est.*" Each determination entails a negation, said Spinoza. But Man's capacity for self-consciousness implies that Man is also aware of this elusive part of himself which is not limited. Hence, consciously or unconsciously, the human being will try to regain the original state of cosmic unity. But how can he merge in his infinity still being a determined being? Many thinkers tried to achieve universality through the mediation of reason, overlooking the fact that the mind itself generates particular forms and limitations.

"We cannot think about the Universe without assuming it is articulated and at the same time, we cannot defend the articulations that we find or make in it against the charge that these are artificial and arbitrary, that they do not correspond to anything in the structure of Reality. It can always be shown that they break up something that is invisible and let slip something that is essential. Yet without articulations of the universe, we ourselves, cannot be articulated—i.e. either think or will. We cannot go on thinking or willing if we regain the unity of the mystical experience. So we have to dissect and in dissecting, misrepresent Reality in order to be able to apprehend Reality as far as we can discern it. Our inability to apprehend Reality completely is, of course, not surprising. It is a paradox that one part of a whole should be able to distinguish itself from the rest and should then be able to achieve even a partial apprehension of the whole including itself."[3]

In the post World War II period Man lost a great deal of his naive confidence in the virtue of Reason and quite a few people are unconsciously seeking the feeling of cosmic unity through sex. But as St. Paul reminds us the union of the flesh is not the one of the spirit and to pretend to achieve the latter through the operation of the first is nothing but the old tantric confusion; certainly the dilemma is not an easy one to solve!

Dostoievsky would perhaps have been helped in his trials if he would have felt around him the community of seekers who raised the age old question of the Finite-Infinity relation.

From the time of the Ramayana down to the existentialism of Jean Paul Sartre, the human mind struggled with the hypothetical

---

[3] Arnold Toynbee—Reconsiderations.

nature of the puzzling antinomy between the Infinite and the Finite which records itself in a number of paradigmic binomial oppositions i.e. being and change, spirit and matter, cosmos and microcosm, universal and particular, actuality and potentiality, necessity and freedom, substance and accident, noumena and phenomena. In the West the ancients stated the terms of the debate with Parmenides who emphasized the immovable perfection of Being on the one hand, and Heraclitus who underlined the perpetual flux of phenomenal change on the other. As we said, the metaphysical riddle was not simply a matter of academic controversy; its contradictory terms weave the very tissue of human existence, because not only is Man split by the contradiction, he is aware of it too. Goethe's Doctor Faust, the magisterial herald of the modern seeker, exclaims "Two souls, alas, are struggling within my breast".

The opening statement of Emmanual Kant's *"Critique of Pure Reason"* soberly expresses the fact:

"Human reason has this peculiar fate, that in one species of its knowledge it is burdened by questions which, as prescribed by the very nature of reason itself, it is not able to ignore, but which, as transcending all its powers, it is also not able to answer".

We could not avoid being attracted like magnets by the knowledge of the Infinite, while being at the same time unable to deal with this longing.

Goethe began to work on Faust in 1769 AD and the Critique of Pure Reason was published in 1781 AD. The 18th Century is the period in which the glorification of the enlightened Rationalism reached its peak, while at the same time the intrinsic limits of Reason were rationally stated in a definite form. Before Kant, philosophers tried to synthesize the duality between the Infinite and the Finite in some impressive intellectual monuments such as Aristotle's works or Aquinas's Summa Theologica. But like a Phoenix born out of its own ashes, the debate would reopen again after each synthesis. Kant rationally laid down that the noumena, the things in themselves, Reality (the Infinite) was beyond Man's grasp because he did not have the proper categories of perception to reach them. This finding was correct to the extent that, indeed, human reason, the mind, the intellect cannot reach the Infinite. This finding was dangerous because the western seeker totally misidentified himself with his mind's reason, without seeing that Man is more, and knows more, than his mind's reason. Thus western Man reached a dead end in his quest for the Primordial Things, from which he could not escape. He soon decided that the whole question was irrelevant. The main current of western reflection lost the kind of perception which would have kept some contact with metaphysical reality. Metaphysics became synonymous with illusion, and physics synonymous with reality. Having forgotten Socrates and ignoring Lao-Tzu, the modern man made a mountain out of his conceptual mole-hill. There were no Zen masters around to tell him how foolish reason can be. It was overlooked that, in order to go beyond conditioned thought one ought to ground the cognitive process outside of its spatio-temporal framework[4] and that this can be achieved only by the "metaphysical" deepening of the consciousness's intensity.

Considering the Infinite—Finite relation in the post-Kantian philosophy, we find three main attitudes.

The Synthetic Assertion: In his *Phenomenology of Spirit* G.W.F. Hegel made an ultimate attempt to reconcile the Finite and the Infinite. The dialectical movement of the phenomenology of spirit culminates in a higher synthesis. The "Unhappy Consciousness" (*das Ungluckliche Bewusstsein*) is the consciousness's awareness of the radical contradiction of its essential nature. But eventually through the mediation of "Reason", the internal opposition which the Self so deeply experiences in unhappy consciousness will be "*AUFGEHOBEN*", overcome. Once the self-consciousness has acknowledged itself to be "Reason" the individual consciousness is reconciled with the Universal by the synthetic assertion. Hegel's "Reason" is at the same time the Idea, the Infinite energy of the Universe, the Tao, the Divine Wisdom; its spirit is freedom and self-consciousness. The actualisation of Man's self-consciousness (*Selbstbewusstsein*) is the door to the freedom of the Spirit. The Finite is reconciled with the Infinite, because "Reason is the conscious certainty of being all reality". This self-actualisation of consciousness overcomes the contradiction of the split human identity.

[4] cf the concept of "Standortsgebundenheit des Denkers" developed by the German historical and sociological schools.

Hegel's intuition might have been quite correct but his system could not work out for a simple reason. The state of unhappy consciousness is the state of the human mind. To go beyond this state requires the ability to evolve a category of perception beyond that of the mind. Hegel tried to realise by an intellectual synthesis the higher synthesis which can only be brought about by a meta-intellectual breakthrough such as, say, the "satori" experience of the Zen Buddhist praxis, or today, the vibratory awareness of the Sahaja yogis. Without this breakthrough, Reason (*Vernunft*) cannot identify itself with Spirit (*Geist*). Or, in other terms, the human mind cannot merge into cosmic consciousness, that is into the universal unconscious. Hegel's work bears witness to the attempts made by one of the greatest minds of the XIXth Century to solve the old enigma. Left-and right-wing Hegelians tried to realize their own synthesis at a much lower level. The right-wing Hegelians emphasized the state as a supreme factor and paved the way for the Fascist theory of Sorel and Mussolini. The left-wing Hegelians emphasized the dialectic of matter and the outcome of this trend is Marx's communist theory.

The Dichotomic Assertion: The Hegelian synthesis was rejected by the great current of existentialist thought. The dilemma acknowledged as radically insoluble is viewed as the dead end of man's existential adventure. Attention is focused on alienation. The Latin word "alienus" means foreign; to be alienated means to be foreign to one's own Self. Philosophy becomes the rationality of despair. For the Dane Soeren Kierkegaard, Man is the Absolute (and ironical) Paradox. As an existing spiritual being, he is a failure under all respects but contradiction, the eternal becoming temporal, the universal becoming the existing particular.

In a life constantly facing him with an "either/or" Man is "Neither/nor." The ways to escape these existential throes are not too promising. With a sort of sad cynicism Kierkegaard writes in the *concluding unscientific postscriptum*:

> "You shut your eyes, you seize yourself by the neck and then— and then you stand on the other side, on the other side of common sense, in the promised land of systematic philosophy (or Christian faith)."

Salvation seems to mean the abdication of intelligence and freedom and appears almost to be a degradation.

With a Cartesian care for strictness and intellectual honesty the Frenchman Jean Paul Sartre led the existentialist position to its desperate consequences; the conclusion of Sartre is quite simple; being excludes non-being; to the extent that there is being within us, we want to join being. We read in *Being and Nothingness*:

"The being of human reality is suffering because it is perpetually haunted by a totality which it is unable to be, precisely because it could not attain the in-itself without losing itself as for-itself." For Sartre any attempt to escape this condition of despair is doomed to failure or expresses the "bad faith" of the faint-hearted who takes refuge in mechanisms of identification such as religion, job, politics, etc. No room is left for the escapist acrobatics of the intellect:

"Many men, in fact, know that the goal of their pursuit is Being...But to the extent this attempt still shares the spirit of seriousness, they are condemned to despair; for they discover at the same time that all human activities are equivalent and that all are on principle doomed to failure. Thus it amounts to the same thing whether one gets drunk alone or is leader of Nations." —*Being and Nothingness*.

Existentialism is a masterpiece of demystification. Once the intellect is elaborate enough to relativize its own construct, it is left with the immense and silent world that contemporary science and philosophy unveiled: relativity and nihilist existentialism. This world resounds with Macbeth's cry:

"Life is but a waiting shadow, a poor player
That struts and frets his hour upon the stage
And then is heard no more; it is a tale
Told by an idiot, full of sound and fury
Signifying nothing."—Shakespeare: *Macbeth* v. 5.24

The One-polarity Assertion: Of course, few are those prepared to exist through the courage of despair only. Hence contemporary thought did not dwell on the correct but frightening statement of the dichotomic assertion. The human ostrich can better stand existence with the head buried in the sand of "bad faith". Therefore the human dilemma is negated and supposedly solved by emphasizing one element of the pair to the detriment of the other. The Infinite dimension is negated and the Finite has to give an account of the totality of the real. Indeed the Positivist XIXth Century was quick to conclude that if one cannot know God it means that God is dead for all practical purposes.

The European continental philosophy after Rousseau, Kant, Hegel and Feuerbach, culminates in Karl Marx. He took over Hegel's dialectic. But whereas Hegel expressed the phenomenology of spirit, Marx stressed the phenomenology of matter. The Cosmic, Infinite, Godly dimension is utterly negated. Hegel's famous statement says in the preface of The *Philosophy of Right*: "philosophy too is its own time apprehended in thoughts". It expressed Man's concern to reach an integrated understanding of his position in the Creation. This concern would be translated by Engel's materialist formulation into a very reductive conceptual scheme: "Modern Socialism is nothing but the reflex, in thought of...the conflict in fact, between productive forces and modes of production (*Socialism: Utopian and Scientific*). This is the Marxist one-cause explanation for the present day human condition.

Anglo-Saxon philosophy did not negate the Infinite but completely ignored it. After David Hume, the heavy emphasis one experimental reasoning excludes the Infinite-oriented metaphysics because the British Philosophers could not conceive that there were experimental ways to relate to the Infinite. Lacking the proper categories of perception and having, anyway, lost all interest in the matter, they evolved a microcosmic, finite thinking focused on quantity and number, logic, linguistics and the philosophy of science. Down to this day Anglo-Saxon analytical philosophy does not escape its methodological limitations and cannot go out of its narrowly defined scope of enquiry; this explains the unstimulating intellectual atmosphere we find in the Universities of the capitalist world, where numerous students try to avoid intellectual asphyxia by adopting the Marxist vision. In *Phenomenology and the Crisis of Philosopy* Edmund Husserl had remarked that:

> " 'the crisis of European existence', which manifests itself in countless symptoms of a corrupted life, is no obscure fate nor impenetrable destiny. The reason for the downfall of a rational culture does not lie in the essence of rationalism

itself but only in its exteriorization, its absorption in 'naturaliasm' and 'objectivism' ".

2. *The impact of the perceived contradiction*

So, this is the present state of 20th Century thought and consequent actions. With the rejection of the Hegelian synthesis we reached what we could call "the entropic state of modern speculative thought". By this we mean that contemporary philosophy reached a point which, not being crossed, marked the starting point of a regression process. Indeed once the overcoming of the unhappy consciousness is rejected, Western thought remains caught in the dilemma of the Infinite-Finite relation and any further elaboration seems to be a regression, an additional chapter to the phenomenology of "bad faith". In the cosmology, ontology, epistemology and corresponding political philosophy that these three fields evolve, the I-F relation represents "the limit" which cannot be thought or crossed, the heart of the essential dilemma and its subsequent contradictions, the realization of the second principle of thermodynamics (entropy) in the phenomenology of consciousness. It is completely overlooked that this state of things is at the root of the evils we are facing in contemporary societies, because it affected the model these societies implement.

Entropy, is a mathematical function used in thermo-dynamics to express the principle of degradation of energy. The degradation gets translated by an ever growing state of disorder within matter. Any supplementary input of energy within the system corresponds to a further disorganisation. To relate to an Eastern religious scheme, entropy is the state of a system which has lost its "Dharma", its sustenance. Dharma is what makes one fit to evolve so that it harmonises the dynamics of the particular within the whole[5]. But the greater the entropy of a system, the smaller is its capacity for spontaneous change. With-out Dharma, neither evolution nor integration are possible. Today human sciences such as psychology or sociology are constantly dealing with the pathology of Adharma but their conceptual apparatus does not yet encompass the real cause of the phenomena they are studying; any malfunction within an organism is caused by a deviation from the path of Dharma.

[5] By evolving Dharma only evolution took place.

Both Marxist society as the product of European continental philosophy and capitalist society as the result of British political philosophy, appear to be the consequence of this entropy. By ideologically negating or methodologically ignoring the Infinite dimension, both these models offer us a materialist society where life, knowledge and social relations are managed in a relative and microcosmic way. But to negate or ignore the dilemma of the human condition only aggravates it in the long run. Neither the political commissar, nor the psychiatrist, or the priest are going to solve for us the great problem we are facing. By cutting himself off from the Infinite, Modern Man and his Finite society evolves in a closed system.

The second law of Thermodynamics informs us that in a closed system the only reactions that can occur spontaneously are those that increase the total entropy of the system. Statistical thermodynamics suggest that the entropy of a system is a measure of the randomness of energy-distribution in the system and so perceives entropy as a measure of the disorder of the system. The present state of Man and the biosphere indeed could provide a little illustration of the law of Clausius which states that the Universe progresses towards "entropic doom". We are all aware of the ecological degradation of the biosphere. We can also note that according to many research reports from international institutions the developed societies are drawing nearer to a state which could be described as "near-saturation" i. e. things cannot go on much longer without being confronted in certain directions by a set of fundamental limits. There are signs of saturations in total population, population space ratio, degradation of environment, exhaustion of natural resources, as well as in the size of urban agglomerations, or in overload of information for the intellect.

Indeed we are confronted by the phenomenon of entropy, but this time it is the entropy of civilisation. The process will also affect the individual as an energy system: by negating or avoiding to face the true problems of the psyche, the human brain is becoming stunned and will no longer register any mental or emotional stimuli. Ultimately man will lose physical awareness as well. Alienated from Infinity, from the knowledge of Reality, failing to recognise this very alienation, we are missing the rule of right action (Dharma), the sustaining power which ensures the dynamic integration of the social organism as a whole. Hence, not surprisingly, society is running out of control and our microcosmic mechanical devices cannot prevent its march towards disintegration and destruction. The marginalization of the spiritual dimension is paid for every day in heavily growing social and ecological dues. This development, ironically enough, was carried through and implemented by the spirit of rational and scientific enquiry. This spirit led mankind through the industrial and technological revolutions, the essential steps to be made if the complete mastery over the material world was to be achieved. Now that this mastery had been acquired, it is time for Man to master himself.

We could now bring together our argument in the following way:

—As in other great philosophical traditions, the Western mind has struggled for a better mastery of knowledge and for the grasp of the "Primordial Things".
—The failure to do so on a strictly rational basis has itself been rationalized and glossed over in the eighteenth century, to the extent that the Primordial Things, after having been declared unknowable, were conveniently considered nonexistent.
—On this conceptual basis the XIXth Century evolved a materialistic society which under the capitalist or Marxist form, has lost its faculty for dynamic integration, a society which lacks an intuitive conformation to the rule of right action, has lost its Dharma (sustenance power). This is because it was erroneously assumed by the XIXth Century positivists that the greatest good for a human being is of a material order. The crisis of affluent societies and the revolutions of the 1960's in the USA and Europe, among other indicators, show clearly that any degree of economic plenty does not prevent social disruptions and Man's desperation or frustration. Human satisfaction cannot be found in a scheme of society which does not include the spiritual dimension in its notion of "quality of life". If the fundamental element of happiness is absent from such a model, it is not surprising that such a society is unhappy. Psychological and social alienations endanger more and more an immensely complex and therefor vulnerable social structure. When an organism is no longer connected to a great evolutionary line, to the "in-built

program" which is its power of sustenance. It begins generating its own destruction. From a biosociological point of view, advanced capitalist societies are suffering from a rampant cancer in which the malignant cells are beginning to work independently on their own, thereby threatening the very cohesion of the whole. In a Marxist society the human beings are dwarfed and disintegrated by the oppression of the system...They lack the minimum conditions required to evolve any they are thrown into entropy by fear.

Logically enough, biological and human eco-systems are upset when Man has no cognitive tool to relate to the whole. How to evolve a cognitive tool to relate to the whole is what the epistemological break-through is all about. "Eco" comes from the Greek word "oikos" which means "the house". Western Man could no longer conceive of the Universe as a single house because he could not situate himself in it (who is the landlord? Where are the stairs? What is the rent? etc. etc....). Well, it is fair enough to say, as a conclusion, that the alternative to the cognitive revolution is a slightly sophisticated version of the by-now-well-known classical doomsday scenario. However expected this may be, it will not be a lot of fun.

What we are saying is this: Today, human societies go wrong because human action went wrong. Action went wrong because human thought went wrong. And this happened because this thought could not solve the Infinite-Finite dilemma. Indeed, in order to think beyond the "Infinite-Finite" limit, one had to think both sides of the limit and the mind could not do it being itself on this side of the limit: hence the entropy.[6]

We can propose two further remarks:

If the Finite entity defines itself for-itself i.e. in antithesis to the Infinite, this position amounts to negating the Infinite as Infinite. The finite will practically tend to view itself as its own infinity and therefore, will be threatened by the existence of other finite entities which appear to negate its self-evolved infinite perception. This is the paranoid syndrome at the roots of competitivity, disorder and wars.

On the other hand the Finite might acknowledge its belong-

---

[6]See Wittgenstein's similar argument in his *Tractatus Logico—philosophicus*.

ing to the Infinite. The microcosmic human perceives itself a part of the cosmic totality. However, without being able to experience the nature of the relationship, the finite microcosm undergoes a feeling of split identity. This schizophrenic syndrome throws Man into the psychic refuges of the mechanism of misidentification: "I am a brahmin, a member of the communist party, an American, a great lover, an administrator, etc..." The brain seem to need above all some kind of security but artificial securities and misidentifications do not lead anywhere.

Nietzsche's Zarathustra was right: Man is something to be overcome. But it has to be overcome by Man's realization, Man's entry into the Real, by the "Selfman"; this is the oldest problem but today we are doomed to solve it or perish.

Can we overcome the contradiction of human consciousness? Can we solve the Infinite-Finite dilemma? If so, how?

3. *Apparent and real contradictions*

It should be remembered that the world unveiled by Einsteinian physics is very consistent with the one presented by the great spiritual traditions; the Universe is nothing but a dancing pattern of ENERGY. What would a scientist of the beginning of the century have thought in reading the following statement:

"In those far reaches of the universe are places where a teaspoon of matter weighs as much as 200 million elephants... where a tiny whirling star winks on and off thirty times a second...where matter and light are continually sucked up by devouring black holes, never to be seen again..."[7]

The author of the above quoted article on Astro-physics goes on "how can the human mind deal with the knowledge that the farthest object we can see in the universe is perhaps ten billion light-years away?"

This question dramatically illustrates the degree to which we can trust our mental constructs. If physics relativizes the two basic dimensions in which we evolve our understanding of the physical world—time and space—could we not expect from a

[7] K. Weaver—The Incredible Universe. *National Geographic* May 1974 Vo. 145.

science dealing with Man that once again, reality goes beyond fiction, the fiction of our limited mental constructs, the fiction of our limited philosophical and social-pseudo-science. If this is so we should dare pass the present frame of references that the present social and psycho-sciences provide, keeping in mind the remark of C. G. Hempel: "In his endeavour to find a solution to his problem the scientist may give free rein to his imagination and the course of his scientific creative thinking may be influenced even by scientifically questionable notions."[8]

In *Physics and Philosophy*, Werner Heisenberg makes the following statement :

"It is probably true, quite generally, that in the history of human thinking, the most fruitful developments frequently take place at those points where two different lines of thought meet. Those lines may have their roots in quite different parts of human culture, in different times or different cultural environments, or different religious traditions; hence, if they actually meet, that is if they are at least so much related to each other that a real interaction takes place, then one may hope that new and interesting developments will follow."[9]

Let us thus bring together the findings of contemporary science and of the millenial spiritualities.

Science tells us that matter is nothing but Energy. Spirituality tells us that spirit is nothing but Energy. Now, the human consciousness too, is some kind of Energy which permeates at the same time the material and the spiritual field.

The great problem of the opposition between the finite matter and the infinite spirit Man being seemingly cornered by this contradiction will appear, in the last analysis, to have been a wrong problem, created by human ignorance which opposes and separates. Between matter and spirit there is, so to say, only a difference in the frequency of vibration. Matter itself represents a specific coefficient of energy and so does, at a different level, psychic activities. Consciousness itself is yet another—we could say a higher-form of Energy. Between matter and

---

[8] Carl G. Hempel—*Philosophy of Natural Sciences*, p. 16.
[9] W. Heisenberg—*Physics and Philosophy*, p. 187.

spirit, the Finite and the Infinite, the outlet for Man is a mutation. Man carries within himself the means to conduct it succesfully. It has been said in many scriptures that, when the human consciousness takes the Infinite for its object, it becomes itself Infinite. (Of course the only snag is: how to do it?) This mutation should not occur by the negation of the physical body or overpowering the mind but through its transformation by enlightenment. We must change, not negate, and everybody should undergo this change according to one's own spontaneous rhythm. Mutation and not breaking off! It is because many religious dogmas could not assume this harmonic line that we have lived out the rupture that we know in the modern world between the Finite and the Infinite, the body and the soul.

On the intellectual level we should understand that, the conceptual tools to deal with the Infinite-Finite issue escape from the classical and modern logic which rests on the principle of identity and the principle of non-contradiction stated by Aristotle (*Metaphysics* N 10052; XI 1061, 635): "It is impossible to be and not to be at the same time." Precisely, the double assertion of the Infinite and the Finite within man (Spirit and Matter, Cosmos and Mocrocosm) challenges the ground axiom of bivalent logic: "*non est simul affirmare et negare idem de eodem.*"[10] The infinite and the finite exist at the same time and in the same place within the same being and to come to terms with this logical impossibility asks for new logical tools.

In China and Japan the "*Koan*" or enigmas given by the Zen master for the disciple to solve, had eventually the salutary effect of breaking the logical patterns of thought in the disciple's mind. In the West the sharp awareness of logical distinction appears to be a legacy of the Aristotelian principles and of the Ionian

---

[10]This axiom is not only challenged by spirituality but also by science: "certain aspects of quantic and undulatory mechanics, Heisenberg's relations of uncertainty, the probability character of the laws of physics do not seem any more adequately expressed on the present forms of the bivalent logic where everything is formulated in terms of the true and the wrong. Certain physicists concluded... that one had to add a third value, the probable or possible to the values of true and wrong.' Roure *Logique et Metalogique* Vitte edit (Paris 1957); p. 157. (my translation).

Bivalent logic has also of course, been challenged in the field of mathematics by Godel's theorem which establishes that a somewhat complex formal system cannot be at the same time non contradictory and complete.

philosophy which opposes the parmenidean intuition to the heraclitian fact. However, the principle of analogy would be a better tool to express the actual inter-penetration of several strata of Energy within the tissue of the living. The same Reality expresses itself through several levels of manifestation and we should not lose the perception of the underlying unity by reifying the conceptual distinctions by which we apprehend the different states of its manifestation. Concepts such as "finite" and "infinite" appear to be mutually exclusive only because the thinking subject at his specific level of ratiocination operates within the finite. It is irrelevant to wonder what is infinite and what is finite; we should wonder, from which epistemological standpoint does the subject wonder. Logically enough only the Infinite subject will know the Infinite. The goal of the enquiry should be: How can the subject concretely realise its infinite dimension? The subject who lives in the finite world of thoughts has to achieve the state of mind in which his attention enters into the infinite. How?

As previously said, on this side of the cognitive border, the rational man cannot go further than stating the problem without being able to solve it. Kant said that man is an animal which needs a master but the master himself is an animal: when we try to transform ourselves we are bringing our old weaknesses to bear on this very attempt. When we try to overcome old conditionings we only create new ones. When we make revolutions to free people we generally introduce a new dictatorship, etc... The teachings of history are clear enough: the common man cannot solve the Infinite-Finite dilemma. And yet there has been a tremendous historical expectation for that kind of happening. And yet the greatest scriptures in the world (The Tao-Te-King, Bhagavad Gita, The Torah, The Koran, the Bible, etc...) are metaphorical sayings on the possibility for man to break through the existential entropy, that is, to establish communication with Reality. Roughly described the cognitive precondition for this happening was usually described as follows:

Thought (intellect, mind, reason) and Feeling (emotion, sensitivity) as the finite psyche must be connected in the perceiving subject with whatever is the Infinite or, more exactly, with the way in which the Infinite consciousness within man perceives itself. When man, as a new cognitive unit, (after his rebirth) realizes the overcoming phase of this synthesis, his self-consciousness has entered the new stage of the Infinite-Finite synthesis.[11] If we extend this thinking to the collective and social dimension, the answer to the question "how to master the human mind in a way that can be historically implemented"? can only be "By a new type of awareness which can be operative within the wordly scene." This answer implies that the common man should be able to break through the limit. Be it said in passing, if this next step cannot be crossed, it is difficult to see how the contemporary planetary issues in ecology, the economic and social fields can ultimately be solved; ideed they deteriorate quicker than the pace with which man's instrumental capacity of adaptation can face them.

It seems now that we have isolated the terms of the real contradiction. The paradox is not between the Finite and the Infinite but in the fact that although man is not yet able to overcome this contradiction, this contradiction is to be overcome. Such a statement is, to be sure, the very finding which leads to existentialist despair. But why not consider a new hypothesis: why not expect that a historical happening could trigger, on behalf of Reality, the process of a breakthrough of consciousness? After all, between the ape and man, something somehow happened a long time ago. We evolved from the amoeba to the present stage without any planning exercises on our side and it is not unreasonable to expect that our further evolution will also take place spontaneously by the play of Reality. That which led evolution from animal to the human stage would it not lead it further from the human to the super human?

In other words, we should not exert ourselves too much for the sake of reaching the higher consciousness. But it seems wise to keep ourselves disponible and ready for the event. That means may be developing a proper understanding of the human condition but it implies above all, living the kind of life which will keep us fit for the evolutionary purpose.

It seems that the main task of the past spiritual instructors of mankind has been to explain, describe or even dictate what such a life should be which has been called the virtuous or dhar-

---

[11]Various mystical language sets would say: to join the Pure Land of Amrithaba, to enter the Kingdom of Heaven, to enter Satori, to merge into Buddahood, Nirvana, Samadi, the Atman, Brahman, the cosmic, the Pan, the All, Reality, Al Haqq, the Tao, etc....

mic life. Of course, a further consequence of our hypothesis is to be wakeful. If the event which will trigger our collective ascent is an historical one, that is, located within time and space, we should not fail to recognize it when the opportunity arises.

Can we not guess what that event could be? "It is because man cannot move towards God the God has to come to him in a human incarnation." So tell millenial religious traditions. So many of us are looking for a Deliverer! The theme pervades books, movies, science fiction and daily day-dreaming because the expectation is very much alive in our unconscious. Could this smoke be without a fire? Quite a few esoteric communities claim that the "white Fraternity" (the invisible masters from the supraconscious realm) provided them with startling information: the Divine Incarnation who will redeem Mankind has already been in our midst for over half a century! But how does one recognize the true Incarnation? Are we sure that we would have recognized the son of God when He entered Jerusalem seating on a donkey? I really wonder...

Open-mindedness and disponibility are thus very necessary. We can maintain ourselves in these helpful dispositions by challenging a couple of unwarranted premises which have biased the understanding of the modern mind.

PART SEVEN

ASSUMPTIONS TO CHALLENGE

"My proposal is, therefore, surely the mildest possible —Oh! It is so weak! My proposal is that at least we should make the true state of affairs known."

Soeren A. Kierkegaard

13

Assumption number one :

Past Mythologies and Religions are nothing but Superstitions.

"There are more things in heaven and earth, Horatio,
Than are dreamt of in your philosophy."

—Shakespeare, *Hamlet 1.5.166*

    Science, philosophy, religions, mythologies are different avenues of knowledge leading to a central square called Reality. It does not matter whether you climb the house's walls or use the staircase as long as you get on the roof; but what is important is that we ought to remember, using the staircase, that we want to reach the roof. The means is not the end nor is the part the whole: when we enlist in scientific or philosophic pursuit, when we adhere to such and such religion, should we not remember that it is reality which is the object of knowledge and that reality is not to be naively reduced to the extent to which we can perceive it? Nor is it to be uniquely identified with the type of knowledge we are using to get at it. The map is not the territory. Let us forget our parochial attitude towards knowledge. A modern scientist would tell an Ancient Inca: "You propose the sun is a god merely because the sun provides the biological conditions for earth's life." And the Inca would answer: "The sun provides the biological conditions for earth's life merely because he is a God." They are both right, why can they not agree? In perceiving Aton, the sun-disk, as the father of life, the Pharaoh Akhenakon in his Amarnian heresy was perceiving the deep biotic relation between man and the sun without being able to explain it whereas the modern astro-physicist and biologist can explain but not perceive it. Would it not be nice to reconcile the Pharaoh and the scientist in one single awareness?

Many great thinkers of today say that the one and same reality is perceived differently by science and philosophy; it is translated into an iridescent pattern of human expression such as arts, thought systems, music, political and economic structure, literature; is it not dwelling in the eyes of the children, the flight of the clouds? May be it is time that we had better realise what mythologies and religions wanted to tell us about this very same reality.

The Rigvedas, the legends of Precolombian America and Budhhism, the Book of Genesis, the Zen-Avesta, the Koran, the Greek mysteries and Roman cults, all these and other traditions are telling us a tale that few can understand for the code to read the ciphered message is not known. It has been perceived however that every myth in its initial purity, is expressing some aspect of the elusive cosmic reality. The existence of non-human strata of existence (gods, angels, demons, etc.) has been assessed at all times by different religious and cultural traditions in ways and terms which express a pattern of consistency. Because consistency can be found in the ritual messages of cultures which were not historically related and corresponded to widely different socio-economic conditions, the hypothesis that these messages are actually telling something about reality should be investigated with great seriousness. A hypothesis emerging from observable facts (archaeological and anthropological findings) and communicable data, might, after all, lead to some sort of scientific observation. Is it not a good index of the anthropological naivety and cultural provincialism of modern man that he assumes that any religious utterance before the 18th Century's dawn of rationalism expressed merely the ignorance of superstition?

For the first time in history we have the extraordinary opportunity to evolve a world culture. We can integrate the various religious, philosophical messages and psychic experiences of the globe's numerous regional civilisation. In his *Discours de La Methode* (1637) Rene Descartes tried to make a fresh start for modern epistemology and, in the process, gave out the odd hypothesis that spirit meets matter within Man's pineal gland. If Descartes could have known the teachings of Shankaracharya or the poems of Kabir, the 15th Century religious reformer of India, his speculations of the role of the pineal gland could have opened to Western thought a new domain of psychosomatic enquiry. Similarly, when Spinoza and Leibnitz sought to lay a new foundation for metaphysics, they had no way to find out that the direction of their research would have been endorsed by the monism of the Upanishads.

After all, it may be that the Universe is one big house with one history; from the generation of galaxies to the appearance of man is it not one and the same drama? Some of the previous acts of the show have been performed by actors who were not human beings and their deeds have been carried to us in various terms by the different mythologies and religions. It is conceivable that more than ten thousand years ago, superhuman beings had the possibility to commonly take a physical form on this earth and the ancient cosmologies are relating some of the happenings. For instance, in the Greek and Hindu versions of the Indo-Aryan pantheon, the gods (devas) are fighting the titans (asuras) which seem to be of Iranian origin. Zeus, like Indra, rules over the paradise of the gods and is endowed with the thunderbolt weapon. The Inca and Aztec veneration for a powerful creature in the shape of a man-jaguar strangely reminds us of Vishnu's fourth incarnation as Narasimha in the form of a man-lion. In precolombian America as well as in the Bible, we find the story of the sons of God and the daughters of men : "the sons of God saw that the daughters of men were fair; and they took to wife such of them as they chose."*Genesis* 6.2. The Great Flood is recalled by several unrelated legends and there are other instances of such odd similarities. The Bible and the Koran mention the story of Adam and Eve and the last judgement. Here we are just mentioning these similarities without, of course, entering into a comparative study of religions.

The gods appear as perfect but finite beings who are living in a supremely enjoyable stratum of existence; they are in charge of the elements (the wind, fire, ocean, etc.) and they derive part of their energy from the dutiful performance of sacrifices by the human beings. The titans could have been extremely powerful beings which constantly challenge the supremacy of the gods and usually ended up demons. The demons' *(Rakhasa)* origin is traced back by the christian and muslim traditions of Lucifer, "the bearer of light", the fallen angel, the prince of the first revolt.

Indo-christian scriptures have mentioned superhuman beings under other names: seraph cherub[1], angel, etc. As there are numerous states of existence both toward hell and heaven (not God's

---

[1] CF books of Ezekiel, Daniel, etc.

Heaven) the different human seers, rishis, saints and prophets of the past have not always seen the same beings or they might also have seen the same being under different forms.[2]

The next question in mind is of course : why is this myriad of beings so conspicuously absent from the contemporary world? Our daily experience does not bear witness to extra-human beings or immaterial entities. The great silence of the Universe resounds only with man's noise. The answer to this riddle points towards one of the main themes of this book: MAN HAS BEEN GIVEN THE CENTRAL ROLE IN THE DRAMA. Since the advent of Christ, the picture of the cosmic struggle between "the forces of light" and "the forces of darkness" seem to have followed a consistent trend: the fight has gradually ceased to be external to man and is increasingly taking place in man's psyche. It has descended from the superhuman stage to invade the human one. This development corresponds to the millenial message that, from all eternity, man was designed to be the focal point of universal evolution and it also emphasizes the importance of man's awareness as the new battlefield: the human being is in itself a KURUKSHETRA[3] in the sense that the human psyche harbours cosmic conflicts.

Modern psychological research is gradually providing evidence to support this proposition. In psycho-analytical observations made on countless patients C.G. Jung already found out that the collective unconscious (which encompasses all non-human strata of existence, good and bad) can make irruption into the subject's consciousness and eventually initiate a process of mental illness. It has been reported that in 1975 Britain lost more working hours because of emotional and mental stresses than because of strikes! Many indicators point out that, in the present time, man is to internalize the major conflicts of cosmic evolution: has the drama shifted from the macro-cosmic (epic fight on open fields) to the

---

[2]For instance HH Mataji mentions that the same Messenger appeared differently to Sita in the form of Hanumana or to the Virgin Mary in the form of Saint Gabriel. The great Fighter Angel has been perceived in Nepal as Bhairawa and in Medieval Europe as Saint Michael.

[3]Six thousand years ago, on the field of the Kurukshetra, a major battle took place between the right cause of the Pandavas, and the wrong cause of the Kauravas. In the words of the Bhagvad Gita, Krishna exhorts the hero to act with detachment and self-control.

microcosmic stage (man's psyche and nervous system)? That would be why maybe, the Greek and Indian traditions declared man to be a microcosmos.

In other words, the seemingly unspectacular present time might well boil down to a tremendous nexus of possibilities. In that case, never have demonic forces been closer to their ultimate success or their ultimate failure. Never has man been closer to "the second death" nor closer to his real ascent. And the fermentation of multiple futures is ripening while men are quite busy with more important things such as getting a job promotion, trying a new camera or changing mate.

With regard to the above considerations, a better grasp of the messages of past mythologies would certainly be helpful in providing man with some criteria of orientation for handling his psychic life. C.G. Jung made a major contribution in trying to integrate ancient religions and modern psychology into a coherent conceptual whole.[4] He perceived under different traditions a basic morphology of meaning that he could relate to the mechanisms and perturbations of the human psyche such as neuroses, schizophrenia, paranoia, etc. The different stories tell the same history. Thus, for instance, Mithra killing the bull is overcoming animal instinctivity and in a similar way, Horus-Osiris manifests, through death and resurrection, the triumph of the conscious over the subconscious. So does Jonah going out of the whale (see the similar Polynesian myth of Rata). Hanumana expresses the same symbol in fighting the monster on his way to Lanka: he enters into the mother of Rahu, swells, tears her apart and pursues his flight: swallowing up and resurrection. The hero who dies to rise again has been called Tammuz in Sumar and Akkad, Attis in Asia Minor, Osiris in Pharaonic Egypt and Adonis in Syria. Some of the findings of Jung are enlightening, some are bound to be misleading. It is not easy to identify the thematic unity underlying such complex symbols as the fire, the serpent, the tree of life, the water, the sphinx, etc. The serpent, for instance, cannot be merely reduced to a symbol of libido. Truly, he is the "Ancient Serpent", the Devil of Genesis and the Apocalypse. But he is also a symbol of life and regeneration as the Agathodaimon of the Greek and

---

[4]See *Symbole der Wandlung* (Rascher edit, Zurich) and other works such as *Psychology and Religion, Psychology of the Unconscious*, etc.

Roman medicine, as the gnostic symbol for the Kundalini rising in the spinal chord : he is Quetzalcoatl, the Aztec tutelary God of rain or Sesha, the naga of Shri Vishnu resting in the cosmic waters in the Vaikuntha. It is rather difficult to come up with a precise set of interpretations and, as a rule, the psychologist cannot go much beyond laying down a frame of hypothesis. The reason for those limits appears to be the following: the intuitions of Jung as well as those of the great scientists spring from something he called the collective unconscious. This unconscious is encompassing each individual's unconscious. Thus these intuitions can be lit in the individual unconscious of each and every human being. However without an "esoteric" knowledge, without a direct inward cognitive link with the collective unconscious,[5] messages can be received in dreams or intuitions, truly, but they cannot be deciphered; and the past messages of former civilisations can only be dealt with at an "esoteric" level, that is, with an inevitably superficial rational computation of the few perceived variables. Jung himself was aware of the epistemological difficulties of this sort of enquiry. He probably also knew that an imperfect grasp of these basic forms, ideas, or archetypes led mankind along the path of dogmatic quarrels and war. Indeed, to mention but one example, the world religions played with a powerful element of the human finite nature: his emotional side. As they could not rationalize themselves, they prospered by pumping imaginery emotional visions which adorned the archetypes and created realms of mythical satisfactions.

What is an Archetype?

The messages from the collective unconscious are pouring into the human psyche under the form of Archetypes, images, symbols, and are manifesting to men the primordial laws of life. They provide the basic canvas for mankind to evolve its greatest systems of thought, works of Art, scientific discoveries; the Archetypes are the signals reality is broadcasting on our psychic waves. They surface from the collective unconscious into the individual psyche. Let us take the example of the law of the conservation of Energy discovered by Lavoisier and Robert Mayer: it was unveiled to this latter by a hunch, a clue, an intuition that had to come from

---

[5] Of course Sahaja yogis know vibratory awareness to be this cognitive link.

somewhere[6]. Furthermore this discovery which is at the basis of modern chemistry and physics can be related to the "Weltanschauung" of the primitive dynamist religions that is, to their perception of a magic force, an all pervading energy (mana) that we find in the more elaborate religions under the symbol of fire; e.g. the Persian "haouma", Moses' burning bush and the Holy Spirit's tongues of fire in the Old and the New Testament, the aura of the angels, saints, boddisattvas which are represented in medieval paintings and Tibetan thankas as a radiation of light. It can be said, indeed, that science unveils at a specific level of material manifestation, aspects of this very energy which is the object of religious beliefs.

Jung defines the Archetypes as inherited, universally present forms whose ensemble constitutes the structure of the unconscious. They are like beds in which flow the river of psychical happenings!They are also, as in Plato's system, emblematic models and focuses of psychic energy. They mobilize the spiritual libido. Hence, they are generating the highest monuments of human creativity. For instance, in Christendom, the Archetype of the Mother has inspired some of the noblest masterpieces of universal Art such as Memling's *Adoration of the Magi* in Bruges (Belgium) or Michelangelo's *Pieta* in the Vatican.

It should be made very clear that the Archetypes are very alive in the contemporary world and that they provide us with information on the present time and the bearings of the future. A careful analysis of some of the specific manifestations of contemporary creativity such as cinema or science fiction novels would unveil their presence. For instance, in Tolkien's masterful feat of imagination, the trilogy of *the Lord of the Rings*, we can, with some fun, try to identify a couple of archetypical meanings. The epic fight between the forces of darkness and the forces of light, evil and good, get polarised in the last analysis, as a conflict between two opposite waves of psychic energy, two conflicting will powers : Sauron, the lord of the foul hosts has not even a physical body! He can bend the will of weaker beings. The ring of power means that to use or claim a power external to one's own leads to self-destruction (cf. thema of psychic possession). Gandalf represents the teacher, the

---

[6]Cf: C. J. Jung *Psychologie de L'Inconscient*. Libraire Georges (Geneve 1973) p. 125 SS

good wizard, the one who is powerful enough to resist the seduction of evil power, the guru, while Saruman is his opposite. Arathorn is the classical figure of the mythological cosmic hero, matured through toils and hardships (including a journey through the kingdom of the dead like Attis and Osiris!) and he returns to his city as the resurrected King, the Saviour. The hobbit Frodo is the symbol of man as the microcosmic hero. He seems to be the weakest of all actors in the formidable struggle but he is the ultimate key to the victory over the forces of evil. This is so because although loaded with the Ring (Man is a victim of psychic interferences and possessions) he has been able to resist the devilish temptation to use the ring and has resisted the ring's suggestions. Galadriel, the noble lady of the Elven Wood (who lives at the top of a huge tree) incarnates the crystalline power and amazing grace of feminine innocence and she is the very one who assists the microcosmic hero in the worst part of his journey: the horrible tunnel of Shelob.

I wish now to take a specific case of a paramount importance, the Archetype of the Mother, in order to illustrate the cognitive significance of the mythologies and the dangers of limited rationalisation such as Freud's theory of the Oedipus complex. But let us first introduce the matter.

The first manifestation of religious Archetypes in the history of mankind appear to be the neolithic figurines portraying the fertile Mother. From the very onset it should be stated that the Archetype of the Mother is universally pervading the consciousness of mankind. It has been manifested through tribes, peoples, cultures and civilisations all over the five continents; we find it in African, Polynesian, Amerindian legends as well as in the German or Nordic sagas and in the middle Eastern and Oriental cosmologies. The Hindu religion is the religion of the Mother: the Devi Bhagavati as the very Primordial Divine Energy (Adi Shakti) manifests herself in countless motherly Divine forms (Jagadamba, Gauri, Parvati, Laxshmi, Saraswati, Kali, Durga) or incarnates as a human being (Seeta, Radha); in Ancient Egypt She is Nun, Nunet, Hathor, Isis. She can be Demeter or Persephone for the Greek, Athene for the Athenians, Artemis for the Ephesians, Ceres for the Romans, Astarte for the Chaldeans, Kuan Yin the buddhist Chinese Mother of Mercy, etc., etc. In the time of the Prophet Muhammad, Fatima, daughter of the Prophet and mother of Hussein and Hassan appears to be the model of Islamic motherhood. It is to be emphasized that, although the Judeo-Christian world is dominated by Yahwe, the Heavenly Father, the Mother is not absent. Among the essential symbols of primitive Christianity, the New Jerusalem is of a feminine nature. The Virgin Mary appears to be permanently present in Christian and especially Catholic and Orthodox worship. Furthermore in the Apocryphal Acts of Saint Thomas the Holy Spirit is invoked as a Mother. Motherly symbols commonly worshipped are: the City[7], the Water of life (the Ocean as the all encompassing infinite, the baptism ritual), the Earth (Prithivi in India, Demeter in Eleusis, Cybele in Phrygia), the Cow (Hathor, Surabhi) etc. of course the Universal representation of this thema could be tentatively explained by the simple fact that human mothers exist everywhere but the argument in itself does not solve anything because it does not prove in any way the non-existence of this Divine Mother which is explicitly asserted by the mythologies.

The above indications only provide a little glimpse of the mythological, religious and symbolic expressions of one of the many components of psychic life, the Relation to the Mother. The Archetype of the Mother is manifested in manifold ways by elaborate rites and customs and is represented as well in various thought systems but there is no point here in going into philosophic anthropology. Such a wealth of information appears to be somewhat confusing and many scholars have been confused indeed. However, again, beyond the startling diversity of forms, the message asserts a thematic unity, a substantial homogeneity. Could we not resume this central meaning as follows :

Through a complex nexus of relation to the Father and the Mother, to the libido, the conscious and the unconscious, through death and resurrection, the figure of the Son Hero-Saviour pursues his initiatic pilgrimage towards his higher Self, thus showing the path of evolution to the human race.

The theme of the hero as a god incarnate appears in the person of Pharaoh at least as early as the beginning of the Fifth Dynasty. The hero is usually identified with the solar principle as expressed by the Aryan heroes of the Ikshawaku line in which Lord

---

[7] In that case she can be mother of virtue or of sin; the New Jerusalem is contrasted with "Babylon the Great, mother of harlots and of earth's abominations." John 17. 7.

Rama took his birth. In the West we can recall the "sol invictus", the unconquerable sun of the Roman emperors from Aurelian to Constantine the Great. Mithra, Osiris, Vishnu or the bodhisattva Amithaba have represented the saviour, the Messiah, the incarnated hero but not Shiva or Yahwe who never incarnate as they represent the infinity of the spiritual reality behind forms and nature. The completed achievement of the Hero Saviour as the resurrected one has culminated in the christic stature of Jesus, the good shepherd. The story of the cosmic hero, be it historic or mythical, always expresses a deeper meaning which enlightens the sense of the purpose of human evolution in the following way.

The cosmic stage on which the hero is evolving symbolises the microcosmic stage of the individual psyche on which man is to perform the drama of his ascent! Indeed the hero is the Model for the individual human being. On the path of his ascent the human hero has to master the dragon of instinctual energy and uncontrolled libido (e.g. the Germanic legend of Siegfried, the legend of Saint George) he has to emerge from the whale of the engulfing subconscious (e. g. the prophet Jonah).

We are all waiting for the hero to come and save us. But what about the hero being born within us? Could it be that the saviour within would be awakened by the touch of the Saviour Incarnate?

Now, surprisingly enough, sometimes mothers behave in strange ways. Isis threatens Horus and Ishtar tries to seduce Gilgamesh. To be sure, the myths of Tammuz, Mithra, Adonis, Attis, Osiris, Dionysios, Siegfried are showing a double relation between the hero and the goddess: she is a mother and a wife. Therefore many psychologists are relating these ambiguous findings to what they think to be the sources of neuroses and other mental illness: the main problem of the human psyche is of a sexual nature, says Freud, and its core appears to be a tension of repressed incestuous tendencies. This theory seems to be corroborated by the conclusions of Levi-Strauss's structural anthropology: in all human communities, the primal rule at the roots of any society is the prohibition of incest and more specifically with regard to the son and the mother. Today social scientists, psychiatrists, etc., have erected the "Oedipus complex" hypothesis to the respectable status of a scientific psychological dogma. This issue puzzled me for quite some time. I found out in Baltimore that some youngsters had been frightened and shaken during their drug trips because they were afraid to become doomed Oedipus! I could see that anthropology and psychology insistently pointed towards the Mother-child relation. As if this relation was the key to the understanding of the unfathomable depths of the psyche. As if some important secret was hidden in the beauty of this relationship. But I could not believe that psychological theories had found out this secret.

The reduction of the universal meaning of the beautiful Mother-Son relationship to a more or less happy incestuous drive is nothing but sheer nonsense and nonsense does not become common sense by the mere virtue of the fact that too many people indulge in it! We have no intention here to elaborately refute the positions of Freud, Reich and Co. The big mistake is to be attributed to Freud. In seeing the libido as essentially sexual he arbitrarily reduces the libido to only one of its aspects. This reduction distorts the perception of energetic phenomena. Sexual energy is only a little aspect of the libido and the libido only a part of psychic energy, and psychic energy only one of the very many manifestations of Energy. Such cases of misunderstanding usually happen when Man is looking at the big Universe with his little conceptual glasses and proudly declares that the Universe is about the size of the glasses.

The psychologist comes in contact with absolutely abnormal people. He is not aware that he is subtly but deeply affected by them. He often catches a psychic infection from his patient and no one can detect the contamination. Then the psychologist's theory rationalises the abnormal behaviour in a way that almost legitimizes it. And the joke goes on unnoticed: the doctor has become the patient and his diagnosis proudly tells "in order to be healthy, indulge in your sickness."

Clinical findings—when they have not been spoiled by the methodological bias of the psychiatrist—do not legitimize on experimental grounds the primacy of the sexual interpretation. When one considers the very little number of pathological cases which are *actually* related to incest, it cannot sensibly be held that this statistically marginal type of deviation provides any factual support to an incest-oriented interpretation of the mythologies' universal Archetype of the Mother. After all, how can animal behaviour guide human beings to understand themselves? If we are to rise, there must be a higher model, symbol of our perfection.

But then the question arises: how to explain the explicit sexual allusion in so many universal mythologies and, above all, how to explain that the prohibition of the mother—son incest is the absolute taboo at the basis of all social rules?

Having tackled these questions and having being exposed to the knowledge of some of the phenomena of consciousness I would propose to the reader the following answer.

In the pre-natal stage of his mother's womb the child is still connected with the all pervading cosmic Energy and he is perfectly integrated with his Foetal environment as well as with the whole universe. The birth and the rupture of the umbilical cord comes as a traumatic shock because the new born is cut from the cosmic to become himself a microcosm. The after-birth handlings are even more frightening for the baby who has been propelled into an entirely new world. The interaction between him and his environment starts developing his ego and his super-ego. But in his deepest unconscious, man remembers the uterine Eden and thus, the "return to the mother" expresses the yearning of the separated being for cosmic integration. In this respect we can say that the relation to the mother carries a feeling of relation to the cosmic. Hence, the various mythological symbols of the mother are expressing the feeling of the all pervading oneness: the sea, the earth, and also the communal feeling of the city. The mother is all enveloping, integrating, protective. The universal prohibition of incest as an absolute taboo imperatively states that SEX IS NOT AND CANNOT BE THE WAY TO REGAIN THE COSMIC INTEGRATION MAN IS LONGING FOR. On the contrary it is a universal warning that the confusion between sex and spirituality is the absolute error. As a spiritual child of God the human being has to assert himself as a separate entity; he is to develop to the fullest extent the potentialities of the microcosm that he represents (the myth of the hero). He rises in his freedom. He raises his energy and awareness towards the highest synthesis. It is because the boundless intensity of this highest synthesis and the true nature of the cosmic union could not be conceived by mankind in the earlier stages of evolution of the human awareness that the fundamental theme of the Union has often been depicted by the Ancient mythologies in exoteric sexual symbols which are commonly identified with the notion of intensity.

So, it could well be that the cosmic drama has been partly revealed, partly concealed, on the cosmic stage of mythologies and religions and it is to be performed at the microcosmic level by each and every individual. For this last purpose however mythologies are not actually helpful. We can confidently state that incest is not the key to the understanding of the psyche. We can also propose that Union is the goal of the hero's quest, a Union which is sought in a revelation of the consciousness. We can also guess that the spiritual process is mysteriously connected with gods and demons, our familial relationships, the forces of nature and the movements of the mind. Many further hints can be given. But when it comes to actually experiencing this revelation, here and now, in my consciousness, I do not find any key in the unfathomable messages of the past. They merely point out a way and mess up the tracks. This is, or so I am suggesting, their most significant contribution. It might well be that the unconscious is warning us: "do not seek me in scriptures, teachings, the past. Do not try to reach me through frantic efforts. For I lead myself the drama of your ascent".

14

Assumption number two :

The devil does not exist.

"I am the Spirit who always negates."[1]
—Mephistopheles, *Faust*

The devil believes in the ineluctability of the devil; asserting himself he denies the rest. Therefore he is the Spirit who constantly denies. He denies the Divine and its attributes such as Innocence, Love, Righteousness; he denies the perfectibility of Man and those dispositions which are conducive to it; and, last but not the least, he denies the existence of the devil. There is a saying in French which goes : "the greatest cunning of the devil is to let believe he does not exist".

We can imagine that, would the devil manifest himself in a conformist physical form (a sulphur smelling, horned gentleman or any sort of unkind descriptions you find in universal mythologies). Man would not run after him. Therefore he comes in disguise or, more elegantly, as the Prince of Seductors, the Prince of this World, the *"Princeps huius mundi"*. It is necessary for the Devil to negate himself because, in order to be accepted by Man, evil must seem to be good, mild and sweet, the ugly, beautiful and attractive, the dull exciting and the rotten apple tasty. In other words, without a radical state of ignorance and confusion within man's mind, man could not do or think the wrong because he would see it as wrong; i.e. not conducive to his "TRUE" happiness. The devil is an expert in camouflage because the point that he is at pains to make—and possibly actualise—is that it is man

---

[1] "Ich bin der Geist der immer verneint."—Mephistopheles, *Faust*.

who is devilish and that the extent of the demonic is not limited to the devil's person but encompasses the whole world.

As we think we are so very clever it is difficult for us to conceive of somebody who is so much more clever than we are i.e. the devil.

Does the devil exist? Of course not...of course yes. Some distinctions must be drawn here.

There is no Devil without a God and the very extension of God's metaphysical perfection precludes the logical possibility of an Absolute Principle of Evil which would be the match of an Absolute Principle of Good as represented by God. If there is anything like the Devil it cannot appear but within God's creation, as a creature, and hence the inferior existential status of the devil cannot be compared to God's intrinsic existential plenitude.

However, if it is true that the Devil as God's match does not exist, it has also been reported that there exists a host of demons. A few of them are so pre-eminently powerful that they are perceived in various religious traditions as God's equals. Primitive and early religions which represent the stage of human conceptualisation before the advent and manifestation of Lord Krishna. were not anyway in a position to conceive of God's metaphysical perfection; thus they would often conceive of Good and Evil as two equivalent opposite principles. Ultimately we might say that the dichotomic balance of the cosmic forces of Good and Evil as expressed in the strictly dualist cosmologies such as the Zoroastrian System[2] or the Manichean heresy were more reflecting a reification of Man's intellectual need for symmetry than an insight into the dynamics of evolution. The brain has a taste for sharp distinctions and it is easier to grasp black or white alternatives. Furthermore we should also remember that some demons have over-lordship over the foul folk. Satan rules over Behemoth, Leviathan, Belzebuth; in the great epic of the Ramayana, Ravana is the leader of the demonic hosts, etc.

Confronted with these traditions, the curious mind raises a major question; how can Man relate to the existence of demons he cannot see, nor hear, nor touch?[3] It is hard to bump into something being obviously satanic walking down Fifth Avenue or Les

---

[2] Ahuramazda (Good) against Ahriman (Evil).
[3] A few people are sadly privileged to have these capacities.

Champs Elysees or any less famous street of our cities, while demons haunted the backyards and alleys of medieval boroughs not to mention earlier days when they swarmed in dark forests, deep valleys, moonlit hilltops and other uncongenial places. In order to account for the volatilisation of the dark folk any comment on the reality of demons should be put in an evolutionary perspective.

Demons do not take incarnated forms in their likeness any more. That aspect of their prodigious interventions on the historical stage of evolution[4] is over. Most probably the change operated between the Ramayana (8,000 years ago) and the Mahabharata (6,000 years ago). In the first epic the fight takes place between fantastic beings, Monkeys (vaanaras), and Demons (rakshasas), while in the second one, even though the fighters are endowed with extraordinary powers, they are human beings. Following this trend today certain demons have come much closer to the human race in two ways:

They incarnate themselves as ordinary human beings and as a consequence they undergo the weaknesses of the human race; although much more powerful than human beings they have lost or are losing most of their past demonic powers (it should be understood here that power is an equation awareness-energy). In other words, the mighty Ravana who once shattered Shiva's abode by the depth of his concentration could just be today some kind of lusty guru preaching salvation through sex. Obvious cases of manifested demonic personalities include, let us say, Nero, Aurangzeb, Rasputin or Hitler.

In the present time, a lot of these demons are turning out to be male and female spiritual leaders, prophets and other gurus, and indeed, this would not come as a surprise to us for the following warning from Jesus is well known:

> "Then if any one says to you, 'Lo, here is the Christ' or 'there he is' do not believe it, for false Christs and false prophets will arise and show great signs and wonders, so as to lead astray, if possible, even the elect. Lo, I have told you beforehand."—Matthew 24.25.24

---

[4] See for instance a classic of the Sanskrit scriptures: *The Devi Mahatmyam* or *Shri Durga-Saptasati*. The Devi (Goddess) incarnated to fight the demons: Mahisasura, Shumba and Nishumba, etc. They are all incarnated today in a human form.

These false prophets have themselves succumbed to that ultimate temptation by which Satan had vainly tried to seduce the Christ: the temptation of Spiritual power.
Today, demonic forces do not need so badly to incarnate. They are much more dangerous for the human race because they have an increased faculty to enter as psychic forces into the human psyche. This, in the long run, represents a very effective threat because no one but man can oppose them: gods and angels *do not* enter the human psyche because they respect human freedom. And, meanwhile, how is man to oppose them when he is not aware of external interferences within his own psyche? "The greatest cunning of the Devil" is thus revealing its full meaning.

These phenomena have collective as well as individual consequence for they can proliferate when the social attitudes and common beliefs which used to keep them in check are no longer effective. Unfortunately, this comment applies particularly to the contemporary state of affairs in our "advanced" societies. With the dawn of the positive man, in the 19th Century, moral values were disregarded as irrational. The churches, mosques, and temples had long ago started to compromise for they did not have any method by which they could prove that "moral values are good for you". Beyond Good and Evil, the late 20th Century Western Man abolished the old moral rules and settled himself in a world where the devil, the wrong and the bad did not exist except in relative socio-economic terms. This evolution was possible because the deepest spiritual foundation of morality was never perceived as being related to our psycho-somatic system. It was carried through by the smartest intellectuals of past generations, a fact that fully illustrates the comment of Aquinas "Corruptio optimi pessima": the corruption of the best man is worst...in terms of its extent and consequences. As a consequence of all this "enlightenment" and "liberation", modern man is not yet aware of the detrimental effects that the break down of moral rules is exerting on the psyche.

In order to propose a conceptual alternative to the positivist model of "laissez faire laissez passer" let us try to sketch a scheme between spiritual evolution, moral values and social rules.

Very briefly, let us call, "good" or "right" what is conducive to Man's further evolution (i.e. growth in awareness) and "evil" or "wrong" what is preventing it. These terms of reference are actually assuming the existence of a general evolutionary line and a relation to the psychosomatic factors that we have already discussed. As there are in the world energies at work-emblematically expressed by the demons—which are not conducive to Man's evolution, we say that Evil exists as something transhistorical, transcending Man and society.

To negate the existence of Evil does not make it disappear. The tolerance of evil is the repression of good because wrongness constantly tries to overcome good; the struggle cannot be avoided. Let us describe the battlefield as follows :

In its illusion of being a separate autarchic identity, the individual identifies himself with any physical, emotional or psychological phenomenon of which however he is only the theatre. He considers that whatever takes place within the physical limits of his material body expresses his Self, comes from him, manifests him. This myth has already been destroyed by the findings of contemporary psychology which has been working with the notion of conditioning to such an exaggerated extent, sometimes, that man appears to be nothing but an internalized accumulation of external conditionings (socio-cultural, psychological, genetic, etc.) Avoiding both the extremes of psychological conditioning and psychological autarchy, the one who truly seeks the answer to the question "who am I"? is going to gradually drop all false identifications : "I am not this I am not that"...Ultimately, Reality is reached: "I am That". "Unwavering discrimination between Self and non-Self, destroys ignorance." says Patanjali (*Aphorisms* 11.26). But still, the question remains, what are the "this" or "that" which we are carrying say, in our psyche, but which are not truly our own since we can get rid of them without losing our integrity? Not everything can be explained by chromosomes or economic relations of production! Now and then perceptive people begin to wonder what is the source of divers trouble such as psychic stresses, uncontrolled tensions in inter-personal behaviour, lack of self-confidence, unexpected anguish, sleeplessness, irrational fear, boredom, envy, lust, frustration, etc. What are these things which sometimes generate condemnable thoughts, feelings, or action that our deeper attention would reject as alien to us? Saint Paul wonders in the same terms as Arjuna: "How is it that I do the bad I do not like and do not do the good I like?"

The point I am trying to bring out is the following: the bone walls of our brain, the flesh of our body, express the physical limits of the body: as such they represent a physical obstacle for physical things to penetrate into us: if they do, we are hurt or killed. But neither flesh nor skull have the capacity to prevent our mind or any other part of our person to be penetrated by "things" much more subtle than physical matter. These things can enter into us; actually they do enter into us but we are not aware of it, because we have not yet a sharp enough discriminating power of attention to isolate the interference. There are different levles of intensity by which we can be affected by what is not our own, from benign cases of conditioning to instances of possession. Ultimately I am sure you would agree in saying that the only index we have to know what is "ours" is the extent of awareness-control we have over it. Whatever names we give to a number of these units of psychic interference "bad vibrations" "identities", "entities", "bhoots" "badhas", "spirits", "pretas", "djins", "demons", "goblins", they do exist and the more so since we are not aware of them: very often we identify ourselves with their suggestions or we do not understand what is happening to us. In the confusion thus generated, the power of the Self often does not get its chance although the energy belonging to the Self's power of attention can wipe them off. It should be understood that the UPI are trying to settle into and proliferate within the field of the human awareness i.e. ego and super-ego because it is the only way open to them to avoid dwelling in those strata of existence where they belong (i.e. the seven stratas of hell) and to enjoy through the human nervous system the sensations they are deprived of because they are mere awareness without a physical body. UPI are but the parasites of psychic energy in the same way that viruses are parasiting the physical energy of the body.

Man is largely unaware of the external conditionings he might be undergoing because these conditionings exercise themselves within that part of the human psyche which is below the threshold of consciousness.[5] The subject, as a rule, cannot turn his attention inside, towards the processes which are shaping the phenomena of

---

[5] I should refer here to Lyall Watson's stimulating book *The Romeo Error* which deals extensively with the after death. As Watson says "The chances are that, if a personality does continue to exist, its character will be so different from the living one that it might be impossible for us to recognize it." op. cit. Hodder & Stoughton (Great Britain 1974) p. 105.

UPI could also stand for: Unidentified Psychic Intruder.

his psychic life and thus when intruded by UPI vibrations, he is a passive agent. If there is in-built in the subject an intuitive knowlege of the Right (Dharma), the UPI vibration, badha, spirit, etc., cannot get a hold over him, that is, cannot parasite the subject's psychic energy. If such a link with the good is weakened, the UPI vibration can settle itself within the energetic field of the subject's awareness and gradually programme the subject's attention and behaviour in those types of attitudes which are congenial to the UPI. The subject usually resists it and the resulting tension at the unconscious level, can generate mental and emotional stress and, in serious cases, physical, nervous and mental sickness. As the French poet Baudelaire wrote it, "La victime et le bourreau" the victim and the torturer share the same soul. In case his organism does not react anymore, the subject will end up identified with the UPI and the induced behaviour: the wrong course of action will seem normal to him.

Jesus, Buddha, Guru Nanak, etc., warned us to have nothing to do with spirits.

Certain research departments of militarily powerful countries are making intensive research in ESP (extra sensory perception) in the hope of tapping new sources of power. But without the guidance of the Power which is beyond all powers such research is really dangerous. The supra and subconscious realm cannot be tamed by these men; only the inverse proposition is true; men will be enslaved. However, such a disastrous issue—nothing less than hell—can be avoided. Actually our bodies (physical, emotional and mental) serve as the setting of a play where a certain number of unauthorised actors are trying to get the leading part. If they can appear on the scene it is only because they manage to tap the attention for their own sake; by withdrawing my attentiom from them, I am withdrawing the power they have over me, and all identifications—from the grossest to the most subtle—are gone. In order to be king in my kingdom, in order to be chief actor in my own life's drama, I have to rely on my self's attention. In order to confront UPI's I have to stay on my field and not follow them on theirs. My field is the field of my own Self. It can be expanded by attention. When this Self's attention grows, my self-mastery grows gradually, and when this attention takes the very Self for its object, within me and outside me, then I have begun to recognise Reality or rather, Reality recognizes itself; this is the Kingdom of God.

But it is impossible to reach such a level of awareness without mobilizing some kind of Divine Power; only such an awakening and the opening of the inner channel of awareness is the sure road to liberation, only then an individual has the power to fight his own weaknesses; to become one with Reality. HH Mataji says: "You do not have to fight others but yourself, your own misidentifications." When misidentifications are dropped, the UPIs have no psychic space in which to survive. They are automatically expelled and cannot enter back.

We are quite aware that this book's denunciation of the actual interference of UPIs can appear surprising and that it might be very difficult for the reader to relate to it but it should be said that, anyway, verbal identifications cannot adequately cover these phenomena which can be really detected only by an adequately evolved vibratory awareness. Before my awakening to it I was not aware of UPI's. I would just register the consequence of their interferences: feeling very uneasy with some people without being able to find out why; going through periods of intense boredom, etc. I suffered from these moods, the more so that I could not understand them.

While most UPI are parasiting the super-ego, the ego offers to Man the other possibility to become devilish. The type of ego-inflated people are often in charge of administrative economic or political affairs. To begin with they are not interested in truth: how could their ego accept truth because for them truth does not exist but as their own creation, suiting their own purpose. Without truth, righteousness cannot be; thus the blinding ego has finished the sense of righteousness in them without giving them the slightest pain. But they know how to play games. They can be very charming and attractive, mild and patient actors who know all the tricks of the trade of deception. They live with fake righteousness, deceiving themselves. Hence they cannot go into honest introspection as they are subconsciously afraid of what they could find within themselves. They dominate their wives and their cunning destroys their home life which is the source of happiness. Outwardly they will be well behaved every time their own success matters. Jung describes many cases of those "successful" characters.

Machiavelli who freed his "Prince" from morality assumed nevertheless that he would be guided by some sense of "virtue". But once the ego is on its own it does not accept any limit. It shows successful results to the world, preens itself and boasts; it exploits and dominates without any remorse. To this extent the ego is even more misleading than the super-ego which eventually makes people uncomfortable and sick. The egoistical monster might do just whatever he pleases, lured by the appearance of worldly success. Dictators, imperialists, colonialists were typical examples of such egoists who, in the name of leadership, overpowered their fellow men or people belonging to the so-called lower races. As the overdeveloped ego usually directs the mental activity, this latter merely rationalises the vagaries of the former. The mind accepts the dogma or theories which suit the ego. Weaknesses and sins, all kinds of noxious or depraved behaviours can be legitimized or even glorified by big theories. This is where the extremes of ego rejoin the extremes of super-ego to develop the kind of personality structures which are most destructive. The egoist overpowers others and is aggressive to himself as well: he destroys others and himself by injurious indulgences. The Devil as ego is never identified because the egoistical person has been given free latitude by modern pseudo-psychology: as it was found out that controls created conditionings it was suggested that controls should be removed but no one realizes that absence of control helps to create the egoistical monster.

When blind people are the leaders of society it is not difficult to see that societies are heading towards chaos, injustice, famine, disorders and wars. This millennial proposition is finding today its forceful expression as Man has tremendously increased his power of action, that is, of unenlightened action. In this respect the forces of Evil have found a vastly expanded field of interference in human affairs.

Without going into details I wish to state now that what has been named "dharma" is the absolute antidote to the forms of Evil in the human psyche and behaviour.

—What is Dharma? Why should it matter to us? What is the reality behind the word?
—At this point of my development it should merely be said that "dharma" means "doing the right thing". That is, the right thing to keep the human substance intact, the right thing to keep Mankind fit for evolution. It is quite simple: whatever is not congenial to our physical, emotional and

mental being is to be avoided and whatever brings concord in a human life (such as, say, a happy married life) is to be accepted. Dharma embodies at the same time the laws of Manu and of Moses; the ancient stoic and Christian virtue, the Chinese way of equilibrium called the Tao, or the middle way of Buddha, etc. All these concepts imply a human commitment to a right, ideal behaviour. The further point to understand is that such behaviour is right or ideal by virtue of its conformity to the general laws or universal evolution. This link between righteousness and history is expressed as Lord Vishnu. He is that aspect of God which embodies the perfection of Dharma while leading the cosmic evolution. He represents the sustaining power of evolutionary Ascent.

In its historic dynamic extension human Dharma manifests the Universal principle of evolution towards good, a principle clearly expressed for instance, in Teilhard de Chardin's Parousie or the return of the Christ-King. In its metaphysical extension Dharma could be what was identified by Plato as the supreme Archetype of the Form of Good, embodying the essence of Goodness, Justice and Righteousness. Dharma is the sustenance of all the things that are born or created; in matter it is the valency of the atom which determines the specific quality of an element. We can in this respect compare dharma with the aristotelian and thomist concept of essence: "that which makes a thing be what it is." It is, for example an atom of hydrogen and not of oxygen. More concretely with respect to human beings, dharma establishes the further actualisation of Man's existential potentials while opposition to it delays Man's perfectibility. Hence the great instructors of Mankind have taught those mental attitudes and social behaviours which keep Man in harmony with the laws of dharma. For instance, Buddha's noble eightfold Aryan path is actually a means to keep one's attention in balance, that is to say, in harmony with Dharma, thus helping to liberate oneself from karma and the cycle of rebirth. In China, Confucius proposed an ethical conception of aristocracy, raising the standards of social conduct so as to stimulate a congenial dharmic milieu, etc., etc., whatever was understood of the teachings of these masters formed the basis of religious beliefs and consequent systems. The differences in emphasis laid by the different teachings are due to the different needs to correct different societies at different periods. Moses' ten commandments however have a truly universal value.

Dharma, as human nature's essential goodness, lies in every human being but it will be enhanced or marginalized by the social environment precisely because the social environment generates most of the conditionings and vibrations that the subject is exposed to while providing him at the same time with the criteria to judge what is good and to be accepted and what is bad and to be avoided. When the social environment legitimizes practices which are not conformable to dharma, the threshold of the individual's psychosomatic resistance to negative or aggressive interferences tends to be lowered. The subject will be more inclined to negative thoughts, feelings and behaviours thus contributing to build up the momentum of a snow-ball social effect which will affect other individuals. The interaction between individual and society works as a reciprocal feedback system. The social and collective dimension of dharmic behaviour has been magnified by the fact that the Dharma aspect of God, Lord Vishnu himself, took his seventh incarnation as Shri Rama, twelve thousand years ago, to provide Man's sociopolitical consciousness with the socio-political rules of right action (*samaj Tatha Rajkaaran Dharma*).

We should also understand the Vedic caste system! In the times of old, the brahmins knew that human beings literally bombard each other with all kinds of vibrations and they tried to keep the vibratory interactions under control by social check; a non-brahmin could not come into a brahmin house, etc. Of course the system became useless when the perception of the underlying rationale could no longer be related to vibratory awareness.

We can now better guess the link between evolution, morality and society. Moral values are to maintain social rules and manners on the central path of optimal evolution. The adequate instrument to this end is the law. The moral imperative represents the factor of social cohesion: If we make the assumption that Man has evolved from the animal kingdom we could then say that Morality is the attempt of the mind to restructure (in a relationship pattern) the proper type of environmental behaviour which was once secured by biological and instinctual certainties.

> "Honour your father and mother. You shall not kill, you shall not commit adultery, you shall not steal, you shall not bear false witness against your neighbour, you shall not covet your neighbour's house..."
> —*Exodus* 19.12

From the time of the laws of Manu, the commandments of Moses, the Babylonian code of Hammurabi, the Roman Twelve Tables, etc., rulers and legislators have tried to enforce those patterns of behaviour conducive to Dharma in implementing within the human psyche an awareness of the criteria of goodness which could maintain the togetherness of the human tribe.

Man's existence unfolds in a collective as well as in an individual dimension and therefore dharma is to be mediated by some sort of social instrument in order to be reflected at the collective level. Thus it gets embodied in moral values which typically deal with the man-community relationship and assure the biological homogeneity of the human horde. The set of dharma-oriented rules and practices that morality generates, are enforced by rites, customs and laws, and offer the best protection to immunize Man against noxious UPI vibratory interaction within the community and thus, against the consequent disruptive behaviour. Dharma regulations seek to destroy the vibratory environment in which the UPI can proliferate.

This is the psycho-spiritual imperative at the roots of the very notion of law. In *the Pure Theory of Law*, the positivist H. Kelsen reached the logical conclusion that the "Grundnorm", the basic rule at the roots of all constitutional, legislative and judicial dispositions was of a psychological nature; "The law is to be obeyed" but would not give a reason for it. The psychological rationale behind any legal dispositive is to enforce within society the conditions congenial to dharma. It is in this imperative that one has to find the ground for the legitimacy of Law and that is why the earliest legal systems such as, say, the "jus quiritium" of the first Romans, were interwoven with liturgical exorcisms and religious rituals. These exorcisms were bending the psychic energies against the adharmic UPI's! The power of the Law also kept the ego in check.

The erroneous, sinful behaviours have been described in consistent terms by different traditions. For instance, the scholastic fathers of the Middle Age claimed, "Greed is the root of all evil"[6] and the Buddhist bonzes spoke of greed, anger, lust, etc. A Persian saying goes: "Do you know what can never be satisfied? The eye of greed. All the world's goods cannot fill the abyss of its desire." In the sanskrit classics six foes have been identified: Kama (lust and greed), Krodha (anger), Mada (vanity or false pride), Matchara (jealousy), Moha (selfish attachment to family or clan), Lobha (coveting others' possessions). Those are the internal foes which corrupt and blind the mind, lead us to wrong action and entangle us in sin. But today greed is magnified by capitalist rationality, unbridled lust is called "liberation" and the worst forms of anger i.e. violence are officially enforced in totalitarian regimes and unjust societies.

It is indeed high time that we relate ourselves to dharma. And, most probably, we should not rely exclusively on a legal system to enforce righteousness: the best system can be manipulated by the worst men. Let us in all our freedom understand that right is good for us.

Alternatives to this understanding look rather gloomy. As it was blatantly proven by the history of the Roman or the Chinese Empires, the enlightened respect of law is one of the pillars of civilisation. Ultimately civilisation rests on the degree to which social organisation can successfully set up a psycho-spiritual, moral and legal protective structure against the energies of Evil in whatever forms they take. When this protective structure is dismantled, civilisation is on the way to collapse. The French poet Paul Valery exclaimed: "We, civilisation, we know that we are mortals."[7] And we also should know why: the very pattern of moral breakdown and social dissolution which, very often, attended the destruction of the old empires is exhibited in the contemporary societies to an unprecedented extent.

[6]"Cupiditas radix omnium malorum est".
[7]"Nous autres civilisations, nous savons que nous somme mortels." P. Valery, *Considerations*.

In the above considerations we have been talking about Evil, Units of Psychic Interference, Evolution, Morality, Law and Civilisation. It might be relevant to summarize what we have been trying to say.

Evil exists: it is at work here and now and it exerts itself at an individual and collective level, chiefly through the medium of human psyches: It conditions the super-ego and inflates the ego of Man. Because these phenomena interact at the collective level human societies attempted to preserve themselves with a collective response, by a complex system of religious beliefs, moral values and principles, rites and rituals, customs, rules and laws. The maintenance of such a system is what civilisation is all about.

Rousseau and Freud correctly saw that civilisation is built on repression and they had a strong tendency to view repression as a bad thing; but it all depends what it is that we are repressing! If I repress a furious desire to kill my neighbour's dog because he is walking unscrupulously around my tenderly manicured lawn, then repression, being civil to the poor animal after all, might not be altogether wrong. Christianity imposed upon the Roman Mediterranean world some decent notions about the respect of the human person that existing barbaric practices certainly resented as repression e.g. suppressing the slave's owner's legitimate right to sell his slave's daughter to a brothel. In the same way, during the Middle Ages, the Church enforced "the truce of God" which seriously "repressed" during certain days of the week the lords' freedom to conduct endemic feudal warfare; that was not a bad thing either. The great empires of Sumer, Akkad, Egypt and China rested on the level of repression necessary to build up and maintain an irrigation network. True enough, totalitarian repression is an accursed evil but so might be libertarian tolerance in much subtler ways; the contemporary belief in Western societies that just about any type of behaviour should be legally tolerated in the name of freedom is worth a closer look. Indeed these behaviours are often an open-ended invitation for the UPI's worse conditionings which will injure innocent people. Freedom to liberate oneself from conditionings, ignorance and limitation reveals itself as Man's highest attribute, Man's great noblesse...and freedom to enslave oneself with chains of lust and intoxications, to precipitate oneself in further ignorance, further conditionings and limitations, can be considered as Man's deadliest illusion.

Such illusions cannot create a civilisation that helps human evolution. Quite on the contrary, the civilisations which encourage those illusions do retard the human progress by which Man liberates himself from his self-made bondage in order to become his own master.

To speculate that the state of Nature preceding the man we know was good as Rousseau proclaimed or evil as Hobbes warned cannot be warranted on logical grounds because good and evil appear only within consciousness, with man's ability to make ethical distinctions: a non-conscious being cannot be either wicked or virtuous whereas man can be both. Henceforth the element of consciousness which distinguishes man from the other living species implies the freedom to choose between good and evil, a typically human choice that neither beasts nor angels have to face. For the stoics, freedom is man's greatness. For the existentialists it is man's bane. They are both right. Those who are wrong are the libertines who mistake licence for freedom.

The paradox of the human condition appears to be that it follows one and the same path to doom or salvation: it is called freedom. It follows that words such as repression and tolerance involve a qualitative meaning only when considered in relation with the teleology of freedom; freedom from what, freedom for what? It is precisely in order to answer this question that an awareness of Dharma is so important. During the trial period when man is free between good and evil, man strives to reach freedom from evil. At the individual level, dharma manifests the strength to achieve human freedom from evil; it represents the only disposition that maintains human wisdom which can triumph over evil: when the power of discrimination is enlightened by Dharma, it casts its loving, gentle light of wisdom in the dark corners of the mind; then, the Devil is shown to exist and is thereby reduced to powerlessness. Knowledge of Evil as such implies its repression. Upon that, Dharma opens the central path of optimal evolution at the individual spiritual psycho-somatic level as well as at the collective level (socio-political and economic). What we need now is a concrete tool to raise dharma consciousness within ourselves because we have really lost it to a great extent. Don't you agree that things are pretty bad? Do we still know what to seek and what to avoid?

Man projects his own image on the world he creates. There is no civilisation without repression, no society without a rule because, in the last analysis, there is no human being without the need for some degree of self-control. It is to assert the control of the Self over the pysche and thus the freedom of the psyche from external interferences that the individual consciousness has to master the lower involvements of the psyche's attention in order to preserve the integrity of the individual's psyche as a whole. And it is to preserve the integrity of society as a whole that social rules and legal dispositions are devised to prevent or repress noxious social behaviours. In this respect self coercion should be a desirable feature of any society in the same sense that self-control is a desirable feature of any human being.

Moreover, history showed that we are not safe with this latter statement because noxious groups in power appear to define noxious social behaviours according to their own class interests and the very structure that they generate to protect their own good (i.e. the state) happens then to generate evil. Hegel was at pains to demonstrate that the state was the instrument to bring about the common good (the *"bonum comune"*). One century later, the very state of Hegel's country was the instrument of Nazi sadism. This in turn sadly proves our point : on the social level, it is dharma alone which guarantees the common good and not any rule, social system or political structure in themselves be they the ancient civitas, capitalist free enterprise or Marxism. The common good cannot be ensured without a social awareness of Dharma in all sectors of social life:how could a corrupted mind possibly evolve a virtuous social action? Indeed, we have quietly forgotten what Plato stated in the *Republic* :

> "Blind' is just how you would describe men who have no true knowledge of reality and no clear standard of perfection in their mind to which they can turn as a painter turns to his model, and which they can study closely before they start laying down in this world about what is admirable or right or good where such rules are needed or maintaining, as guardians, any that already exist."

Without dharma-consciousness the best social organization proves itself almost paralyzed, incapable of ensuring the greatest happiness of the greatest number, the common good, because it cannot deal at the psycho-somatic root of the individual's consciousness with those dispositions which are destructive of the common good. A superficial manipulation of the institutional superstructure at the collective level (laws, economic mechanisms, social and political organization) is bound to fail if the individual psycho-somatic infrastructure remains perverted and corrupt. This dilemma has grown today to the full size of a historical drama because the increased power of action that man has secured for himself through the mechanisation of industrial production during these three last centuries has not followed the laws of dharma but those of greed.

It is time to raise a few simple questions.

After all what do we need a civilization for? Should not a civilization empower the individual to develop the human potential for happiness, bliss and fulfilment? How could that be?

A civilization based on Dharma integrates the individual within society by creating a feeling of security, balance and harmony. People develop a sense of belonging and participation to such civilizations. They feel protected. They develop pure relations of companionship. Problems of disturbed or perverted relationships disappear. Family life is supremely enjoyable and in this beautiful nest children blossom to fruitful life. Such civilizations can be created by proper, loving education and not by force or compulsion. Mahatma Gandhi's attempt at launching such an education pattern failed because of the betrayal of the westernized bureaucrats. If a dharmic society (Ram Rajye) could have been achieved then the Indian civilization could have offered optimal conditions for the evolutionary destiny of Self awareness.

Ultimately in the ideal society, one would transcend Dharma and reside in the Kingdom of God. There one cannot be conditioned or tempted. One is neither aggressive or threatened. One becomes the witness (sthit pragya) watching the working of the Divine Love through oneself. Then Man emits divine dharma and love.

This may sound a bit far out but there are ways a human society can prepare itself for the Kingdom of God. It is worth noting here that the education system in ancient India was entirely based on Dharma. Perhaps the life pattern itself was based on the contemplative findings of the great sages.

Life was divided into four periods called Ashramas.

—After the age of five the child was sent to a school belonging to a University (gotra) situated in the forest amidst the most beautiful natural surroundings. These gotras were established by sages who were high realized beings. No one could marry a student of the same University; that would have been considered an incest. Hence natural celibacy *(Brahmacharya)* preserved the innocence of the pupil.
—At the age of twenty-five the students would return to their homes, get married and raise children with great care until they reached five.
—After the age of fifty both the parents, endowed with maturity, dignity and wisdom would go to the forests as vanaprastha. There they looked after their grandchildren studying in the Universities. They showered their love on the children who would surround them with respectful loving attention.
—At last, when they reached an advanced age, blessed by satisfaction and happiness, they would take to renunciation and reclusion, becoming meditating sages *(Sanyasashram)*.

This interesting pattern lasted for a few millenia and was entirely woven around dharmic life.

Let us refer for a while to what the Indian ancient thought perceived of the cosmic laws. While Brahma—Saraswati manifests the Creative power of God, Shiva-Kali the destructive power, Vishnu-Laxmi manifests the protective and sustenance power of God. As before said Dharma, as the aspect of Vishnu, is the aspect of God which sustains, protects, and evolves the Universe. Within us it is the essential disposition of righteousness which will lead on the path of further evolution. Beyond that, it is the cohesive power of cosmic integration and harmony. Thus Dharma, within the human microcosm and within the macrocosm, represents the principle of divine ecology. Without Dharma there is no ecology; the delicate, self-regulating and self-maintained balance of energetic cycles cannot be preserved. The drama of the present time is that we have acquired an increased power of action in the world without correspondingly increasing our perception of

Dharma. Thus the foes of Vishnu, the forces of Evil (which, they will tell you, do not exist) have settled within the realm of Man. They are sitting upon our heads, enthroned by our technical achievement and mechanical powers. They have ruined our family life, our *civitas*, they are attacking our nervous system and, if not destroyed, they will destroy the very habitat of earthly life. We are already endangering earth's very biosphere, that is the film of land, water and air enveloping Mother Earth in which exist all the known species of living beings including Man.

Indeed, to quote A. Toynbee's words, the present time reveals itself to be "the grand finale that is heading towards a climax"...

> "This climax might be the annihilation of life through the wrecking of the biosphere by human wickedness and folly now that the devil incarnate in Man has armed itself with sufficient technological power. Alternatively, the climax might prove to be a transition from the first epoch of human history to a second, or, more probably, to a long series of successive epochs...we cannot foresee the future, but we can argue that we are approaching an ethical parting of the ways that will be as decisive as the biological parting, twenty or twenty-five million years ago".[8]

The alternative in front of us is wide open, frightening but clear:

> "It looks as if man will not be able to save himself from the nemesis of his demonic material power and greed unless he allows himself to undergo a change of heart that will move him to abandon his present objective and to espouse the contrary ideal. His present self-inflicted plight has confronted him with a peremptory challenge. Can he bring himself to accept, as necessary practical rules of conduct for people of ordinary moral stature, those precepts, preached and practised by saints, that hitherto have been regarded as being Utopian counsels of perfection for "l' homme moyen sensuel"? The

---

[8] A. Toynbee— *Mankind and Mother Earth*: Oxford University Press (*New* York and London: 1976) page 26.

ASSUMPTIONS TO CHALLENGE 385

long-drawn-out debate over this issue that seems to be approaching a climax in our day is the theme of the present chronicle of Mankind's encounter with Mother Earth".[9]

A change? But how?
Before we can overcome greed and lust, we need a radical mutation of our cognitive relation to ourselves and the outer world. This knot is at the core of the human dilemma and it is to be cut through now.

Indeed, the key to the cosmic struggle lies within the human microcosm. Our psychosomatic being encompasses the field where two apparently different and opposite realms, the material and the spiritual, are joined; human consciousness has been trying to cope with this odd marriage. We had the choice to turn our attention towards the material mastery over our external environment or towards the spiritual mastery over ourselves. Today the choice no longer exists. We are already ruthlessly endangering the protective biosphere sheet in which Mother Earth shelters the life of her children. We have appropriated the energy of Father Sun and stored it in the atomic war heads of our missiles. We conquered matter which is what we were supposed to do according to the Book of Genesis but, meanwhile, matter conquered us, which is what we were supposed to avoid.

Scientists, statesmen, thinkers of various schools are slowly realising that there are no alternatives to man's self-made Apocalypse...but a spiritual revolution which is beyond Man's power to initiate. And yet if Man does not gain mastery over himself, the Devil-man will extinguish the species "homo sapiens".

Maybe this is the time when the last Rider of the Apocalypse, is to come?

Or do we really believe that we are just in a brave new world where life is better than ever before?

---

[9]op. cit. page 20.

15

Assumption number three :

We have made the World a better place to live in.

"They thought they were the masters of Destiny but it was the master of all of them"[1]

—*Greek Wisdom*

1. The Freedom to destroy oneself

Somewhere, in the throbbing infinity of galactic spaces, Man a living being among the living, a beat at the heart of life, a part of this organism whose pulses are the floodtide, the music of the stars, the bird's song, the breathing of the cells, the tree's growth and the swarming of the atoms. . . ., Man is a part and parcel of cosmic ecology. He belongs to the Universe.

But Man is also a microcosm on his own, the only free agent who can programme himself as an independent variable. He can ignore the fact that he is a part of the whole and consider himself as the whole itself[2]. This freedom, when coupled with ignorance, generates mistakes. Without proper consideration for a global, transhuman equilibrium, we deprive ourselves of the possibility of knowing what is our position in the general picture what is our location in time, space, destiny, finality. Consequently we cannot identify our inner space as the truth within is the same as the truth without. Deprived of the knowledge of our inner space, we are a geometric point without density or dimension, lost without guidances and rules, floating in the Universe like an

---

[1] Greek tragedies expressed in all possible ways that man is crushed by his own ego.

[2] "Es ist doch lange hergebracht, dass in der breiten Welt, man kleine Welten macht" *Faust*. Goethe. It is an old story that one creates little words within the big one. (my translation.)

errant spaceship, with our creation floating around us in increasing disorder. The multiple forms of this disorder projected into the world are shaping the history of the present time.

This time is the first in which this odd variety of living being, homo sapiens, can rationally foresee in which way he is bringing about the extinction of his own species and the destruction of the sustaining biosphere.[3]

The perspective of mankind facing its doom in scientifically stated terms of planetary magnitude results from a very rapid acceleration of history whose cumulative effects made themselves felt in an extremely short period of time: 1870-1970 AD.

The Australopithecus, two or three million years ago, already shaped stones suitable for usage, thus showing a spark of consciousness. It is probably a remarkable feat of human consciousness that a hundred years of modern man's activity could bring about a global threat to the very survival for which that consciousness fought during hundreds of millenia. We might wish to have a quick look at the historical genesis of this somewhat surprising development.

2. *An historical overview*

During all but the last tiny fraction of its time span, mankind has lived in the static way of life of the Paleolithic Age. Then, 40,000-70,000 years ago, the technological discoveries of the Upper Paleolithic Age marked the beginning of a new era: improved tools, bow and arrows, the domestication of the dog, etc., eased the struggle for survival. In the Neolithic Age, the domestication of more plants and animals, the invention of agri-

[3] "It is becoming evident that man's activities, based on the massive leverage which science and technology have made available to him, have reached a scale and intensity at which they are significantly modifying many of the elements within the biosphere that are essential to sustaining human life. Increased consumption of fossil fuels, proliferation of nuclear reactors, the introduction into the environment of more than a thousand new man-made chemical compounds every year, vast man-made changes in the surface of the planet and its plant and animal life-all impinging on the natural systems in ways we cannot fully evaluate and understand. But there is increasing evidence that they are giving rise to serious risks to human health and well-being in such areas as possible climatic change, marine pollution, contamination of the food chain, polluted water supplied, and damage to the Earth's ozone buffer." The United Nations Environment Programme. *The State of the Environment* 1975 p. 15.

culture together with the invention of new tools, spinning, weaving and pottery, provided the infrastructure of rural life as it is still known today in parts of the globe.

Agriculture and animal husbandry provided the basis for the first regional civilisations that archaeology can recall with a relative wealth of information: Sumer, Pharaonic Egypt and China, a period stretching from 4000 to 1500 BC. (our knowledge of the Indus, and Meso-American civilisations is still very fragmentary).

From that period onwards, cumulative technological improvements contributed to the generation of an economic surplus on which new forms of activities and social organisations could be built. The increased pace of introduction of technological innovations and the socio-economic adjustments they generated accelebrated the rhythm of historical transformation.

However it appears that, very soon in history, Man's increased technological power could not be kept in check by a corresponding rise in ethical standards. Unidimensional technical[4] progress could not cope with the various requirements of an increasingly multidimensional society. The division of labour, the differentiation of social functions and a more complex mechanism of wealth distribution institutionalised the economic disparity and social inequity which broke the togetherness of the Paleolithic community. Also, newly discovered needs and the expanding mobility of political groups augmented the possibilities of war: the domestication of the horse brought, from off the Eurasian steppe, the invaders who sacked Babylon (the Hittites in 1595 BC.), ravaged Memphis (the Hyksos in 1730 BC.) and destroyed the Indus civilisation (Indo-Aryan tribes around 1500 BC.). Mobility brought about an increase in trade and a corresponding wealth but also the greed corresponding to the latter, a keener competition for goods and above all, for land. The civilisations' response to these challenges marked the dawn of imperialism; confrontation and wars developed on a grand scale. Skilful display of violence became the seal of statesmanship.

The Chinese, Roman, Persian or Maya Empires, the Arab Caliphates, Mongol Khanates or Japanese Shogunate differed widely in cultural and social terms but, during the millennia 1500 BC.—1500 AD. such regional powers exhibited a consistent

---

[4]See the thesis of Herbert Marcuse in *One Dimensional Man*.

degree of homogeneity and parity among themselves in terms of military power, level of technology and organisational capacity. It is when this parity broke down in favour of one of the world's regions, namely Europe, that the speed of historical change found the momentum which brought about the modern world.

In the 13th Century AD when the Mongols almost conquered the whole of the Eurasian continent, nobody could have dreamed that the small nations of the remote European peninsula would conquer the globe. And yet, in the 15th and 16th Centuries, the process was initiated whereby the geo-political configuration of the orbis terrarum was drastically modified—for the best or the worst—to the profit of the European colonialist powers. The non-European societies which could have opposed alternative models of society to the western one were often crushed well before the tidal wave of the industrial mode of production.

By the time of the 15th/16th Centuries nobody was aware that the real victor—and master of the society to come—was not the European Christendom but a new kind of faceless knowledge, invisible within social classes but omnipresent in social organisation, initiated by Man but not controlled by him: today, we would call this knowledge "technical", and its leverage on social action is not an easily identified church but "something" called technology.

In Europe itself, in a matter of a few decades the old social patterns of organisation were crushed: The new warfare technology (muskets and artillery) smashed the military overlordship of the feudal nobility, the ruling class of that time. The invention of typography (Gutenberg, Aretino) broke the information monopoly of convent and monastery and weakened the Catholic Church more surely than its potential religious rival,Protestantism. Furthermore, the technologically induced commercialisation of agriculture, and the appearance of banking in Northern Italy and Flemish cities, modified the immediate social life pattern more surely than any political or religious revolution before.

In 1498 AD, thanks to a newly discovered technique of oceanic navigation, Vasco de Gama landed in Calicut, after having circum-navigated Africa from West to East. Columbus reached America with Bibles and guns in 1492. Magellan went round the globe in 1519-22. The Iberian navigators started the scramble of the European nations for world dominion. In a matter of four centuries (1500-1900) this undertaking succeeded.

The regional civilisations which could not westernize themselves (that is, in concrete terms, which could not quickly adopt the superior war technology) were simply annihilated; with the help of luck and treachery, Hernando Cortez conquered the Aztec Empire, (1519-21 AD) Montezuma was killed and Tenochtitlan destroyed: with the help of luck, treachery and smallpox Francisco Pizarro conquered the Inca Empire; which had been torn apart by the war between the Inca Huascar and Atahualpa. Atahualpa was killed and Cuzco destroyed. The invaders slowly (sometimes quickly) exterminated the native Amerindians. Meanwhile Africa became a hunting ground for buccaneering slave traders.

The civilisations which could not westernize quickly and thoroughly enough sank into decay: such was the case of the prestigious Islamic world. Russia defeated the Ottoman Padishah of Istanbul (1768-74) and the British subjugated the Timurid Mughal Emperor of Delhi (1798-1818). China failing to understand that the world was not ruled by the decrees of Peking's "son of Heaven" but by the guns of the "barbarians", was to fade for one century (1839-1939).

The civilisations which could westernize survived. The non-Europeans who could oppose the West were those who understood that the West could only be matched by westernization. This meant a Western-style army, technology, economy and administration. Tsar Peter the Great westernised Russia in 1694 and the Meiji Revolution did the same for Japan's benefit in 1868. In due time these two countries became imperialist powers. Moscow and later on St. Petersburg conquered the Asian hinterland while Tokyo's "sphere of coprosperity" led to the Manchurian war and the Asian theatre of World War II.

In the 19th and 20th Centuries, cultural idiosyncracies, local traditions, beliefs and social systems were gradually discredited because they could not evolve a political entity capable of opposing the technological and industrial might of the West. Until this very day, the claim to adopt the assembly-line while preserving one's national cultural integrity has proved futile; cultures and religions have been shown to lose their impact on society when the socio-economic process develops independently from them.

Through a painful churning process, the non-European agrarian societies cast themselves into a mould of economic development which is likely to destroy the remnants of spiritual ecology preserved in their traditional values. These values provided an intelligible life-framework to the common people who understood their place between the gods and nature, the good things to do and the bad things to avoid. These values are not being replaced by modernisation and it is by no means clear that there will ever be any social remuneration for this agonizing process of change in which the individuals lose their criteria of personal and social identity. But, anyway, the process of social change and development cannot (and should not) be reverted; the question is: how to handle it?

The world has opened itself wide to mechanical and technological modes of production and thus western values are ruling the world despite the decolonised state's lure of political sovereignty. The implications of Western values should be understood: the God that the West has exported is not Christ but Matter. Both capitalism and Marxism are committed to the increase of production of material wealth, and the societies which borrowed from this model have also acquired its shortcomings.[5]

We should perhaps elaborate now on what these shortcomings are by taking the advanced industrial society as a model.

3. The collapse of the materialist millennium

The technological and economic revolution that started around 1760 in Great Britain transformed agriculture and industry. In 1870, it had spread beyond Britain and continental Europe and by 1970, its momentum was even more powerful and still accelerating. The transformational impact of the Industrial Revolution on the world, society and the individual's psychosomatic equilibrium has been inexorable and tremendous. It has given Man an unprecedented mastery over his environment, dramatically enhancing his capacity to rule over the material world

---

[5]Despite Mao Tse-Tung's attempt to blend the Western dialectic (Hegel-Marx-Lenin) with the Chinese one (Taoism) it is by no means certain that the Chinese experiment is going to offer a feasible alternative model of society. Marxism remains a direct offspring of the European continental philosophy. A true alternative for a free, balanced, harmonious society would, most probably, ground itself on Gandhi's principles.

that—as recalled in the book of Genesis—God delivered to him. After millennia of struggle for mere survival, Man has brought himself to a point where he can virtually master any aspect of material life. Man has filled the earth with his image while exorcising God and devil. In the countries where the conditions of living have reached standards without any precedent, Man's achievements are hailed as a feat of genial creativity. And yet, Arnold Toynbee's remark is pertinent: Man overcame all his old natural foes, all except one: himself. And this foe is now unbound, without adequate perception of God or Nature to contain its possible follies.

The one question one must raise appears to be: what is the purpose of development and of mastery over matter? The truth, deep down, is that material development allows us to save labour and time for spiritual growth and contemplation. Alas, quite on the contrary, we have become life-long slaves of working habits, material comfort and artificial needs. We are so very busy without even reflecting upon what we are busy about! All the while we gladly float adrift in the inflated balloon of the ego, flying over the mythical landscape of our achievements.

The industrial mode of production and capitalist society, as Karl Marx rightly saw it, irremediably altered the existing patterns of life, social structures and value systems which were less obviously productive. Meanwhile the baby was thrown away with the bath water; the old forms of social organisation had their own virtues precisely because they were not systematically organised according to the rationale of maximized profit and accumulation of wealth. Considerations of human relationships were preeminent, thus spontaneously taking into account the fact that the optimal environment for Man is not merely economic but also psychological. For George Wilhelm Friedrich Hegel (1770-1831) the very notion of "Gemeinschaft", community, implied that selfishness should be transcended by enlightenment; but enlightenment is unlikely to take place within a materialist society built on the rationality of selfishness. This is of course a direct criticism of the capitalist mode of production while the attempt of "communist" societies to transcend selfishness by ideological repression historically failed to bring about the Gemeinschaft of authentic communism. In both these forms of societies, human relationships have been strained by the asphyxiating conditioning of the materialist environment.

The scientific and technological break-through changed Man's relation to time and space, Self and destiny, hunger and thirst, day and night, life and death. This proved to be a dangerous mutation. The new Icarus[6] with the wings of technology is coming to terms with Mankind's old dream to escape the prison of the body. However, he is doing so not by deepening his spiritual dimension, and self-knowledge, which is the way to liberation suggested by the ancient wisdom, but by projecting a mechanical, technologically monitored extension of himself over the whole world; he travels upon earth and sea, reads the language of the stars, of the molecules and chromosomes, builds huge cities, flies in the sky... and all the time flies nearer the sun of his doom.

We will not elaborate here on the well-known planetary dangers of over population, exhaustion of natural resources, pollution, poverty, atomic, bacteriological and chemical warfare or genetic engineering. But it has to be summarised briefly at least.

The intellectual polemic has been raging between adherents and opponents of the newly discovered doomsday scenario theory. All the while, administrators, scientists and professionals of all kinds are confronted with the following hard facts. The world population has now reached 3.8 thousand million people and, barring some unforeseen malthusian disaster, is projected to reach 6.5 thousand million by the end of this century[7]. With the increase of population, the provision of basic human necessities (food, shelter, clothes, space, health, education) demands more and more food, energy and raw materials which are already in short supply. With the world population doubling in the next forty years the increase in economic activity is bound to further disrupt the natural ecosystems (water, natural vegetation, etc.,) which maintain the biosphere's conditions of life.

Then we might as well look at the perspective of growing disorders in urban areas.

---

[6] Icarus wanted to fly and made himself artificial wings; it worked quite well but as Icarus drew nearer the sun the heat melted the wax which retained the wings, and Icarus fell into the sea. The fool is dead.!' Long the live fool. We seem to be all headings towards the same end.

[7] "The Grounding Arithmetic for the Year 2000". *UNESCO Courier*, May 1974, p. q.

"What does it mean, that the population of the world will double in the next thirty years, adding 3,500 million people to the human family?

First, nearly all these new millions are going to live in towns and cities. That means building the equivalent of 3,500 cities of one million inhabitants each. In the world today, there are still fewer than 300 cities with one million population.

What about housing? Even with an average family of six (too many, say demographers), 3,500 million people would need nearly 600 million housing units, more than exist in the entire world today.

Then, think about children. At current birth-death ratios, the number of children who will be born and survive through childhood in this 30-year span will exceed 5,000 million. How many doctors, teachers, schoolrooms and playgrounds are needed for such a number of young people?

The challenge of the future is awesome. Towns and cities of the world already are in crisis, failing to provide basic facilities and services. Problems of unemployment, pollution, congestion, slums and squatter settlements, inadequate transportation, social alienation and crime are mounting everywhere. Past solutions have not worked. We need new techniques, new ideas and new forms of social organisation."

These remarks were to introduce "Habitat" in the United Nations conference on Human Settlements in Vancouver (1976). But the conference itself plainly exhibited the fact that the decision-making power structure of the contemporary states is not politically equipped to deal with global and regional issues of such magnitude. Already now, the urban environment threatens to go out of control. Surrounded by polluted air, polluted water, polluted cities, unbearable noise and congestion, man in our cities is threatened by cardiovascular, glandular, respiratory and neurological troubles. The crisis is far more serious for the Third World cities plagued by squalor, poverty, hunger, disease and unemployment. In Calcutta, Lagos, Manila, Cairo, Guayaquil or Kinshasa, the demand for even the basic necessities of life far outstrips available supplies. (In 1971, for instance, 600,000 people were sleeping on the streets of Calcutta). It is estimated that mass migration from rural to urban areas cannot be prevented in the existing conditons of economic discrepancy between the city and the countryside.

The urban crisis is but one of the crucial issues present societies are facing or rather, are failing to face. The gravity of these various crises worsens daily because of the incapacity of today's world political elites to face them in an appropriate way.

For instance the alarming tide of poverty which is submerging the majority of mankind today could be reverted. The World Bank figures show that it does not cost all that much to deal with poverty. A figure of about $125 thousand million over a period of ten years, or $12.5 thousand million a year is needed. This figure should be compared with the world's spending on armaments. At present (1976) the sum is roughly $250 thousand million a year. Thus the entire proposed spending to deal with poverty for an entire decade would amount to no more than half the world's *annual* bills for weapons. Is not such a world institutionalizing madness?

If Man were wise he would handle himself as well as the problems he generates for himself. But the pathetic irony of this present condition is that Man has made wisdom increasingly difficult to get. Wisdom is the inward knowledge of dharma and dharma within oneself is difficult to perceive when dharma outside of oneself is gradually eliminated as a result of Man's impact on the environment. For instance, nature's organic cycles and ecological balance appear as a manifestation of dharma at the micro and macro-biological level. Man's sense of what is and is not "natural" —in that sense, dharmic—depends upon whether Man's environment is natural or not; it depends upon the possibility of living in psychic osmosis with nature. A balanced physical environment which provides you with the right models and criteria of sound environmental cycles and interactions is needed. Once nature is replaced by a man-made environment, the intuitive criteria provided by nature, which were spontaneously incorporated in Man's life pattern, are lost. At the time of the aristotelian "polis", for instance, the Ancient Greeks knew well that there existed an optimal size for a city, a dharmic social setting in which the citizen could best participate in the life of a community. In short the city would be shaped according to the dimension of Man. But today, the human urban environment has gone out of control as proven by the inhuman living conditions in the modern megalopolis. In a world without God or nature, we are left without any objective points of reference to assess the quality of our actions.

Today, the old biblical promise is fulfilled; Man has inherited the earth, provided, of course, that earthquakes, droughts, floods, locusts and climatic variations do not upset the conditions of the last decades. We have the technical ability to triumph over almost any material obstacle Mankind is facing. Nature has been transformed and harnessed. However the question is no longer how to master nature but how to master the one who masters nature. E. Kant[8] knew that this question was the most difficult to solve... and the fact that this master does not know himself does not help its solution.

Indeed, while transforming the world, Man was not aware of the extent to which he was transformed himself. The sequence can be described as follows: the change in the environment modified Man's conceptual structure; and both these modifications affected Man's neuro-psychic equilibrium. It is necessary to emphasize the negative developments of the contemporary "advanced" society so as to present the dialectic interactions between the kind of world (concepts-society-environment) we are generating and our decaying neuro-psychic status...decaying, that is, in comparison to what it was and above all, what it could be. We certainly should not negate the positive trend of evolutionary history or ignore the view that our deficiencies are necessary pre-requisites for a breakthrough of awareness leading to a higher form of human consciousness. Let it be emphasized that our time is ripe for the best as well as for the worst in terms of historical development; but it should be plain from the start that existing conditions are bad enough to warrant a deeper understanding of the problem.

5. The threat to Man's neuro psychic system

While projecting himself outwards, Man did not pay sufficient attention to the manner in which his own metabolism reacted to the far-reaching changes he generated; because, anyway, the externalized awareness could not be readily directed on to the inner life of the psyche. This internalisation of the attention was not thought to be necessary as Man's concept of Self was defined by

---

[8]See E. Kant's Proposals for Universal Peace from a cosmopolitan point of view.

external action and not by knowledge of Self. All the while, the human psycho-somatic instrument was affected by Man's creation in ways which steadily diminished Man's ability to control the latter; the creation of the sorcerer's apprentice began to work on its own:[9] The greater the extent to which Man is manipulating the outer world the more he isolates himself from the harmonic laws of dharma which represent the spontaneous in-built mechanisms against conceptual and behavioural mistakes. The sad paradox is that Man immensely developed his ability to implement virtue or sin on earth while losing the perception of either. History points out that the major aspects of this process are developed within Man's mind.

It might not be irrelevant to provide a few indications about the ways Man has undergone essential neuro-psychic modifications without being aware of the change.

Let us start for instance with the problems of the relation between Man and his destiny. In the cosmology of the ancient Greeks, Destiny is all powerful. In the plays of Aeschylus, Euripides, Sophocles, dramatic heroes such as Orestes or Antigone, Electra or Oedipus can all bitterly exclaim with Shakespeare's Romeo: "I am Fortune's fool." The universal morality of the ancient tragedies is expressed in the fact that Man is inevitably eushed by Destiny and that the capital sin, hubris, is to challenge it. Such a theme is developed also by the myth of Prometheus.[10] Fortune was again pre-eminent in Roman times (*fortuna* or *fatum*) until Augustinian Christianity humanized it in the notion of Divine Providence. Although the Weltanschauung of the Ancients was a bit grim it provided a healthy buffer against human presumptuousness: men were advised to watch out, to take refuge in the rectitude of their conduct and the firmness of their soul.[11] Useful indeed was such advice to keep human beings on the right evo-

---

[9] What is happening in the field of entomology provides an expressive image to illustrate the story: we are presently manufacturing all sorts of insecticides which are slowly but surely laying down the genetic conditions for the insecticide-proof insect.
[10] Prometheus, tried to steel the fire from the gods and was condemned to have his liver eternally devoured by an eagle.
[11] The stoic ideal of psychic self-reliance seems to have crossed the borders of social classes: Marcus Aurelius was an Emperor, Seneca a court grandee and Epictetus slave.

lutionary track, at a time when the subtler psychosomatic foundations to legitimize morality were utterly unknown.

In the contemporary world things are a bit different. The much respected "Fortune" loses her veils and is laid bare. The welfare state and the Insurance Company substitutes for God's providence, providing us with the comforting illusion that life's risks and accidents can be accommodated by statistical computation and social security schemes. Chance exists but only to be computed and dealt with accordingly; we discover instead parameters, variables and random factors. Probability calculus and electronically monitored mathematical projection can unveil the hidden face of Hazard, this powerful god who collapsed before the integrated circuits of the computers. In other words, the human mind and its technological extensions appears to be a better buffer against adversity than righteousness and prayer. Hence technology and not righteousness would shape and define the scope of action. But then, should we wonder why righteousness is absent from a world secreted by such an action? Should we complain about ecological disequilibrium, growing social alienation, etc.?

Furthermore, as Man could not eliminate the ultimate risk, death, he chose to ignore it also as we shall explain presently.

Let us consider, say, the period of the High Middle Ages. Man—be it the overlord, the Lord, the guild companion or the serf—had a strong sense of the religious order of the world and of his own place within it. His feeling of religiosity, unenlightened and confused as it may have been, nevertheless kept the subject's attention on its trans-human destiny and the widespread concern for death and the after-death mitigated Man's total involvement in wordly pursuits. It offered men a balanced perception of the futility of mortal things ("vanitas vanitatum") and of the ineluctability of his own transcendency.

Today, what is our awareness of Death?

In 1977's developed industrial countries the social consciousness of death has disappeared because of the results of the secularisation of life and of the tremendous (and welcome) successes of health engineering. The average child of man very rarely sees a corpse unless the grandmother dies or unless there is an accident on the highway. Anyway. death is something which happens to others, a fact which is confirmed by life-expectancy statistics. As a consequence, modern man lives as if he is not meant to die. Meanwhile, ignorance of one's mortality does not imply one has become immortal· it implies above all, that we do not feel any more the necessity to clearly set up our life priorities with regard to the after-death, that is, actually, with regard to the soul's cosmic destiny and its transmigratory cycle of births and deaths.

Death corresponds merely to a change in the basic conditions of life. It is the mutation from one stratum of existence to another, and the impact this mutation has on our further destiny depends upon what kind of life has preceded the mutation[12]. Hence the traditional exhortation to lead a good life. When such concerns are eliminated from Man's consciousness they surface in the subconscious where they act as an element of the individual's psychic insecurity. This element of instability is too deeply rooted in the unconscious to be easily cured by psycho-therapy or often even detected but it can be briefly described as follows: without a sharp contrast of light and darkness, of life and death, the subject has trouble evolving a well defined concept of Self in the context of Destiny and time. He builds the world for himself and thus finds himself isolated, trying to find security in beliefs, conclusions, erotic behaviour or creative action. But the security the brain needs cannot be found in the fruits of the (conceptual and physical) actions of an insecure subject. The resulting determination helps generate an identity crisis which weakens the subject's resistance to psychic interference. This consequence tends to start a chain reaction at the collective level.

The ignorance of death is only one of the numerous unperceived ways by which modifications of the material environment and life-styles influence the human mind. This influence may be considered to be ominous because it is surreptitious and largely unnoticed. We could list many such examples. For instance, the awareness of death and of time as the messenger of death gave former generations a more poignant and vibrant perception of the present. This psychic disposition has remained to this day, true, but it is blunted and dulled except for those few sensitive people who painfully survive the growing tedium of life.

At the height of the Renaissance in Florence, Lorenzo di Medici, the Magnificent, sang the flow of time, pleasure and melancholy:

---

[12]The idea of the process is nicely described in the Bardo Thodol: The Tibetan Book of the Dead.

"How beautiful youth
Which ceaselessly slips away
Have fun if you will
Of tomorrow there is no certainty."[13]
    (my translation)

In many languages, time has been sung of as the slow death. In the Indian mythology the God of time, Kala, is also an aspect of the God of destruction. An awareness of the motion of time implies the heightened awareness of the present transience of existence. A few poets, belated in our century, remind us of our mortality. Like Heraclitus, Guillaume Appolinaire contemplates in the river-flow, the story of things passing by.[14]

Also the awareness of time, the feeling of the futility of material existence and the threat of a difficult material environment made it possible for man in past times to enjoy the material world much more intensely than we seem able to: as Ronsard and most poets put it you cherish your rose more dearly today if you know that it will be faded tomorrow.

When the world was a couple of hundred years younger, experiences—whether of pleasure or pain—were made with a more striking immediacy. Sensations had yet, to the minds and nervous systems of man, a vivid quality of directness and absoluteness[15]. We do not know how much a 14th Century burger of Magdeburg or Utrecht enjoyed his evening pint of wine but the overall impression that one gets is that he did a lot. He was endowed with a capacity to fully savour earthly things and life's pleasant moments. We find evidence of this by getting familiar with the way the literature of those times described man's relation to life.

Today our faculty to enjoy the intensity of simple pleasures has significantly decreased. We do not notice it because the sheer quantity of goods supplied by the materialist consumption society

---

[13]"Quant e bella giovinezza/Que si fugge tuttavia/Qui vuol esser lieto sia/Di doman non e certezza".

[14]"Sous le pont Mirabeau/Coule la seine/Et nos amours/Faut-il m'en souvienne/Le joie venait toujours apres la peine/Vienne la nuit sonne l'/heure/Les jours s'en vont je demeure."

[15]"We, at the present day, can hardly understand the keenness with which a fur coat, a good fire in the hearth, a soft bed, a glass of wine, were formerly enjoyed" J. Huizinga *The Waning of the Middle Ages*. p. 9.

is supposed to compensate for our decreasing ability to enjoy them. Logically enough, because he enjoys less, the modern consumer-man yearns for more. Hence a socio-economic structure to guarantee a system of external material gratification has been institutionalised to make up for man's inability to feel an inward intensity of satisfaction. If we define sensuality as the faculty to fully enjoy sensations we can say that the flight forward of ever increasing consumption is built on the ever spreading sensual impotency of the actors of economic life. And, of course, the mode of economic production which corresponds to this state of affairs involves a vested interest to perpetuate it and the corresponding society it generates magnifies quantity—and not quality—oriented values. But the mere quantity of the opportunities for satisfaction cannot ensure their quality. This is the cardinal paradox of materialist life as it has been pointed out by past religions. Desire and greed cannot be quenched. But since people are educated to believe in the value of the materialist system in which they evolve, how can they be provided with the conceptual tools to identify the impossibility of fulfilling the faithful expectation for a materialist millennium? A socio-economic system which is based on the premise that accumulation of goods is the chief achievement to be secured by society because it is the basis for individual happiness, is a system which is based on the logic of Absurdity. A system based on a wrong assumption about human happiness cannot find the right means to ensure this happiness. It does not provide the congenial setting in which happiness can bloom. Happiness is inside and you cannot go inward by running outside after material desires which are insatiable. They produce toxic psychological effects: they create habit formation, dependence, addictions. To ignore this very simple truth (expressing ages of human common sense) results in heavy economic and environmental costs. The rationale of the advanced industrial society is to perpetuate irrational economic behaviour: produce anything, produce more. The production of goods for the sake of production is legitimized if necessary by artificial manipulations of demand.[16] These manipulations will tend to encourage all the human weaknesses. Indeed profit seeking industries cash in on man's degenerated taste for the vulgar and the arti-

---

[16] See the theories of G.K. Galbraith and the well-known preoccupations of Ralph Nader in the USA.

ficial. Such taste is cultivated by clever advertising; new weaknesses are created to generate more profit. Productive capital will be readily invested in intoxicating products which cause psychological dependency (alcohol, cigarettes, etc.,) because the enslavement of the consumer guarantees a steady market. In the process, the innocent is aggressed, the intelligent befooled and the poor are robbed by the master minds of sales promotion. In the name of beauty, entertainment or freedom the consumers are thoroughly cheated!

Thus waste becomes an intrinsic feature of the system it is a waste of goods and a waste of energy and the material resources which helped to produce them. Although the process is not self-evident, there exists a very real link between the individual's fading nervous sensitivity and the senseless depletion of natural resources which is threatening the future of man on this planet.

As a result the delicate sensitivity of the nervous system is being damaged. This is literally the psycho-neurological cause as well as consequence of the materialisation of man's mind, of man's world. When human attention is diverted and overloaded without the reward of any real satisfaction how can we expect to achieve tranquillity and bliss? In this maddening world many people try to escape reality by losing themselves in power trips, drugs or sex mythologies. But how can we blame them? In our crazy, self-destroying society everyone makes everyone else sink further into confusion and insecurity.

The deterioration of our neuro-psychic apparatus is the contemporary concrete dimension of the old contradiction expressed in the scholastic and Hegelian opposition of Spirit and Matter. If Spirit does not rule over matter i.e. if man's mind cannot keep a true control over man's action upon matter, matter asserts itself to the detriment of the spirit of man.

Unfortunately the decline in man's general sensitivity has not only been limited to the appreciation of material satisfaction; it has also drastically affected man's ability to find psychological fulfilment in inter-personal relationships and this dismaying development appears to be sadly ubiquitous in the advanced societies.

Again, we should refer to the testimonies of the past such as the literature and poetry of previous centuries, which are bound to tell us something about the society in which they evolved. We should then discover that the pattern of inter-personal relationships was somewhat different from what it is now; feelings such as generosity, modesty, friendship, fidelity, chivalry, honour and dignity forced such an effective social recognition that in many cases the social actors would value these attitudes higher than the satisfaction gained from unethical material profits or power games. There were certain barriers that one could not cross without losing one's self-esteem and these barriers were rarely crossed. Neighbourly togetherness, mutual consideration born out of love and other psychological aspects of "the quality of life" were integrated as a matter of course in daily life and there was no need to coin a new word or any need for the present horde of social scientists trying to find out what the quality of life is all about and why it is missing. Today also we can witness a genuine quality of social life in the societies which have not yet "developed". I have seen in the remote valleys of Nepal or in rural India young girls endlessly playing with small children; mothers spending hours in the company of their babies or grown-up children: two boys and girls would enjoy a sweet conversation, lovingly teasing each other in an atmosphere of pure friendship. Alas, the sense of pure companionship that gives complete relaxation to the mind is only too often missing from today's western families and society. In a pure relationship man is the most beautiful object of enjoyment but in our society, direct rapport and spontaneous contact are rather different. We need a third agent (cinema, theatre, party, cards, drinks, sports and God knows what) in order to communicate with each other.

In olden days the little episodes of life such as visiting a friend, giving hospitality to somebody as well as great events such as weddings, feasts, going to church or to war, were all solemnized by some sort of social rituals and they seem to have been thoroughly felt and thoroughly enjoyed. Symbols and rites were of paramount importance because they were acting as social emblems of and focus for the individual's feelings of personal identity and social integration. For instance, the European "Ancien Regime's" system of reward was directly based on a ritualisation of symbols reflecting the subject's social recognition within the community.[17] All this contributed to ensure a fair degree of psychological cohe-

---

[17]Examples can be caricatural: as the Duc de Saint-Simon sarcastically reports, it was quite a big affair for a French Duchess at the time of Louis XIV to sit at the King's Court in Versailles on the appropriate emblazoned stool the height of which would conform to her rank.

sion in the little world of man. What is to be emphasized is merely that human relations had a value recognised by the social system, and were not merely organised as a function of economic productivity. This simple fact made personal relations vivid and enjoyable[18]. The same remark holds for the hierarchical agrarian societies of Asia and meso-America. Certainly, according to our criteria, past societies were built on social repression but as this repression was not perceived as such by the actors of that time they seem to have been much less unhappy than we assume they were.

Human beings seem to have loved and hated genuinely with a great intensity of passion and quite generally been more aware about and enjoying each other than we are. In universal literature we find sublime monuments sanctioning genuine friendship, fully dedicated love between man and woman, holy relationships between brother and sister, parents and children, as well as strong evidence showing the unity and importance of the familial cell; intensity existed in these relationships because of their purity. Shakespeare's heroes cannot have been created out of the blue: an element of sublime and total heartfelt commitment pervaded the lovers' stories. The relationships we find, say in the 17th Century Racinian drama, represent a very strong type of committed involvement: intensity was enjoyed through the intimacy of exclusiveness: one man one woman. True enough the royal courts and the Kings in the West were far from always corresponding to the above type of lovers yet the sort of "interchangeable mates" gamble which is not unusual in our sexually liberated countries would have been considered as a strange way to waste one's opportunity to love and to be loved fully. The 18th Century libertinage in the upper classes appears to be one of the numerous ways the old values were destroyed and not too surprisingly it was also the time when the old order broke down in the French Revolution. The reason for the moral degeneracy of the elites appeared to be the takeover of these people's psyches by their inflated egos. Ego negates virtue and wisdom. Today—perhaps thanks to the democratic decentralization of power—everyone seems to be loaded with that treacherous ego and shamelessness is no longer confined to the court of the King!

---

[18] It is not logical to found one's assessment of the nature of the Ancient Regime on the sole analysis of the period before the French Revolution when, indeed, it was completely rotten.

The major acceleration in the crumbling process of European desensitisation took place in the 19th Century. It is significant to note that as far as literature is concerned, the first half of the century burst into a blazing apotheosis of passions in Germany (Sturm und Drang), Italy (Risorgimento), France (Romantisme) and in the England of Shelley and Byron, while the second half of the century exhibits the first symptoms of the debilitating illness which was to infect the 20th Century: it has been called "spleen" or "mal du siecle" and it swarmed into our time under the famed label of boredom or "l' ennui". Interestingly enough, the years following the romantic upsurge corresponded to those decades where capitalist industrialisation conquered Europe, while in Paris poets such as Baudelaire, Rimbaud, Verlaine or Mallarme suffocated in an asphyxiating world turning more and more dull, oppressive, stupid, ugly, vulgar and boring. The poetry of that time betrays a desperate reaction of the individual against materialistic alienation, it sobs and shrieks, beseeches and anathemizes, it mourns the lost azure in a song of incomparable sadness and beauty. The fallen angels woke up and found themselves caught up in matter. Charles Baudelaire sinks in sombre grief, Arthur Rimbaud staggers in the inebriety of helpless revolt; Paul Verlaine's music sends forth frail notes of a bygone era of tenderness and refinement, bursts into obscene songs and weeps; Stephane Mallarme stretches towards the inaccessible purity of Being or Nothingness. (May all of them incarnate again to know the blamelessness of the new morn). These poets rang the toll bell at the very time when materialism, industrialisation, mechanisation, rationalism and positivism triumphantly invaded the stage.

All the while, in Copenhagen, Soeren Kierkegaard was philosophising on how ridiculous it is to exist. The feeling of the helplessness of existence was to culminate in the pathology of the 20th Century sensitiveness which has been superbly magnified by French existentialism. Here the degradation of man's relation to life and himself finds its masterful philosophical formulation. The human intellect brilliantly elaborated upon man's fading nervous and psychic sensations. What is felt to be the insipidity of existence itself leads to a creeping sensation of existential "Nausea". The existentialists added an acid touch of bitterness to Pindar's elegiac sights which depicted Man as the dream of a shadow erring in the night. Life is a passing dream, so better not wake up. Between birth and death time is given to you to raise questions you cannot answer...or, unfortunately, ignore; so, try to be silly, that is try to find a meaning to your life which is basically meaningless.

Of course men are quite happy being busy doing something but their activities are radically useless, a meek attempt to escape despair through blindness. It is a manifestation of what B. Pascal in the 16th Century called "divertissement" (from the latin disvertere: to turn away from); to turn away from the true dimension of existence in the vain agitation of worldly involvements. J. P. Sartre called this escapist attitude "mauvaise foi": bad faith: the human ostrich buries its head into the sands of religion, job, politics, wealth, etc., so as not to see the emptiness of life and its Absurdity. Despair, at least, asserts its own dignity (and drapes itself in the sombre pride of a Spanish flamenco). To be sure despair leads to nothingness but it does, after all, express a certain kind of human beauty. For the greatness of Man is to accept his own insignificance.

The greatness of man in Reality is to accept the insignificance of his ego and super-ego so as to merge in the greatness of his Self, but this the French intellectuals could not grasp precisely because they were using the intellect only. As a consequence they were left with the difficult task of surviving the finding that life is hopeless. A Camus happened to kill himself against a tree during a night drive but Sartre and others did not have this luck. Sartre led the way for many European intellectuals: he took refuge in the creed of Marxist militancy, thus collapsing into the very bad faith he keenly denounced in *Being and Nothingness*. In the post World War II period, Marxism heavily capitalized on the intellectuals' willingness to escape the existentialist nightmare.

French existentialism is certainly worth emphasizing here because the French genius for Cartesian rigour, and ruthless logic delivered to the world a philosophical monster which exerted a devastating influence during the period after the Second World War. The Anglo-Saxon public who could not cope with such sharp intellectual surgery preferred to ignore existentialism and dwelt quietly in the comfort of un-acknowledged bad faith.

Existentialism however remains significant in universal philosophy as the most veracious account of man's present neuro-psychic degeneracy, that could develop in the confusion of a Godless, materialistic society. It is an honest and lucid attempt to tell the

20th Century Man: "here we are! What is there to be proud of?".

There is nothing to be proud of and people are trying to forget it in "more": more money, more sex, more speed, more noise. Alas this also means less peace, less love, less harmony, less joy and evermore boredom.

5. *The alternative for the post war generation*

The fear of boredom, "l'ennui", still haunts the Western psyche even in the (not) so happy America which has built up a very sophisticated system of anti-boredom technology; to watch TV for instance helps you to ignore that you would be left with boredom, if, by mistake, you were left with yourself.

The established culture and the by-now established counter-culture are struggling differently against the same ghost. The only difference between Timothy Leary (the drug Revolution) and any conformist grocery-store owner is that the first tried harder than the second to find a meaning to life where there cannot be any. But anything will be preferred to the atrocious "Ennui"! The great thing about the sixties and its train of drugs and fake gurus is that by now, in a last attempt to catch hold of the wrong philosophical stone, we found a way to directly damage our Autonomic Nervous System more effectively than we ever did before. We have succumbed to the dangerous illusion of the great Alchemy in taking our own psyche as the guinea-pig. In an attempt to overcome the basic insignificance of life we have half opened the gates of hell, a risk that the supposedly dull bourgeois, the standard coca-cola drinking TV watcher was wise enough not to take. The story appears to be as senseless as any other, only just a lot more pathetic.

We should remember the 17th Century fabulist Jean de La Fontaine: we need the new even if there is nothing new left in the world (my translation); ("*Il nous faut du nouveau n'en fut-il plus au monde*"). In *The Cultural Contradiction of Capitalism* (New York 1976) Daniel Bell recognises that the ever expanding quest for the new is a factor of psycho-social dis-equilibrium in the American society as people cannot cope with the pace of change.

The affluent society, the leisure society, is to cope with boredom by more consumption, more activity, more superfluity or more experiences, other experiences, new experiences, ever renewed experiences leading further and further away from the central path of dharma, further deep into confusion, neuroses, mistakes and sin. But as nothing is more boring than sin the wolf you want to chase from the yard enters the house through the back door. Eroticism, pornography, drugs are extreme but excellent examples of the process of the flight forward whereby we seek powerful sensations at the cost of further ruining the subtle psycho-somatic equilibrium of dharma which is the only buffer against "l'Ennui" as well as the source of true satisfaction and joy and the instrument of further ascent in awareness. A whole generation is going down the drain and does not know it.

The process, of course, has gone generally unnoticed for many reasons. For one, many people wrongly tend to assume their own personal experience of life to be an index of what life is all about. They lack any cultural points of comparison and generally live in an anthropological ethnocentrism which ignores alternative modes of life-style in space and time. Then, because of fading sensitivity and corresponding mental thickness, they have settled in a world of relative opinions, half-truths and lesser evils. They are happy enough not to be thoroughly unhappy.

Neither technology or drugs, neither capitalism or marxism, neither anything which has been generated by the advanced industrial society or man himself appears to be in a position to extract man and its doing from the self generated Absurdity of the present condition. Enjoyment is an attribute of awareness: any conceptual or behavioural pattern of involvement which is not enhancing the subject's awareness cannot connect man with the hidden spring of knowledge and joy; but it is not possible to deepen one's awareness as long as it is not sensitive to one's dharma. We have made dharma increasingly difficult to perceive because of our decreased awareness. Thus we close the vicious circle.

The punishment of the modern *hubris* (false pride) is that, by refusing to respect the divine outside himself in the world and in others, the individual is prevented from recognising his own divinity. The gods did not have to send any eagle to devour the liver of the new Prometheus; because man is chastised by the very result of his own actions.

As a result we find that the internal psycho-somatic world and the external material world are running out of control. The dialectic inter-action between these two aspects of the same destructive trend (as expressed by the interaction between individuals and society and the environment) cannot be prevented by new ideologies or superstitions or by any display of mechanical socio-economic devices. Yet everybody feels something is to be done. The need for a radical revolution asserts itself. But what kind of revolution do we mean?

Many seekers in the past have tried to bring an end to social injustices and miseries by launching political revolutions. Marx, for instance, thought that a social class, as the basic unit of social life, would be the chosen instrument of the historic revolution; he believed the proletariat would be this revolutionary class.

Let us however consider here that the foundations of any human edifice happens to be the individual and not the social classes. Man, as an individual, and not as a member of a class, is the basic unit of social life. When one merely changes class relations while man himself cannot be regenerated, the outcome of this revolution will prove somewhat disappointing. Liberty, equality, fraternity did not follow the French Revolution or the Russian, or the Chinese. There is no great point in elaborately working on the house when the underlying foundations are not firmly established. Human institutions are interchangeable and the old forms of vice will simply flow into the new structure. Napoleon or Stalin exhibited a good many of those autocratic features which were denounced in the previous regimes. Revolutions and new ideologies helped people to internalise the coercion but that was not what the revolution was originally about.

Perhaps we did not realize then as we do today that we need a more thorough, more fundamental revolution. We have found out now that, spiritual and not political, concentrated within and not scattered without, the Revolution we need is the inner revolution of Man: we need to start the Copernican[19] revolution of the human psyche through which the autocentric, isolated microcosm will discover its cosmic dimension and its place in the cosmos, its place in the great primordial being (Virata) of the Indian Cosmology. Like planets around the sun, our attention should start revolving around our divine Self. It is time to very humbly accept and realize that the ego is not the centre of the galaxy.

[19] A Polish Astronomer, Nicholas Copernicus (1473-1543) abolished the old premise of the Ptolemean astronomy according to which the earth laid at the centre of the Universe by finding out that the earth was revolving around the sun as any other planet of the solar system.

How can we concentrate our energy on what is essential in us so as to recognise what is essential outside of us? How do we know beauty, harmony and integration within us so as to spread it in our creation, so as to recognise it in nature? Somehow, once we realize that knowledge is a postulate towards integration, that truth is one and that we are one with it, we would perceive who we really are. In perceiving our Self we would know that we are not the centre of the Universe for the centre of the Universe is everywhere; including in us. Unlike the limited ego, the Self is limitless. It will connect us with the all pervading substance of the Universe. Is it then that we would gleam through the moon, dance with the planets, that we would know each other, would know that we are one?

It is said that the Self is the primordial manifestation of existence within man. It has been asserted that in relating to the Self we relate to Existence itself, in relating to Existence, we relate to joy; Parmenides, Plato, Aquinas and many other great philosophers knew it too; their metaphysical equation of being reads: Being=beautiful=good=true. How are we to reach the state of holiness in which to know it is to merge with it? How can we experience this instantaneous act of knowledge whereby the knower, the known and the knowing melt together in the recovered unity? Thinkers such as Pascal, Gilson, Maritain or Heidegger were lucky indeed! Have they not been graced by the metaphysical intuition of Being? The awareness of existence, the feeling that one is existing, provides the substance of any true satisfaction. We read in the *Brihadaranyaka Upanishad* these golden words:

> "The perfection which is the Self is the goal of all beings... this Self, which is dearer to us than anything else is indeed dearer than a son, dearer than wealth, dearer than all besides it. Let a man worship the Self alone as dear."

It is through the Self that anything which is dear is dear! These words of wisdom give us a great vision of our liberation. After all the vicious circle between neuro-psychic decay and uncontrolled material creation can be broken through a Self-oriented cognitive Act. The knowledge of Existence implies the highest plenitude of bliss for it finds its deepest roots in the presence of the Self, the Atman; God within us.

In its total simplicity the awareness of Existence opens the door of total intensity, because—as it is beautifully expressed in the form of Lord Shiva and Parvati—Existence and Divine Love, the Witness and the Energy, are one and the same thing. United with and within the cosmic divine ecology, Man is meant to enjoy the creation as a beautiful divine play (Leela), music to the glory of God and to the joy of his children. So we reach the conclusion that if we do not recognize God within, we cannot realise God without. If we are not prepared to recognise God, we will not be able to bring into the world the godly attributes of satisfaction, peace and beauty or prevent the impending destruction we are calling upon ourselves and our children. How can we turn our attention towards the Self? How can we merge in it? How can the impossible revolution be conducted? These questions have been raised again and again by the successive generations of seekers of the previous millennia.

Thank God our prayers are heard. Our problems are being taken seriously by God Almighty. Or, perhaps, He cannot allow this creation to be destroyed: so, the knowledge of spontaneous salvation, "Sahaja yoga" has been revealed. He has granted it to the human race for its emancipation. It sounds fantastic, impossible! We are so much doomed, in so many ways, that we cannot believe it. Whatever the reason may be, I do not know, but believe me, the Power of God has really brought this knowledge, this breakthrough within the reach of the desperate human seekers. This book is proclaiming the great news of this stupendous happening. Eureka!

APPENDIX

Chakra	Deity	Qualities	Gross Expression
7 Sahasrara	Shri Kalki (Shri Mataji)	Collective consciousness, integration, silence	Limbic area
6 Ajnya	left: Shri Mahavira centre: Lord Jesus (Mother Mary) right: Shri Buddha	Non violence to self Forgiveness, resurrection, truth Non violence to others	Right temple crossing of optic thalamus left temple
5 Vishuddhi	Shri Krishna (Shri Radha)	Divine greatness, playful witness, self respect	Cervical plexus
4 Anahath or Riddhaya	left: Shri Shiva (Shri Parvati) centre: Shri Durga or Jagadamba right: Shri Rama (Shri Sita)	Existence, joy, mother Motherly protection Dutiful life, father	Heart organ Cardiac plexus Right chest
VOID	Adi Guru	Primordial Master authority	—
3 Manipur or Nabhi	Shri Vishnu (Shri Laxshmi)	Dharma, right behaviour, welfare, well being, sustenance	Solar plexus
2 Swadhistan	Shri Brahmadeva (Shri Saraswati)	Creativity, knowledge, beauty	Aortic plexus
Mooladhar	(Shri Gauri)	Virgin purity, holiness of mother, motherly love	Coccyx
1 Mooladhara	Shri Ganesha	Innocence, eternal childhood, contentment, wisdom	Prostate gland
NADIS			
I Ida nadi (moon channel)	Shri Ishwara (Shri Mahakali)	Existence, joy Auspiciousness	Left sympathetic nervous system
II Pingala nadi (sun channel)	Shri Hiranya Gharba (Shri Mahasaraswati)	Attention, creativity discipline	Right sympathetic nervous system
III Sushumna nadi (central path)	Shri Virata (Shri Mahalaxshmi)	Truth, evolution, religion, revelation	Parasympathetic nervous system

N. B. This Chart is only a first draft which will be corrected and completed on the basis of further teachings and new experiences.

APPENDIX

Location on Hand	Manifestations	Some causes of Catch	No. of Petals
Centre of palm	Cool vibrations	Atheism, dogmatism, doubt in HH Mataji	1000
—	Super ego	Conditioning	
Ring finger	Sight, intellect	Roving eyes, misled thinking, drugs	2
—	Ego	Worries	
First finger	Arms, neck, ears, nose, mouth, face	Wrong use of the tongue guilt, arrogance, wrong mantras, smoking	16
—	Heart beat	Physical stress, Hatha yoga	
Little finger	Breathing	Insecurity, UPI from dead relatives	12
—	—	Disturbed relationship	
Outer part of the palm	As Nabhi + Swadhistan	Failing as a disciple, false guru, drugs, religious fanaticism	
Middle finger	Stomach, liver (part)	Household and money worries, alcohol, drugs, UPI in food, corruption	10
Thumb	Liver, kidney, spleen, pancreas, uterus	Too much thinking, planning, using spirits, psychiatry, tantrism, heavy drinking, crude behaviour, artificiality	6
Heel of Palm	Kundalini	Imbalance of sympathetic	
Heel of Palm	Elimination, generation	"Sex liberation", constipation, tantrism	4
Whole left hand	Tamo guna, past, subconscious mind, emotional body	Lethargy, mother's problems, licentiousness, superstition, habits	
Whole right hand	Rajo guna, future, supraconscious mind, physical and mental bodies	Overactivity, father's problems, repression, egotism, expectations	
Cool hands	Satwa guna, present, conscious mind.		

Glossary

Adharma	anti-dharma
Adi Guru	Primordial Master
Adi Shakti	Primordial Power, power of God the Almighty
Amrit	Nectar, flow of bliss
Apocalypse	Coming of Kalki
Archetype	Model, form, fundamental symbol
Atman	The Self
Auspiciousness	The Quality of being tuned to the Unconscious.
Avatar	Divine incarnation
Bhairawa	Archangel Saint Michael
Brahmadeva	God's aspect of creation
Brahman	God as undifferentiated, all pervading consciousness
Brahmarandhra	apex of the brain
Buddha	Incarnation of the Ego of God
Chaitanya	Divine Vibrations, life force
Chakra	Subtle centers of energy within the human body
Collective consciousness	State in which the awareness encompasses other beings
Collective subconscious	Superego of the Virata
Collective supraconscious	Ego of the virata
Cosmos	The total field of the creation, the universe
Darshan	Physical presence of a divine incarnation
Dattatrya	Primordial Master

GLOSSARY 417

Deities, devatas	Aspects of God
Dharma	Righteousness as the sustaining factor of ecology and evolution
Dhyana	Meditation
Dialectics	Study of the law of contradiction within nature and men
Durga	Name of Parvati when manifesting without Shiva
Ego	Side of the Psyche which manifest and develop the individual identity
Entropy	mathematical function expressing the law of degradation of energy
Eschatological Scheme	Scenario of the last days
Existential dilemma	The condition of man being both Finite and Infinite
Ganesha	God's aspects of innocence, wisdom and contentment
Gauri	The Divine virgin, power of purity, the Kundalini
Guna	Mood of the Virata
Guru	Teacher, Master
Griha Laxshmi	Laxshmi's aspect of the goddess of the household
Hanumana	Archangel Saint Gabriel
Hatha Yoga	Yoga of the sympathetic nervous system
Holy spirit, Holy Ghost	See Adi Shakti
Jagadamba	Durga as the Mother of the Universe
Jesus	Incarnation of the son of God
Ida Nadi	Moon channel presiding over emotions, the past
Kali	Fierce form of Parvati
Kali Yuga	Age of Darkness
Kalki	Forthcoming tenth Incarnation of Vishnu
Karma	Consequences of past actions
Kingdom of God	State of consciousness of the Sahasrara chakra
Koan	Short enigma given in the buddhist teaching practices
Krishna	Incarnation of the Father aspect of God
Kundalini	Residual divine consciousness of the Holy Spirit within man

Laxshmi	Shakti of Vishnu
Loka	Cosmic realm
Mahakali	Divine seed energy of existence and destruction
Mahalaxshmi	Divine seed energy of evolution
Mahasaraswati	Divine seed energy of creation
Mahavira	Incarnation of the super ego of God
Mandala	System of awareness-energy around a chakra
Mary	Shakti of Jesus
Maryada	Boundaries
Mataji	Holy Mother
Maya	Illusion, delusion, confusion
Microcosm	The total field of the human condition, the mini-universe
Nadi	Channel
Ontology	Province of philosophy studying Being
Paramatma	The Universal Unconscious
Parasympathetic	Part of the autonomous nervous system balancing and restoring the energy
Parvati	Shakti of Shiva
Pingala Nadi	Sun channel presiding over physical and mental activities, the future
Prakriti	Nature
Psychosomatic Instrument	Instrument controlling the physical and psychic bodies
Purusha	Spirit
Radha	Shakti of Krishna
Rajo Guna	Mood, mode of operation of Mahasaraswati
Rama	Seventh incarnation of Vishnu
Ravana	King of the demons
Sadashiva	God the Almighty
Samadhi	Self-realisation
Sahaja	Spontaneous, inborn
Sangha	Community of the realised souls
Saraswati	Shakti of Brahmadeva
Satan	Collective principle of evil
Sat Chit Ananda	Truth, consciousness, bliss
Satguru	True guru, Adi Guru
Sattwa guna	Mood, Mode of operation of Mahalaxshmi

GLOSSARY

Sattya Yuga	Age of Revelation, Golden Age
Self	God within man
Self-realisation	Opening of the Brahmarandhra
Shakti	Power
Shiva	God's aspect of existence and destruction
Siddhi	Superhuman Power
Sita	Shakti of Rama
Shri	Lord, Lady; also a name of the Goddess
Spiritual Libido	Desire to be the instrument of necessity, fate, the unconscious
Sri Chakra	Instrument of the Holy spirit
Standard Psychic State	State of mind of the common man
Subconscious	Field of ida nadi and the superego
Super ego	Side of the psyche which stores conditionings, past experiences
Supraconscious	Field of pingala nadi and the ego
Surrender	Disposition, attitude leading to the opening of the Sushumna Channel
Sushumna nadi	Central channel of evolution and revelation
Sympathetic nervous system	Part of the autonomous nervous system controlling voluntary functions
Tandava	Shiva's dance of destruction
Tamo guna	Mood, mode of operation of Mahakali
Tantra	Instrument
Thoughtless awareness	The state of awareness beyond mental activity
Unconscious	See Universal Unconscious
Tree of life	The sushumna nadi and the chakras
Units of Psychic Interferences	Entities, spirits intruding the psyche
Universal Unconscious	Mind of the Virata
Vaikuntha	Celestial abode of Vishnu
Vibratory awareness	Awareness of the chaitanya
Vilamba	Space of silence between two thoughts
Virata	The Great Primordial being, God manifested
Vishnu	God's aspect of evolution
Water of life	River of chaitanya and also the amrit
Yantra	Technique
Yoga	Union

ABBREVIATIONS

UPI	Unit of Psychic Interference
PNS	Parasympathetic Nervous System
SNS	Sympathetic Nervous System
SPS	Standard Psychic State